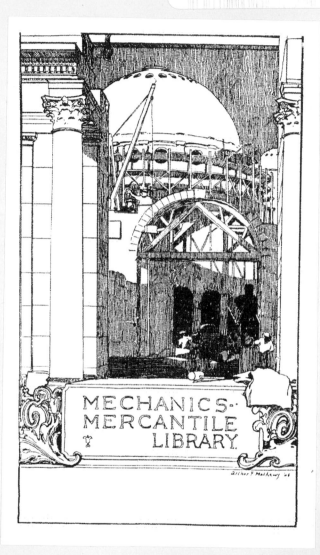

MECHANICS·
MERCANTILE
LIBRARY.

THE TWILIGHT
WARRIORS

ALSO BY ROBERT GANDT

NONFICTION

SEASON OF STORMS
The Siege of Hong Kong 1941

CHINA CLIPPER
The Age of the Great Flying Boats

SKYGODS
The Fall of Pan Am

BOGEYS AND BANDITS
The Making of a Fighter Pilot

FLY LOW, FLY FAST
Inside the Reno Air Races

INTREPID
The Epic Story of America's Most Legendary Warship
(with Bill White)

FICTION

WITH HOSTILE INTENT

ACTS OF VENGEANCE

BLACK STAR

SHADOWS OF WAR

THE KILLING SKY

BLACK STAR RISING

THE DEADLIEST NAVAL BATTLE
OF WORLD WAR II
AND THE MEN WHO FOUGHT IT

THE TWILIGHT WARRIORS

ROBERT GANDT

BROADWAY BOOKS   NEW YORK

BROADWAY

Copyright © 2010 by Robert Gandt

Published in the United States by Broadway Books,
an imprint of the Crown Publishing Group,
a division of Random House, Inc., New York.
www.crownpublishing.com

BROADWAY BOOKS and the Broadway Books colophon
are trademarks of Random House, Inc.

Library of Congress Cataloging-in-Publication Data
Gandt, Robert L.
   The twilight warriors : the deadliest naval battle of World War II
and the men who fought it / Robert Gandt.— 1st ed.
      p.   cm.
   Includes bibliographical references and index.
   1. World War, 1939–1945—Campaigns—Japan—Okinawa
Island. 2. World War, 1939–1945—Naval operations, American.
3. United States. Navy—History—World War, 1939–1945.
4. United States. Navy—Biography. I. Title.
   D767.99.O45G36   2010
   940.54'25229—dc22   2010014062

ISBN 978-0-7679-3241-7

Printed in the United States of America

DESIGN BY BARBARA STURMAN

10 9 8 7 6 5 4 3 2 1

First Edition

FOR PAULA AND PHOEBE

WITH LOVE

OLD MEN FORGET: YET ALL SHALL BE FORGOT,
BUT HE'LL REMEMBER WITH ADVANTAGES
WHAT FEATS HE DID THAT DAY.

—HENRY V TO HIS TROOPS ON THE EVE OF THEIR VICTORY
AT AGINCOURT, 1415 (SHAKESPEARE, *KING HENRY V*)

MANY OF THESE THINGS I SAW
AND SOME OF THEM I WAS.

—VIRGIL, *THE AENEID*

CONTENTS

PART THREE
FLOATING CHRYSANTHEMUMS

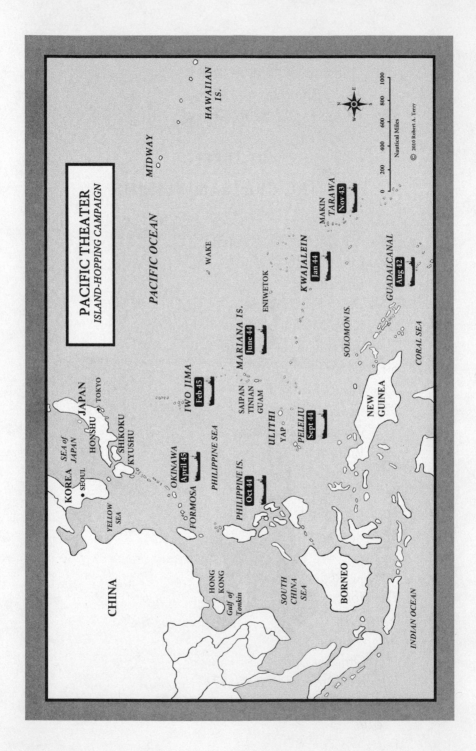

PACIFIC THEATER
ISLAND-HOPPING CAMPAIGN

CHINA

KOREA
SEOUL

SEA of
JAPAN

JAPAN
HONSHU
TOKYO
SHIKOKU
KYUSHU

YELLOW
SEA

HONG
KONG

Gulf of
Tonkin

SOUTH
CHINA
SEA

FORMOSA

OKINAWA
April 45

PHILIPPINE SEA

PHILIPPINE IS.
Oct 44

BORNEO

IWO JIMA
Feb 45

SAIPAN
TINIAN
GUAM

MARIANA IS.
June 44

ULITHI
YAP

PELELIU
Sept 44

PACIFIC OCEAN

WAKE

ENIWETOK

KWAJALEIN
Jan 44

MIDWAY

HAWAIIAN
IS.

MAKIN
TARAWA
Nov 43

NEW
GUINEA

SOLOMON IS.

GUADALCANAL
Aug 42

CORAL SEA

INDIAN OCEAN

N
W   E
S

0   200   400   600   800   1000

Nautical Miles

© 2010 Robert A. Terry

TIME LINE

1944

JUNE 17 ▸ At Saipan, Admirals King, Nimitz, Spruance discuss Okinawa as next major stepping-stone.

SEPTEMBER 15 ▸ Air Group 10 re-formed under Cmdr. J. J. Hyland.

OCTOBER 23–26 ▸ Battle of Leyte Gulf. IJN suffers calamitous defeat.

NOVEMBER 25 ▸ USS *Intrepid* severely damaged by two kamikazes off the Philippines.

1945

JANUARY 26 ▸ Spruance assumes command of U.S. Fifth Fleet; Mitscher takes over Task Force 58.

FEBRUARY 10 ▸ Vice Adm. Ugaki takes command of IJN Fifth Air Fleet.

FEBRUARY 19 ▸ U.S. Marines land on Iwo Jima.

FEBRUARY 20 ▸ *Intrepid* deploys to join Task Force 58 at Okinawa.

MARCH 16 ▸ Iwo Jima declared secure.

MARCH 18 ▸ Air Group 10 flies combat missions against Japanese mainland.

MARCH 19 ▸ USS *Franklin* struck by Japanese dive-bomber.

MARCH 26–29 ▸ U.S. 77th Inf. Division captures Kerama Retto.

APRIL 1 ▸ Love Day. U.S. invasion of Okinawa begins.

APRIL 6–7 ▸ *Kikusui* No. 1. First massed kamikaze attack.

APRIL 7 ▸ IJN battleship *Yamato* and five escorts sunk by Task Force 58 aircraft.

APRIL 12–13 ▸ *Kikusui* No. 2.

APRIL 15–16 ▸ *Kikusui* No. 3.

APRIL 16 ▸ *Intrepid* struck by kamikaze, withdraws from Okinawa.

APRIL 16–21 ▸ 77th Infantry Div. captures Ie Shima.

APRIL 18 ▸ Ernie Pyle killed on Ie Shima.

APRIL 20 ▸ 6th Marine Div. secures Motobu Peninsula.

APRIL 27–28 ▸ *Kikusui* No. 4.

MAY 3–4 ▸ *Kikusui* No. 5.

MAY 4–6 ▸ Japanese counterattack in southern Okinawa.

MAY 10–11 ▸ *Kikusui* No. 6.

MAY 11 ▸ *Bunker Hill* hit by two kamikazes, out of the war.

MAY 23–25 ▸ *Kikusui* No. 7.

MAY 17 ▸ Vice Adm. Turner relieved by Vice Adm. Harry Hill.

MAY 27 ▸ Spruance and Mitscher relieved by Halsey and McCain.

MAY 27–29 ▸ *Kikusui* No. 8.

MAY 30–JUNE 4 ▸ Japanese 32nd Army withdraws to southern positions on Okinawa.

JUNE 3–7 ▸ *Kikusui* No. 9.

JUNE 18 ▸ Lt. Gen. Buckner killed on Okinawa. USMC Maj. Gen. Geiger takes command.

JUNE 21–22 ▸ *Kikusui* No. 10.

JUNE 21 ▸ Lt. Gen. Ushijima and Lt. Gen. Cho commit ritual suicide.

JUNE 21 ▸ End of organized resistance on Okinawa.

AUGUST 6 ▸ Atomic bomb dropped on Hiroshima.

AUGUST 9 ▸ Atomic bomb dropped on Nagasaki.

AUGUST 15 ▸ Cessation of hostilities in the Pacific.

AUGUST 15 ▸ Vice Adm. Ugaki conducts last kamikaze mission.

SEPTEMBER 2 ▸ Japanese surrender aboard USS *Missouri*.

THE TWILIGHT
WARRIORS

PROLOGUE

ALAMEDA NAVAL AIR STATION, CALIFORNIA
FEBRUARY 19, 1945

I t was late, nearly ten o'clock, but the party was going strong. You could hear them singing a hundred yards down the street from the officers' club.

> I wanted wiiiings
> till I got the goddamn things,
> Now I don't want 'em anymoooore . . .

Getting plastered before deployment was a ritual in the wartime Navy, and the pilots of Bomber Fighting 10 were no exception. It was the night before their departure aboard the aircraft carrier USS *Intrepid*. The entire squadron had suited up in their dress blues and mustered in the club for their farewell bash.

The party began like most such occasions. Pronouncements were made, senior officers recognized, lost comrades toasted. The liquor flowed, and then came the singing. It was a form of therapy. For the new pilots, the booze, bravado, and macho lyrics masked their anxieties about what lay ahead. For the veterans, the singing and the camaraderie brought reassurance. Most knew in their secret hearts that they'd been lucky. They'd lived through this much of the war. There were no guarantees they'd make it through the next round.

Leaning against the bar and clutching his drink, Ensign Roy "Eric" Erickson bellowed out the verses of the song. Erickson was a gangly twenty-two-year-old from Lincoln, Nebraska. He was one of the new pilots in the squadron. They called themselves "Tail End Charlies." They flew at the tail end of formations, stood at the tail end of chow lines, and now were catching the tail end of the war. They'd spent the past year and a half training to be fighter pilots. Their greatest fear, they liked to boast, was that the war would be over before they got there.

The Tail End Charlies were seeing a new side to the squadron skipper, Lt. Cmdr. Wilmer Rawie. Rawie liked to drink, and now that he'd had a few he was leading his boys in his favorite drinking song, "I Wanted Wings."

They taught me how to fly,
And they sent me here to die,
I've had a belly full of waaarrrr . . .

Rawie had gotten a brief tour of combat duty in 1942, flying off the *Enterprise* in the early Pacific skirmishes. But then he was relegated to two tedious years as an instructor back in Florida. Finally, in the twilight of the war, he'd gotten a squadron command. Now Will Rawie was playing catch-up.

But I'll take the dames,
While the rest go down in flames,
I've no desi-ire to be buuurrrned . . .

Watching from across the room was the CAG—air group commander—Cmdr. John Hyland. A dozen years older than most of his pilots, Hyland wore the bemused expression of a father chaperoning teenagers. The only one near his age was Rawie, who had begun his commissioned career after a stint as an enlisted man. Hyland had seen lots of these parties, and he had nothing against them. It was a tradition. Let the boys get shit-faced, herd them back to the ship, then get on with the war.

Though most of his pilots didn't know it, Hyland was also playing catch-up. When the war began, he was on a patrol wing staff in the Philippines. Since then he had served in a succession of Washington staff jobs. Now Johnny Hyland, who had never flown fighters in combat, was another twilight warrior.

The singing grew louder.

Air combat's called romance,
But you take an awful chance,
I'm no fighter, I have learrrned . . .

By the time they closed the bar a few minutes before midnight, the party had gotten rowdy. A drunk pilot had to be subdued after demonstrating how to smash the mirrors behind the bar. Another stuck his fist through a plaster wall. One of the junior officers nearly drowned when he passed out over the toilet. Several had to be hauled nearly comatose back to the ship and loaded aboard like cordwood.

The *Intrepid*'s departure the next morning was a hazy, indistinct memory for most of the Tail End Charlies. As the ship entered the heaving ocean, the hangovers magnified to bouts of barfing. Eric Erickson, who had never been aboard a vessel larger than a canoe, stayed sick for three days.

After a week of provisioning and training in Hawaii, *Intrepid* was under way for the western Pacific. In the smoke-filled ready room of Bomber Fighting 10, the pilots learned for the first time where they were going. The intelligence officer stuck a chart on the bulkhead. It was a map of southern Japan and the Ryukyu island chain.

The Tail End Charlies stared at the map. The men knew some of the place names—Shikoku, Kyushu, Okinawa. Until then that was all they'd been, just names. Now reality was setting in. Those places on the map—the ones with the hard-to-pronounce names—were where they would see their first combat.

But there was more. What none of them yet knew—not the pilots or the intelligence officers or the flag officers planning the operation—was that the island in the middle of the chain, the one called Okinawa, was where the Imperial Japanese Navy would make its last stand.

Kamikaze crashes into USS *Intrepid*, November 25, 1944.
(*INTREPID* SEA, AIR & SPACE MUSEUM)

PART ONE
THE WAY OF THE WARRIOR

WHEN REACHING A STALEMATE, WIN WITH A
TECHNIQUE THE ENEMY DOES NOT EXPECT.

—MIYAMOTO MUSASHI,
LEGENDARY JAPANESE SWORDSMAN AND
MILITARY STRATEGIST (1584–1645)

MY ONLY HOPE IS THAT THE JAPS DON'T QUIT
BEFORE WE HAVE A CHANCE TO WIPE THEM OUT.

—ADM. JOHN S. McCAIN

1 ▸ THE NEXT ISLAND

The flies were everywhere. Vice Adm. Raymond Spruance maintained his stone-faced silence as he waved the insects away from the table. They were large and black, and entire squadrons of them were swarming into the wardroom of Spruance's flagship, the cruiser *Indianapolis*.

Indianapolis was anchored in the lagoon on the eastern shore of Saipan. The heavy tropical air was seeping like a dank cloud through the spaces of the non-air-conditioned warship. Spruance's guests were his two immediate bosses, chief of naval operations Adm. Ernest King and the commander in chief of the Pacific Fleet, Adm. Chester Nimitz. Dinner had been served early in the hope that an ocean breeze might still be wafting through the portholes of the wardroom.

Instead of a breeze, they got these damned flies. Splotches of perspiration were staining the admirals' starched khakis as they waved at the insects. King and Nimitz had just completed a Pacific inspection tour. They had stopped to confer with Spruance, whose Fifth Fleet had just won a resounding victory at the Battle of the Philippine Sea. Joining them in the wardroom was Vice Adm. Richmond K. Turner, who had commanded the amphibious landings on Saipan.

In keeping with wardroom tradition, the admirals were avoiding high-level military discussions at dinner. They were also avoiding the subject of the black flies and where they came from. King and Nimitz had taken a tour of Saipan that afternoon. Most of the island's thirty thousand Japanese defenders and twenty-two thousand civilians were dead, and their decomposing bodies had been moldering in the tropical heat for nearly a week. Saipan and the adjoining lagoon where *Indianapolis* was anchored were swarming with flies.

Eager to be done with dinner and the flies, the admirals evacuated the wardroom and returned to the business of war. Spruance was aware that his actions in the recent Battle of the Philippine Sea had come under heavy criticism. Instead of dispatching Vice Adm. Marc Mitscher's Fast Carrier Force in an all-out attack on the Japanese task force, he had held them back to cover the landings on Saipan. By the end of the engagement, the air strength of the Imperial Japanese Navy had been crushed—six hundred aircraft destroyed and three carriers sunk—but in the view of many senior officers, it wasn't enough. Spruance had allowed the Japanese to escape with most of their fleet intact.

It wasn't the first time Raymond Spruance had been accused of excessive caution, nor would it be the last. At the 1942 Battle of Midway, after his dive-bombers had sunk four Japanese carriers, Spruance chose not to press his advantage and pursue the remainder of Adm. Isoruku Yamamoto's fleet after nightfall. The remnants of the Japanese force survived to fight another day.

If Spruance was worried about his boss's judgment, he could relax. The Navy's senior officer put the subject to rest. "You did a damn good job there," he said. "No matter what other people tell you, your decision was correct." Coming from the hard-boiled Ernest King, it amounted to high praise.

Few officers could have been more different in style and temperament than King and Spruance. Ernest King was tall, arrogant, fond of hard liquor and loose women. He was also a notorious bully who ruled the Navy with an iron fist. By contrast, Raymond Spruance was a cerebral, mild-mannered officer whose demeanor seldom changed. He was an oddity in the 1940s Navy, an officer who neither drank nor smoked, and in a generation that disdained exercise, he was a fitness fanatic. If his fellow officers didn't warm up to Ray Spruance's personality, they never doubted his brilliance.

Even the arrogant King acknowledged that Spruance was the smartest officer in the Navy—though King put himself second.

It was precisely because Spruance was so well regarded that King was aboard *Indianapolis* this evening, the flies notwithstanding. The conquest of the Marianas was complete. The decision had already been made that the island of Luzon in the Philippines was next. But then what? King wanted to know what Spruance thought should be the next objective in the ultimate conquest of Japan.

Spruance answered without hesitation. "Okinawa."

King's eyebrows rose. So did Nimitz's. It wasn't what they'd expected to hear. The Joint Chiefs of Staff, including King, were on record as favoring an invasion of Formosa. Why Okinawa?

In his usual low-key monotone, Spruance laid out his case. Formosa was a heavily fortified, mountainous island that would take months to capture. Bypassing Formosa and seizing Okinawa was the quickest way to strangle Japan.

As a prelude to an Okinawa invasion, Spruance thought they first should take Iwo Jima, a volcanic island with an airfield that was within bomber range of Okinawa and Japan. After they'd captured Okinawa, they would be in position to blockade all shipping in the East China Sea. Japan would be cut off. It might preclude a bloody invasion of Japan itself.

An uncomfortable silence fell over the flag compartment. King was dubious. So was Nimitz. Bypass Formosa?

The admirals peered at the map on the bulkhead. Okinawa nestled like a protected pendant in the middle of the Ryukyu island chain, dangerously close to the Japanese mainland. Even if Spruance was right, an invasion of Okinawa would be a hell of a battle. The Japanese would fight back with every weapon they had left.

Daylight was fading over Mabalacat airfield, 50 miles from Manila, when the black limousine pulled up. The officers standing outside the command post snapped to attention. The fluttering yellow pennant on the front of the vehicle indicated an officer of flag rank. In unison they saluted the short, stocky figure that emerged from the back of the limousine.

Vice Adm. Takijiro Ohnishi looked older than his fifty-three years. He had the gnarled, deeply lined face of a man who had spent years at sea. Ohnishi was a complex man, known for his bluntness and coarse manners as well as for his sensitivity. A product of his generation, he was an example of the classic samurai—a warrior capable of horrific deeds who could also shed tears at the sight of a falling petal. Like many of his peers, Ohnishi was a poet who rendered in lyrical verse his deepest feelings about war and death.

This day, October 19, 1944, was Ohnishi's first visit to Mabalacat. Gazing around, he saw that the place was a mess. The airfield was part of the sprawling complex of the formerly U.S.-owned Clark Air Base, and for the past few weeks American carrier-based planes had been bombing on a daily schedule. Now, in the waning light, Ohnishi saw ground crewmen scurrying to conceal the surviving fighters in revetments, readying them for the next morning's missions.

Ohnishi had arrived in the Philippines only two days before to take command of the First Air Fleet. The battle—the *real* battle—for the Philippines was about to begin. A powerful American invasion fleet was moving into the Leyte Gulf. Within a few days, U.S. troops would be swarming ashore.

In response, the Japanese high command had devised a complex counterthrust called Sho-1. The plan called for coordinated attacks from the west by three separate heavy surface fleets and a decoying action by a carrier group in the northeast to draw away the American carrier task force. *Sho* meant "victory," and it reflected the delusional thinking of the high command. Any victory in the coming battle would result more from divine intervention than from Japanese execution.

Sho-1 contained a fatal flaw. The battleships and cruisers of the Japanese fleet had only their own guns to fend off U.S. planes. Ohnishi's air fleet in the Philippines would be unable to provide any significant air cover for the Sho operation. His squadrons had been decimated in almost daily attacks from U.S. forces, and the total inventory now amounted to fewer than a hundred fighters. He'd been promised reinforcements from the Second Air Fleet in Formosa, but Ohnishi knew that was a pipe dream. The Formosa squadrons had just endured their own mauling, losing more than five hundred airplanes in three days of attacks by American carrier-based planes.

Knowing all this, it was hard for Admiral Ohnishi not to be discouraged. His meager air forces—his *conventional* air forces—had no chance of turning back the American carrier fleet. But now, in the twilight of Japan's dominion in the Pacific, Ohnishi's thoughts had turned to something unconventional.

Japan had one remaining potent weapon, and it was as ancient as the Japanese culture. What Ohnishi had in mind was a Special Attack Corps—a dedicated unit of airmen who would crash their bomb-laden airplanes into American ships.

The desperate strategy had a name—*tokko*. It was interchangeable with *kamikaze* and meant "divine wind." According to legend, the name came from the wind god, who in the thirteenth century had sent a typhoon to destroy the invasion fleet of Kublai Khan. The divine wind had saved Japan.

Tokko was an echo of the ancient Japanese code of *bushido*—the way of the samurai. Already embedded in the Japanese military ethos was the idea that a warrior, especially one already wounded, was willing to sacrifice his life for the emperor. But the decision to die was expected to come in the heat of battle when all else had failed. Deploying entire Special Attack units—*tokkotai*—on predetermined suicide missions was something new. And controversial.

To Ohnishi, it amounted to making the best of an impossible situation. The cream of Japan's experienced pilots had already been killed in combat. Most of the remaining young airmen were insufficiently trained and lacked superior aircraft and weapons. They faced almost certain annihilation in the coming weeks. The *tokko* missions would allow them an honorable death while dealing a powerful blow to the enemy. Before Ohnishi departed Tokyo, he had obtained the blessing of the minister of the navy for a Special Attack Force.

What Ohnishi still didn't know was how the pilots would respond. The admiral kept an impassive face while he presented the idea to the squadron commanders of the 201st Air Group, the officers who would direct the *tokko* missions.

The officers stared back, showing no expression. Seconds ticked past. Finally the air group executive officer broke the silence. He asked a staff officer how effective a plane carrying a standard 250-kilogram (551-pound) bomb might be if it crashed into a carrier's flight deck. The officer answered that the chances of scoring a hit were greater than by conventional bombing.

No one was surprised. Conventional bombing against the American fleet had produced dismal results. Still, no one seemed happy about Ohnishi's *tokko* proposal. The executive officer asked for a few minutes to consider. He then went to his room and discussed the proposal with other pilots.

Finally he returned. The pilots, he reported, were enthusiastic about a Special Attack Unit. The executive officer asked only that he be allowed to organize the new unit.

A feeling of relief swept over Ohnishi. The hard part was over. He had his first cadre of *tokko* warriors. A divine wind might still save Japan.

2 ▸ TAIL END CHARLIES

Eric Erickson could feel the parachute thumping the back of his legs as he walked across the flight line. It was still a new feeling, and he liked it. This was the day he would make his first solo flight in the Stearman N2S biplane, the trainer the Navy cadets called the "Yellow Peril."

Flying was the only thing the cadets liked about Pasco. The remote base was enclosed with a galvanized wire fence. There was nothing there but a few two-story barracks for the cadets and for the enlisted men who worked on the yellow-painted Stearmans. The town of Pasco had no bars, no entertainment, and, worst of all, no available women. The closest real town was Yakima, a two-hour bus ride away, but the cadets had learned that Yakima wasn't much of an improvement over Pasco.

They were there to learn to fly, and that's what most—but not all—did at Pasco. Washing out of the program meant an end to the cadet's status as an officer candidate. Washouts went back to the fleet as seamen second class, the next-to-lowest enlisted rating in the Navy.

Back in Nebraska, Erickson had been an aspiring artist. He was the son of hardworking parents who traced their roots to Sweden. His father was a foreman for the Iowa Nebraska Light and Power Company, a veteran of World War I, and deeply suspicious of anyone who didn't earn a living by physical labor. That one of his sons actually wanted to *paint pictures* for a living disturbed him.

The war changed everything. Erickson was studying art in a California academy when the wave of patriotic fervor swept America after the attack on Pearl Harbor. By the summer of 1943 he was marching with his fellow cadets on the parade ground of the Navy's Preflight School in northern California.

Erickson was a tall, skinny kid, six foot two and 160 pounds, lithe and agile enough to handle the strenuous physical training program. His previous college work gave him a leg up on the engineering and mathematics classes.

Then came flight training. The former art student seemed an unlikely candidate to be a Navy fighter pilot. On *every* training flight, he became violently airsick. Each time they went aloft, he'd have to lean out and vomit over the side of the little Aeronca training plane. Erickson's classmates gave him a nickname: "Bucket." His job after every flight was to wash down the barf-stained fuselage of the Aeronca.

The airsickness continued until the day his instructor cleared him for his first solo flight. It was as though his gut experienced an epiphany. From that day on, he was finished with the bucket.

By the time Erickson and his class got to the Yellow Perils at Pasco, flying had become great fun. There were close calls, but none were deadly. Engines sometimes failed. Once in a while someone "ground looped"—caught a wing tip on landing and went swirling to a stop in a cloud of dirt, sagebrush, and torn fabric. Naval aviation, they believed, was not inherently dangerous. Sure, there were risks, but if you were good—*really* good, like they were—nothing bad would happen.

Then one day one of Erickson's buddies, a fellow Nebraskan named Paul Hyland, was practicing a solo acrobatic routine. He inadvertently put the Yellow Peril into an inverted spin—a rotating, disorienting maneuver—and was unable to recover. The Stearman plunged into a wooded field near Pasco, scattering pieces of the wood-and-fabric biplane over the field like yellow confetti. Hyland was killed instantly.

The accident stunned them all. They had been together since preflight training school. Hyland was a good-looking, well-liked kid who seemed blessed with above-average skills both on the ground and in the air. Of all the class, he seemed one of the least likely to be killed in a flying accident.

For the cadets, it was their first brush with a hard truth. Okay, naval aviation *was* dangerous. If they stayed with it, finished training, and went into combat, they could expect more such losses. Next time it might be *them*.

A few quietly dropped out and were not seen again. Others, like Erickson, wrestled with their misgivings, then stopped dwelling on it. If it happened, it happened. Anyway, Erickson rationalized, weren't his parents the beneficiaries of his government $10,000 insurance policy? Hell, it was more than his father earned in a year.

Erickson and about half his class made it through Pasco and went on to Corpus Christi, Texas, for advanced training. They flew the "Vultee Vibrator," the fixed-gear SNV, in which they learned instrument flying. Then they graduated to the big North American SNJ Texan trainer, learning formation flying, gunnery, and radio navigation. A few more cadets washed out, but by now most of the fainthearted had been eliminated.

Meanwhile, the war in the Pacific was tilting inexorably in favor of the United States. The new *Essex*-class carriers were joining the fleet, and the Japanese were on the defensive. To Erickson and his classmates, it was something to worry about: after all this training, the damned war would be over before they got there.

Almost to a man, each wanted to be a fighter pilot. Flying dive-bombers or torpedo planes took guts and skill, but the real glory was in the Corsair and Hellcat fighters. In newsreels, comic books, and recruiting posters, fighter pilots grinned down from cockpits covered with rows of swastika and rising-sun victory symbols. Absolutely nothing matched the pure testosterone-loaded glamour of being a World War II fighter pilot.

On a steamy May afternoon in 1944, Erickson and his classmates stood on the hot tarmac at the Corpus Christi Naval Air Station and received their gold bars as newly commissioned ensigns and their naval aviators' wings of gold. The big prize, though, was the orders: Erickson and four of his buddies—Maurie Dubinsky, Jack Ehrhard, Bill Ecker, and Joe Arvidson—received the top assignments in the class. They were going to be fighter pilots.

They were sleek and sexy and, at first sight, intimidating. They were lined up at the naval air station, each in blue livery and adorned with white lettering and broad bars with a star. The newly winged naval aviators stared in awe at the voluptuous objects. They were Chance Vought F4U Corsairs, and they were, arguably, the hottest fighters in the world.

It was what Erickson and his buddies had been training for all these months. They'd been through fighter combat school in the Grumman F6F Hellcat in Vero Beach, Florida. They'd been up to Lake Michigan to qualify in carrier landings aboard a vessel called the *Wolverine*, a makeshift carrier converted from a paddle-driven passenger ship.

Now they had orders to a combat squadron, the famous VF-10 Grim Reapers, which would soon be split into two units—a fighting squadron and a bomber-fighting squadron, each equipped with the new Corsair fighter. And here they were, standing on the ramp at the Atlantic City Naval Air Station, gazing at the row of long-snouted fighters.

The Corsair had several nicknames, some complimentary, some not. They called it "Hose Nose," "U-bird" for its frontal shape, "Bent-Wing Bastard," and sometimes "Hog." The name that bothered the Tail End Charlies was "Ensign Eater." The Corsair was harder to fly than more forgiving airplanes such as the Hellcat, and it had a reputation for turning on inexperienced pilots like a mean-tempered pit bull.

As fighters of the 1940s went, the Corsair was *big*. Powered by the Pratt & Whitney R-2800 Double Wasp radial engine, the Corsair mounted a 13-foot 4-inch three-bladed Hamilton Standard propeller. To accommodate the massive propeller, Vought came up with the Corsair's unique inverted gull-wing design. The design permitted a shorter landing gear while allowing clearance for the long prop blades. The stubbier gear could retract straight aft into the wing, leaving no bulges and still allowing room for internal wing tanks.

The Corsair was fast—faster than almost any other fighter in the world. On its fifth test flight back in 1940, it became the first single-engine production fighter to exceed 400 mph in level flight. The Navy was sufficiently impressed that they placed an order for 584 Corsairs in June 1941.

But then came the problems. During the Corsair's carrier suitability tests, the test pilots found that they couldn't see the carrier deck or the landing signal officer over the 14-foot-long nose. Worse, when the Corsair was at landing speed, about to plunk down on the deck, the left wing would drop like a rock, resulting in a swerving, heart-stopping arrival and sometimes a collapsed landing gear. Even when the Corsair came down on both wheels, the oleo shock absorbers sometimes bounced the fighter back into the air. The tailhook would skim over the arresting wires, causing the fighter to crash into the cable barricade stretched across the forward deck.

This was not suitable behavior for a carrier-based fighter. There was a war on, and the Navy urgently needed fighters on the new *Essex*-class carriers. They opted for the reliable Grumman F6F Hellcat and banished the temperamental Corsair to shore duty with Marine and Navy squadrons in the Solomons.

In the hands of Marines such as Pappy Boyington and Ken Walsh and Navy aces such as Tommy Blackburn and Ike Kepford, the Corsair proved itself to be one of the most lethal aerial killing machines ever designed. And it was then that the big fighter earned another nickname, this one from the Japanese—"Whistling Death," for the high-pitched howl from its wing-root air coolers.

Meanwhile, Vought and Navy engineers were working on the Corsair's carrier landing problems. The nasty wing drop was fixed with a simple 6-inch stall strip mounted on the leading edge of the starboard wing. The dangerous bouncing tendency was cured by reengineering the oleo shock absorbers in the landing gear. The visibility over the long nose was much improved simply by raising the pilot's seat 18 centimeters and giving him a Plexiglas bubble-type canopy.

The best fix came not from engineering but from technique. British Royal Air Force squadrons had been operating Corsairs from their own carriers since mid-1943. The Brits had learned to make a continuously turning approach to the carrier deck, not leveling the Corsair's wings until they were almost over the ramp. The pilot had a clear view of the deck and the landing signal officer all the way to landing.

The fixes worked. After two years of being sidelined, the F4U was cleared for U.S. Navy carrier duty. And just in time.

From his new office on the Atlantic City naval air station, Lt. Cmdr. Wilmer Rawie could see the row of new Corsairs. They were arriving one or two at a time, and so were the pilots, many of them fresh out of flight training.

But not all. Rawie's previous job had been superintendent of training in Green Cove Springs, Florida, where he'd been responsible for training Corsair pilots for the fleet. When he received orders to be skipper of the newly formed VF-10 Grim Reapers, Rawie cherry-picked the best instructors and students to take with him.

Will Rawie had come up from the ranks, serving a hitch as an enlisted man before going to the Naval Academy. After graduating in 1938, he'd put in two years as a surface officer before going to flight training. He saw a brief flurry of combat flying F4F Wildcat fighters from USS *Enterprise* at Wake, Marcus, and Midway, and he flew cover when Jimmy Doolittle's raiders took off for their raid on Tokyo.

But then the war passed Rawie by. He was rotated back to the States to be an instructor, and there he stayed for two years. A lieutenant commander with no command experience, Rawie had reached a dead end.

His break came in late 1944. An air group was being formed under the command of Cmdr. John Hyland, an old squadronmate of Rawie's from the *Enterprise*. Hyland tapped Rawie to lead the new fighting squadron. When their training was complete, they would deploy to the Pacific aboard one of the fast new *Essex*-class carriers, the USS *Intrepid*.

Through the autumn and into the gray winter of 1944, the new Corsair pilots drilled on gunnery, air-to-air tactics, night flying, and dive bombing. And they learned one of the grim statistics of the war: the Navy was losing nearly as many airplanes in accidents as they were in combat.

One day Erickson and a lieutenant named Al Blackman were practicing dive bombing on a target complex in the New Jersey marshes. They were flying a racetrack pattern, diving on the bull's-eye target on the ground.

Erickson was behind Blackman when he saw something—an object, maybe a piece of the aircraft—come off Blackman's airplane. The Corsair abruptly went into a flat spin. Erickson saw the canopy open, and he watched the tiny figure of Al Blackman trying to climb out.

He didn't make it. The Corsair exploded into the ground, sending up a gush of oily black smoke.

Erickson was astonished. Blackman wasn't a Tail End Charlie like Erickson. He was one of the guys who were supposed to know how to stay alive. Later, they learned what had happened. When Blackman's Corsair pulled out of its dive, the starboard horizontal stabilizer separated from the tail. No one knew why, whether it was the result of previous damage or a flaw in construction, but Al Blackman had been doomed from the moment he entered the dive.

Erickson thought about it for a while. *If it could happen to him, it could happen to anyone. Even me.* Then he stopped thinking about it. If he let it bother him, he couldn't do this job.

One final challenge remained: the Big One—carrier qualification. Without the ability to launch and land back aboard a carrier, none of a Navy fighter pilot's other skills counted. Until now, the Tail End Charlies' belief in their own invincibility had not been shaken. They were still bulletproof. Landing the Corsair on a carrier was going to be a piece of cake.

Then they saw the carrier.

The USS *Core* was a "Jeep carrier," an escort carrier converted from a merchant ship hull. Jeep carriers were intended to escort convoys and support amphibious landings. Their designation was CVE, which, according to their sailors, stood for "combustible, vulnerable, and expendable."

Most of the pilots didn't mind the day landings. They didn't even mind the fact that they were out in the tossing Atlantic on a butt-freezing winter day, with a low cloud deck that was spitting rain and sleet. Beneath the clouds the visibility was okay, and in the landing pattern they would try to concentrate on the LSO—the landing signal officer—and ignore the fact that the *Core*'s stern was heaving up and down like a yo-yo in the heavy seas.

From his platform on the aft port deck edge, the LSO coached the pilot with a pair of "paddles"—canvas-covered signal boards— signaling whether the plane was too high or low, fast or slow, angling his outstretched arms one way or another to align the plane with the deck. When the airplane was over the deck edge, the LSO gave the "cut"—a paddle across his throat. The pilot chopped the throttle, and the airplane dropped like a dump truck onto the deck.

Carrier qualification was tough on the airplanes. Several blew their tires after especially hard landings. One of the Tail End Charlies bounced back into the air, coming down nose low and gouging a hunk of wood from the deck with the big three-bladed propeller. With amazing efficiency, the deck crew hauled the wounded birds to the forward deck and soon had most of them flying again.

As soon as a pilot got his three landings, he'd climb out of the seat and another would take his place. When Erickson's turn came, he strapped into the still-running Corsair, ran through his cockpit checks, then gave the deck officer the signal that he was ready. When the deck officer swung his flag forward, pointing down the deck, Erickson shoved the throttle forward and released the brakes. Hurtling off the bow, Erickson nudged the Corsair's nose up, and the big fighter lifted into the gray sky.

He turned downwind, passed abeam the carrier, and started his turning approach. He spotted the LSO, who was giving him a "roger"—paddles level, no urgent signals to add power or slow down. Nearing the blunt, unforgiving ramp of the ship, he saw the cut signal and yanked the throttle to idle. The Corsair thudded into the wooden deck, and Erickson felt the hard tug of the shoulder straps as the tailhook snagged a wire. Less than a minute later, he was roaring back into the sky.

Each pilot needed three landings for day qualification, then had to make two at night. After Erickson's third day landing, he thought it was almost becoming fun.

Then came nightfall, and the fun ended.

It looked like the carrier had sailed into an inkwell. The only lights the pilots could see were the line-up lights on the landing deck, which were visible only within a cone of 12 degrees. German submarines were reportedly lurking off the U.S. Atlantic coast, so neither the *Core* nor her escorts were showing any running lights. The destroyers ahead and behind the carrier were each marked with a tiny blue light.

Everyone was having trouble. The LSO was waving off one pilot after another. Some were taking as many as five passes to get their first landing. To the pilots watching from the darkened deck, awaiting their turn, it looked dangerous as hell out there.

It was. While they watched, one of the Corsairs turning into the groove—the short final approach to the deck—abruptly wobbled its wings. Before the LSO or anyone else could react, the fighter stalled and crashed into the fantail—the stern—of the carrier. There was a shuddering explosion, a brief orange flash, then nothing. The pilot, Lt. (jg) Larry Meade, was killed instantly.

Night operations were suspended—but not for long. Two hours before sunrise it was Erickson's turn. After a botched first pass, he found his way through the murk and managed to land aboard. Then he repeated the process, completing his two required night landings. Following the director's signals, he folded the fighter's wings and taxied to the bow. Despite the freezing temperature, sweat steamed from beneath his helmet. Erickson knew he should have felt jubilant, but he wasn't. He was just glad to be alive.

The next day the Tail End Charlies said goodbye and good riddance to the *Core*. They were finished with training. The next time they saw a carrier, it would be the real thing—the USS *Intrepid* in the Pacific.

They were headed for the war. But first a tradition had to be observed.

Partying was as much a part of squadron life as flying. Still, the historic Atlantic City bash would be discussed in hushed tones at reunions for the next half century. Most of the pilots had only blurred memories of the event, but one thing they agreed on later: it was probably a mistake to have invited everyone—especially the senior officers and their wives.

Of course, they should have known what to expect. The man responsible for planning the party was the squadron executive officer, Lt. Timmy Gile. Gile was an ace from the fighting in the Solomons, a bachelor, and a renowned hell-raiser.

The party started out fairly subdued, with the usual toasts and pronouncements. The officers were in their dress blues, their ladies wearing semiformal dresses. Then it gathered momentum. Gile had booked a sixteen-member female group called the

Philadelphia Debutantes. They were followed by the second act, a voluptuous stripper who went by the name of Toni the Tease.

By eleven o'clock most of the pilots were soused, the senior officers' wives scandalized, and Timmy Gile's place in squadron history secured. Not only had he organized the party to end all squadron parties, but he disappeared with Toni the Tease.

3 ▸ YOU ARE ALREADY GODS

Lt. Yukio Seki took his place in the front rank, a step ahead of the others. Seki wore his flight suit, helmet, and goggles, with a billowing white scarf tied about his neck. Since dawn he and his pilots had been ready for departure.

Seki was exactly the kind of officer Admiral Ohnishi had been looking for to command the first official kamikaze unit. He was a graduate of the Eta Jima naval academy and had already distinguished himself as a gifted naval officer.

Now Seki had under his command twenty-four volunteer pilots, with twenty-six Mitsubishi A6M Zero fighters, given the American code name "Zeke." The unit was divided into four sections, all with poetic names: Shikishima, a poetic name for Japan; Yamato, the ancient name for Japan; Asahi, the morning sun; Yamazakura, for mountain cherry blossoms.

Tears welled in Admiral Ohnishi's eyes as he delivered the orders to the volunteers. "You are already gods without earthly desires," he said in a quavering voice. "But one thing you want to know is that your crash-dive is not in vain. Regrettably, we will not be able to tell you the results. But I shall watch your efforts to the end and report your deeds to the Throne." They lined up for a farewell drink from a ceremonial container. Their fellow pilots took up an ancient Japanese warrior's song:

> If I go away to sea,
> I shall return a corpse awash;
> If duty calls me to the mountain,
> A verdant sward will be my pall;

Thus for the sake of the emperor
I will not die peacefully at home.

The mournful notes of the song still hung in the air as the pilots manned their planes. Seki gave his commanding officer a folded paper, which contained strands of his hair. It was a traditional samurai gesture, a farewell gift to his fiancée and his recently widowed mother.

One after the other the Zeroes, each armed with a 250-kg. (551-lb.) bomb, roared down the runway and headed off for their targets.

And then returned.

They had combed the area where the enemy fleet was reported until their fuel was depleted, then returned to Mabalacat. Seki was mortified. With tears in his eyes he apologized for his failure.

The next day Seki sortied again—and once more returned. Four times this happened, day after day, because of the same problem. The weather over the Philippine Sea bedeviled them. With no radar and little reconnaissance support, the Zero pilots had to pick through the towering cumulonimbus clouds that swelled over the ocean. Every gray shadow and shaft of sunlight looked like a target. Each time they returned to Mabalacat in bitter disappointment.

Meanwhile, beyond their view in the Leyte Gulf, the greatest sea battle in history was unfolding.

Sho-1 had begun. The ambitious Japanese operation—a three-pronged strike of surface ships—was converging on the American amphibious force at Leyte. Two separate Japanese surface forces were coming from the south, while Admiral Takeo Kurita's northern force, led by the world's mightiest battleships, *Yamato* and her sister ship *Musashi*, charged into the Sibuyan Sea, headed for the San Bernardino Strait. A fourth force, a decoy fleet of carriers with a smattering of warplanes, was positioned several hundred miles northeast of the Philippines to draw Adm. William "Bull" Halsey's carriers away from the fray.

In the early hours of October 25, 1944, the southern striking force, commanded by Admiral Shoji Nishimura, was wiped out in a classic night surface battle in the Surigao Strait before they could reach the critical Leyte landing ships. Kurita's northern force was hammered in the Sibuyan Sea by U.S. carrier-based warplanes. By the end of the day, *Musashi* and a third of the force had been sunk. The pride of the Imperial Japanese Navy, the mighty *Yamato*, took two bomb hits but managed to control the damage and stay in the battle. Admiral Kurita reversed course, appearing to withdraw to the west from the battle.

Halsey had taken the bait. He sent his fast carriers roaring after the Japanese decoy carrier force, leaving the critical San Bernardino Strait unguarded. That night, Kurita again reversed course and passed through the strait. At dawn the Japanese force was bearing down on the virtually undefended fleet of escort carriers called Taffy Three.

They took the Americans by surprise. Kurita's warships poured fire into the hapless escort carriers, sinking the escort carrier *Gambier Bay* and three destroyers. Then the Japanese admiral made his own critical misjudgment. Thinking that he was engaging the main American carrier force, Kurita ordered a retreat. With a stunning victory in his grasp, he cut his losses and withdrew to the north.

It still wasn't over. Passing back through the San Bernardino Strait and into the Sibuyan Sea, Kurita's fleet again came under attack from U.S. carrier planes. Though his warships took more damage, Kurita managed to escape with most of his fleet intact.

The Battle of Leyte Gulf was a crushing defeat for the Imperial Japanese Navy. Conventional weapons and tactics had failed to inflict serious damage on the American fleet. But on the morning of October 25, 1944, while Kurita's warships were in full retreat, Lieutenant Seki's unconventional weapons were headed for their targets.

This time Seki was determined that he would not return. His five bomb-laden Zero *tokko* aircraft were escorted by four conventional fighters. They would comb the ocean to the east of the Philippines, and if they failed to find the carriers, they would strike at the flotilla of enemy supply and amphibious vessels supporting the landings on Leyte. These ships were nowhere near the value of enemy carriers, but they would be convenient targets.

It was midmorning when Seki spotted what he was looking for. Down below in the gray seas off the coast of Samar were the telltale flat-topped shapes of aircraft carriers. What he didn't know was that these were the escort carriers of the Taffy Fleet, still recovering from their surprise battle that morning with Kurita's fleet.

Each of the five *tokko* pilots selected a target. On Seki's signal, they began their attacks.

Kamikaze. It was a new word to Rear Adm. Tom Sprague. Like most of the men aboard his flagship, the escort carrier USS *Sangamon*, Sprague had never seen a kamikaze. He was the commander of Task Unit 77.1, known as "Taffy One," and had overall command of the three escort carrier units.

Sprague's carriers had already had a close call that morning. Their only losses from the Japanese battleships and cruisers were Taffy Three's *Gambier Bay* as well as two screening destroyers and a destroyer escort. Now that the Japanese had withdrawn, Sprague had given the order to stand down.

Suddenly, a new threat: from out of the gray sky appeared a Zero, weaving through a belated storm of antiaircraft fire. As Sprague watched, the Zero dove toward USS *Santee*, one of the Taffy One escort carriers. The Zero's 20-millimeter cannons opened fire, spraying the flight deck.

Every observer, from Sprague to the lookouts on *Santee*, knew what would happen next: the Zero's pilot would release his bomb and pull out of the dive.

He didn't. Without wavering from the dive, the Japanese plane plunged straight into *Santee*'s deck. The bomb crashed through the wooden deck and exploded on the hangar deck below. In the ensuing carnage, sixteen men were killed and dozens more wounded.

The attack astonished the men of the Taffy Fleet, but no one attached special significance to it. Japanese planes had been known to crash into their targets, especially after they were already hit.

And then, minutes later, it happened again. Another Zero dove into the deck of the escort carrier *Suwannee*.

The attacks continued. In quick succession, Japanese planes dove into the escort carriers *Kalinin Bay*, *Kitkun Bay*, and *White Plains*.

By now it was clear: the Japanese had launched a wave of suicide attacks.

At 1051, a low-flying Zero roared toward the stern of the escort carrier *St. Lo*. A half mile astern, the Zero pulled up, rolled inverted, and dove straight into the carrier's flight deck.

Just as with *Santee*, the kamikaze plane penetrated the thin wooden deck and exploded in the confined hangar bay, but the crash on *St. Lo* was even deadlier. A compartment of torpedoes and bombs exploded, ripping through the bowels of the carrier, sending an aircraft elevator and flaming hunks of metal and bodies a thousand feet into the sky.

St. Lo was doomed. Within half an hour the carrier had sunk and 143 crewmen were dead or dying.

Tom Sprague and the men of the Taffy Fleet were bewildered. They were among the first to witness a terrifying new weapon. How did you defend yourself against an enemy who was determined to die?

At Mabalacat, there was jubilation. Seki's mission had succeeded beyond their dreams. Not only did all five of the *tokko* planes succeed in hitting enemy ships, but some of the fighter escorts had chosen to join them. A Japanese ace named Hiroyoshi Nishizawa, who witnessed the attacks, thought it was Seki who had dived on the *St. Lo*. If so, Yukio Seki would enter history as the first kamikaze to sink a major enemy ship.

The *tokko* warriors provided the only bright moment in a disastrous week. In the four engagements that became known as the Battle of Leyte Gulf, the Imperial Japanese Navy lost three battleships, ten cruisers, thirteen destroyers, and five submarines. U.S. losses amounted to one light carrier, USS *Princeton*, the Jeep carriers *St. Lo* and *Gambier Bay*, and two destroyers and a destroyer escort. For the Americans, whose fleet now commanded the Pacific, it was a pinprick. For the Japanese, it was a blow from which they would never recover.

But the success of Seki's kamikazes sent a thrill of pride through the demoralized Japanese forces. In the Battle of Leyte Gulf, the little cadre of *tokko* warriors—Ohnishi's young gods—had caused more destruction to the enemy than all the navy's battleships and cruisers.

Now, more than ever, they wanted to continue the hunt. Waiting for them off the eastern shore of the Philippines were the real trophies—the big *Essex*-class aircraft carriers.

The bullhorn blared in every compartment aboard *Intrepid*: "General quarters! All hands man your battle stations!"

The announcement was becoming routine. Since midmorning on November 25, Japanese snooper planes had been probing the carrier group's defenses. Each time the ship's crew had gone running to general quarters.

Intrepid was the flagship of Task Group 38.2, under Rear Adm. Gerald Bogan. In the group were *Intrepid*'s sister ship *Hancock*, the light carriers *Cabot* and *Independence*, the battleships *Iowa* and *New Jersey*, the light cruisers *Biloxi*, *Miami*, and *Vincennes*, and seventeen destroyers.

The antiaircraft guns were firing again. On the flight deck, pilots waiting to take off were peering nervously into the sky. They had become unwilling spectators to the show over their heads.

A kamikaze was diving on *Intrepid*. The Japanese fighter took a hit from a 40-millimeter round and crashed into the sea off *Intrepid*'s starboard side. Behind it came another, a Zero fighter-bomber, weaving through the tracers and mushroom bursts of gunfire, coming almost straight down. Less than a mile away was *Hancock*. *Hancock*'s pilots, just like those on *Intrepid*, were watching the descending apparition. *Which carrier is he going for?* In a few seconds, they had the answer.

At the last instant, the Zero disintegrated, but its flaming hulk crashed onto *Hancock*'s flight deck. Amazingly, the only casualty was the kamikaze pilot, Flying Petty Officer 1st Class Isamu Kamitake, whose remains were still in the wreckage of his airplane.

More kamikazes were inbound. The antiaircraft bursts closed in on a low-flying Zero, exploding it 1,500 yards astern. Another appeared, and it too went into the water close to the stern.

Then came a third Zero, flying low from astern. Every aft and starboard gun on *Intrepid* was blazing away, tracers converging on the low-flying Zero. Somehow the Zero kept coming. The sky behind *Intrepid* roiled with black smoke and explosions. The surface of the sea frothed from the hail of spent ordnance.

As he came closer, the kamikaze pilot pulled up in a steep climb, then rolled over and dove toward *Intrepid*. By now every eye on *Intrepid*'s topside area, including the admiral's, was riveted on the incoming Zero. The kamikaze and its bomb exploded into the flight deck aft of the island, a few feet forward of the mid-deck number three elevator. The mass of the wrecked fighter punched through the wooden deck, penetrating the gallery deck suspended beneath the flight deck, spewing flame and shrapnel into the hangar deck below.

In Ready Room 4, on the gallery deck beneath where the kamikaze first struck, death came instantly for thirty-two sailors, most of them radarmen waiting to start their duty shift. On the flame-filled hangar deck, armed and fueled airplanes were exploding. Fire-fighting crews rushed to the scene of the worst conflagration. The ship's fire marshal, Lt. Don DiMarzo, reported to the captain that the damage was bad, but he would get it under control.

And he might have if it hadn't been for what happened three minutes later.

The pilot's name was Kohichi Nunoda. Even at this low altitude, less than a hundred feet off the water, Nunoda had no trouble spotting his target. A thick column of black smoke was rising from the enemy carrier's flight deck where it had been crashed into minutes earlier by Nunoda's squadronmate Suehiro Ikeda.

Today was the most concentrated *tokko* raid to date—125 dedicated pilots plus their accompanying reconnaissance and fighter escorts. Not since the Leyte Gulf battle a month earlier had so many Japanese warplanes been launched against the U.S. fleet.

As the ship swelled in his windshield, Nunoda hauled the nose of the Zero into a steep climb, rolled up on a wing, judged his dive angle, then plunged downward. He aimed for the middle of the flight deck, which was already ablaze from Ikeda's attack.

Nunoda was taking no chances that his mission might fail. With the deck of the carrier rising to meet him, he released his bomb. Then he opened fire with his 20-millimeter cannons. Nunoda's guns were still firing when his Zero crashed into the ship.

The devastation was immediate and spectacular. The bomb drilled straight through *Intrepid*'s wooden flight deck. It ricocheted off the armored base of the hangar deck, then hurtled forward to explode where the firefighters were still battling the blaze from the first kamikaze.

Lieutenant DiMarzo and his firefighters were blown away like chaff. Nearly every airplane on the hangar deck burst into flame. Secondary explosions from airplane ordnance turned the cavernous hangar bay into a maelstrom of fire and shrapnel.

The worst killer was the smoke. It gushed into passageways and filled compartments, trapping men on the shattered gallery deck with no route of escape. The smoke billowed into the sky through the open holes in the flight deck. Firefighting crews manned hoses on the open deck, trying to keep the flames from spreading to more airplanes and ammunition stores. The debris of the wrecked Zero—the second kamikaze—still smoldered on the forward deck. In the wreckage someone discovered the mostly intact body of the pilot, Kohichi Nunoda. His remains were given an unceremonious burial at sea.

The second kamikaze strike jammed the ship's sky-search radar. Sailors were drafted as lookouts, their eyeballs serving as *Intrepid*'s primary warning system. The towering column of smoke was a beacon for more kamikazes. "For God's sake," said a gunnery officer, "are we the only ship in the ocean?"

They weren't. The massed wave of *tokko* aircraft had fanned out to other targets. At 1254, another pair of Zeroes dove on the light carrier *Cabot*. The first crashed into the forward flight deck among a pack of launching airplanes. Less than a minute later, a second Zero attacked from nearly straight ahead. At the last second, the gunners put enough rounds into the plane that the Zero veered off course and crashed into the port side at the waterline. Still, the intense shower of flame and debris wiped out the gun crews on *Cabot*'s exposed port rail. By the time the flames were extinguished, the toll of *Cabot*'s dead and missing, mostly men of the gun crews, had swelled to thirty-five, with another seventeen seriously injured.

While *Intrepid* and *Cabot* were fighting their fires, yet another carrier in the same task group, USS *Essex*, was under siege. At 1256, an Asahi D4Y "Judy" dive-bomber, a sleeker replacement for the fixed-gear D3A "Val" bomber, flown by a young man named Yoshinori Yamaguchi, came slanting out of the sky toward *Essex*. Trailing a dense stream of smoke from its burning left wing, the kamikaze dove straight and true into *Essex*'s port deck edge. A geyser of fire and smoke leaped into the sky and enveloped the carrier's flight deck.

Later it was determined that Yamaguchi's plane carried no bomb. Intelligence officers searched for an explanation. Was he not a kamikaze? Had he already dropped his bomb, then spotted *Essex* and decided to crash into it? The mystery only added to the aura that was growing around the kamikazes. What sort of people would turn themselves into human bombs?

In less than a half hour, four carriers had been struck. *Cabot*, *Hancock*, and *Essex* could be patched and returned to duty, but *Intrepid*'s wounds were more serious. The hangar deck was a scene of horror. Decks and bulkheads were warped from the intense fires. Bodies and body parts were still being recovered. Sixty-nine men had perished in the attacks, and 150 were wounded. Many of the dead had simply vanished, blown overboard or their bodies never found.

Intrepid was headed back to San Francisco for extensive re-pairs. When she returned, *Intrepid* would have a fresh air group embarked. The war was entering its final act. And halfway around the world, the stage was being set for the last great sea battle of history.

By the time Chester Nimitz arrived in Washington in October 1944, the debate about which Pacific island would be next was officially over. Nimitz was accompanied by Fifth Fleet com-mander Vice Admiral Spruance and a square-jawed Army lieuten-ant general named Simon Bolivar Buckner Jr. Buckner had just been given command of the newly formed Tenth Army, which would make an amphibious assault on either Formosa or Okinawa.

Nimitz, Spruance, and Buckner were all of the same mind: Okinawa should be the target. All they had to do was convince the hardheaded chief of naval operation, Adm. Ernest King.

To their surprise, King needed no more convincing. He had al-ready studied the logistics reports and reached the same conclusion.

An invasion of Formosa would entail unacceptably high American casualties and would only lengthen the war. Formosa would be bypassed. After capturing the island fortress of Iwo Jima in early 1945, Nimitz's forces would invade Okinawa.

With the Joint Chiefs of Staff in agreement, the planning began in earnest. The invasion of Okinawa now had a code name: Operation Iceberg.

4 ▸ TINY TIM

The Grim Reapers were splitting up. The news came while the squadron was still on the East Coast, packing up to fly to California and board the *Intrepid*. Instead of one big Corsair squadron, the legendary Fighting 10, a new outfit—Bomber Fighting 10—was being spun off.

The new squadron reflected the current thinking about air group composition. Task forces needed more fighters to protect them from the growing specter of kamikazes. The F4U Corsair was both an air-superiority fighter and a bona fide bomber. Unlike the plodding SB2C Helldivers and TBM Avengers, which needed fighter cover while they hauled bombs to their targets, the Corsair provided its own protection. Since the air-to-air and air-to-ground missions were distinctly different, someone in Washington had decreed that they should be performed by different squadrons.

Wilmer Rawie was tapped to command the new squadron, now designated VBF-10. True to form, Rawie grabbed up most of his cadre of handpicked students and instructors from his former training unit. Meanwhile, the fighting squadron, which got to keep the VF-10 designation and the old Grim Reapers logo, received a new skipper, a heavyset, mustached lieutenant commander named Walt Clarke, another veteran with four kills from the Solomons campaign.

No one was happy about it. To the old hands, splitting up a legendary outfit like the Reapers was the same as breaking up a family. It didn't seem right. Despite the hoopla about bombers and fighters, weren't the airplanes and the missions the same?

Not exactly. What they didn't yet know was that the experimental new bomber-fighting squadron had been selected to fire an experimental new weapon, a rocket called the Tiny Tim. And as the pilots would find out, there was nothing tiny about it.

Like most of the Tail End Charlies, Erickson was in awe of his senior officers. Within the squadron, the skipper, Will Rawie, occupied the top rung on the ladder of official respect. Just beneath him came the executive officer, Lt. Timmy Gile, architect of the famous Atlantic City party and an ace with eight kills. Close behind were guys such as Paul Cordray and William "Country" Landreth, old hands with combat time on their records.

One figure stood out above all others. With the possible exception of God Himself, no one received greater deference than Cmdr. Johnny Hyland, who went by "CAG," the acronym for air group commander. Hyland was one of those rare commanders who seemed to have it all—good looks, a quick, focused intelligence, a charismatic personality, and the skills of a natural leader. The son of a naval officer, Hyland was a 1934 graduate of the Naval Academy. He'd put in a year as a surface officer aboard USS *Lexington* and then the four-stack destroyer *Elliot* before going to Pensacola for flight training. His first assignment after earning his wings was a made-in-heaven job—flying with the Navy's most prestigious fighting squadron, VF-6, aboard *Enterprise*. He should have been in the sweet spot for quick advancement when war came.

But Hyland's timing was off. On the day Pearl Harbor was attacked, December 7, 1941, Hyland was in the cockpit of a lumbering PBY patrol plane attached to Patrol Wing 10 at Olongapo in the Philippines. He flew the last patrol plane from the Dutch naval base at Ambon before the Japanese swarmed over the Dutch East Indies. Of the wing's original forty-six patrol planes, only three escaped.

Sent to Washington, D.C., Hyland became the operations officer, then the executive officer at Anacostia Naval Air Station.

Instead of rotating to a combat billet in the Pacific, he was chosen as the personal pilot for the chief of naval operations, Adm. Ernest King. Hyland was missing the war, a victim of his own competence.

He pulled every string, including a request to King himself. Finally, in the summer of 1944, came the orders Hyland had been praying for. A new air group was being formed aboard USS *Intrepid*. John Hyland would take command.

The assignment came just in time. If Hyland was to have any chance at ascending to high rank in the postwar Navy, he had to collect his share of combat ribbons. He'd come dangerously close to missing out.

By now the new bomber-fighting squadron had been sorted into four-pilot divisions. Each division was split into a pair of two-plane sections, with a senior pilot leading each division and section. The junior pilots—the Tail End Charlies—were assigned as their wingmen.

Erickson learned that he would be the wingman of a veteran of the Solomons campaign, Lt. (jg) Robert "Windy" Hill. Hill had been in VF-17, a famous squadron called the Jolly Rogers. He was one of the more flamboyant pilots in the squadron, earning the nickname "Windy" for his fondness for over-the-top storytelling. Hill was the epitome of the World War II fighter pilot—cocky, aggressive in the air and on the ground, with movie-star good looks.

"If there were two good-looking women in the room," remembered one of the Tail End Charlies, "you could count on them both going for Windy. The smart thing was to stay close and grab the one he didn't take."

Being Hill's wingman suited Erickson just fine. Then he learned the rest of his assignment. The leader of their four-plane division was none other than the air group commander himself.

Erickson didn't know whether to cheer or moan. The CAG could have picked anyone he wanted as his Tail End Charlie. It meant that Hyland trusted Erickson to cover his tail. It also meant that if Erickson somehow screwed up and *didn't* cover Hyland's tail, he was dead meat.

O ff they went, in flights of four, headed for California and the USS *Intrepid*. It was not a smooth journey. Before they reached Alameda and their new carrier, two more Tail End Charlies were gone.

One was an ensign named Charles Jensen, who decided to take a detour over his hometown of Mesa, Arizona. In a classic case of boldness exceeding judgment, Jensen was buzzing the floor of the desert when he clipped the ground. The Corsair crashed and exploded in full view of the pilot's horrified family.

Almost as soon as they reached California, they lost another. Ens. Spence Mitchell took off on a training flight over the cloud-covered Pacific. He was never seen again, and no trace was found of his fighter. The best guess was that he'd become disoriented in the clouds and spun into the ocean.

Meanwhile, the pilots of the new bomber-fighting squadron had one more square to fill. They flew out to the Navy's ordnance testing facility at Inyokern Naval Air Facility, in the California high desert country, for indoctrination in the new weapon called the Tiny Tim. Inyokern was part of the Navy's China Lake ordnance test base. The place looked like the set of a movie Western. There were a couple of bars and a motel, but not much else of interest to young fighter pilots.

No one got a good feeling when they first saw the Tiny Tim rocket. The weapon already had a bad reputation. In one of its first test firings at China Lake, it had killed the crew of the SB2C launch plane when the rocket blast destroyed the Helldiver's control surfaces. The fix the engineers came up with was to drop the weapon far enough to clear the aircraft before igniting the rocket with an attached lanyard. The fix didn't always work. If the rocket wasn't released from a precise 45-degree dive, the missile could fly through the airplane's propeller. Or it could veer off and hit an unintended target, such as the plane that launched it.

Even the name seemed like a joke. The Tiny Tim was a monster—over 10 feet long and more than half a ton in weight, with a diameter of 11.75 inches, which by no coincidence was the dimension of a standard 500-pound semi-armor-piercing bomb, the warhead of the Tiny Tim. It also happened to be the diameter of standard oil well steel tubing, which was used as the casing for the rocket. The Tiny Tim had a solid-propellant motor that could accelerate it to nearly 600 mph, with an effective range of over a mile. When it leaped from beneath its launching aircraft, streaming a trail of fire, the Tiny Tim looked like a creature from hell.

Between classes and missile-firing sorties, the pilots had time on their hands. They played cards, checked out the drinking establishments, and pursued the local girls. It was mostly a futile chase. After Atlantic City, Inyokern seemed like a desert outpost, which in fact it was.

Finally came the end of Tiny Tim training. Someone decided that the newly qualified pilots should conduct a firepower demonstration for the Navy brass. Eight Corsairs, each armed with a Tiny Tim and eight 5-inch HVARs—high velocity rockets—dove in formation on a practice target. Led by Johnny Hyland, they salvoed their weapons on signal.

It was spectacular. Spewing flame and smoke, the rockets roared toward the earth at nearly supersonic speed. More than six tons of high explosive slammed into the target like the broadside from a battleship. The concussion rumbled across the desert floor, rattling every window in Inyokern and sending a eruption of dirt, sagebrush, and black smoke hundreds of feet into the sky. The senior officers watching the demonstration were flabbergasted. Even the citizens of Inyokern, long accustomed to loud noises from the Navy weapons range, were startled.

Most of all, it shocked the pilots in the Corsairs. A single collective thought passed through their brains: *Holy shit!* It dawned on them that this thing could do a hell of a lot of damage. And not just to the enemy.

Vice Adm. Matome Ugaki poured himself another sake. It was evening, and he was alone in his small wood-and-fabric home in the coastal town of Atami, 60 miles southwest of Tokyo.

Drinking had become one of Ugaki's preoccupations since his return from the disastrous battle at Leyte Gulf. Unlike his mentor, Adm. Isoruku Yamamoto, who was a teetotaler, Ugaki loved sake. When he had nothing else to do, he frequently drank himself into a stupor. This evening, like most evenings lately, he had nothing else to do. Nothing except think about the war and write in his diary.

The war news was all bad. The Americans were in Subic Bay, on the main Philippine island of Luzon. The Red Army was within 15 miles of Berlin. American B-29s were flying nightly over Japan. From his garden Ugaki could hear the drone of the bombers on their way to raze another city.

Ugaki had started the diary during the months before the war in 1941. Like a good navy man, he began most entries with an observation about the weather. Amid cynical comments about the course of the war and the damage inflicted on Japan's homeland, he inserted snippets of poetry, thoughts about nature and the changing seasons, and notes about his health problems. He disliked going to Tokyo, he wrote, because the lack of warm water aggravated his piles.

Even when he was drunk, Matome Ugaki seldom smiled. Photographs showed a bullet-skulled man with a stern, unyielding countenance. The expression was common to senior Imperial Japanese Navy officers, most of whom wished to emulate the fierce image of a samurai warrior. The nickname bestowed on Ugaki by his subordinates was the "Golden Mask."

There was more, however, to Matome Ugaki. Behind the mask was a man of intelligence and sensitivity. Like his colleague, Vice Adm. Takijiro Ohnishi, founder of the Special Attack Corps, Ugaki embodied all the ancient contradictions in Japan's culture—the warrior's bloody *bushido* ethic balanced against an aesthete's tears over the changing of the seasons.

Ugaki was a classically educated scholar who had made a life-time study of Buddhist philosophy. He was also a devoted family man, inordinately proud of his son Hiromitsu, who had just become a naval surgeon. Ugaki had never stopped mourning his wife, Tomoko, who died five years earlier. He made regular visits to her tomb to clean the grounds and offer prayers.

Ugaki had begun the war as chief of staff of the Combined Fleet, serving under the brilliant Yamamoto. He remained in that post, surviving the Battle of Midway, until April 18, 1943, when Yamamoto's and Ugaki's planes were ambushed by American P-38s over Bougainville. Yamamoto's Mitsubishi G4M "Betty" bomber was shot down in flames and crashed in the jungle. Ugaki's bomber also went down, ditching offshore. Ugaki managed to crawl out and survived by clinging to floating wreckage.

Though badly injured, he recovered from his wounds, was promoted to vice admiral, and took command of a battleship division in time for the Battle of Leyte Gulf. Again he escaped death, though his fleet was pounded by American carrier-based planes, sinking the 72,000-ton dreadnought *Musashi*. En route back to Japan, Ugaki endured the further ignominy of losing more ships— the battleship *Kongo* and the destroyer *Urakaze*—to American submarines in the East China Sea.

Then Ugaki's career slid into limbo. For the rest of 1944 he was attached to the navy general staff, with no specific duties. Each day passed much like the one before, puttering in his flower garden, writing in his diary, drinking sake. He took long walks and gazed balefully into the sky. American bombers were a steady presence. On the last day of 1944 he wrote in his diary, "However impatient I might be hoping to save this crisis by all means, I can't do anything now. All I can do is to send off the outgoing year, expecting to exert efforts next year. My thoughts ran wild seeking ways to save the empire."

To save the empire. As if by a miracle, a way to save the empire came to Ugaki on the night of February 9, 1945, while he was still finishing his bottle of sake. It arrived in the form of a phone call, via the local police station. The admiral was to proceed to Tokyo immediately for an audience with the emperor. Ugaki would be appointed commander in chief of a newly established unit, the Fifth Air Fleet, with the responsibility for guarding all of Japan's southern shore.

Although the new command was called a "fleet," Ugaki knew there was no fleet. The Fifth Air Fleet was a suicide force composed of *tokko* aircraft and pilots, Kaiten manned torpedoes, and *Ohka* flying rocket bombs.

Ugaki considered the assignment a gift from heaven. He already believed that the only strategy left to Japan was to bleed the Americans until they sued for peace. In Tokyo he had heard the whispers and veiled suggestions from certain officers that Japan should avoid total ruin by negotiating a conditional surrender. Ugaki had only contempt for these weaklings. In his view, Japan's honor demanded that every fighting man and citizen be willing to sacrifice his life.

Matome Ugaki was a religious man. Like most senior officers, he worshiped at the Yasukuni Shrine, where, according to Shinto belief, the *kami*, or spirits, of Japan's fighting men resided. Ugaki mused in his diary that if he, too, could be honored to be enshrined with the other spirits at Yasukuni, he would be content.

"I'm appointed to a very important post," he boasted that night in his diary, "which has the key to determine the fate of the empire, with the pick of the Imperial Navy available at present. I have to break through this crisis with diehard struggles."

Ugaki already had an idea where the diehard struggles would occur. The Americans were bringing the war closer to Japan. Their next target would surely be in the Bonin Islands, perhaps Chichi Jima or Iwo Jima. And then would come the stepping-stones to southern Japan, the Ryukyus—and the island of Okinawa.

5 ▸ YOUR FAVORITE ENEMY

A steady barrage of thunder pulsed in Erickson's skull. His stomach churned, and he had the dry heaves. The twenty-two-year-old fighter pilot was an inexperienced drinker, and now he had a hangover of seismic proportions.

He wasn't alone. The squadron's deployment bash at the Alameda officers' club had left most of the Tail End Charlies in a near-comatose state. As *Intrepid* slid away from her berth at Alameda, the forty-man junior officers' bunkroom they called Boys' Town looked like a death ward. From the lavatories came a steady litany of gagging and retching.

Despite their nausea, Erickson and a few others mustered the strength to go topside to watch *Intrepid*'s departure. The ship's crew, wearing their dress blues, lined the edges of the flight deck. As the carrier steamed across San Francisco Bay, past the rocky hump of Alcatraz, someone yelled, "So long, Big Al." For the old hands who had made this passage several times, it was a tradition. It didn't matter that the prison's most famous inmate, Al Capone, was no longer in residence.

The men on the flight deck and in the island watched the great spans of the Golden Gate Bridge looming ahead. There was always a crowd on the bridge to observe warships departing, but this time was different. The people lining the rails of the bridge were *girls*, dozens of them. They were waving brassieres, scarves, panties. They yelled and blew kisses to the men on the deck.

The men whistled and yelled and waved back. Even the carrier's new skipper, Capt. Giles Short, who had the best view of anyone, was laughing. Minutes later the Golden Gate and the rocky shoreline of Marin County were receding in the distance.

Then came the open ocean. As *Intrepid* took on a gentle roll, the hangovers were compounded by violent seasickness. Erickson, a kid from the Great Plains, lay in his bunk feeling deathly ill for three days. Then one morning, halfway to Hawaii, he woke up feeling fine. By the time *Intrepid* pulled into the channel at Pearl Harbor, Erickson felt like an old sea dog.

While most of the pilots hit the beach and prowled the bars at Waikiki, the former art student packed up his sketchbook and watercolors and spent his liberty time touring the mountains of Kaneohe. At the highest point on the island's mountain ridge, Erickson spent an afternoon sketching the magnificent scenery. It was hard to imagine, gazing around at the tranquil mountainscape, that somewhere beyond the western horizon a war was raging.

The air group was scheduled for a five-day operational training session aboard the *Intrepid*. After the first day, the exercise was abruptly canceled and *Intrepid* was ordered back to Pearl Harbor. The crew was told to prepare for immediate departure.

The pilots and aircrewmen were herded into an open-air theater on Ford Island for a briefing on escape and evasion techniques. The next morning, March 3, 1945, *Intrepid* was under way, joined in her voyage by the carriers *Franklin*, *Bataan*, and *Independence*, the battle cruiser *Guam*, and eight destroyers. They were on their way to an atoll called Ulithi, in the Caroline Islands group. Since late 1944, when Marines seized Ulithi from the Japanese, the atoll had become the U.S. Navy's principal anchorage in the western Pacific.

Now Ulithi was brimming with warships staging for what would be the largest amphibious operation of the Pacific war. The ships of Raymond Spruance's Fifth Fleet would converge on the island of Okinawa, where, on April 1, 1945, 182,000 troops of the U.S. Tenth Army would storm ashore.

The Ulithi atoll was more than a thousand miles from the

closest enemy air base in Japan. Their vital anchorage, most senior U.S. commanders believed, was safe from attack.

They were wrong.

Vice Adm. Matome Ugaki studied the map spread out on his desk. The tiny atoll looked no bigger than a flyspeck. Reaching the enemy base at Ulithi would be a demanding feat of navigation for his *tokko* airmen, but it could be done.

Ugaki had arrived at his new command post in Kanoya in mid-February 1945, just as the American invasion of Iwo Jima was about to begin. Frustrated and angry, the admiral followed the inexorable progress of the battle. By March 6, 1945, the vital airfield at Iwo Jima was in American hands. In two more weeks the battle for the island would be over.

With carrier-based close air support no longer necessary, the American carriers were withdrawing from Iwo Jima. A Japanese reconnaissance plane had just reported that sixteen U.S. carriers were entering the lagoon at Ulithi.

To Ugaki, this was an irresistible opportunity. It would be glorious! Such an audacious *tokko* mission would send a single, shining statement to the world: the Japanese people would never surrender.

Ugaki gave the order to prepare the operation, which took the name Tan No. 2. (Tan No. 1 had been a similar strike on the U.S. anchorage at Majuro from the Japanese base on Truk but was aborted because the U.S. fleet departed Majuro before the attack.) Called the Azusa Special Attack Unit, the *tokko* pilots would fly two dozen twin-engine Yokosuka P1Y "Frances" bombers nonstop from Kanoya to Ulithi, a distance of 1,350 miles. Each bomber had a crew of three and carried an 800-kilogram (1,764-lb.) bomb. The Tan operation would be the longest and boldest kamikaze raid ever attempted.

The first component of the mission, a Japanese flying boat, took off at 0300 from Kagoshima, on the southern tip of Japan, to scout the weather en route to Ulithi. Four land-based bombers left

Kanoya at 0430 to patrol in advance of the main force. Four more flying boats launched from Kagoshima at 0730 to serve as pathfinders for the twenty-four kamikaze bombers, led by Lt. Kuromaru Naoto.

The Tan No. 2 mission began to unravel early. Plagued by the same problems that afflicted every Japanese air combat unit—bad gasoline and shortages of parts—thirteen of the Frances bombers developed engine trouble. Most were able to divert to the Japanese-held island of Minami Daito. Two ditched in the ocean.

As the remaining eleven bombers neared Ulithi, a system of heavy rain squalls forced them to climb above the clouds, depriving them of visual navigation cues. When they guessed they were near Ulithi, they descended back through the clouds—and saw nothing. Finally spotting the island of Yap, 120 miles west of Ulithi, they turned toward their target.

By now the mission was well behind schedule. Darkness was descending over the Pacific. Because of the diversions around weather, the bombers were at the extreme end of their range. One by one the Nakajima NK9B engines coughed and went silent. Nine of the bombers splashed into the darkened sea.

Two were still flying. As the shape of Ulithi lagoon loomed out of the darkness, the fatigued pilots peered down, trying to pick out the ships in the anchorage. Their targets were almost invisible. Almost, but not entirely.

I t was dark on the flight deck of the USS *Randolph*. Radioman Second Class V. J. Verdolini had just gotten off watch. He was walking along the starboard edge of the flight deck, on his way to the Radio 3 compartment near the stern, when he heard music. It was coming from the hangar bay below. A movie—*A Song to Remember*—was playing, and more than a hundred crewmen were crammed into the open bay. Verdolini hesitated, then decided to go below and catch the end of the movie. It was a decision that saved his life.

The movie was nearly over. It ended with Cornel Wilde, as the composer Frédéric Chopin, playing the "Heroic Polonaise." Verdolini was standing in the back of the crowded hangar bay, about to head back to the stern, when a white flash blinded him. A thunderous explosion rocked the ship. Verdolini was slammed to the steel deck.

Dazed, he staggered to his feet, dimly aware of the klaxon sounding the general quarters alarm. Bodies were lying around him. Except for flash burns on his face and arms, Verdolini wasn't seriously injured. By the time they extinguished the blazes on *Randolph*, twenty-five men were dead and more than a hundred were wounded.

Not for several more hours did they piece together what had happened. The kamikaze bomber—one of the two that made it to Ulithi that night—crashed into *Randolph*'s starboard side aft, just below the flight deck. With almost no fuel remaining, the Frances bomber didn't burn, but its bomb exploded with horrific results. They later found the remains of the three Japanese crewmen in the wreckage of the bomber.

The second kamikaze was less successful. Searching for a target on the darkened atoll, the pilot zeroed in on what appeared to be the silhouette of an enemy warship. It was, in fact, tiny Sorlen Island. The Frances bomber plunged straight into the uninhabited islet and exploded.

The brazenness of the attack shocked everyone. To fleet and task force commanders, the attack was an eye-opener. Before they invaded Okinawa, they would have to stamp out the bases where the kamikazes lived.

Smoke was still spewing from the charred fantail of *Randolph* the next morning when *Intrepid* pulled into the Ulithi anchorage. Sober-faced sailors stared from the rail at the wreckage on *Randolph*'s stern. For those who had just joined the carrier in San Francisco, it was a first glimpse of the reality of war.

The voyage from Pearl Harbor had taken ten days. To the "plank owners"—sailors who had been aboard *Intrepid* since her commissioning in August 1943—pulling back into the Ulithi lagoon evoked a flood of memories, some good, some painful. Ulithi was where they had come between battles to rest and replenish. The recreational facility on Mog Mog Island was where they sloshed around in the surf, drank their ration of two warm beers, and swapped news and war stories with sailors from other ships.

Ulithi was also the place where *Intrepid* had come five months earlier, her decks smoldering and the stench of death filling the hangar bay, after enduring two consecutive kamikaze strikes off the Philippines.

Ulithi looked different now. Everywhere, from one end of the big heart-shaped lagoon to the other, were ships—carriers, destroyers, battleships—all part of the the vast fleet assembling for the invasion of the last stepping-stone to Japan, Okinawa.

The U.S. military's path to Japan had been divided since 1943 when the joint chiefs dictated that forces of the U.S. Army, under Douglas MacArthur, would advance via the Solomons, the Bismarck Archipelago, New Guinea, and the Philippines. The U.S. Navy, led in the Pacific by Chester Nimitz, would drive across the central Pacific, landing Marines in the Marshalls, the Carolines, and the Marianas, and now on Okinawa.

It was an awkward, two-headed command structure, unlike the situation in Europe, where Gen. Dwight Eisenhower had supreme command of all U.S. forces. At Okinawa, the Army-Navy command sharing would continue. A U.S. Army general, Simon Buckner Jr., would command the ground forces, while Fifth Fleet commander Adm. Raymond Spruance would have overall responsibility for the invasion.

Just as confusing was the Navy's habit of changing the fleet designations. When Spruance was in command, the armada was called the Fifth Fleet, but when he was relieved by his counterpart,

Adm. Bull Halsey, it became the Third Fleet, and the designation of each task force and task group was similarly changed.

The name changes gave everyone headaches, including the enemy. Halsey likened it to changing drivers and keeping the horses. "It was hard on the horses," he explained later, "but it was effective. It consistently misled the Japs into an exaggerated conception of our seagoing strength."

Neither Halsey nor hardly any other American in 1945 had trouble using words such as *Japs* or *Nips*. No one would forget that it was the Japs who had perpetrated the sneak attack on Pearl Harbor. Magazine articles and intelligence reports confirmed that rampaging Jap troops bayoneted babies, beheaded prisoners, and raped their conquered people. Hating Japs made it easy to kill them.

The hatred and racism were mutual. Japanese fighting men held Americans, as well as most other Westerners, in contempt. Japanese soldiers and sailors were fed a steady stream of salacious stories about how barbaric U.S. troops rolled over civilians and prisoners with their tanks. Americans were spoiled, decadent, uncivilized. They would go down in defeat because they lacked the courageous spirit of Japanese fighting men.

We welcome *Intrepid* to the Okinawa area," said the silky voice on the radio. "Kamikaze division number 147 will join you on your arrival."

The voice belonged to Tokyo Rose, whose broadcasts from Japan were coming over the ship's radio. The announcer was supposed to sound like an evil seductress who knew the location of every U.S. ship and planted thoughts about what the GIs' wives and girlfriends were up to while they were at war. The idea was to erode the morale of the U.S. fighting men, but it produced the opposite effect. Most thought it was great entertainment.

Tokyo Rose, who was actually a composite of eight or more female broadcasters, had a mocking, sardonic humor that made them laugh. "Hello again," she would start out, "this is your favorite enemy." The shows had music, popular and classic, and news from home, mostly concerning disasters and privations of the war, and then accounts of all the American ships sunk and battles lost. Sailors cracked up when they heard, often for the third or fourth time, that *their* ship had been sent to the bottom.

Still, the Tail End Charlies had to wonder. How did she know *Intrepid* was on its way? What else did she know about them? Was it true about the kamikazes joining them? What was so important about Okinawa?

The answer was geography. The Great Loochoo—the name the ancients bestowed on the island of Okinawa—was 340 miles from Japan. The island was 64 miles long, set in the middle of the Ryukyus, the chain that dangled like a stinger from the rump of the Japanese home islands.

For seven centuries the Great Loochoo had been an autonomous kingdom, maintaining a precarious balance between the competing powers of China and Japan. The militaristic Meiji dynasty of Japan swept down to annex the Ryukyus in 1879 and since then had governed it in colonial fashion. Okinawans became second-class citizens of the Japanese empire, whose administrators considered the Okinawans to be ignorant and racially inferior. As a result, the natives of the Great Loochoo retained their own customs and dialects. For the most part they had no use for the abstract Japanese notions of *bushido* and loyalty to an emperor.

The majority of the 450,000 Okinawans lived in the south. Most were farmers living in thatched huts or small frame houses. Private automobiles were virtually nonexistent. Two of the three primitive railroads were horse-drawn. There were only three towns of any significance: Toguchi, on the sparsely populated northern peninsula; Shuri, ancient seat of the Great Loochoo and site of a castle; and Naha, the modern capital.

Okinawa's major assets were its three airfields and half dozen natural harbors. But the real prize was its proximity to the enemy homeland. The Great Loochoo would be the springboard to Japan.

By mid-March 1945, the man responsible for the amphibious assault on the Great Loochoo was making his final preparations.

They called him the "Alligator." In a war that demanded the invasion of the enemy's ocean empire one island at a time, Vice Adm. Richmond K. Turner was the acknowledged master. Though Kelly Turner earned the "Alligator" label because of his mastery of amphibious operations, those who knew him thought it also described his personality. His subordinates had their own name for him, never used in his presence—"Terrible" Turner. A *Time* magazine article commented about Turner, "To his colleagues (who know how to use monosyllables respectfully) he is known as 'a mean son of a bitch.'"

Turner had a high, receding hairline, bushy eyebrows, and steel-rimmed spectacles through which he could direct a withering glower like a barrage from his guns. Ships he commanded were remembered as "taut" rather than "happy."

The Alligator, for his part, had no interest in happy. His reputation for arrogance nearly matched that of his old boss, Adm. Ernest King, the chief of naval operations, who once described Turner as "brilliant, caustic, arrogant and tactless." Coming from King, it was the highest form of compliment. It meant that he saw in Turner a version of himself.

Turner and his equally cantankerous counterpart, Marine Maj. Gen. Holland "Howlin' Mad" Smith, had been a formidable team in the invasions of Betio, Makin, Majuro, Kwajalein, Roi, and Namur. In March 1944, Turner commanded the nearly flawless landings on Saipan, Tinian, and Guam. In February 1945, he directed the bloody campaign at Iwo Jima.

Here at Okinawa the Alligator would be running the greatest invasion of them all. As usual, he had developed a plan that covered every detail of the complex operation, leaving his subcommanders no gray area or need for improvisation. He was still, as naval historian Samuel Eliot Morison observed, "the same driving, swearing, sweating 'Kelly' whose head could conceive more new ideas and retain more details than any flag officer in the Navy."

Aboard his flagship, the cruiser *Eldorado*, Turner was making final preparations for the invasion when his eye was drawn to a cluster of mountainous islands 15 miles southwest of Okinawa called the Kerama Retto. *Retto* meant "archipelago," and what interested Turner was the natural anchorage between the largest island of the group and the five smaller ones to the west.

It looked to Turner as if the anchorage—"roadstead" in naval parlance—might be able to shelter seventy-five or more of his ships. Even better, both ends of the anchorage could be protected by antisubmarine nets. Another feature he liked was the Aka Channel, a two-mile clearway ideal for seaplanes and their tenders.

The trouble was, none of Turner's task group commanders agreed with him. Trying to take the Kerama Retto only a few days before the April 1 invasion of Okinawa was too great a risk. If the Japanese put up a tenacious defense, it would tie up the invasion force and divert resources from the critical landings on Okinawa.

It wasn't the Alligator's style to be dissuaded when he knew he was right. True to form, he listened to the arguments, then dismissed them all. Hell, yes, it was a risk, but it was worth it. One thing he'd learned from Iwo Jima was that an invasion fleet needed a sheltered anchorage for replenishment.

In any case, Turner doubted the Japanese would put up a fierce resistance. The whole damned Retto, he told his staff, could probably be captured by a single battalion. Still, to be on the safe side, he would agree to a division-sized amphibious assault.

The major threat to Turner's ships would be the kamikazes based in southern Japan. And the carriers of Mitscher's Task Force 58—the Fast Carrier Task Force—were already on their way to Japan to hit the kamikaze bases.

Among them was the newcomer, USS *Intrepid*.

6 ▸ FIRST BLOODING

The squawk box blared at 0415. Erickson climbed down from his third-tier bunk in Boys' Town and joined the line in the head. No one had gotten much sleep. The chatter this morning was subdued, not the usual raunchy banter. After a quick breakfast in the wardroom, Erickson made his way to the squadron ready room.

The pilots looked like aliens, all wearing red-lensed goggles to protect their night vision from the glare of the ready room lights. They were also wearing something new—a green nylon anti-blackout suit. Called a "G-suit," the garment was supposed to inflate during high acceleration, squeezing the pilot's legs and torso and preventing a blackout because of blood draining from his brain.

Being a lowly ensign, like a full third of the squadron pilots, Erickson knew his place. He went to the back of the ready room and took a seat in the last row. The leather-upholstered ready room seats were another anomaly that was peculiar to the flying Navy, like the brown shoes and green uniforms worn by naval aviators. The high-backed seats looked more appropriate for an airliner than a naval vessel.

A few minutes before 0500, the squadron skipper came barging in. If Will Rawie was nervous, he didn't show it. In fact, Rawie seemed more nonchalant than ever, keeping a matter-of-fact demeanor as he told them where they were headed on their first combat mission.

They were going to Japan.

The mood in the ready room turned even more somber. No one was really surprised. They'd already been briefed that their first targets before the Okinawa invasion would probably be the airfields in Japan. That was where the kamikazes came from.

Until that morning, that's what it had been—*probably*. Now Rawie had just cleared it up for them. He stuck a map of southern Japan up on the bulkhead.

From the back of the ready room, the Tail End Charlies stared through their red-lensed goggles. Reality was setting in. Any of them who still worried that he was missing the war could officially stop worrying.

The primary target was Oita airfield on the southernmost island of Kyushu. In case of bad weather, the secondary would be Saeki airfield. Erickson jotted the flight information on his knee board. With a grease pencil he marked on his plotting board the coordinates of Point Option—the position where the carrier was supposed to be at the end of the four-hour mission. If the carrier had to duck into rain squalls for cover or run from an enemy threat, Point Option could be 75 miles off when a strike came home low on fuel.

Rawie read off the aircraft assignments. Twelve Corsairs were headed for Kyushu. Another eight Corsairs as well as four F6F-5N Hellcat night fighters would fly CAP—combat air patrol—over the task group. *Intrepid* and her task group were dangerously close to Japan. The job of the CAP fighters was to intercept enemy aircraft before they could get to the carriers.

The Japanese already knew they were there. All through the night enemy aircraft had been probing the task force defenses. The snoopers were driven off by antiaircraft fire from the destroyer screen. No one doubted that they would be back in force now that they'd located the fleet.

At 0520 the gravel-voiced order came over the ready room squawk box: "Pilots, man your planes." Each man pulled on his parachute harness, Mae West life preserver, and .38 revolver. They dropped the red-lensed goggles in a box outside the ready room. In silence they trudged down the dimly lighted passageway and up the steel ladder to the catwalk at the edge of the flight deck.

A chill wind swept over the deck. Beyond the rail they saw only the empty void of the ocean and sky.

The flight deck was covered with warplanes. Ordnancemen were scrambling over them, hanging bombs, rockets, loading .50-caliber guns. The Corsairs were in the front of the pack, wings folded, noses tilted up, looking like raptors in the darkness.

Country Landreth was one of the CAP pilots. As a combat veteran with three and a half kills to his credit, he had been a natural choice for the critical job of fleet defense on their first day of action.

Picking his way through the parked airplanes, Landreth found his Corsair in the front of the pack. The CAP fighters would be first to catapult, then take their station over the task group while the strike aircraft were launching. The wings of the CAP fighters were clean—no bombs or rockets, just the single 160-gallon drop tank on the center station beneath the fuselage.

Erickson's fighter was further back on the deck. He found it in the darkness, gave it a once-over, then climbed up to the cockpit. The plane captain—the Navy term for a crew chief—was an enlisted man a good ten years older than Erickson. Erickson was surprised to see that the man was in tears and shaking. He'd heard the sky was thick with Japanese airplanes headed for the *Intrepid*. He was afraid for his life.

Erickson was struck by the absurdity of the situation. He was about to launch on a combat mission into the heartland of the enemy. But before he took off he had to console an anxiety-stricken sailor who would remain behind on the carrier. Erickson told the man not to worry, everything would be fine.

After he'd strapped in, Erickson flicked on the instrument panel lights. Seconds later a voice boomed over the flight deck bullhorn: "Erickson, turn off those goddamn lights!" He flicked off the lights. *Damn.* He'd forgotten that the flight deck was supposed to be blacked out. He wondered for a moment how the air boss knew who he was, then he remembered: up in the island they had every plane and pilot's position on the deck plotted. His first mission, and everyone on the flight deck had just heard that he'd screwed up.

Minutes later over the same bullhorn came the order to start engines. Up and down the deck the big three-bladed propellers whirled. Tongues of flame spat from exhaust stacks. The rustle of wind was dissolved in the sound of chuffing, belching radial engines. A cloud of sweet-smelling exhaust smoke drifted down the deck and through the open cockpits.

Erickson's engine settled down to a low, steady throb. Following the lighted wands of the plane director, he taxied to the number one catapult on the port side of the forward deck. On signal, he unfolded the Corsair's wings, then checked to make sure they were locked in place.

Nearly an hour remained before sunrise, but the eastern sky was turning pale, offering a tiny pencil line of horizon. Except for his night carrier qualifications aboard USS *Core* nearly four months before, Erickson had no experience at launching in darkness.

One after another, the Corsairs hurtled down the catapult track. Erickson's flight leader, CAG Hyland, was already airborne. Windy Hill had just launched from the starboard catapult. Erickson waited while the crewmen hooked the catapult shuttle to the belly of his airplane. On signal he pushed the throttle up to full power, checked his gauges, then shoved his head back against the headrest. He gave the ready-to-launch salute.

The catapult fired. Erickson felt like a stone in a slingshot. He sensed the dark shape of the carrier sweeping away behind him. The hard thrust of the hydraulic catapult abruptly ceased, and the Corsair hurtled into the night sky.

Minutes later, Erickson was joined up with Hyland's flight, tucked in behind Windy Hill's right wing, on his way to Japan.

From his CAP station at 20,000 feet, Landreth squinted into the pinkening sky. It was still too dark to pick out the shapes of warships against the blackened ocean. All the carriers in *Intrepid*'s Task Group 58.4 had launched their strikes. Now the aircraft were en route to the targets.

Most of the time, combat air patrol was an exercise in boredom. You droned in an orbit over the task force, conserving fuel, waiting for a sudden urgent call from the FIDO—fighter director—whose radar showed incoming unidentified aircraft, called bogeys. When the bogeys were identified as hostile, they became bandits. In the space of seconds, boredom was replaced with a surge of adrenaline-charged excitement.

For Landreth, no such call had come. In the warm solitude of his cockpit, he had time to reflect. Like most pilots in the wartime Navy, he was a reserve officer. When the war ended and the military shrank back to peacetime size, they would return to civilian life. Now that Landreth was in his second tour of combat duty, he had reached a decision. He wanted to stay in.

The night before, he'd brought up the subject with the skipper over a toddy in Rawie's stateroom. Technically, it was a breach of regulations. Drinking aboard Navy ships had been banned since 1914 when Secretary of the Navy Josephus Daniels issued General Order 99: "The use or introduction for drinking purposes of alcoholic liquors on board any naval vessel, or within any navy yard or station, is strictly prohibited, and commanding officers will be held directly responsible for the enforcement of this order."

It was one of those rules that begged to be broken. Most squadron pilots had stashes of booze for the purpose of late-night debriefings, celebrations of promotions and victories, and toasts to fallen comrades. Few commanding officers made an issue of it, and Will Rawie was no exception. Rawie, in fact, was a firm believer in the salutary benefits of a libation with his pilots and kept his own supply for that purpose.

Rawie told Landreth he had his blessing to become a regular

officer in the Navy. It was exactly what Landreth had hoped to hear. He left the skipper's stateroom with a warm contentment from the drinks and the knowledge that he had a career ahead of him in the Navy.

Landreth was still feeling the contentment as he and his flight continued their orbit on their CAP station. It was quiet in their sector, although the Hellcat night fighter pilots on the opposite side of the task force had been sent after a pair of intruders, a twin-engine Kawasaki Ki-45 "Nick" fighter and a Mitsubishi G4M Betty bomber. They only managed to get a quick burst into the Nick before both aircraft escaped in the clouds.

Landreth's orbit was bringing him back to an easterly heading. As he watched, the rim of the sun broke through the horizon. In a matter of minutes, the sea was bathed in an ethereal orange glow. One by one, the gray ships below became visible.

Landreth was astounded. "From horizon to horizon," he recalled, "the ocean was covered with the might of the United States Navy. Five task groups—twenty-one carriers and all their escorts." Until that moment, the ultimate victory of the United States over Japan had been only a vague assumption. Gazing down at the armada of warships, Landreth was struck with a sudden realization: the outcome of the war was a certainty. It was almost over. The day was close when the fighting would be over.

What Landreth didn't know was that for him that day was today.

Erickson was hearing noises. He was in his assigned slot—Tail End Charlie—in CAG Hyland's four-plane division. They were droning over the open ocean, en route to Japan. And Erickson kept hearing these worrisome sounds from his Corsair.

With them were more flights from the fighter squadron, VF-10, making a total of nineteen fighters. All were armed with eight of the new 5-inch HVARs, which someone had aptly nicknamed "Holy Moses," describing their reaction the first time they fired the rockets.

Erickson was still hearing the worrisome noises. He knew what they were, of course, but they didn't go away. Such noises were a joke—and a common phenomenon—among fighter pilots. On your first long mission over water, you heard things. You heard a roughness in the engine, a buzz in the controls, a rattle that didn't belong. After you stopped worrying about the noises, you worried about other things: losing fuel, magnetos shorting out, oil leaking.

Erickson knew all this, but he worried anyway. For a while he worried that his guns might not work. After running out of things to worry about, he started wondering about his parachute. Would he be able to open it? He practiced reaching for the D-ring of the chute. Just in case.

After an hour over the water, they spotted the shoreline of Kyushu. The primary target, Oita airfield, lay on the northeast coast, looking across the Bungo Strait at the island of Shikoku. Oita wasn't visible. It was obscured beneath a heavy cloud cover, and Hyland made his first decision as a strike leader. They would go for the secondary target, the Saeki naval base and airfield. Saeki was thirty miles south of Oita and visible through the broken cloud deck.

Erickson armed his guns and set his rockets to fire in salvo. One after the other the Corsairs pushed over in their dives. As the airfield, buildings, and revetments swelled in his windshield, Erickson could see the parked Japanese airplanes lined up, red meatballs on their wings.

He squeezed the trigger. The six .50-caliber guns rattled in a staccato beat. He saw his tracers arcing down toward the parked airplanes. As in a dream, he watched one of them explode in a roiling fireball. Then another.

The Corsairs swept over the airfield. In the harbor beyond, Erickson spotted a tanker. He salvoed his rockets at the ship, then opened up again with his guns. Peering over his shoulder as he pulled up, he saw that the tanker was ablaze. Crewmen were diving over the sides into the water.

But the enemy was firing back. One of the Tail End Charlies, Ens. Loren Isley, was diving on his target, guns firing—and didn't pull up. Isley's Corsair dove straight into the harbor and exploded.

Stunned, the other pilots stared at the blackened slick on the water where the Corsair had hit. No one knew—nor would they ever know—whether Isley had taken an antiaircraft round or just pressed his attack too close.

They came back to strafe the field, expending most of their .50-caliber ammunition, until Hyland gave the signal to pull off and rejoin.

But they weren't out of harm's way yet. As they were clearing the Japanese coastline, another Tail End Charlie, Ens. Rob Harris, called that he was losing gasoline. His fuel system had taken a hit, and he was down to only 20 gallons.

A couple of minutes later, Harris's engine quit, and he put the Corsair down in the frigid water off Shikoku. Overhead, another Tail End Charlie, Ens. Les Gray, circled, keeping an eye on Harris. He could see the pilot scrambling out of the cockpit, but the Corsair was sinking quickly. Harris wasn't dragging his life raft out with him.

Within seconds the Corsair had vanished. And so had Rob Harris.

7 ▸ THE MOOD IN BOYS' TOWN

The men in the gun tubs couldn't believe it. Their first damned day back in the war, and it was happening all over again. A Japanese plane was skimming the water, somehow dodging the curtain of antiaircraft fire, headed straight for *Intrepid*.

It seemed like the replay of a bad dream. Most of the men on the deck had been aboard *Intrepid* four months earlier when two kamikazes, five minutes apart, plunged through the carrier's flight deck, snuffing out nearly a hundred lives and taking the ship out of action.

This one was a twin-engine bomber, and its pilot seemed to be blessed with divine protection. Oily black bursts were exploding all around him. The ocean below the bomber frothed with the splashes of spent ordnance. He kept coming.

Japanese planes had been stalking *Intrepid* all morning. Fresh yellow blips kept showing up on the radar screens in CIC—the combat information center. CAP fighters from all the task group carriers were intercepting the bogeys, which were quickly tagged as bandits. As the intruders flew into range of the antiaircraft guns on the screening ships, the CAP fighters were forced to withdraw and let the gunners blaze away. Most of the attackers were shot down or chased away.

But not all. Through the CAP screen and then through the hail of antiaircraft fire came a Yokosuka P1Y Frances bomber. *Intrepid*'s 5-inchers hammered away, mostly missing. As the Frances came closer, every Bofors 40-millimeter and rapid-fire Oerlikon 20-millimeter gun on *Intrepid*'s starboard side opened up.

The Frances was taking hits, trailing smoke—but still flying. The men on *Intrepid* could see the two round cowlings with the radial engines and the distinctive long, slender wings. As the bomber bored closer, they could make out the figures of the pilots in the glass-enclosed cockpit.

The gunners braced themselves for the inevitable. This thing was clearly not a torpedo plane or a bomber. It was another kamikaze, and he had them bore sighted. Just when it seemed that the Japanese plane would smash into *Intrepid*'s flight deck, a round from one of the 5-inch guns clipped the Frances's tail.

The bomber's nose pitched straight down. In a scene that lasted less than two seconds but would remain fixed in their memories for the rest of their lives, the gunners had a plan view of the Japanese bomber. It was so close they felt they could reach out and touch it. The moment was captured by a combat photographer—the orange ball of the rising sun emblazoned on the starboard wing, port wing tip shattered by gunfire, Japanese crewmen hunched inside the cockpit.

The bomber hit the water 50 feet from *Intrepid*'s starboard bow. The explosion showered fire and debris against *Intrepid*'s starboard side and into the exposed hangar bay. Flames enveloped the forward hangar bay, lighting off the fabric control surfaces of parked airplanes and scorching painted surfaces.

By a miracle, none of the airplanes exploded. There were casualties, but not all were caused by the kamikaze crash. One of *Intrepid*'s escorts, the cruiser *Atlanta*, was also shooting at the incoming kamikaze and fired a 5-inch shell too close to *Intrepid*'s fantail. In the brief action, one sailor was killed and forty-four others wounded.

Intrepid's seasoned damage control crews had the fires extinguished in fifteen minutes. The worst damage was to the hangar deck curtain—the screen that shrouded the open hangar bay during night operations. No airplanes were destroyed, and the flame-damaged aircraft control surfaces would be quickly repaired.

The hangar bay and forward starboard hull were fire-blackened and required new paint.

The morning had just begun. While *Intrepid* was fighting off her attacker, a Yokosuka D4Y Judy dive-bomber put a 500-kilogram bomb into the carrier *Enterprise*, operating only a few thousand yards from *Intrepid*. *Enterprise*'s long string of luck held. The bomb punched a neat hole in her flight deck, then crashed into a machinery space without exploding.

A few minutes past 1300, it was *Yorktown*'s turn. Three Judy dive-bombers dove on the carrier, and two missed their target. The third put its bomb through *Yorktown*'s signal bridge, penetrating one deck before exploding and blowing two big holes in the ship's side. Five *Yorktown* crewmen were killed, and another twenty-six were wounded.

Returning from the strike on Kyushu, *Intrepid*'s Tail End Charlies were learning another lesson the hard way: a wingman used more fuel than his leader. This was because wingmen were forced to make constant throttle changes to keep their position in the flight. Each throttle movement consumed precious gasoline. After four and a half hours in the air, Hyland's wingmen were almost out of fuel.

But the *Intrepid* wasn't ready to take them aboard. The flight deck was still packed with airplanes waiting to be launched. Watching his fuel quantity gauge, Erickson wished he'd leaned out his fuel mixture and been more prudent with the throttle. It was too late. His tanks were almost empty. So were those of Ens. George Tessier, the young North Carolinian who was flying on Hyland's left wing.

Hyland put his flight into a low-power, fuel-conserving orbit, waiting for a clear deck on *Intrepid*. While they were still in the orbit, Tessier's engine abruptly quit. Dropping like a rock from the formation, Tessier's Corsair splashed down next to one of the screening destroyers. Minutes later the pilot was plucked out of the water by the destroyer crew.

Erickson knew he'd be next. Close to *Intrepid* was *Enterprise*, which had already launched her own strike planes and had a clear deck. Erickson received immediate clearance to land aboard.

After he'd safely made it down on *Enterprise*'s deck and checked his fuel, he found that he had five gallons left. If he hadn't made it aboard on his first pass, he would have been in the water with Tessier.

Erickson spent the rest of the morning aboard *Enterprise*. By comparison to *Intrepid*, the older *Enterprise* seemed smaller, her flight deck shorter and more narrow. Even her spaces belowdecks seemed cramped. Famished after his four-and-a-half-hour mission, he gobbled down peanut butter sandwiches and cocoa while the deck crew refueled his Corsair. Catapulted back into the air, he was assigned to a CAP station for another hour and a half before finally landing back aboard *Intrepid*.

The kamikazes kept coming. Following the first bomb strike on *Enterprise*, two more raiders were picked off by *Enterprise*'s gunners. One was a Judy dive-bomber whose crew, obviously not kamikazes, bailed out of the shattered airplane.

As the two Japanese parachutes floated down through the smoke and gunfire, one of *Enterprise*'s destroyer escorts came racing up with the apparent intention of capturing the enemy airmen.

They didn't. While the parachutes were still descending, the destroyer escort's gunners opened fire with their battery of 20-millimeters. The shredded bodies of the Japanese airmen hit the water, floated briefly, then disappeared beneath the waves.

None of the commanders who witnessed the incident expressed any outrage. To a man, each was filled with the same boiling fury at this maniacal enemy who was crashing into their ships. They were Japs, and you exterminated them wherever you found them.

A t 1045, *Intrepid* launched its fourth strike of the morning. It was Country Landreth's second mission, and this time he was leading a strike against the Japanese airfield complex at Uwa Jima, on the home island of Shikoku.

Arriving at the target, Landreth swept across the airfield, his .50-calibers rattling the fighter's airframe as he strafed buildings and parked airplanes. As he skimmed over the field at low altitude, he spotted something in the estuary ahead of him. It was a speedboat, racing across the water at high speed, leaving behind it a rooster tail of white water. Guessing that it must be a target of value, he went for it.

Then he noticed something else—a small island in the estuary. Protruding from the vegetation were a few round tanks and tile-roofed buildings. "I decided to give them a squirt on the way to the speedboat," he recalled.

It was a decision Landreth would regret for the rest of his life. He fired a burst into the tile roof, then shifted his attention back to the boat. In the next second, the innocent-looking building, which happened to be an ammunition storage facility, erupted in a cataclysmic explosion. Flame and debris shot hundreds of feet into the sky. As Landreth's Corsair flew through the fireball, the G-forces hit him like a giant sledgehammer. His spine compressed, and the airframe of the Corsair shuddered from the impact.

When his vision cleared, Landreth knew he was in trouble. "I looked at the oil pressure dial," he remembered, "and it read zero." Thirty seconds later, right on schedule, the big twin-row Pratt & Whitney engine, now out of oil, chuffed once and then stopped. A ghostly silence filled Landreth's cockpit.

He pointed the Corsair toward the open sea. Landreth's back was broken, and he had no feeling in his legs. Unable to use rudder pedals, he managed to turn the Corsair into the wind. He blew the canopy off just before the fighter splashed down in the gray sea off Shikoku.

And then, a miracle. Despite his injuries, he was able to haul himself out of the cockpit, dragging the life raft with him. Somehow he clambered into the raft. He pulled his tarpaulin up over him, blue side out to be less visible to the Japanese.

He waited. It was a long shot, but there was a chance that a U.S. submarine or a "Dumbo"—a seagoing rescue plane—would pick him up. His squadronmates had seen him go down and would have passed on his position via the search-and-rescue frequency. For the rest of the day he bobbed in his raft, in agony from his damaged spine.

Night came, and with it a freezing drizzle. Landreth hunkered down in the exposed raft, tarpaulin up to his chin, and waited. His mission had shrunk down to one overriding objective: stay alive until morning.

The strikes and fighter sweeps continued for the rest of the day. Twelve more Corsairs bombed and rocketed the airfield at Usa, on the north shore of Kyushu, then turned down the coast to make strafing attacks on the parked airplanes at Oita, which had been spared the earlier strikes because of weather. Escorted by the fighters, SB2C Helldivers and bomb-carrying TBM Avengers then swept in to hammer the buildings and hangars at Oita with 500-pound bombs, returning to finish the job with their machine guns.

By the end of their first day of war, *Intrepid*'s newly formed air group had logged more than 120 combat missions.

That evening the officers' wardroom was segregated along the usual lines: black shoes and brown shoes. By long tradition, surface navy officers wore black uniform shoes, while the airedales—officers of the flying branch—wore brown shoes with their khakis or aviation green uniforms. But the culture gap between them extended far beyond the color of their shoes.

The black shoes had something to celebrate. There weren't many days when surface officers on an aircraft carrier could cover themselves with glory, but this was one of them. During the near-death encounter with the kamikaze that morning, the gunnery department and the damage control crews had risen to heroic status. Now the black shoes were in an animated discussion, reliving the incident.

Jabbering at the opposite end of the room were the brown shoes, gesturing with their hands, rehashing the action over Kyushu and Shikoku. Most had flown two combat missions that day. Images of flak bursts and targets viewed through gun sights and the dry-mouthed anxiety of nearly empty fuel tanks were still fresh in their minds.

Even in normal times, the two groups maintained a cordial distance. Black shoes made no secret of their belief that they were the only *real* Navy men aboard the ship. They alone understood the crafts of ship handling, gunnery, navigation, damage control. Without them, the carrier was nothing more than an immobile barge.

The brown shoes, for their part, couldn't care less about arcane nautical lore. Most of them, especially the Tail End Charlies, kept saying things like "left" instead of "port," "floor" for "deck," "wall" when they meant "bulkhead." Mainly to annoy the black shoes, they insisted on calling the 27,000-ton aircraft carrier a "boat."

But what galled the black-shoe officers most about the airedales was their *attitude*. They were like spoiled frat boys. They sequestered themselves in their private berthing spaces, where they played cards, partied, and, if reports were to be believed, actually consumed booze. One of *Intrepid*'s black shoes came up with an analogy: the brown shoes were just like seagulls. Except for flying, all they did was eat, sleep, and crap.

There was no party that night in Boys' Town. The mood had changed. Gone were the horseplay, the banter, the wiseass jokes. There were two empty bunks. "All the ensigns were in quiet conversations, just above a whisper," remembered Erickson. "Except for a few standby pilots who would now be replacing our losses, we were no longer virgins."

Until that day, flying Navy airplanes had been a lark. Even

losing friends in training hadn't dulled the sense that the war was a great adventure.

Now all that had changed. The best buddies of Loren Isley and Rob Harris were removing the personal effects from their lockers. What happened to them could have happened to any of the Tail End Charlies. "Some were seriously writing letters," Erickson recalled, "and it didn't take much to guess what the messages contained. One day of combat had changed boys into men."

Also among the missing was Lt. (jg) Country Landreth, who by virtue of seniority hadn't been a resident of Boys' Town. One of the Tail End Charlies had seen Landreth's Corsair go into the water offshore. Another pilot reported seeing a Japanese submarine a mile and a half from where he went down.

It meant that Landreth was screwed. By now he was either dead or captured.

8 ▸ SHOOT THE SON OF A BITCH

Landreth was alive. Still adrift in his tiny raft, he clung to the hope that a submarine might pick him up. He had already stopped believing that a rescue plane was coming. Even if the crew was willing to risk coming this close to the Japanese shore, they'd never spot him in the murk. The weather was lousy. Freezing rain continued to pelt him.

The second day passed. No submarine showed up. Nor did a rescue plane, even though the weather had cleared a bit. By the time darkness fell again, Landreth was in bad shape. His lower body was numb, and hypothermia was sapping the last of his energy. He had what seemed like pneumonia. He knew he couldn't last much longer.

On the morning of the third day, he was dimly aware of voices coming to him across the water. They weren't speaking English. Out of the gloom appeared a rowboat. The two young Japanese men in the boat stared at him, keeping their guns ready while they warily circled Landreth's raft. Finally, deciding that the bedraggled figure was not a threat, they hauled him into their rowboat and took him ashore.

It was the first day of Country Landreth's ordeal as a prisoner of war.

The morning of March 19, 1945, was a replay of the day before—same predawn wake-up, same breakfast on tin trays, same briefing in the ready room. Wearing their red-lensed glasses to protect their night vision, the pilots again listened to Will Rawie tell them that they were going to Japan. He said it in the same matter-of-fact style as the day before, as if he were giving them directions to the wardroom.

This time the ante was going up. The target was a big one—the Kure naval base. Kure was on the southern shore of Honshu, the main island of Japan, 12 miles from the city of Hiroshima. Kure was the Japanese equivalent of the United States's Norfolk naval base. It was where the greatest ships of the Imperial Japanese Navy were constructed and repaired, and where one, the greatest of them all, *Yamato*, was still home-ported. The complex contained airfields, oil depots, foundries, docks, workshops, slipways, and administrative buildings. Towering over the harbor was Mt. Yasumi, which was covered with antiaircraft gun emplacements. Across the bay was the island of Eta Jima, site of the Imperial Naval Academy, with its own concentration of antiaircraft batteries. Kure was one of the most heavily defended targets outside of Tokyo.

Erickson was again CAG Hyland's number four. The downside of flying with the air group commander, of course, was that any mistake he made would result in a monumental ass chewing back on the ship. The big plus was that the CAG's division was always the first into the air and the first to land back aboard. Everything revolved around Hyland, who was responsible for coordinating the strike. His wingmen were responsible for covering his tail.

For Erickson, another plus was his section leader, Lt. (jg) Windy Hill. For all his faults—a tendency toward mouthiness and a streak of narcissism—Hill was a good fighter pilot. He'd made it through the Solomons and had the enemy aircraft kills to prove it. Erickson trusted Hill to make the right calls when the shooting started.

The ten *Intrepid* Corsairs would be joined by a trio of four-plane divisions of Hellcats from *Yorktown*. As the flights joined up, Erickson was suddenly aware of the number of airplanes in the strike. "The sky was full of planes as far as the eye could see, all making their way toward the home islands of Japan."

But somehow the *Intrepid* strike group and *Yorktown*'s group

became separated. By the time Hyland's ten Corsairs were crossing the island of Shikoku, bound for Kure, they were alone. Directly in their path lay the Japanese airfield of Matsuyama. What
they didn't yet know was that Matsuyama was the home base of the
343rd Kokutai (air group), the Imperial Japanese Navy's most elite
fighter unit. The Japanese fighters were already airborne, waiting
for them.

D awn was breaking as the Corsairs crossed the inland sea between Shikoku and the main island of Honshu. Beneath
their noses sprawled the Kure naval base. Still at 12,000 feet, they
dropped their belly tanks—jettisonable auxiliary fuel tanks—and
armed their .50-calibers. The antiaircraft gunners had already spotted them. The sky over the Kure harbor was filling with bursts of
fire.

Erickson swiveled his head, glancing left, right, then up—and
his heart nearly stopped. Six thousand feet above them, circling
like hawks, was a cluster of dusky shapes. Even at this range, Erickson could make out the red meatballs on the wings. It was his first
sight of an enemy airplane in the air.

In an excited voice, he reported the fighters to Hyland. Hyland already knew about them. He'd been watching them for the
past several minutes. The Japanese fighters didn't seem inclined
to fight. They were in a lazy tail chase, following each other in
aileron rolls. Erickson wondered whether they were working up
their courage or just showing off.

Keeping an eye on the fighters overhead, Hyland led the Corsairs in a wide turn over the bay, then rolled into a dive on the oil
storage tanks at Kure. Half the Corsairs were carrying 500-pound
bombs, and the other half were armed with 5-inch rockets.

After putting their bombs and rockets into the tanks, they all
came back for a strafing attack. By now black puffs of antiaircraft
fire were filling the sky, but without much accuracy. All over the
Kure complex, strike aircraft were pummeling their targets. In

their concrete-sheltered berths, the behemoth battleship *Yamato* and the carrier *Amagi* took hits, although neither warship was seriously damaged.

Hyland was pulling out over Kure harbor when he spotted a prize—a Mitsubishi A6M2-N "Rufe" floatplane fighter flying low over the water—and dove after him. Erickson and Hill, now on their own, were climbing back to altitude. Above them, Erickson again saw the dark shapes still circling. As he watched, two of them peeled off in a dive, coming straight down at them.

Erickson and Hill pulled into a hard vertical climb, meeting them head-on. Erickson raked the bellies of the two oncoming airplanes—Kawanishi N1K-J fighters, code-named "George"—with his machine guns as they swept past.

But Windy Hill was in trouble. He hadn't been able to jettison his belly fuel tank. Now the drag of the external tank was slowing him down. One of the high-performance George fighters was on Hill's tail, closing in for the kill.

Erickson and Hill went into a Thach weave—a mutual-defense technique of crossing each other's path, clearing each pilot's tail. Weaving high to the outside of the turn, Erickson swept back down on the enemy fighter behind Hill.

He opened fire, watching the tracers of his .50-calibers arcing toward the Japanese fighter. In the next moment, the George blew apart. The aft fuselage separated from the cockpit and spun away. No parachute blossomed from the debris of the airplane.

Meanwhile, Windy Hill, despite his still-attached belly tank, had maneuvered behind another of the Japanese fighters. He fired a long burst, and smoke belched from the George fighter. Seconds later the Japanese pilot bailed out.

As the enemy pilot's parachute blossomed, Erickson flashed past close enough to glimpse the pilot's dark brown flight suit and the astonished look on his face. On an impulse, Erickson turned hard, trying for a shot at the dangling figure. He couldn't turn tightly enough. The lucky Japanese pilot made it to the ground, still alive.

On reflection, Erickson was glad he hadn't killed the man in the chute—but not for humanitarian reasons. "I heard it might not be a good thing to do, as it didn't help the treatment given to our POWs below. I had no moment to consider this, either— I was at war."

They were still on their own. Flying a hundred yards abeam each other for mutual protection, Hill and Erickson were passing back over Shikoku when more trouble appeared.

Erickson spotted it first—the dark green form of a Nakajima Ki-44 "Tojo" fighter, slipping in behind Hill's Corsair. A telltale pattern of winking orange bursts was coming from the Tojo's wings. Bright tracers were arcing like tentacles toward Hill's tail.

Again the Corsairs went into a desperate Thach weave. The tracers were converging on Hill, who was turning as hard as he could, trying to escape the deadly fire. For a few seconds Erickson had a shot at the Tojo—and missed.

Hill was desperate. He couldn't shake the Tojo. Tracers were flashing past his canopy. "Shoot the son of a bitch, Eric!" he yelled on the radio.

"What the hell do you think I'm trying to do?" Erickson snapped back. He swung high and wide to the far side of the weave, then returned his sights to the Japanese fighter. It was a high-angle shot, nearly 90-degree deflection. If Erickson missed this time, Hill would be in flames.

He saw his tracers bending back toward the Tojo—and connecting. Abruptly the enemy fighter burst into flame. Erickson watched the burning Tojo enter a steep death dive to the green hills below.

They were safe, for the moment. Low on fuel and exhausted from the long mission, they steered toward *Intrepid* using their

ZB homing receivers, which picked up signals from a transmitter aboard the carrier. The transmitter sent a different Morse code signal every 30 degrees of arc from the ship. A different sector was chosen each day as the official inbound gate to the ship, to prevent the enemy from using the code.

Hill was still rattled by the close call with the Tojo fighter. The belly tank that he couldn't jettison had nearly gotten him killed. Then he found that one of his .50-caliber guns wouldn't fire. Finally, his oxygen system failed, meaning he was forced to remain at low altitude. He was having a bad day, and it only got worse. Arriving back at the ship, he botched his first landing pass and had to come back for another try.

Finally aboard, he climbed out of his Corsair and trudged down the labyrinth of ladders to the squadron ready room. The old fighter pilot swagger was gone from Hill, at least temporarily. He flopped into a seat in the back row and stared at the bulkhead in what infantrymen called the "thousand-yard stare." As in an endlessly looping film, Hill kept seeing flak bursts, tracer bullets, and dark green silhouettes of enemy fighters.

It had been a grim second day of battle for *Intrepid*'s air group. More Tail End Charlies were missing. Ens. Bill York was killed in a noncombat accident. A Helldiver crew, Ens. Bob Brinick and his gunner, Crawford Burnette, of VB-10, had been shot down over Kure harbor and were missing. Another Helldiver crew, also hit at Kure, was luckier. They made it far enough offshore to ditch near a picket destroyer.

Even VBF-10's skipper, Lt. Cmdr. Will Rawie, had been forced to ditch his Corsair. Rawie was picked up by a destroyer and delivered back to the *Intrepid*.

Erickson found that he had sweated off five pounds during the three-and-a-half-hour mission. His tan leather gloves had turned an evil dark brown. His flight suit was so stiff from sweat he could prop it up against the ready room bulkhead.

In recounting the action over Japan, Erickson and Hill found that each thought he had shot down the first Japanese fighter they encountered. Unable to agree on whose bullets did the job, they split the kill. Each would get one and a half victories for the day.

They weren't the only ones who scored kills. CAG Hyland, whom they'd last seen pulling off the target at Kure, had gunned down the Rufe fighter he'd chased across the harbor. It was the thirty-four-year-old Hyland's first air-to-air kill, and there was no mistaking the grin on his face in the wardroom that evening. The old man was keeping up with the kids.

9 ▸ WE WILL SAVE THE SHIP

Rear Adm. Gerald Bogan, standing on *Franklin*'s flag bridge, was one of the first to spot it. The peculiar object was silver-colored, slanting downward from a broken cloud layer.

It was a few minutes past 0700, and *Franklin* had just finished launching her strike aircraft. That morning she had steamed within 50 miles of Shikoku, the closest any U.S. carrier had ventured to the Japanese homeland in the war.

Bogan could see crewmen on the flight deck readying planes for the next launch. They were arming Corsairs with the new Tiny Tim rockets. In the next few seconds, Bogan heard *Franklin*'s anti-aircraft guns open up.

Gerry Bogan was no stranger to kamikaze attacks. He had been the task group commander aboard *Intrepid* during her three kami-kaze strikes off the Philippines. Now he was an observer aboard *Franklin*, which was the flagship of Rear Adm. Ralph Davison's Task Group 58.2.

The silver object was still diving, becoming more visible, some-how evading the hail of antiaircraft fire. Spotters had already tagged it as a Judy dive-bomber, though other observers would report it as an older fixed-gear Val.

But everyone would later agree that the dive bomber's pilot was not a single-mission, poorly trained kamikaze. His attack was a masterpiece of precision. While his two 250-kilogram bombs flew straight and true toward their target, the dive-bomber pulled back up and escaped into the cloud deck.

The results were catastrophic. The first bomb punched through

Franklin's forward flight deck and exploded on the hangar deck. Fires and explosions consumed every man and plane in the forward hangar bay and two decks directly below.

The second bomb struck further aft, just behind the island, exploding as it penetrated the wooden flight deck. The number three elevator, in the center of the aft flight deck, was flung to the side by the explosion. Armed aircraft on the flight deck, preparing to launch, were caught in the conflagration and exploded one after the other. Tiny Tim rockets on the wings of the Corsairs were lighting off and sizzling across the flight deck, adding to the carnage.

Franklin's executive officer, Cmdr. Joe Taylor, remembered the deadly missiles. "Some screamed by to starboard, some to port, some straight up the flight deck. Some went straight up and some tumbled end over end. Each time one went off, the firefighting crews forward would instantly hit the deck."

On the navigation bridge, *Franklin*'s skipper, Capt. Leslie Gehres, was slammed to the deck by the impact of the first bomb. Stunned, Gehres staggered to his feet to find the starboard bow of his ship engulfed in flame and smoke. He ordered full right rudder to bring the wind to the port side and deflect the flames from the airplanes parked aft. Then, to his shock, he realized that the aft part of the ship was also ablaze. He countermanded his order, swinging *Franklin* back to port, putting the wind on her starboard side.

Nothing seemed to help. Explosions were racking the ship. "In a very few minutes," recalled Admiral Bogan, still on the flag bridge, "the forward part of the ship was an inferno." Firefighting crews were thwarted by exploding ordnance. All the ammunition in lockers and gun mounts behind the island structure exploded.

From 20 miles away the men of *Intrepid* could see the smoke and flames. Radarman Ray Stone, watching from *Intrepid*'s flight deck, was shocked. "Hearing the numerous, repeated explosions from the fully-armed, about-to-be-launched airplanes was sickening," he wrote. "You could virtually feel and smell the fire."

Franklin was dead in the water. All communications on the

ship were lost. The cruiser *Santa Fe* was already gathering up survivors who'd jumped into the sea to escape the flames. Admiral Davison advised Captain Gehres he should consider abandoning ship. Gehres declined. After transferring more than eight hundred men, mostly wounded, to *Santa Fe*, he kept seven hundred officers and men with him to try to save *Franklin*.

For the rest of the day and the following night they fought the fires that raged inside the carrier. By morning, the skeleton crew had most of the fires under control. Towed by the cruiser *Pittsburgh*, the shattered carrier began a slow withdrawal to the south. Most of her unexploded ammunition had been heaved overboard.

At midday, *Santa Fe* blinkered Admiral Mitscher's flagship *Bunker Hill*: "*Franklin* says fire practically under control, skeleton crew aboard, list stabilized at 13 degrees. If you save us from the Japanese, we will save the ship."

By early afternoon *Franklin* had four boilers back on line and her steering control back. Still spewing smoke, her flight deck now a shredded wreck, the wounded carrier limped under her own power toward Ulithi. From there *Franklin* proceeded to Pearl Harbor, and then all the way to New York for major repairs. She would never see combat again.

Franklin had suffered the greatest damage inflicted on any aircraft carrier without being sunk. Her losses—724 killed and 265 wounded—were among the most on any single U.S. warship. The carrier owed her survival to a combination of human courage and skilled firefighting. Much had been learned about shipboard damage control since the battles in which the carriers *Lexington*, *Yorktown*, *Wasp*, and *Hornet* were lost. Improved techniques, special firefighting schools, and new equipment including fog nozzles, foam generators, and independent fire mains were saving ships that otherwise would have gone to the bottom. Each carrier's damage control crew received intensive training before going into combat.

Franklin wasn't the only victim that day. Soon after sunrise on March 19, the fast carrier *Wasp* was launching strikes when a dive-bomber appeared directly overhead. No one had picked up the intruder either visually or on radar. The bomber, probably another Judy, put its bomb through *Wasp*'s flight deck, but it penetrated to the hangar deck, then passed through the number three and number two decks before exploding in the crew galley. Despite the slaughter in the mess compartment and fires that spread to five decks, the blazes were quickly extinguished.

But it wasn't over for *Wasp*. Fifteen minutes later, while she was recovering aircraft, yet another bomber dove on the carrier. This one, a bona fide kamikaze, narrowly missed the deck edge and exploded in the water alongside the ship. *Wasp*'s losses from the attacks amounted to 101 killed and 269 wounded, but she stayed on line for several more days before withdrawing to Ulithi for repairs.

The next day, March 20, it was *Enterprise*'s turn again. A swarm of fifteen to twenty Japanese warplanes bore down on the veteran carrier. One managed to get close enough to score a near miss with its bomb and rake the flight deck with its machine guns.

At the same time, yet another carrier, the *Hancock*, was fighting off an incoming Zero. At the last moment, *Hancock*'s gunners managed to pick off the incoming kamikaze. The flaming wreckage skimmed past the carrier's flight deck edge, crashing into the main deck of the destroyer *Halsey Powell*, which had just completed refueling from *Hancock*.

What happened next was a classic example of why Navy men called destroyers "tin cans." The kamikaze's bomb penetrated *Powell*'s thinly armored deck, punching completely through the destroyer's hull without exploding. Still, ten of the tin can's sailors perished in the attack, and twenty-nine more were wounded. *Powell*'s steering gear was wrecked, and the destroyer was out of the fight.

That night Vice Adm. Marc Mitscher pulled his carrier task force southward from their dangerous stations close to Japan. The strikes had been effective but costly. The operation they were here to support, the amphibious invasion of Okinawa, was still a week away, and already four fleet carriers—*Franklin*, *Enterprise*, *Yorktown*, and *Wasp*—would have to retire for damage repair.

To Mitscher, the past three days had been an ominous preview of the coming battle. The Japanese could hurl hundreds of kamikazes at the U.S. fleet and lose almost all of them. If only one slipped through, it could mean the loss of a ship.

Pilots on the strikes against the Japanese bases claimed a total of 528 enemy aircraft destroyed on the ground and in the air. It was an inflated number, mostly derived from the claims of multiple pilots hitting the same targets. The Japanese reported that they'd lost 161 out of 193 aircraft in addition to an undetermined number of unflyable airplanes destroyed on the ground.

The truth lay somewhere in between. Exaggerated action reports were not unique to either side. Both the Japanese and the United States overestimated the numbers of ships and planes destroyed and troops killed by their side. Airmen were like prizefighters who, after landing a punch, believed they'd scored a knockout. A Helldiver pilot would swear his bomb sank a battleship. A torpedo plane pilot refused to believe that after he'd penetrated a wall of flak to deliver his weapon, the enemy vessel could still be afloat. A fighter pilot, seeing his tracers hitting an enemy plane, *knew* that he'd shot the bandit down.

And not just pilots. Intelligence officers, squadron skippers, even fleet commanders were biased toward swollen damage estimates. This sometimes resulted in dangerously flawed decisions. At the Battle of Leyte Gulf, when dive-bomber and torpedo plane pilots, full of hubris and adrenaline, reported fatal hits on the battleships and cruisers of Admiral Kurita's striking force, Adm. William Halsey concluded that the Japanese force was no longer a serious threat.

It was a nearly fatal mistake. Hell-bent on pursuing the Japanese carrier force, Halsey left the San Bernardino Strait unguarded while he chased after a decoy Japanese carrier force. Kurita's still-formidable striking force slipped through the strait and by dawn were firing point-blank into the unprotected ships of the Taffy group.

However, the Japanese were even more susceptible to believing their own exaggerations. One of the most willing believers was Adm. Matome Ugaki, who concluded that after the *tokko* attacks of March 18–19 on the U.S. fleet, his pilots had sunk five carriers, two battleships, and three cruisers. Whether or not Ugaki actually believed such nonsense, it reflected the Japanese high command's detachment from reality.

Because of the finality of the *tokko* missions, results were difficult to assess. When it could be confirmed that a kamikaze pilot did, in fact, crash into a ship, the vessel was usually declared sunk. The Japanese public was fed a steady stream of lies about the successes of the *tokko* warriors. During the battle for Okinawa, *tokko* airmen would be credited with sinking half a dozen U.S. aircraft carriers when, in fact, not one was actually sunk. The carrier *Lexington* received the distinction of being reported sunk four times.

One purpose of the misinformation was to divert attention from the rain of incendiary bombs falling nightly on Japanese cities from American B-29s. Bad news was glossed over or not reported at all. The truth about the Battle of the Philippine Sea in June 1944, in which most of the Imperial Japanese Navy's airpower was lost, was kept from the public. So was the fall of Iwo Jima in February and March of 1945, when almost all of the twenty-one thousand defenders of the island perished.

Action was light for the next few days while Mitscher reorganized his task force into three task groups, leaving one— TG 58.2—to protect the wounded *Franklin*, *Enterprise*, and *Yorktown* as they limped to Ulithi. The only combat missions being flown were those by CAP fighters and a few sweeps over the enemy airfields to keep the Japanese fighters grounded.

Off Okinawa, the armada of attack transports and landing craft was swelling in numbers as new arrivals came from their staging bases at Ulithi, Leyte, and Saipan. Two naval bombardment forces under Rear Adm. Mort Deyo had moved in toward the western shore of Okinawa, and the big guns of Deyo's battleships and cruisers were shelling Japanese positions, preparing the landing zones for the coming invasion on April 1.

Aboard *Intrepid*, Johnny Hyland took advantage of the breather to evaluate his air group's performance. In a dizzying two days of action, his pilots had bombed, rocketed, and strafed targets up and down the coasts of the Japanese home islands. There had been losses, some of them avoidable. Hyland's own wingman, George Tessier, had run out of fuel and put an expensive Corsair into the sea. Several others, including Erickson, had come close to joining him in the water.

It was one of several lessons that were being learned the hard way. Long-range mission planning, particularly fuel management, would take some fine-tuning.

Hyland had also been surprised at the numbers and tenacity of the Japanese fighters who rose to meet them during the strikes on Japan. The Japanese fighter pilots who dueled with Erickson and Hill were skilled airmen, not the neophytes who were flying the suicidal kamikaze missions.

To Hyland, it was an ominous sign. It meant the Japanese were keeping their best airmen in reserve. They were hoarding them for the battle to come.

10 ▸ THUNDER GODS

Ohka. It meant "cherry blossom," and the poetic name disguised a deadly purpose. The men who volunteered to fly the *Ohka* had never imagined such a thing before they saw it. The *Ohka* was both a giant leap in technology and a crude attempt to change Japan's fortunes late in the war.

The *Ohka* was a manned bomb, 19.7 feet long, with wings that spanned 16.4 feet. The flimsy craft's fuselage was constructed with a metal alloy, and the stubby wings were made of wood. The cockpit bulged from the top of the fuselage as if it were stuck there as an afterthought.

The *Ohka* was intended to be lugged beneath a twin-engine Mitsubishi G4M bomber and released 55 miles from its target. The pilot would glide the craft until he was within range, then he'd ignite the three rocket motors, which would hurtle the *Ohka* to over 400 knots, faster than any pursuing American fighter. The *Ohka* carried enough explosive power—a 1,200-kilogram (2,646 lb.) bomb—to devastate virtually any warship. The exotic craft was the brainstorm of an enigmatic navy ensign named Shoichi Ota, who presented the idea to the naval general staff in July 1944. Ota's timing was perfect. The high command was still reeling from the extermination of Japan's naval air forces at the air battle off Saipan called the Marianas Turkey Shoot. The admirals were receptive to any idea that sounded like a wonder weapon. The *Ohka* stirred in them a fresh excitement.

The weapon's very existence was kept secret. The idea was controversial, even to the *bushido*-inclined officers of the high command. It was one thing to send men to their deaths in conventional warplanes; it was another to actually construct a fleet of aircraft for the express purpose of immolating the pilot.

The first *Ohka* unit, the 721st Naval Flying Unit, took the name *Jinrai Butai*—Divine Thunder Corps. The pilots selected to fly the *Ohka* gave themselves an equally grandiose name— Thunder Gods. The commander of the *Jinrai Butai* was a veteran naval aviator, Capt. Motoharu Okamura, who had fought in almost every battle since the war began and was one of the early proponents of *tokko* warfare.

By August 1944, Okamura was recruiting volunteers. Okamura's candidates were given only cursory information: a special new weapon was being developed that could turn the tide of the war. The volunteers who flew it might be able to save Japan.

There was no shortage of volunteers. By now, the stench of defeat was in the air, and young Japanese fighting men were filled with a mixture of frustration, anger, and a desire to strike back at the hated enemy. Okamura likened his volunteers to a swarm of bees. "Bees die after they have stung," he explained.

The Thunder Gods began their training at the Konoike air base, northeast of Tokyo. After rudimentary training in *tokko* tactics in conventional fighters, they received their graduation flight—an actual practice drop from a Betty bomber mother ship.

The graduation flight was almost as dangerous as the real thing. The trainer was a version of the *Ohka* loaded with ballast instead of rockets and a warhead, and it was fitted with a skid so it could land back at Konoike. It was a wild two-minute plunge back to earth. Several graduation flights ended in disaster, strewing metal and wood and pieces of the pilot over the airfield.

The *Jinrai Butai* had a fleet of specially configured Mitsubishi G4M Betty bombers. The new version, the G4M 2E, had its bomb bay doors removed to accommodate the *Ohka* and was wired for communications between the *Ohka* pilot and the Betty crew. A panel of red and green lights was installed in the bomb bay for transmitting last-minute orders.

The *Jinrai Butai* would also require fighters, lots of them. The vulnerable Betty bombers were even more vulnerable with the *Ohka*s strapped to their bellies. Until they shed their loads, they were sitting ducks for Hellcat and Corsair fighters.

Unlike most *tokko* volunteers, the Thunder Gods had to endure an agony of waiting. Nearly six months would pass after their training before any flew a mission. When the day finally came for them to die for the emperor, it was not in the way they had expected.

On the morning of March 21, Vice Adm. Matome Ugaki stood gazing into the sky over Kanoya. The cloud cover was gone and, at least for the moment, so were the enemy airplanes.

This would be the day. For the past three days he had been waiting for the chance to send the *Jinrai Butai* into the battle. Each day the enemy's carrier-based warplanes had raided the airfields on Kyushu, including Kanoya, destroying every airplane they could find in the open. They'd cratered runways, destroyed hangars, and generally raised hell with his Fifth Air Fleet. There had been no opportunity to assemble the *Ohka* rocket-powered missiles, the Betty bomber mother ships, and the fighters that would fly cover.

According to reports from search planes, the American carrier task force was pulling back to the south. To Ugaki, it was a clear signal that they were preparing for the expected invasion of Okinawa. After six months of training and waiting, the time had come to launch the Thunder Gods against the enemy carriers. The Betty bombers were being loaded with their *Ohka* cargoes. The pilots had burned their old uniforms and donned new ones. Each had written a final letter and placed locks of his hair and nail clippings in a box to be delivered to his family.

Then the commander of the Divine Thunder Corps, Captain Okamura, burst into Ugaki's headquarters. Okamura had just come from the flight line. There was not nearly enough fighter protection for the plodding mother ships and the *Ohka*s beneath their bellies. "Can't we have more fighters?" he demanded.

The answer was no. Ugaki's chief of staff, Rear Adm. Toshiyuki Yokoi, informed Okamura that he was getting all the fighters they had left. The last three days of combat had decimated the squadrons. The most they could muster was fifty-five fighters.

Okamura was furious. It wasn't enough. The attack would have to be canceled.

Admiral Ugaki slumped in his chair while he considered the matter. He understood Okamura's feelings. Okamura had shepherded the *Ohka* project through its inception. He had a personal bond with each of the young Thunder Gods, and he didn't want to see them slaughtered for nothing.

But Ugaki felt the time for action slipping away from them. His reconnaissance and intelligence reports all led him to believe the American carriers could be caught by surprise, even in broad daylight. He was certain that they still had no awareness of the *Ohka* weapon.

The admiral rose from his chair and clasped Okamura's shoulder. "If the *Ohka* cannot be used in the present situation," he told Okamura, "there will never be another chance for using it."

Whether it was true or not didn't matter. A look of grim resignation settled over Okamura's face. "We are ready to launch the attack, sir," he said, and stormed out of headquarters.

Returning to the flight line where the 18 G4M Betty bombers were being readied, Okamura was in a rage. Admiral Ugaki was not an aviator. He could not possibly understand the grave risk in sending the bombers with their unreleased *Ohka*s against the enemy fleet without a protective umbrella of fighters.

As he joined his young pilots waiting to depart, he reached a decision: *he* would personally lead the attack.

He hadn't counted on Lt. Cmdr. Goro Nonaka, the officer already assigned to lead the mission. Nonaka was a charismatic leader, a cult figure famous for telling his volunteers, "All right, you little gods, you've had the balls to come this far, now we'll see if you can go all the way!"

Nonaka was even more enraged than Okamura. "Is it, sir, that you lack confidence in me? This is one time I refuse to obey your order."

In the Imperial Japanese Navy, such impertinence could result in arrest, or worse. But these were extraordinary times. Okamura understood Nonaka's feelings, and he acquiesced. The younger man could have his moment of glory.

It was midmorning when Admiral Ugaki gave the order for departure. Each of the Thunder Gods was wearing a ceremonial *hachimaki*—a white headband with the symbol of the rising sun. Nonaka gave Ugaki a farewell salute, declaring, "This is Minatogawa!" Minatogawa was an ancient shrine erected to the fourteenth-century hero Masashige Kusunoki, who supposedly said before his samurai death, "Would that I had seven lives to give for my country!" Nonaka intended to follow Kusonoki's example.

To the steady roll of the traditional warriors' drumbeat, the Thunder Gods ran to the bombers. One after another, the engines of the Betty bombers coughed and rumbled to life. They taxied as fast as possible toward the runway. It was critical that they not be caught in the open by another enemy air attack.

Solemnly Ugaki watched the bombers lumber into the sky. Of the eighteen Bettys, sixteen were carrying *Ohka*s, and two others were specially equipped for navigation. Close behind went the fighter escorts. As the last one left the runway, Ugaki was informed that because of mechanical problems only thirty fighters were now escorting the bombers.

Then came worse news. Fresh reconnaissance reports indicated that the enemy task force now amounted to three complete carrier groups. It meant that fighter resistance would be even heavier than they had estimated. Ugaki's senior staff officers urged him to recall the attack force.

For good or ill, one of the traits that had distinguished Ugaki from his fellow admirals was his reputation for decisiveness. When he chose a course of action, he stayed with it.

Today would be no different. The Thunder Gods would proceed to their target.

The bombers flew southward toward the U.S. fleet. Burdened by the 4,700-pound *Ohka*s protruding from their bomb bays, the Bettys could make no better than 140 knots, nearly 60 knots slower than their normal speed. En route, the fighters escorting them were further reduced in number when several were forced to turn back with engine problems, mostly because of the low-grade fuel they burned.

Fuel was an ongoing problem for the Imperial Japanese Navy, particularly for the sensitive, high-powered radial engines that powered the Zero and George fighters. Because aviation gasoline was in short supply, fuel was being synthesized from coal and organic substances such as pine roots. Now engine failures were occurring at an alarming rate.

While the Bettys droned toward their targets, Ugaki and his staff hovered over the radio in their underground operations office. An hour ticked past. They heard nothing. The time neared when the *Ohka*s should have been released from the mother ships. Still nothing.

Ugaki worried about their dwindling fuel supply. He gave the order that if they hadn't yet sighted the enemy fleet, they should proceed to Minami Daito, a Japanese-held island about 200 miles east of Okinawa and close to the bombers' estimated position.

There was no reply. It was not a good sign.

Lt. (jg) Dick Mason was the first to spot them. The bogeys were at nine o'clock low, about 11,000 feet. As Mason and his flight drew closer, he saw that they were Betty bombers, and they had fighter escorts.

Dick Mason was a slim, garrulous young man from Brookline, Massachusetts. He was one of the squadron's handful of combat veterans, a transplant from the old Grim Reapers squadron on the *Enterprise* to the re-formed VF-10 aboard *Intrepid*. The Tail End Charlies liked flying on Mason's wing.

On Mason's wing was Ens. Don Oglevee, and with them was their second section, Lt. Jim Dudley and Lt. (jg) Eddie Mills. The four VF-10 Corsairs had been on their CAP station at 18,000 feet over *Intrepid*'s task force when the call came from the FIDO. Mason had acknowledged and shoved his throttle forward, swinging his division northward for the intercept.

Spotting the incoming Betty bombers, Mason observed that they appeared to be uncharacteristically slow. They were plodding along as though they were on a leisurely sightseeing trip. A flight of F6F-5 Hellcats from *Yorktown* was already on the scene, and now they were mixing it up with the Japanese fighters.

Mason kept his flight high until they were almost directly above the Japanese formation. Then he rolled his Corsair inverted and dove nearly straight down on the enemy formation. One after the other, his wingmen followed Mason down.

The attack from above took the Japanese formation by surprise. Normally, a disciplined formation of bombers could put up a formidable defensive fire, each supporting the other. Each Betty had a 7.7-millimeter gun in the nose, one in a turret atop the fuselage, another in a waist turret, and a deadly 20-millimeter cannon in the tail. But now that they were scattered like quail, each slow-moving Betty was on its own.

As the Corsairs swept down through the bombers, one of the escort fighters, an A6M Zero, tailed in behind, trying for a shot at the Tail End Charlie, Eddie Mills.

He was too late—and too slow. Mills's diving Corsair left the slower Japanese fighter behind, but one of the *Yorktown* Hellcats spotted the Zero and locked on to his tail. Seconds later the Japanese fighter exploded.

Bottoming out of their dive, the Corsairs soared back up for another pass on the fleeing bombers. Again the Corsairs tore into the bombers with their .50-calibers. While Mason went after one of the Bettys diving away from the formation, Oglevee slid in behind another, hammering it with machine fire from dead astern.

It was then, seeing a yellow twinkling light from the tail of the Betty, that Oglevee remembered the Betty's tail gunner. An instant later he felt the metallic pinging of the 20-millimeter bullets on the Corsair's airframe.

The mano a mano duel—Oglevee trading fire with the tail gunner—lasted for several seconds. Oglevee kicked his rudder pedals, spraying machine gun fire across the Betty's tail while the gunner fired back.

Abruptly the duel ended. Oglevee saw the glass shatter in the Betty's tail turret. Seconds later, the bomber's right wing separated, and the Betty rolled into a death spiral toward the ocean.

The other two Corsairs were having similar results. The fight was turning into a turkey shoot. The remaining bombers were jinking, turning, and skidding in futile attempts to save themselves. More Hellcats were joining the scrap, all eager to pick off surviving Bettys.

Trails of smoke were arcing toward the ocean, marking the funeral pyres of Japanese bombers. A few of the Bettys had turned back to Kyushu, and others were trying to make it to a nearby cloud bank. Most of the Zeroes had disappeared, either shot down or chased away.

The Corsairs were out of ammunition. Oglevee had lost sight of his leader, Dick Mason, so he pulled up above the fray, where he was joined by Mills and Dudley, the other two pilots in their division. The melee was almost over, and fighters from other carriers had shown up to pick off the few remaining Japanese stragglers.

But Dick Mason was missing. The last they'd seen of him was during their final dive through the formation of Bettys. The three

Tail End Charlies circled until they were low on fuel, then headed back to *Intrepid*, still wondering what happened to their leader.

They never found out. No trace of Dick Mason was ever discovered.

Back in their ready room, the three Corsair pilots tried to describe what they had seen. There had been something different about these Betty bombers. They were slower and less maneuverable than they should have been. Several pilots reported observing a peculiar object protruding from the bellies of the bombers.

Whatever it was, it went down with the Bettys. Not a single one made it through.

A dmiral Ugaki's masklike expression remained unchanged while he listened to the reports. None of his eighteen Betty bombers had returned to Kanoya. Only a few Zero pilots had survived to tell the story.

The first mission of the Thunder Gods had ended in disaster. American fighters had pounced on the slow-flying bombers when they were still 60 miles from the enemy task force. When the first few bombers were shot down, the rest scattered, and it became impossible for the Zeroes to protect them.

Some of the Bettys jettisoned their *Ohkas*, but it didn't save them. One by one they were shot down in flames. A few tried to hide in the clouds, but each was caught and destroyed. The battle was over in ten minutes.

Gloom settled like a pall over the air fleet headquarters. Only a few hours before they had been cheering, saluting, and waving farewells to the noble young Thunder Gods. The last words of the indomitable Goro Nonaka—"This is Minatogawa!"—had sent a surge of pride through every man on the field. Now sixteen Thunder Gods, including Nonaka, were gone. Their sacrifice had accomplished nothing.

Abruptly Ugaki rose and left the bunker. Whatever emotions

he may have felt, he was keeping to himself. It wasn't in Ugaki's chemistry to wring his hands over such things. Nor would he display remorse at having ignored the counsel of a subordinate such as Captain Okamura.

The flat countryside outside the bunker was bathed in the soft sunshine of spring. As Ugaki trudged back to his command shack on the hill, he began to shed his anguish at the failed mission. He was no stranger to calamity. Since the Imperial Japanese Navy's first great triumph at Pearl Harbor, he had witnessed crushing defeats at Midway, the Solomons, the Battle of the Philippine Sea, and then Leyte Gulf. Only by the narrowest of margins had he escaped being killed with Yamamoto. He'd been spared again at Leyte Gulf. Ugaki was a religious man, and he chose to believe that he had been saved by divine intervention so that he could deliver retribution to the Americans.

By now Ugaki was ensnared in the same web of delusions that guided the Japanese high command. Even if the *Ohkas* had failed to reach their targets, Ugaki was sure that many of his other *tokko* raiders had inflicted great losses on the enemy. Based on several pilots' final radio transmissions of "I am going to ram a carrier," he concluded that the United States had lost at least five carriers in the past four days. At this rate, the Americans would have no choice except to withdraw.

A s usual, Vice Adm. Kelly Turner was right. The Japanese didn't suspect that the Americans had an interest in the Kerama Retto, the cluster of islands off Okinawa. The Retto was defended by only a small Japanese force. Turner's amphibious invasion at dawn on March 26 took them by surprise.

But the Alligator hadn't taken any chances. For two days before the Army's 77th Division landed on the islands, three destroyers and two cruisers had hammered the coastline with shellfire. Carrier-based fighter-bombers delivered air strikes, and underwater demolition teams surveyed the landing beaches and marked the locations of coral reefs. When the landing ships and troop-filled amphibious tractors hit the beaches, most of the defenders fell back to the hills and caves. Except for a handful of holdouts who remained in hiding, the small garrison was soon wiped out.

The only retaliation came that evening in the form of nine kamikaze aircraft. One managed to hit a destroyer's stern, taking out a 40-millimeter gun mount. Another destroyer took a near miss.

In less than twenty-four hours, the Kerama Retto became U.S. property. An unexpected bonus was the discovery of more than 250 "Q-boats"—18-foot-long suicide boats, built of plywood and armed with 250-pound depth charges. The boats were hidden in camouflaged shelters and caves throughout the islands of the Retto. With a crew of one, they had a top speed of about 20 knots and were intended for a massed night attack on the U.S. transport ships off Okinawa.

Within two days of the invasion, Turner's new anchorage at Kerama Retto was open for business. Tankers, ammunition ships, repair ships, and mine and patrol craft all began crowding into the roadstead. Two squadrons of PBM Mariner seaplanes began operating in the cleared waterway.

It was the last stage of preparation. The Alligator was ready to land on Okinawa.

11 ▸ THREE SECONDS TO DIE

Erickson's confidence was growing. He was still the CAG's number four, and this morning they were attacking the island of Amami Oshima, at the northern end of the Ryukyu chain. It was part of the preinvasion softening up, hitting each of the Japanese island bases north of Okinawa.

The flight of VBF-10 and VF-10 Corsairs rocketed and strafed the barracks complex on the island until all the buildings were ablaze. Then they returned to *Intrepid* for a quick lunch, and an hour later they were doing the same thing to the enemy airfield at Tokuno, one island below Amami Oshima.

It was dangerous work. The Japanese were shooting back with all the firepower they had on the island, but so far none of the Corsairs had been hit. Pulling off the target, Erickson could see the results of their efforts. Smoke was pouring from the shattered buildings and airplanes.

Erickson allowed himself a brief moment of satisfaction. This was precisely what he had been trained for, flying a fighter-bomber in combat, and he was doing it damned well.

Then something caught his eye. Another Corsair, one flown by Ens. Al Hasse, was still in its dive. As Erickson watched, the dark blue shape of the fighter morphed into an orange ball of fire.

Erickson blinked, not sure of what he'd seen. There'd been no telltale trail of smoke, no radio call, no clue that Hasse was hit. It happened in an instant. The Corsair was there, then it was gone, a shower of burning debris. Erickson kept his eyes on the fireball until it hit the ocean. To no one's surprise, there was no parachute.

Al Hasse was one of the residents of Boys' Town. He and

Erickson had been buddies since their flight training days. An old naval aviation adage flashed through Erickson's head: "Three years to train, three seconds to die."

The flight rejoined and headed back to the carrier. For once the tactical frequency was silent. No one felt like talking.

The day didn't get any better. Another Tail End Charlie, Ens. Jim "Ziggy" South, had hung around Tokuno to make an extra run on the target. South was a muscular young man who had been an amateur boxer back in Kansas. He'd earned the nickname "Ziggy," he liked to say, because he zigged in the ring when he should have zagged.

Pulling off the target, he found that he was all alone. While he made his extra run on the target, the rest of his flight had departed. And then, flying solo back to the ship, South started hearing things. A bothersome noise was coming from up front, as if his engine was cutting out.

Nearing the *Intrepid*, he spotted a pair of Corsairs from his squadron, a section led by skipper Will Rawie, with his wingman, Ens. Tommy Thompson. South joined up on Thompson's wing, and together they entered an orbit over the ship while they waited for the signal to recover.

It was then when things went to hell.

Ziggy South never knew whether he was distracted by his engine noises or Thompson made a too-abrupt control input. All he knew was that in the next moment his propeller was whacking like a meat cleaver through Tommy Thompson's starboard wing.

Both Corsairs were finished. Thompson's crippled fighter rolled into a dive, shedding pieces from its destroyed wing. Thompson jettisoned the canopy and went over the side. Seconds later his parachute canopy blossomed, and he floated down toward a waiting destroyer.

South's Corsair was still controllable, but the shattered propeller was shaking the airplane so hard he had to shut the engine down. Preferring to ditch instead of bailing out, he glided the big gull-winged fighter down to the water.

It would have been a successful ditching. The problem was, the Corsair lost hydraulic power when the engine shut down, and the landing gear flopped out. When the fighter hit the water, it flipped upside down and sank like a stone.

South was trapped in the sinking airplane. He was snagged by his parachute, which was caught on something inside the cockpit. Running out of breath, with the water pressure building in his ears, he fought against the panic that gripped him. In desperation, he yanked the handle that would inflate his life raft.

With a pop and an explosion of gas, the raft inflated, shoving him out of the seat. The raft soared to the surface, hauling South with it. Gasping, he clung to the raft, too weak from the struggle even to wave his arms. A sailor from a nearby destroyer dove into the water and swam to him with a line.

South was hauled aboard the tin can, still dazed and wondering what the hell had happened. All he knew was that five minutes earlier he'd been flying on Tommy Thompson's wing, and now they were both on a destroyer.

I t was another somber evening in Boys' Town. This one seemed especially grim, since several of them had watched Al Hasse get blown to bits over Tokuno that morning.

By now, observing the loss of one of the Tail End Charlies had become a ritual. First someone had to empty the missing man's locker and inventory his effects. Then they broke out their stash of Coon Range whisky, which they'd sneaked aboard back in Alameda. They would toast the departed pilot, recall a few good stories about him, and mostly try to numb their own jangled emotions.

Losing a guy like Hasse was tough. He had been with them through flight training, through advanced fighter indoctrination, and through the forming up of the new squadron and air group. Hasse was a short, good-looking kid from South Dakota. He had been something of a ladies' man, with a string of concurrent girl-friends back in the States.

Like most of the Tail End Charlies, Hasse had left a set of just-in-case instructions. If he didn't make it back, his buddies were supposed to retrieve a pack of love letters from his personal effects and get rid of them. No need to break any more hearts than necessary.

And so they did. It took several more rounds of Coon Range and a few more toasts, then they gathered up the letters. In a solemn procession they made their way up to the darkened catwalk at the edge of the flight deck. The night sky was suitably black, without horizon or moonlight. Silently they tossed Al Hasse's love letters over the rail, watching the fluttering paper vanish in the blackness of the Pacific.

Three days later they were on their way back to Kyushu. This time they were in the company of three other divisions, including Helldivers from the bombing squadron, VB-10, and Avengers from the torpedo squadron, VT-10, whom the other airmen called "Torpeckers." The mission was to find the elusive Japanese fleet, which was reported to be assembling to engage the American invasion force at Okinawa.

Led by Hyland, the strike group swept over the designated place in the ocean off Kyushu. A low cloud cover obscured most of the area. They found no sign of the Japanese warships. Hyland then took them inland to their alternative targets, the airfields on Kyushu.

It was a replay of the first two days of strikes. Even though the fields had been hit multiple times, the antiaircraft fire was as intense as ever. Just as before, the Japanese gunners were filling the sky with black bursts of gunfire.

One after the other, the Corsairs rolled in, jinking and weaving, trying to elude the gunners while keeping their sights on the target. Erickson, in his usual slot as Hyland's Tail End Charlie and Windy Hill's wingman, was amazed that no one had been hit.

And then he saw that someone had. An ominous gray stream was spewing from the belly of the fighter directly ahead of him. "Windy, you've been hit!" he yelled on the radio.

Hill didn't need to be told. He had felt the sharp thunk of the shrapnel hitting his airplane. Now he could see his fuel quantity indicator unwinding. He had to get the hell out of Japan, and he had to do it very quickly. During the past week's operations, several *Intrepid* pilots had taken hits over Kyushu or Shikoku and been forced to ditch. They were all dead or captured.

Hill swung the nose of the Corsair back to the southeast. When the shoreline of Kyushu swept beneath him, he began to feel a tiny ray of optimism. He could see the open ocean ahead. Maybe he'd get far enough to be picked up by a friendly ship. Out the side of the canopy he glimpsed the dark blue shape of Erickson's Corsair close to his starboard wing. He could see the worried look on Erickson's face.

Hill took another glance at his fuel quantity. Almost zero. This wouldn't be his first ditching. Back in his first combat tour in the Solomons, he'd put a Corsair down in the water, and he knew what it was like. It was a hell of a ride.

He called Erickson. "This is my last transmission. I'm depending on you to get someone here to rescue me."

In the next moment, the Corsair's engine coughed, stuttered, then went dead. Gliding toward the water, Hill slid his canopy back and locked it. Then, as an afterthought, he unbuckled his parachute. It would be easier to retrieve the one-man raft from the chute container if it was already released, he thought.

Hill aimed for a trough between the waves. The Corsair smacked down hard on its belly but didn't flip over. With the nose tilting quickly below the surface, Hill struggled to haul the raft out. Too late, he realized that unhooking the parachute had been a serious mistake. The whole package, parachute and raft, had slid to the forward footwell of the cockpit, which was now under water.

Forget the raft. He was barely able to kick himself free of the cockpit before the Corsair sank beneath the waves. Inflating his life vest, Hill bobbed like a cork on the three-foot waves.

He gazed around. There was no sign of the Corsair, not even a bubble left on the surface. For the first time he realized it was *cold*. It was still winter in the northern Pacific, and he was freezing. It was then that the reality of his situation struck Hill like a thunderclap. Without a raft, he was going to die in this damned ocean.

E very strike briefing included a standard admonition about radio silence. You didn't blab on the radio. You didn't clutter the tactical frequency. You didn't give the Japs a radio signal they could home in on.

Since their first mission together, Erickson and Hill had a private agreement. If one of them went down, to hell with radio silence—the other would get the word out.

Now Erickson was doing just that—filling the airwaves, making nonstop calls to other airplanes, submarines, carriers, anyone who could hear him. Beneath him, bobbing in a yellow life vest, was his best friend. Helplessly Erickson had watched Hill trying to pull out his raft. Now Hill looked like a speck in the ocean. Without a raft in the frigid water, he had a life expectancy of little more than an hour.

Erickson opened his canopy and tried to pull out his own raft to heave down to Hill. At six feet three inches, he was too tall. Each time he rose in the seat to reach the raft, the wind stream hit his head and shoulders and slammed him back down. He kept trying until he was exhausted. For a moment he considered ditching his own Corsair next to Hill so they could share his raft. Looking at the whitecaps on the surface, he decided it was a bad idea. They'd probably both wind up dead.

His own fuel was dangerously low. He waggled his wings one more time over the tiny figure in the water, then turned southward, back to the ship. By the time he was approaching *Intrepid*'s deck, he estimated that he had enough fuel left for one pass at the deck. He swept over the ramp and plunked down on the wooden deck, snagging a wire. He was still taxiing to the forward elevator when the engine sputtered and quit, out of fuel.

Minutes later Erickson was standing at attention in front of the air group commander. Hyland was livid. Erickson had jammed every goddamn radio circuit in the Fifth Fleet, alerting every submarine, ship, and airplane, and probably the Japs. What the hell had happened to radio discipline?

Erickson had no answer. This had been the worst day of his life. He'd just left his best friend to die in the ocean. He'd barely made it back to the carrier himself. Hyland, his air group commander and the father figure he revered more than any other human on earth, was furious with him.

Despite his best efforts to maintain a manly composure, he couldn't hold back his emotions. The twenty-two-year-old fighter pilot burst into tears.

12 ▸ AND WHERE IS THE NAVY?

IMPERIAL PALACE, TOKYO
MARCH 29, 1945

The air raid sirens were wailing again. Ignoring them, Emperor Hirohito seated himself at the conference table in the shelter adjoining the imperial library. The sirens had become a fixture of life in Tokyo. Nearly three weeks before, on the night of March 10, 1945, American B-29s dropped incendiary bombs on the city. Nothing like it had been seen in history. Over a hundred thousand Japanese perished in the fires. More than a million were made homeless. Sixteen square miles of Japan's capital were turned to charred rubble. The smoke and stench of the blazes still wafted through the Imperial Palace.

Now a month short of his forty-fourth birthday, Hirohito had reigned for nearly twenty years on the Chrysanthemum Throne. He was a fastidious, slightly built man who neither drank nor smoked. His reign was called "Showa," meaning "radiating peace."

How much longer the reign of Hirohito—or the Empire of Japan—might last was very much on the emperor's mind. Another government was teetering on collapse. The previous prime minister, Gen. Hideki Tojo, had been removed in July 1944 after the defeat in the Philippine Sea and replaced with Gen. Kuniaki Koiso. Now Koiso was on his way out for the same reason: Japan had suffered calamitous setbacks at Leyte Gulf and Iwo Jima. The Allies were about to invade Okinawa.

The next government would be headed by a navy man, Admiral Kantaro Suzuki, with whom no one was pleased, including Hirohito and even the senior officers of the navy. Suzuki was eighty years old and more moderate than army militarists like Tojo and

Koiso. The hard-liners were worried that the old admiral was inclined toward a negotiated peace with the Americans.

The militarists in the imperial government still held sway, just as they had when the decision was taken in 1941 to attack the United States. Never mind that their strident talk of *bushido* and imperial glory made them sound as if they'd come unhinged. No senior officer in either the Imperial Navy or Army was willing to speak what they all knew to be the truth: Japan had no chance of winning this war. To express such a thought was tantamount to treason. Even those who secretly favored a negotiated peace knew better than to reveal their feelings. That would make them a "Badoglio," the detested Italian general and prime minister who surrendered his country to the Allies in 1943.

At the conference table with the emperor were his military advisors, the chiefs of staff of the army and the navy and their immediate subordinates. It was the role of Admiral Koshiro Oikawa, Imperial Japanese Navy chief of staff, to interface between His Divine Majesty and the Combined Fleet headquarters, whose commander in chief was Admiral Soemu Toyoda.

The chiefs of staff had presented to Hirohito the plan for the coming counteroffensive at Okinawa. The officers were keeping their eyes averted from the emperor's divine countenance while Hirohito studied the details of the plan.

Occasionally the emperor stopped, squinting through his wire-framed spectacles, to ask questions. How many aircraft would be used in the attacks? Two thousand, Admiral Oikawa told him. Was that enough? the emperor asked. Oikawa explained that an additional fifteen hundred army aircraft would be available.

Hirohito seemed perplexed. More than a hundred thousand army troops were prepared to die to defend Okinawa, and several thousand *tokko* pilots would be sacrificed. He turned to Admiral Oikawa. "And where is the navy?"

Oikawa exchanged glances with his staff officers. None was sure how to answer. Did the emperor understand that the navy had been reduced to only a handful of ships? Did he know there was nothing the navy could do that would alter the situation at Okinawa?

Perhaps, but it didn't matter. The emperor's meaning was clear. It was not acceptable that the army should make so great a sacrifice while the navy's ships remained clear of the battle.

The audience with the emperor was over. Oikawa and his staff returned to the Navy Ministry. They had only a few days to decide what the Imperial Japanese Navy should sacrifice in the battle for Okinawa.

A *nd where is the navy?* The emperor's question demanded an answer. In his office a few miles southwest of the capital, the commander in chief of the Combined Fleet, Adm. Soemu Toyoda, agonized over the navy's options.

Toyoda was, if nothing else, a survivor. He had been one of those opposed to a war with the United States, viewing it as unwinnable. Thereafter he had been relegated to administrative positions, too senior to receive a division or fleet command. He was thrust into the topmost naval command post by virtue of attrition after Yamamoto was killed at Bougainville and his successor, Admiral Mineichi Koga, was lost on a flight to the Philippines.

At age fifty-seven, round-faced and thick-bellied, Toyoda was neither a great strategist nor an inspiring leader. His job consisted mainly of mediating between the hard-liners who demanded an all-or-nothing decisive battle with the Americans and those who wanted to hoard the navy's assets for the defense of the homeland.

With his staff assembled at a long conference table, maps on the wall behind him, Toyoda was hearing both sides. As usual, the shrill voices of the hard-liners were drowning out the others. Neither Toyoda or Oikawa or even the new prime minister, Admiral Suzuki, was willing to challenge them.

The spokesman for the hard-liners was the Combined Fleet chief of operations, Capt. Shigenori Kami. Kami was proposing that the

Second Fleet, which included most of the navy's still-battleworthy warships, throw its full weight behind the upcoming offensive. A force of ten warships, with the great battleship *Yamato* as its flagship, would hurl itself at the American fleet off Okinawa.

Yamato's guns had greater range than anything the Americans possessed. After inflicting maximum damage on the U.S. ships, she would be beached. The great battleship would become a stationary artillery platform, and most of her crew would join the garrison defending Okinawa.

The sea assault would coincide with Admiral Ugaki's massive aerial *tokko* attacks, while General Ushijima's 32nd Army on Okinawa would take advantage of the situation and counterattack on the ground. It would be glorious. A last *banzai*! The enemy would be hurled back into the sea.

A stunned hush fell over the conference table. Then the more rational officers in the Combined Fleet staff spoke up. They thought it was preposterous. What possible effect could these ships have on the outcome of the Okinawa campaign? It would be a meaningless waste.

It would be even more meaningless, countered the hard-liners, to have them destroyed at anchor by enemy warplanes. Or, infinitely worse, surrendering them whole to invading American troops.

As usual, the hard-liners prevailed. Whether anyone believed such an attack could succeed hardly mattered. The plan had an almost mystical appeal—the mighty *Yamato* charging like a seaborne samurai directly at the enemy fleet, all guns roaring, sending the terrified enemy into a disorderly retreat. It was the kind of seductive, romantic theme that dwelled in the heart of every Japanese warrior.

Admiral Toyoda nodded his agreement. The hard-liners would have their way. Toyoda would sign off on what would be his last operational order of the war.

S he was the mightiest warship ever constructed. Displacing 71,659 tons and capable of 27 knots, the superbattleship *Yamato* had the greatest firepower ever mounted on a vessel—more than 150 guns, including nine 18.1-inchers that could hurl 3,200-pound armor-piercing shells on a trajectory of 22.5 miles. Her massive armor was the heaviest ever installed on a warship, making her virtually impregnable to the guns of any ship in the world.

She was 863 feet long at her weather deck. Her bridge tower, rising 80 feet above the deck, had two elevators and six separate decks for command and control of the ship and her fleet. Her single massive smokestack swept aft at a rakish 25 degrees. *Yamato*'s interior contained five decks divided into a bewildering warren of spaces and watertight compartments. Mounted on her aft deck was an aircraft crane and two catapults over a hangar that accommodated six floatplanes.

Protruding from her bow was the golden two-meter-wide *kikusui* crest, a chrysanthemum-shaped symbol taken from a Japanese legend about a fourteenth-century warrior and martyr. Even the ship's name, emblazoned in gold on her hull, possessed a mystical power. *Yamato* was a poetic and spiritual metaphor for Japan itself. In her gray, armored magnificence, she symbolized Japan's early dreams of conquest. While *Yamato* still lived, so did Japan.

Yamato was the prototype of five such dreadnoughts that Japan intended to build. She was the product of the mid-1930s belief that if Japan were to face the United States in a future war, domination of the Pacific required that they build battleships larger than anything the United States might possess. American battleships were limited in size for practical reasons—the Panama Canal permitted passage of vessels no larger than about 63,000 tons.

She was designed and constructed in secret, in violation of the Washington and London treaties that limited the size and number of battleships. *Yamato*'s hull was laid down in 1937 at the Kure shipyard. Her sister ship, *Musashi*, was begun the following year in Nagasaki, and *Shinano* at Yokosuka. Construction of the remaining two *Yamato*-class battleships was canceled. Ultimately, only *Yamato* and *Musashi* entered service as battleships. After the historic Battle of Midway, when it became apparent that aircraft carriers held the key to victory at sea, the unfinished *Shinano* was converted to an aircraft carrier. *Shinano* would have been the largest carrier ever deployed in World War II, but while transiting from Yokosuka to Kure in November 1944 to complete her fitting out, she was torpedoed by the U.S. submarine *Archerfish*.

Throughout *Yamato*'s construction, she was shielded by a massive canvas screen to prevent observation. Still shrouded in secrecy, the battleship was commissioned a few days after the attack on Pearl Harbor. Although she served as Admiral Yamamoto's flagship at the Battle of Midway, *Yamato* was kept at the fringe of the battle and never saw action. In November 1943 she and *Musashi* were relegated to transport duty, hauling troops and supplies to the Solomons. The next month, while transporting troops to the Admiralty Islands, *Yamato* received her first blooding—two torpedoes in her starboard side from the U.S. submarine *Skate*—forcing her to retire to Truk for emergency repairs.

Not until October 1944 did *Yamato* finally fire her guns at an enemy. As the flagship of Admiral Kurita's First Diversionary Striking Force, *Yamato* fought the U.S. fleet at the Battle of Leyte Gulf. Although Kurita's warships were able to ambush the ships of the Taffy Fleet, sinking the escort carrier *Gambier Bay* and three destroyers, *Yamato* missed most of the glory. Dodging a torpedo, her captain steered her *away* from the thick of the battle. By the time he reversed course, Admiral Kurita had ordered a withdrawal.

Passing back into the Sibuyan Sea, *Yamato* received another chance to fire her guns into the sky when she came under attack from U.S. carrier planes. Again her luck held. She made it back to Kure, damaged but intact.

The "decisive battle" that Japanese admirals rhapsodized about—the mythical great clash between Japanese and American surface fleets that would send the enemy reeling in defeat—was a faded dream. The Imperial Japanese Navy no longer had a fleet. Its handful of surviving ships spent most of their energy darting around the Inland Sea, the long passage between Honshu and Shikoku, hiding from American bombers.

Yamato had become a ship without a mission. Now, finally, the great battleship had received her call to arms.

Ens. Mitsuru Yoshida took a last look up and down Pier 1 at the Kure naval port. As the officer in charge of the last boat to shore, it was his job to make sure no sailors from *Yamato* were left ashore. Missing the sailing of a warship was an offense punishable by death.

As Yoshida expected, there were no stragglers. By now all *Yamato*'s crewmen were surely on board. Yoshida stood for another long moment on the pier gazing around. Kure had been his home since he arrived three months earlier as the new assistant radar officer. The streets of the naval port were eerily quiet this morning, as if everyone was still asleep. In the pale morning light, the surface of the harbor was a slate gray. Yoshida felt a pang of homesickness. He had the feeling that this might be the last time he would ever stand on his native land.

The twenty-two-year-old officer stepped back into the motor launch and ordered the coxswain to return to their ship. As they sliced back across the slick water, Yoshida was struck once again by the sight of the great vessel moored at Buoy 26. The silver-white hull of *Yamato* dominated the harbor. Passing the cruiser *Yahagi*, moored next to *Yamato*, Yoshida could see blinker flashes being exchanged between the ships. Newly graduated from officer candidate school only three months ago, Yoshida could read the signals: "Preparations for getting under way completed."

At 1500 that afternoon, March 29, 1945, *Yamato* eased away

from her mooring. Yoshida was at his duty station on the bridge, an officer of the most junior rank in the midst of captains and admirals. Turning westward, the battleship followed the southern shoreline of Honshu, past the port of Hiroshima.

Along the way, *Yamato*'s skipper, Rear Adm. Kosaku Ariga, ordered drills for the crew. While the ship turned and circled, the crew practiced antiaircraft and antiship exercises.

That evening, after they'd dropped anchor at the Mitajiri anchorage, near Ube on the narrow gulf separating Honshu from Kyushu, Captain Ariga assembled his crew of three thousand men. A stillness settled over the men on the deck as Ariga made his announcement: *Yamato* would be the mainstay of a task force sailing to counter the expected American landings on Okinawa. He hoped that they would rise to the occasion and live up to the expectations of the navy.

For a moment the only sound on deck was the collective breathing of the men. Ariga's announcement came as no real surprise. Everyone knew what was happening at Okinawa. For the past week they'd heard the rumors: *Yamato* would soon be going into action. Now it was official.

Then the cheering began. Like all Japanese fighting men, they had been demoralized by the steady drumbeat of bad news—the Philippines, Saipan, Iwo Jima, now Okinawa. The pent-up frustration and anger came spilling out of them. The sailors yelled and laughed and applauded. Finally they were going to teach the Americans a lesson. The big guns of the *Yamato* were going to blow the enemy to hell.

The truth still hadn't sunk in. The captain had stopped short of actually saying that they were going on a suicide mission. Seconds later, the voice of the executive officer, Capt. Jiro Nomura, cleared up any doubt. "The time has come," he said. "Kamikaze *Yamato*, be truly a divine wind!"

That night Yoshida lay in his bunk reading a biography of the philosopher Spinoza. It was a rare moment. Between standing watches, exercising his division of sixteen men, and performing endless antiaircraft and damage control drills, there had been little time for the pleasure of reading.

In his brief time aboard *Yamato*, Yoshida had learned that his fellow junior officers fell into two categories. There were the professionals, most of whom came from the Eta Jima naval academy, and there were those like Yoshida, who had been plucked from civilian life and rushed through officer candidate school. Most of the academy graduates were hard-liners who embraced the samurai ethos. They loudly proclaimed their willingness to die for the emperor, and they heaped scorn on anyone who suggested that suicide was a senseless tactic.

Most of the recently commissioned officers were of a different mind-set. Like Yoshida, they were university students whose lives had been interrupted by military service. Most had no use for the *bushido* nonsense of the hard-liners, but they had the sense to shut up about it. To Yoshida, there was a difference between being willing to die in the line of duty and throwing yourself at the enemy in a suicidal charge. He hadn't volunteered to die.

It no longer mattered. Yoshida was a loyal son of Japan. His fate was bound with that of *Yamato*.

13 ▸ GIMLET EYES AND THE ALLIGATOR

From the bridge of his flagship, the cruiser *Indianapolis*, Adm. Raymond Spruance had a panoramic view of the amphibious force. The ships looked like brooding whales, one gray shape after another, stretching from horizon to horizon. On the opposite side of Okinawa were the flattops and escort ships of Mitscher's Task Force 58. Together they constituted an armada of more than thirteen hundred ships.

The man whom destiny had placed in command of this force was not a charismatic figure in the mold of Horatio Nelson, John Paul Jones, or even Bull Halsey. Raymond Ames Spruance, in fact, was the reverse image of the flamboyant Halsey, possessing none of Halsey's ebullient temperament or flair for self-promotion. Though he and Halsey were fast friends, Spruance worried about the effect an adoring press had on a senior commander. "His fame may not have gone to his head," Spruance wrote, "but there is nevertheless danger in this. Should he get to identifying himself with the figure as publicized, he may subconsciously start thinking in terms of what this reputation calls for, rather than of how best to meet the action problem confronting him."

By personality and style, Spruance was a cautious commander. Halsey, who had been criticized for the opposite tendency, alluded to this when he wrote, "I wish that Spruance had been with Mitscher at Leyte Gulf, and I had been with Mitscher in the Battle of the Philippine Sea." Coming from Halsey, it was both a rueful comment on his own actions at Leyte Gulf and an implicit criticism of Spruance at the Philippine Sea. The aggressive Halsey was undoubtedly thinking that he would have pursued and destroyed the Japanese carriers at the Philippine Sea, and the Leyte Gulf battle never would have been fought.

Spruance's lean face had a sober, calculating expression, with darting eyes that always seemed to be absorbing new information. "Gimlet Eyes" was a nickname staff officers gave him, but never to his face. The mild-mannered Spruance never indulged in the profane, tough talk of admirals such as Kelly Turner or John "Slew" McCain. His only noticeable vice was a passion for exotic coffees, which he was able to indulge as his forces seized one coffee-growing island after another in the Pacific.

No one, including his bosses Chester Nimitz or Ernest King, doubted Spruance's brilliance. Spruance himself never took credit for being bright, claiming that he was actually just a good judge of men. "I am lazy," he wrote, "and I never have done things myself that I could get someone to do for me." It was Spruance's style to choose bright officers for his staff, then get out of their way.

On the gray morning of March 31, 1945, as Spruance's fleet was preparing to invade Okinawa, a warning was flashed from the CIC of Spruance's flagship, *Indianapolis*: four bogeys were inbound. In the next few minutes, CAP fighters splashed two of the enemy planes. A third was shot down by gunners on the cruiser *New Mexico*.

The fourth somehow slithered through the screen. Dodging the combined gunfire of the task force's heavy ships and their screens, the kamikaze crashed into *Indianapolis's* port quarter.

The kamikaze plane itself did little damage. The starboard wing clipped the cruiser's port bulwark, and most of the wreckage plunged into the water. Its bomb, released just prior to impact, smashed through several decks, including two messing and berthing compartments, before exploding in an oil bunker. Nine men were killed and twenty wounded.

Indianapolis could still fire her guns, and she could make her own way to the newly captured anchorage at Kerama Retto. Inspection revealed that her propeller shafts were damaged, her fuel tanks ruptured, and her water-distilling equipment ruined.

The cruiser was ordered back to the United States. When she returned to war in July 1945, *Indianapolis* would carry the components of a world-altering instrument—the "Little Boy" atomic bomb that was detonated over Hiroshima. In a tragic finale to her career, *Indianapolis* would be sunk by a Japanese submarine two weeks before the end of the war, incurring the greatest seagoing loss of life aboard any U.S. warship.

For Spruance, the kamikaze strike on his flagship was a minor deterrent. Without missing a beat, he transferred his flag to the battleship *New Mexico* and continued planning the next morning's invasion.

A board *Eldorado*, Vice Adm. Kelly Turner was keeping the pressure on his staff, firing off his daily blizzard of memos that his officers called "snowflakes," monitoring the arrival of the amphibious forces as they converged on Okinawa from staging bases at Ulithi, Saipan, Leyte, and Guam. A heavy weather system with high seas in the western Pacific had slowed their progress. True to form, the Alligator was accepting no excuses from his task group commanders.

Love Day—the day the first U.S. troops would hit the beaches at Hagushi, on the western shore of Okinawa—was now twenty-four hours away. Turner's gunfire and covering force, Task Force 54 under Rear Adm. Mort Deyo, was on station off the western shore of Okinawa delivering a preinvasion bombardment of enemy positions.

The problem was, there were no readily identifiable targets. And the enemy wasn't cooperating by firing their shore batteries and revealing their positions. As far as anyone could tell, the western shore—and the landing beaches at Hagushi—were deserted.

The Alligator knew better. He'd seen this before. The Japanese never showed their hand until the battle had begun.

The mood in Boys' Town changed again that night. Out from the lockers came the stashes of Coon Range, but not to mourn the loss of another Tail End Charlie. This was a night for celebration. The report had just reached *Intrepid*: Windy Hill, last seen floating in the Pacific off Kyushu, was alive and aboard an American submarine.

Hill's life, in fact, had been saved by one of the VF-10 Grim Reaper pilots, Lt. George "Bee" Weems, who relieved Erickson on station over the place where Hill went down. Realizing that Hill had left his sinking Corsair without a raft, Weems managed to haul his own raft free and drop it to Hill. With the last of his energy, Hill had made a hundred-yard swim through the high seas and clambered aboard the raft. Thirty minutes later, he was astonished to see the gray shape of a submarine swell up from the ocean.

Eric Erickson's incessant jabbering on the radio had produced results. Alerted by the transmissions, USS *Sea Dog* proceeded to the area. The sub skipper spotted the circling Corsairs through his periscope and made directly for Hill's raft.

Hill had been rescued, but it didn't mean he was coming home to the *Intrepid*. Not for a while. The *Sea Dog* had embarked on its war patrol only a few hours before picking up the downed pilot. Now the submarine was heading back into the Pacific. Like it or not, Windy Hill was along for the ride.

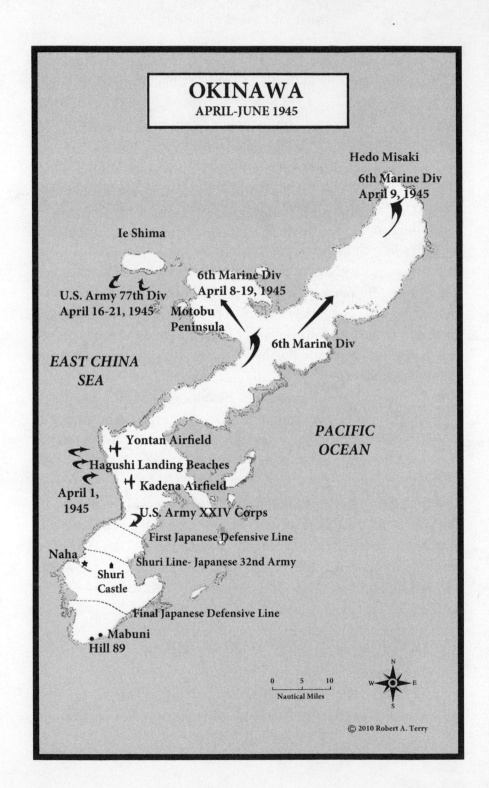

OKINAWA
APRIL-JUNE 1945

Hedo Misaki

**6th Marine Div
April 9, 1945**

Ie Shima

**6th Marine Div
April 8-19, 1945**

**U.S. Army 77th Div
April 16-21, 1945**

**Motobu
Peninsula**

6th Marine Div

*EAST CHINA
SEA*

*PACIFIC
OCEAN*

Yontan Airfield

Hagushi Landing Beaches

Kadena Airfield

**April 1,
1945**

U.S. Army XXIV Corps

First Japanese Defensive Line

Naha

Shuri Line- Japanese 32nd Army

Shuri
Castle

Final Japanese Defensive Line

Mabuni
Hill 89

0   5   10
Nautical Miles

N
W   E
S

© 2010 Robert A. Terry

PART TWO

STORMING THE GREAT LOOCHOO

Marine Corps general, explaining the reason for invading Okinawa: From Okinawa we can bomb the Japs anywhere—China, Formosa, Japan.

Marine Corps gunnery sergeant, nodding: Yes, sir. And vice versa.

The prospects of a long and illustrious career for a destroyer assigned to radar picket station duty is below average expectancy. That duty is extremely hazardous, very tiring, and entirely unenjoyable.

—CMDR. FRANK L. JOHNSON,
COMMANDING OFFICER, USS *Purdy*

Robert Bailey A.S.A.A. ©1998

VBF-10 Corsairs attacking *Yamato* in the painting *Imperial Sacrifice.* (PAINTING © ROBERT BAILEY)

14 ▸ LOVE DAY

It was a perfect morning for an invasion. The sea was glassy smooth, shimmering in the glow of the early spring sun. Waves of LCIs (landing craft infantry) and LVTs (landing vehicle tracked) were moving in parallel paths toward the beach, each craft trailing a long ribbon of foam. In the fore of each column were LCI gunboats, blazing away at the beach with 40-millimeter guns, .50-caliber machine guns, and Mark 7 rocket launchers.

The code name for the timing of the invasion was "Love Day." The fact that the landings were also on April Fool's Day wasn't lost on the grim-faced soldiers and Marines hunched down in the landing craft. Some were veterans of the bloody landings on Peleliu, Saipan, and Tarawa. They all knew about Iwo Jima, where casualties had been horrific. Okinawa, they had no doubt, was going to be a bigger, bloodier version of Iwo.

One of the men in the landing craft of the 1st Marine Division was a skinny forty-five-year-old war correspondent named Ernie Pyle. Pyle was not one of the twilight warriors—latecomers to the war. He'd already seen more combat than most of the men in the landing craft. As a columnist and reporter for the Scripps-Howard newspaper chain, he'd covered the European theater from North Africa to Sicily, Italy, and France. He'd been on the beach at Normandy a day after D-day. His columns had won him a Pulitzer Prize in 1944.

Pyle hadn't wanted to come out here. But after he returned from Europe, he couldn't just stay home. He thought he owed it to the men who were fighting in the Pacific to tell their story.

Now Pyle was hunkered down with the Marines in the landing

craft headed for a beach code-named "Yellow One," on the northern half of the landing zone. "I felt miserable," he reported, "and an awful weight was on my heart. There's nothing whatever romantic in knowing that an hour from now you may be dead."

Center stage of the show was a six-mile stretch of beach on the west central shore of the island, near the village of Hagushi. Under covering gunfire, underwater demolition teams had already slithered ashore to prepare the beaches for the assault. The first key objectives were the two Japanese airfields Yontan and Kadena, directly behind the invasion beaches.

As the landing craft neared the reef that protected the lagoon inside, the thunder of gunfire swelled to a crescendo. Fighter bombers from the carrier task force flashed overhead, firing 5-inch rockets and blazing away with machine guns. Cruisers and battleships kept up a steady barrage with their heavy guns. The baritone rumble of the amphibious crafts' diesel engines wafted over the surface of the water.

Each tracked landing craft, one after another, motored up to the reef, paused, then scuttled like a crab over the barely submerged coral. Plowing back into the sea, it made its final charge to the beach.

In his wallowing amphtrac—amphibious tractor—Ernie Pyle peered ahead through the smoke. So far there had been no enemy shelling of the landing craft. "We had all expected to go onto the beach in a hailstorm of tracer bullets, mortar shells throwing sand, and artillery shells whistling into the water near us," he wrote. "And yet we couldn't see a bit of firing ahead. We hoped it was true."

At 0832 came the radio call, "First wave has hit the beach!" The thunder of the ships' heavy guns abruptly ceased. Up and down the beach, amphtracs waddled onto the shore, discharging their loads of soldiers and Marines. As soon as each was empty, it turned and motored back over the reef, out to where transports waited to load the amphtrac with more troops.

It was exquisitely controlled chaos. For miles in each direction, hundreds of craft were churning the water like swarms of otters, crossing wakes, coming and going, missing each other by scant feet.

Aboard his flagship *Eldorado*, the Alligator was presiding like a conductor over the vast operation. At Iwo Jima, Turner had been accused by infantry commanders of hoarding his ammunition, saving it for the coming invasion of Okinawa. Nothing was being held back now. The bombardment of Okinawa was the most intense of any amphibious campaign in the war. Turner's ships had fired more than forty thousand rounds of heavy shells, breaching seawalls, destroying farms and shacks, razing entire villages. Fighter-bombers from the Fast Carrier Force were sweeping over the island, strafing, rocketing, and dropping bombs.

It was mostly for nothing. Other than a few parked Japanese airplanes on the Yontan, Naha, and Kadena airfields, the warplanes were finding few identifiable targets. By all appearances, the island of Okinawa appeared to be uninhabited.

Hundreds of troops were now ashore, swarming inland. Japanese gunners were still not returning fire, keeping their positions hidden. So far the only enemy counterfire was a few rounds from mortars, which were quickly silenced by the ships' guns. Meanwhile, more waves of troops were arriving, piling out of the landing craft, sprinting to the first available cover.

Despite the lack of resistance, the men on the beach felt exposed and vulnerable. The beach sloped steeply upward in places, making it hard to run with heavy packs and weapons. No one could shake the feeling that the Japanese were setting them up. A murderous enfilading fire would surely come in the next minutes from hidden nests in the hills and limestone bluffs above the landing zone.

The fire didn't come. More troops hit the beach, and behind them came amphibious transports to disgorge tanks and artillery pieces. The beaches were becoming congested. By 0900, spotter planes reported that advance troops were already several hundred yards inland. U.S. tanks could be seen motoring up the slope of the overlooking hillside. Bulldozers and cranes were assembling on the beach. Offshore, the long parallel wakes of more than seven hundred landing craft stretched beyond sight.

Still no resistance. No one was ready to believe it. Men stormed out of their amphtracs on the beach, only to find the Marines and soldiers who'd preceded them moving at a leisurely pace, smoking and talking, making their way unopposed up the enemy slope. Nowhere were the killer mushrooms of enemy mortars, the dreaded rattle of machine guns. New arrivals on the beach exchanged wary looks. Where was the horde of fanatical Japs they'd been told to expect?

One of the most astonished was Ernie Pyle. His amphtrac lurched up on the beach, and the ramp dropped open. "We stepped out," recalled Pyle. "We were on Okinawa an hour and a half after H-hour without getting shot at, and we hadn't even got our feet wet."

It was too good to be true. A Marine first lieutenant, Lawrence Bangser, had seen other invasions, and this one didn't feel right. "Either this Jap general is the world's greatest tactician," he told a reporter, "or the world's stupidest man."

Time correspondent Robert Sherrod waded ashore with the Marines on northern Hagushi beach. He made his way up to a regimental command post. "From the high ground I could see about 1,000 of the 1,400 ships involved around Okinawa. The colonel said that some of his men were browned off because there had been no opposition on the beaches. They had been built up to such a high pitch of combat efficiency that they were bound to feel let down and slightly sheepish. Said the colonel: 'This is the finest Easter present we could have received. But we'll get a bellyful of fighting before this thing is over.' "

A few minutes before 1000, Marines in the northern sector reported that they were on the edge of Yontan airfield. The battleships and cruisers of the task force had to suspend covering fire because the assault troops were moving too fast. At 1035, the invaders had reached the edge of the second objective, Kadena airfield. Along the way they encountered only Okinawan peasants, most of them shell-shocked by the barrage. The Okinawans stared at the Americans as if they were seeing aliens from another galaxy.

The fight for the airfields was over quickly. Yontan was seized at a cost of two Marines dead and nine wounded. The capture of the critical airfield happened so quickly it surprised even the Japanese. Marines at Yontan watched in astonishment as a dusky-colored fighter with a distinctive red ball on its right wing and fuselage glided down to a landing on the still-uncleared runway.

The Zero taxied up to the flight line. Too late the startled pilot realized what had happened. When he jumped from the cockpit with his gun drawn, he was mowed down by the new owners of the airfield.

It was the same story everywhere. Casualties were light. Few units were encountering any significant resistance. By noon both Yontan and Kadena airfields were in U.S. hands. The battle plan allowed three days, and it had taken less than four hours.

One Marine battalion, hunting for Japanese defenders, managed to find and kill four. An army colonel sent them a message: "Please send us a dead Jap. A lot of my men have never seen one. We'll bury him for you."

The landings continued without opposition. While the invasion force was rumbling ashore at Hagushi, another wave under Rear Adm. Jerauld Wright was making a simulated landing further to the south, to draw Japanese forces away from the real landing beaches at Hagushi. Wright's decoy unit had all the elements of an amphibious force—a heavy pre-landing bombardment by surface ships, transport ships, and LSTs (tank landing ships) loaded with Marines.

The ruse brought no response from the enemy ashore, but it attracted attention from the sky. While the decoy force was still maneuvering for its final approach, a kamikaze appeared overhead. Diving on the clustered vessels below, the Japanese *tokko* plane smashed into the port quarter of LST-884, which had three hundred Marines aboard. Fire and exploding ammunition nearly destroyed the craft before a rescue party from the destroyer *Van Valkenburgh* were able to board and extinguish the fires. Twenty-four sailors and Marines were killed and twenty-one wounded aboard the unlucky LST.

At the same time the kamikaze was ramming LST-884, another was crashing into the transport ship *Hinsdale*, killing sixteen men, wounding thirty-nine, and leaving the ship without power. Tugs came to haul both stricken vessels to the new repair facility in nearby Kerama Retto.

None of this could diminish the Alligator's high spirits. At 1600 he sent a message to Spruance and Nimitz: "Landings on all beaches continued, with good progress inland against light opposition. Beachhead has been secured . . . Approximately 50,000 troops have landed over beaches . . . 420th Field Artillery Group with two battalions 155-millimeter guns on Keise Shima in support ground troops . . . Unloading supplies over Hagushi beaches commenced, using LVTs, dukws [six-wheeled amphibious trucks], LSMs [landing ships medium] and LSTs [tank landing ships]."

The chain of command for the invasion of Okinawa was as convoluted as any in the Pacific military structure. Because the Navy had responsibility for the invasion, Adm. Raymond Spruance was in overall charge of the campaign. The officer in command of the ships and men assigned to the invasion was the Alligator, Vice Adm. Kelly Turner. The invading ground force, the Tenth Army, was a mix of Army and Marine divisions, all under the command of a white-haired Army lieutenant general named Simon Bolivar Buckner Jr.

Buckner had not been the choice of Spruance or Turner. Both admirals preferred that a Marine lead the ground forces they put ashore on Okinawa. Their first choice was Lt. Gen. Holland

"Howlin' Mad" Smith, the cantankerous leatherneck who had led the amphibious assaults on the Gilberts, the Marshalls, Saipan, Tinian, and Guam. Smith had also commanded Task Force 56, the amphibious force that charged ashore on Iwo Jima, and had earned the confidence of Spruance and Turner.

But Howlin' Mad Smith had become controversial. At the height of the Saipan invasion, he peremptorily fired an Army division general for what Smith considered to be inept leadership. The incident enraged the Army brass in Washington, including chief of staff George Marshall, who had never believed that Marines had any business commanding Army units. The Army's resentment went all the way back to World War I, when, in their view, the Marine Corps had usurped the Army's rightful glory on the battlefields of France. At Saipan, Howlin' Mad Smith had reignited the old Army–Marine Corps feud.

Pacific commander in chief Chester Nimitz, ever the diplomat, moved to restore peace. Throwing a bone to the Army, he vetoed the choice of Howlin' Mad Smith and chose Lt. Gen. Simon Buckner to command the invasion force at Okinawa.

It was a decision Nimitz would have reason to regret.

15 ▸ BOURBON AND PUDDLE WATER

For Simon Bolivar Buckner Jr., a few months short of his fifty-ninth birthday, just *being* at Okinawa was a personal triumph. By 1945, the handsome, white-haired general was no less a twilight warrior than the kids on the ships and on the beach. Buckner was aware of the controversy over his posting. With minimal battle experience, he had been appointed over a plethora of seasoned combat commanders.

Like Douglas MacArthur, Buckner was a West Pointer and the son of a Civil War officer. His father, Gen. Simon B. Buckner, was named after the South American liberator. He had fought in the Mexican War, joined the Confederate side as a brigadier general, and gained infamy for making a hasty surrender to Ulysses Grant. He was exchanged and returned to fight until the end of the Civil War.

Now his son, Simon Buckner Jr., had arrived at his new command after thirty-seven years in the Army, most of it in staff and administrative positions. He'd missed combat in World War I, having spent the duration giving military training to Army aviators. Like MacArthur, he'd seen two tours of duty in the Philippines. He'd been an instructor at various Army schools and, also like MacArthur, had returned to West Point, serving in the mid-thirties as commandant of cadets.

When World War II began, Buckner was a colonel and a division chief of staff with every expectation of a combat command. Instead of going to Guadalcanal or North Africa, he received a promotion to brigadier general and the unenviable task of defending

Alaska—a region one-fifth the size of the United States, with a coastline nearly as long.

Buckner threw himself into the mission of fortifying Alaska. For a while it even seemed possible that the Japanese might attempt an invasion. They seized the Aleutian islands of Kiska and Attu and made a thrust at the Dutch Harbor military complex before being turned back by airpower. Buckner played only a minor role in the Aleutian action. For most of three frustrating years he paced the tundra while his Army contemporaries were fighting battles—*real* battles—in Europe and the Pacific.

In June 1944, fate finally smiled on Simon Buckner. Now wearing three stars, he was assigned to command the new Tenth Army, which was being formed for the invasion of Formosa. While he was still assembling his army, Buckner learned that Formosa would be bypassed. His first landing would be on Okinawa.

There were other similarities between Buckner and the media-conscious MacArthur. Buckner cultivated an image of himself as a hard-charging, outdoors-living, chest-thumping man of action. A *Time* interviewer profiled him as "a ruddy-faced, white-thatched, driving apostle of the rigorous life."

Buckner's favorite drink was "bourbon and puddle water," with which he made his traditional toast, "May you walk in the ashes of Tokyo." The general had a laugh, a journalist reported, that "starts with a little chuckle in his throat, and then he really lets go and shakes the walls."

Now, with the bulk of his army ashore on Okinawa, Buckner could allow himself to laugh. To his left, Maj. Gen. Roy Geiger's III Marine Amphibious Corps was rolling like a freight train northward through the Ishikawa Isthmus toward the neighborhood of Kim. Opposition to their advance was virtually nil. It was the same to the right, where Maj. Gen. John Hodge and XXIV Army Corps were marching southward toward Naha, the island's capital.

Buckner had good reason to be pleased, but he knew better

than to delude himself. He'd studied the intelligence reports. *Somewhere* on this island were more than sixty thousand Japanese troops. Where the hell were they?

They were there. But Buckner's intelligence reports were wrong. Instead of 60,000 enemy troops on Okinawa, there were nearly 120,000, dug into caves, tombs, and spider holes.

The man who commanded this force, Lt. Gen. Mitsuru Ushijima, watched from his observation post at the ancient Shuri Castle as the Americans advanced toward him. They were meeting only sporadic resistance, which was what Ushijima intended. Not until the enemy reached the open paddies and gentle hills three miles short of the first defensive line did Ushijima intend to show his hand. The approaches to the first defensive line were all pre-sited for artillery, mortar batteries, and machine gun nests to deliver enfilading fire on the advancing enemy.

Ushijima's 32nd Army included battle-hardened veterans of the 62nd Infantry Division, which had seen action in China, and the 24th Independent Mixed Brigade from the home island of Kyushu. In addition to his 34,000 regular infantrymen, Ushijima's force had 10,000 troops drawn from the Navy bases on Okinawa. Another 20,000 soldiers—called the Boeitai—were a home guard conscripted from the Okinawan population. Though the Boeitai lacked the grit and motivation of the homegrown Japanese soldiers, they were useful for the grunt work of digging emplacements and moving equipment.

Ushijima also had guns, more than any Japanese commander of a besieged island had possessed before. Much of the artillery had been destined for the Philippines, but time ran out before it could be delivered. Ushijima had three heavy artillery regiments, a tank regiment, and a regiment of the massive 320-millimeter guns that had been used with devastating effect at Iwo Jima. It was no match for what the Americans would bring with them, but for the first time in any of the Pacific battles Japanese artillery would be a major deterrent to the advancing enemy forces.

Ushijima had studied the previous invasions—Saipan, Leyte, Tarawa, Peleliu, and most recently Iwo Jima. His old Imperial Japanese Army colleague, Lt. Gen. Tadamichi Kuribayashi, had commanded the 21,000-man garrison at Iwo Jima. Outmanned and outgunned, with no hope of reinforcement or replenishment, Kuribayashi had chosen not to contest the American landings. Instead he fought a battle of attrition, resisting the enemy advance from a hidden honeycomb of tunnels, caves, and pillboxes. In the end, Kuribayashi and almost all his garrison went to their deaths.

Here on Okinawa Ushijima faced the same choices. His only option was to turn Okinawa into a Stalingrad for the Americans—a vast bloody pit into which the United States would throw lives and resources until they concluded that an unconditional surrender of Japan was not worth the sacrifice. Like Kuribayashi, Ushijima saw no point in wasting precious resources on the beaches. Nor did he believe in suicidal last-ditch *banzai* charges into the waiting muzzles of the enemy's guns.

Mitsuru Ushijima was not cut from the same cloth as most of the *bushido*-embracing officers of the Imperial Japanese Army. Ushijima was a disciplined, fatherly officer who disdained shows of anger. In a departure from the harsh customs of the Imperial Japanese Army, Ushijima ordered his junior officers to refrain from striking their subordinates.

Ushijima's second in command, fifty-one-year-old Isamu Cho, was his opposite in temperament. Newly promoted to the rank of lieutenant general, Cho was a fiery warrior with a history of extremist leanings. He'd been a conspirator in an unsuccessful attempt at a military dictatorship in 1931. During the infamous Rape of Nanking in 1937, it was Cho who had issued the orders to kill all prisoners. Prone to fits of rage, Cho didn't hesitate to slap subordinates who displeased him.

During strategy sessions in Ushijima's underground headquarters, Cho often clashed with the senior operations officer, Col. Hiromichi Yahara. At forty-two, Yahara was a calm, conservative officer who rejected the *bushido* notion of suicidal *banzai* charges. Such tactics, he insisted, were a stupid waste of lives. He counseled Ushijima that "the army must continue its current operations, calmly recognizing its final destiny—for annihilation is inevitable no matter what is done."

To Cho, such thinking was timid and defeatist, a dishonorable way for Japanese warriors to die. He urged Ushijima to launch a massive counterattack, hurl the enemy back to the beaches, and take the offensive in the battle for Okinawa.

The genial Ushijima presided over the debates in his headquarters more like a moderator than a commander. After listening to the impassioned arguments of both officers, he sided with Yahara. Better to bleed the enemy, making them pay in lives and time for each meter of ground they took.

As the days passed, more Okinawans came out of hiding. Gradually they realized that the invaders weren't pillaging and murdering. The Okinawans stared at the American soldiers in dazed fascination.

Ernie Pyle was with a Marine company working its way north when they found a group of natives hiding in a cave. "They were obviously scared to death," Pyle wrote. "After all the propaganda they had been fed about our tortures, they were a befuddled bunch of Okinawans when they discovered we had brought right along with us, as part of the intricate invasion plan, enough supplies to feed them too!"

The honeymoon continued. Nearly a week had passed since Love Day, and the Americans were still encountering little opposition. After the tense first few hours of the invasion, the men of the Tenth Army felt almost like celebrating.

Spring had come, the weather was benign, and the island

seemed almost friendly. To the old hands who had fought in hell-holes such as Tarawa and Saipan, the absence of thick jungle and oppressive heat was a blessing. Okinawa had a temperate climate. Its hillsides were covered with pine trees and wild raspberries. Flocks of pigeons fluttered overhead, offering the only targets for trigger-happy soldiers. Troops commandeered bicycles and horses. The most notable casualty of the first few days was a Marine who broke an ankle when he fell off a purloined bicycle.

One day passed into another as they made their careful advance across the island, still meeting no resistance. A few civilians, mostly children, approached the soldiers for handouts. Many of the GIs were farm boys from America's heartland. They gazed around at the pleasant landscape, impressed by the efficient cultivation of the arable land. Almost every square inch of tillable ground was neatly terraced and cultivated. It seemed an unlikely backdrop for a great battle.

M eanwhile, several hundred miles to the northeast of Okinawa, in the ocean off Shikoku, Windy Hill had reached a conclusion: he *hated* submarines. They were dangerous, claustrophobia-inducing, smelly steel tubes.

It had taken Hill less than one full day aboard USS *Sea Dog* to make this discovery. He had been having dinner in the officers' wardroom when the klaxon sounded: "General quarters, man your battle stations!"

The sub had been running on the surface, recharging its batteries. Hill watched with growing trepidation while the captain and all the officers charged out of the wardroom. The sub dove to periscope depth, and minutes later Hill heard the rumble of the forward torpedo tubes firing. The target, he learned, was a Japanese submarine that had been sighted on the surface.

Alone in the wardroom with only a steward for company, Hill huddled with his back against the bulkhead, trying to shut from his mind the vision of a torpedo slamming into the hull behind him.

They finally lost contact with the enemy submarine. *Sea Dog* returned to the surface, and the officers resumed their dinner. Gloomily Hill thought about his fellow airedales back aboard *Intrepid*. While he was stuck on this damned boat, they were shooting down Japs, bombing airfields, and collecting medals.

His gloom only deepened when the submarine's skipper informed him that the fun was just beginning. *Sea Dog's* war patrol would last another five weeks.

16 ▸ TEN-GO

Perched in his command chair on the sixth deck of *Yamato*'s bridge tower, Vice Adm. Seiichi Ito watched the crew preparing the battleship for departure. Ito had been one of those who loudly opposed the operation, now called Ten-Go, which literally meant "heaven number one." Ito, in fact, thought the whole *tokko* strategy was stupid, not for moral reasons—he was as much a samurai as the superpatriots—but because it was a waste of precious resources. Japan's warriors—and their weapons—should be saved for the final battle in the homeland.

But Seiichi Ito was, above all else, a loyal officer. Now that the decision was made and the orders received, he had committed himself to the success of Ten-Go. He commanded the Imperial Japanese Navy Second Fleet and, with his flag aboard *Yamato*, would lead the task force into battle against the Americans.

Seiichi Ito was fifty-four, a tall, stooped man with a square-cut, rugged face. Like his fellow admirals Toyoda and Oikawa, Ito had spent most of the war in Combined Fleet and Imperial Japanese Navy general staff assignments. All his requests for a major sea command had been denied. To Ito, it now seemed a stroke of irony that his first sea battle would, in all probability, be his last. It would probably also be the last for the Imperial Japanese Navy.

Ten-Go would be the first of a series of massed kamikaze attacks called *kikusui*, which meant "floating chrysanthemum." Like most Japanese war plans, the enchanting label masked a macabre strategy. The name came from the heraldic device of the fourteenth-century warrior Masashige Kusunoki, who personified the classic self-sacrificing warrior. According to legend, Kusunoki, obeying the command of the emperor Go-Daigo, led his army into certain death against vastly superior forces. Surrounded by the enemy and his situation hopeless, Kusunoke and six hundred of his surviving troops committed *seppuku*—the samurai ritual suicide by disembowelment

The *kikusui* attacks were supposed to emulate Kusunoki's sacrifice, but on an even grander scale. Involving more than two thousand *tokko* aircraft, they would attack the U.S. fleet in ten waves.

The *kikusui* operation had been envisioned purely as a series of airborne *tokko* attacks directed from the Kanoya base by Admiral Ugaki. No one had suggested that they be accompanied by a surface attack of Imperial Japanese Navy warships.

Not until a few days ago. Now the mighty *Yamato* and her entourage were about to embark on their own *tokko* mission.

A board *New Mexico*, Adm. Raymond Spruance read the decoded message. It had been transmitted that afternoon, April 5, from the Imperial Japanese Navy Combined Fleet commander to the commander in chief of the Second Fleet. Like almost all Japanese military communications, the intercepted message was deciphered by U.S. cryptologists in Makalapa, Hawaii, then flashed to Chester Nimitz's headquarters in Guam, where it was relayed to Raymond Spruance off the shore of Okinawa.

It was the official order for an operation called Ten-Go.

*Yamato and the Second Destroyer Squadron will sally
forth in a naval special attack via Bungo Channel at
dawn of Day Y-minus-one; at dawn of Day Y they will
charge into the seas west of Okinawa and will attack and
destroy the enemy's invasion fleet. Day Y will be 8 April.*

The intercepted report came as no real surprise to Spruance and his intelligence officers. For the past week reconnaissance aircraft had observed the Japanese fleet maneuvering in the Inland Sea as if preparing for the long-expected breakout. That they were coming through the Bungo Strait, the wide passage between Kyushu and Shikoku, was also no surprise. Their only other route would have been westward through the narrow Shimonoseki Strait, between the tips of Honshu and Kyushu, which were dangerous waters for a warship the size of *Yamato*. The strait was shallow, only 10 fathoms in places, and had been sown with mines by B-29 bombers. The strait was already littered with the hulks of unlucky ships that had stumbled into mines.

So the Imperial Japanese Navy fleet—what remained of it— was coming out to fight. To an old battleship sailor like Spruance, it presented a tantalizing possibility. He could send Task Force 54, Rear Adm. Mort Deyo's formidable array of battleships and cruisers, to confront the Japanese in what would likely be the last great surface engagement of the war. Or he could use the more expedient weapon—the warplanes of Marc Mitscher's Fast Carrier Task Force.

Or both, and let the quickest take the prize.

In either case, he had more to worry about than the *Yamato* surface force. He also had a report that the Japanese would be timing the surface attack with a simultaneous massive air assault and a counterattack from the Japanese ground forces on Okinawa. The battle for Okinawa was heating up.

The crew of the *Yamato* stopped in midstride. The voice of their executive officer, Capt. Jiro Nomura, was booming over the bullhorn: "Distribute sake to all divisions."

It was an announcement seldom heard aboard a warship of the Imperial Japanese Navy. On this, the eve of *Yamato*'s last battle, both Nomura and *Yamato*'s commanding officer, Rear Admiral Ariga, had decided to memorialize the occasion. Except for a skeleton crew of lookouts and duty officers, the crew of *Yamato* was going to have a monumental party. The galleys were ordered open.

Cooks were instructed to break out all the extra rations. There was no longer a need to keep the best food and drink in reserve. Crates of sake were opened and bottles distributed to all the divisions on the ship.

The cooks prepared delicacies of *sekihan*, a red bean paste, and *okashiratsuki*, sea bream served with the head still intact, all washed down with vast quantities of warm sake. Emboldened by alcohol and the brash hubris of youth, the sailors on the mess decks were making boisterous toasts, drinking to one another's death.

Whether any of them actually *welcomed* death was immaterial. By training and upbringing each was ensnared in a complex code of loyalty to his fellow sailors, his family, and ultimately to the emperor. The fear of disgrace held more sway over them than the fear of death.

One of the celebrants on the mess deck was eighteen-year-old Kazuhiro Fukumoto. It took only a couple of sakes, and the inexperienced young sailor was soused. Fukumoto was finding it hard to take all this mawkish talk about honor, death, and disgrace seriously. He was convinced that *Yamato* was unsinkable. It was an unreasoning belief, a gut feeling that came just from being aboard such a dreadnought. How could a warship of this size and firepower be sunk? It was impossible. Sure, in the thick of battle some of the crew might be killed by bullets and bombs. Still, the odds were in his favor. Given the number of crew aboard, his chances of being one of those killed were very slim.

He hadn't discussed *Yamato*'s mission with his parents, who lived in Kure, *Yamato*'s home port. With most of the crew, Fukumoto had been given a few days' shore leave to say farewell and settle his affairs. He'd had dinner with his parents and younger sister and told them to watch after his things while he was gone. For Fukumoto, it wasn't an emotional farewell. He didn't expect to be away for long.

In the officers' main wardroom, they were drinking not only sake but real Scotch whisky, part of the loot seized from the British after the capture of Singapore nearly four years earlier. Someone had pulled out the hand-cranked turntable, and they were singing along to the scratchy music from their collection of 78-rpm vinyl records. Even the skipper, Rear Admiral Ariga, and the executive officer, Captain Nomura, showed up, each bearing a huge bottle of sake.

Most of the officers were drunk, and Ariga, known as a hard drinker himself, was no exception. Forty-eight years old, Ariga had been in command of *Yamato* for only four months. He was a stern but fatherly commanding officer, revered by most of his young sailors. Their nickname for him was "Gorilla," for his stout, ungraceful build and hairless head.

For once the stiff formality of navy protocol went by the boards. Nomura was swept up in a mock scrimmage, his jacket getting ripped. Junior officers took turns thumping Ariga's bald, dome-shaped head. It was a wild, one-of-a-kind bash.

Soon after midnight, while most of the besotted crew was still stumbling to their bunks, the shadowy, taper-winged silhouette of a four-engine airplane passed high overhead. It was a B-29 reconnaissance bomber snapping pictures of the anchored battleship below, radioing its exact position back to Allied headquarters.

The early hours of April 6 were spent off-loading combustible materials and unnecessary stores. The deadline for mail was 1000, and the executive officer urged each officer and man to write a final letter to his family.

In his cramped quarters, Ens. Mitsuru Yoshida struggled to find words for a letter to his parents. He tried to push out of his mind the picture of his mother bent over in grief. Finally he wrote, "Please dispose of my things. Please, everyone, stay well and survive. That is my only prayer."

One of Yoshida's friends was Ens. Kunai Nakatami, who was a *nisei*—a Japanese American. Nakatami had been studying in Japan when war broke out. Conscripted into the navy, he was an assistant communications officer whose job was to interpret American emergency transmissions. Nakatami was a man whose homeland and enemy were the same. Two of his brothers were U.S. soldiers fighting in Europe. Most of his fellow officers aboard *Yamato* despised him for being an American.

Nakatami had just received a letter from his mother, via neutral Switzerland, which only added to his misery. "How are you?" his mother asked. "We are fine. Please do put your best effort into your duties. And let's both pray for peace." Nakatami broke down in tears, certain that he would never be able to reply to his mother's letter.

Similar scenes were playing out on the nine other ships that would sail with *Yamato*. Aboard *Yahagi*, the cruiser that would lead the attack force into the East China Sea toward Okinawa, Capt. Tameichi Hara wrote a last letter:

> *The Combined Fleet has shrunk unbelievably in the past*
> *two years. I am about to sortie as skipper of the only cruiser*
> *remaining in the fleet—8,500-ton* Yahagi. *With my good*
> *friend Rear Adm. Keizo Komura on board, we are going on*
> *a surface* tokko *mission. It is a great opportunity as well*
> *as a great honor to be skipper of a ship in this sortie to*
> *Okinawa. Know that I am happy and proud of this*
> *opportunity. Be proud of me.*
> *Farewell.*

In his cabin, the commander of the task force was also writing letters. Vice Adm. Seiichi Ito had been married to his wife, Chitose, for twenty-three years. They had three daughters, two of whom were still teenagers, and a son, a twenty-one-year-old navy pilot based in Kyushu. Ito was inordinately proud of his son, but he also had a father's gnawing trepidations about what would happen to him. As the aerial offensive shifted more and more to *tokko* tactics, Ito knew that his son would be a prime candidate for a one-way mission to Okinawa. Like his samurai model, the fourteenth-century general Kusunoki, who faithfully obeyed his emperor's orders despite the overwhelming certainty of death and defeat, Ito accepted his fate. And by the same reasoning, he could also accept whatever fate awaited his son. It was the way of the warrior.

Later that morning, the executive officer gave the order for fifty-three cadets from the Eta Jima naval academy who had boarded two days earlier to disembark. The cadets were crestfallen. Aware of *Yamato*'s coming mission, several begged the executive officer to be allowed to remain. Nomura shook his head. He understood their sentiments, and he would feel the same way in their position. As untrained officers, they were more hindrance than help in the coming battle. They were Japan's future skippers, and they should remain ashore.

Bitterly disappointed, the cadets made their way to the destroyer alongside, which would take them ashore. Along with them, *Yamato*'s Captain Ariga ordered another fifteen seriously ill men to disembark, as well as several over the age of forty whose large families would suffer undue hardship.

Standing at the rail of the destroyer, the cadets, most still hungover from the previous night's party, rendered a long final salute to *Yamato*.

They were running late. The task force was supposed to be under way at 1500, April 6, but there were delays off-loading nonessential supplies and combustibles. Not until 1524 did the captain give the order, "Unshackle from the buoy. All engines ahead slow."

A rumble passed through the great ship, and a gray foam boiled up from beneath her stern. Slowly she eased away from her mooring and into the channel to join the waiting formation. *Yamato* and her nine escorts turned their bows southeastward, toward the Bungo Strait, making a speed of 12 knots. In the lead was *Yahagi*, with a row of destroyers trailing on either side. The flagship *Yamato* was securely positioned in her place of honor in the center.

Twilight was descending over the task force when the executive officer, Capt. Nomura, mustered the crew. The evening breeze swirled over *Yamato*'s bow, ruffling the uniforms of the men assembled on the deck. Against the setting sun, silhouettes of the hills on Kyushu were gliding past *Yamato*'s starboard rail.

Standing atop the number two turret, Nomura read the orders from the task force commander, Vice Admiral Ito: "This task force of the Imperial Navy, in cooperation with the army, is about to stake its entire air, sea, and land might on an all-out attack against enemy ships in the vicinity of Okinawa. The fate of the empire hangs in the balance."

The crew faced the east, bowed to the emperor, and sang the Japanese anthem, "Kimi Ga Yo." Then, as one, they shouted, *"Banzai! Banzai! Banzai!"*

From across the water, like echoes, came the same shouts from the other ships. It was an emotional moment. The men shook hands and assured each other that the next time they met would be at Yasukuni, the sacred shrine near Tokyo where the spirits of Japanese warriors resided.

Returning to his duty station on the top deck, Lt. Naoyoshi Ishida felt the same emotions, but he had no illusions about what lay ahead. At twenty-eight, Ishida was a decade older than most of the sailors who were cheering a fate they could only dimly imagine. Unlike many of *Yamato*'s junior officers who had been snatched from civilian universities and professional studies and hurriedly trained as officers, Ishida was a professional naval officer who had begun his career before the war.

Ishida's wife and son were back in Kure. Like most of the ship's officers, Ishida had been given three days' leave before *Yamato*'s departure. During his leave, Ishida had purposely not allowed his thoughts to dwell on what lay ahead in the sea off Okinawa. He was a product of his culture and class. A willingness to die in the service of the emperor was an integral component of his being. The prospect of death in battle had never caused him a moment's anguish—until his visit with his family was nearly finished.

Darkness had come to Kure when Ishida said his farewell to his family in the doorway of their tiny wood-and-paper home. He felt a pang of grief as he realized that his infant son, whom he had not seen until this visit, would soon be fatherless. He struggled for the words to say farewell to his wife. Even if he had been allowed to reveal the secret that neither he nor *Yamato* would return from the next sortie, he wouldn't have been able to say it. It would simply have been too difficult for both of them.

He'd kissed his wife, then walked away. After she closed the door, he came back. He walked around the house, taking a last look at the fragile structure. He peered through the window to fix in his memory a last image of the family he would never see again. He said a silent goodbye and made his way to the *Yamato*.

Back aboard the battleship, he wrote a final letter to his parents. It wasn't difficult. In the traditionally respectful language with which Japanese addressed their elders, he requested their forgiveness for not having said farewell. He asked that they please live long lives. He sealed the envelope, then began writing a letter to his wife. "You can marry again," he wrote, "but whatever you do, please raise our son to be a good man."

Ishida laid down his pen, stared at the letter, then tore it up. He tried writing another letter, then tore it up also. He couldn't do it. Such a letter would cause her too much pain. The image of his beloved wife weeping over the letter would make it harder for him to perform his duties when *Yamato* entered battle.

Forget it, Ishida decided. There would be no farewell.

17 ▸ DIVINE WIND

The drums rolled. The *tokko* pilots stood in a long row awaiting their final orders. Each was dressed in a bulky flying suit and helmet, a ceremonial white *hachimaki* headband tied around his head. The first wave would take off at 1320.

As he always did when dispatching young men to their deaths, Vice Adm. Matome Ugaki wore a somber expression. With him was Combined Fleet chief of staff Vice Adm. Ryunosuke Kusaka, both admirals wearing their starched whites, swords, medals, and white gloves. On long tables before them stretched the row of empty cups, the plates of rice wafers.

Ten-Go was the first and most ambitious of the ten planned *kikusui* operations. It would be a mass air attack by both *tokko* aircraft and conventional warplanes, coordinated with the surface attack by the *Yamato* task force. At the same time, General Ushijima's 32nd Army was supposed to counterattack on Okinawa and retake the airfields at Yontan and Kadena.

Ugaki was skeptical about Ten-Go's chances for success. Like most Japanese operations, the complex plan depended on precise timing and careful coordination. From experience Ugaki knew how poorly the army and the navy coordinated their operations. He doubted that General Ushijima would seize the moment to regain the lost ground on Okinawa. He was even more pessimistic about *Yamato*'s chance of success. Ugaki, an old battleship sailor, had been opposed to the mission. It was "superficial," he declared, to regard the battleship as useless.

Ugaki spoke to the assembled pilots. In the same low voice he always used when delivering final orders to the *tokko* warriors, he told them that this was the first of a series of *kikusui* operations. More than two thousand warplanes were being assembled for the campaign, three-quarters of them dedicated to *tokko* missions. In a succession of blows they would annihilate the American fleet off Okinawa. The enemy would be paralyzed and unable to proceed with their invasion. The noble young *tokko* airmen would be in the vanguard of saving the empire.

They gazed back at him in respectful silence. Whether or not they actually believed him didn't matter. Questioning such an order was not an option. Nor was reneging on their pledge to die for the emperor.

The cups were filled. Solemnly Ugaki raised his to the assembled pilots. "We shall meet at Minatogawa," he told them.

They had heard Ugaki make this promise several times now. The *tokko* volunteers who had not yet flown their missions accepted it as an article of faith that the admiral would follow them into death. They would be reunited in spirit at the shrine commemorating the legendary battle of Minatogawa.

The pilots drank from their cups. They saluted Admiral Ugaki, then bowed respectfully. The admiral gave the order to man their planes, and in unison the pilots yelled three *banzai* cheers. The drums beat a steady tattoo while they trotted to the camouflaged revetments where the armed and ready airplanes were concealed.

Minutes later, the stillness at Kanoya was split by the sound of radial engines coughing and rumbling to life. The first group of attack aircraft—fifty-six Zeroes, each laden with a 250-kilogram armor-piercing bomb—appeared from beneath the camouflage nets and lumbered over the uneven ground toward the runway.

It was an emotional moment. Well-wishers, ground crew, and pilots awaiting their own *tokko* missions watched and cheered. One after the other the warplanes throttled up and roared down the patched runway. With them went ten Zero fighter escorts. It was insufficient fighter cover, Ugaki knew, but it was a sign of the times. The ten fighters and their pilots were all that could be spared. Experienced fighter pilots were in such short supply that their commanders were refusing to send them into hopeless duels with the superior enemy air forces.

When the last of the *tokko* planes had disappeared in the cloudy southern sky, Ugaki returned to his bunker. He settled himself into his command chair and assumed the position that he had adopted since the first *tokko* operations—sitting upright, hands folded in his lap, eyes fixed straight ahead as if he were in a trance. He would remain there until the first reports came back from the battle.

The kamikazes were coming. That much U.S. intelligence officers had gleaned from the intercepted Japanese communications. April 6 was supposed to be the day of the greatest massed attack yet staged by the kamikazes.

Admiral Spruance put the entire Fifth Fleet on alert. From the radar picket stations to the beaches at Hagushi to the anchorage at Kerama Retto, guns were loaded and pointed skyward. Radarmen in every red-lighted CIC compartment peered into their yellowish green scopes. Lookouts on every ship gazed upward at the scudding clouds. Flights of Corsair and Hellcat CAP fighters droned over each carrier task group.

Early morning—a favorite time for the kamikazes—passed and nothing happened. Afternoon came and the weather worsened. Visibility went down and a northwest wind whipped the surface. A high broken cloud layer obscured the sun, bathing the sea in dark splotches of shadow. Still nothing happened.

Then, a few minutes before 1500, it began. First came the sudden, frenetic radio calls. Radarmen had picked up a wave of incoming bogeys. CAP fighters on the northern stations roared northward to intercept them.

More raiders were showing up behind the first wave. All seemed to be headed southwestward for the Hagushi beachhead and the fleet of transport ships. Their course would take them directly over the northern radar picket stations, called RP1 and RP2.

To Cmdr. R. E. Westholm, skipper of the destroyer *Bush*, the radar picket station designated RP1 had just become the most dangerous place on earth. Westholm could see them coming, a swarm of dark-colored bandits swinging into an orbit around his ship. They looked like raptors swooping down on an easy kill.

During the predawn hours *Bush* and her sister ship USS *Colhoun* had fended off sporadic night raiders. Those were hecklers, mostly feeling out the defenses of the U.S. fleet. These kamikazes swarming around *Bush* were the real thing.

First came the Aichi dive-bombers, code-named "Val." The Val was an obsolete, fixed-gear warplane, easy to identify with its big, flowing wheel fairings. The slow-flying bomber was relatively easy to hit, too, and *Bush*'s gunners flamed two of them. A few minutes later a Nakajima B6N "Jill" torpedo bomber, a tougher target, came skimming in low on the water, somehow penetrating *Bush*'s wall of antiaircraft fire. Westholm swung his ship broadside to give his main battery a clear shot. Every gun on the destroyer was hurling fire at the incoming kamikaze.

Nothing could stop it. The Jill kept coming, weaving and dodging, finally crashing with deadly precision between *Bush*'s twin stacks. The high-explosive bomb penetrated to the forward engine room, killing every man in the compartment and most of those in the two fire rooms. Dead in the water, *Bush* listed to port, seawater flooding her lower compartments.

From 10 miles away, the destroyer *Colhoun* came racing at 35 knots to help while her skipper, Cmdr. G. R. Wilson, frantically called for more CAP fighters. The fighters assigned to cover them were already engaged with incoming bandits. Now they were running out of fuel and ammunition.

The stricken *Bush* was easy to spot. An oily black smoke column marked the position where she drifted, drawing more kamikazes.

As *Colhoun* closed with *Bush,* a swarm of fifteen kamikazes bore down on both ships.

Bush's big guns—her 5-inchers—were jammed. Her gunners blazed away with the Bofors 40-millimeters, and *Colhoun* joined in with her own batteries. It was like swatting hornets. Kill one, and another would appear in its place. The kamikazes were attacking from all directions. *Colhoun's* 5-inchers scored a hit on a diving Zero, splashing it midway between the two destroyers. "One down, eleven to go," *Colhoun's* skipper remarked.

Colhoun's gunners killed another off the starboard bow, splashing him 50 yards abeam. Then another. But a fourth Zero, diving toward the port bow, plunged into *Colhoun's* main deck, wiping out both 40-millimeter gun mounts and their crews. The bomb exploded in the aft fire room, killing every man inside and rupturing the main steam line.

Colhoun was wounded, but she was still making 15 knots, most of her guns still firing. Her damage control crews were getting the blazes under control when three more kamikazes—two Val dive-bombers and a Zero—bored in from opposite sides.

The two Vals went down in a hail of fire, but the Zero didn't. The kamikaze penetrated the hail of fire and crashed into *Colhoun's* forward fire room. The exploding bomb blew out both boilers, ripping a 4-by-20-foot hole in the hull below the waterline.

Now *Colhoun* was as badly crippled as *Bush*. Each of the stricken destroyers was sending up a tall, unmistakable pillar of roiling black smoke, and the kamikazes seemed bent on finishing them off instead of going after fresh targets.

At 1725, *Colhoun* downed a Zero 150 yards abeam, but at the same time two Vals came swooping through the defensive fire. One clipped *Colhoun's* after stack with a wing tip, showering the deck with flaming gasoline. The kamikaze's bomb exploded in the water alongside, ripping a hole in the destroyer's hull at the waterline. The explosion and cascade of seawater blew every man off *Colhoun's* fantail.

The second Val was still boring down, but it missed *Colhoun*. Pulling up, the kamikaze pointed its nose at the nearby *Bush*. Gutted by fire, her main batteries no longer firing, *Bush* was almost defenseless. The Val hit the destroyer amidships between the stacks, nearly cleaving the vessel in half.

Bush was doomed, but the kamikazes weren't finished. At 1745, yet another Zero smashed into the destroyer's forward port side, killing all the wounded men and medics in the wardroom.

It was *Bush*'s death blow. Engulfed in flames and settling at the bow, the destroyer abruptly broke in half and sank.

Meanwhile in the gathering darkness, *Colhoun* was fighting for her life. Another Zero, attacking the dying *Bush*, switched targets at the last moment and went for *Colhoun*. Despite withering 40-millimeter fire, the flaming kamikaze exploded into *Colhoun*'s port side.

Colhoun was finished. With night coming fast, Commander Wilson ordered his crew to abandon ship. *Colhoun* was still blazing in the darkness, a beacon for more Japanese attackers. She received her coup de grace by gunfire from the destroyer *Cassin Young*, which had come to rescue survivors.

The ordeal for the crews of the sunken destroyers wasn't over. Many who survived the attacks were terribly burned. In the darkened ocean they clung to the few rafts and flotsam remaining from their lost ships. Because enemy airplanes were still overhead, search vessels couldn't use floodlights to illuminate the area. By the time the rescue operation ended the next morning, a total of 129 officers and men, most of them from *Bush*, were dead or missing.

The radar picket stations weren't the only scenes of action. From the catwalk outside the bridge of *New Mexico*, Admiral Spruance had a front-row view of the drama off the western shore of Okinawa. CAP fighters had chased four bandits southward from the island of Ie Shima. Almost directly over Spruance's flagship they caught up with them. While Spruance watched, all four kami-kazes, one after the other, were shot down in flames.

But more were on the way. Rear Adm. Mort Deyo had already begun moving his fire support ships away from their exposed stations near the Hagushi beachhead. As the force of battleships and cruisers, surrounded by a screen of seven destroyers, moved northward toward Ie Shima, lookouts on the lead destroyer, *Leutze*, spotted bogeys eight miles out. Within seconds, the graying sky turned red with the fire of every antiaircraft gun in the force.

The raiders were Nakajima B5N "Kate" torpedo bombers and Ki-43 "Oscar" fighters. They were coming in so low that the lookouts had spotted them before they appeared on radar. Like the first wave, they were going for the destroyers instead of the higher-value targets behind them.

The destroyers in the fore—*Leutze* and *Newcomb*—took the brunt of the attack. In the space of a few minutes, a kamikaze crashed into *Newcomb*'s after stack. Another fell to the destroyer's guns, but a third, carrying a larger weapon than the standard 250-kilogram bomb, struck amidships. The explosion blew up both engine rooms and turned the after fire room into a mass of rubble. Every man in the three spaces was killed instantly.

Seconds later yet another kamikaze was boring in on *Newcomb*'s port beam, crashing into the forward stack, spraying the entire midsection of the destroyer with flaming gasoline. *Newcomb* became an inferno, spouting flame hundreds of feet into the darkening sky. The smoke was so dense that nearby ships lost sight of the destroyer and thought she had gone down.

The destroyer *Leutze* came racing to assist the blazing *Newcomb*. As *Leutze*'s crew was passing hose lines to fight the fires, a fifth kamikaze streaked in toward *Newcomb*'s bridge. At the last second, a 5-inch antiaircraft shell caught the attacker. The kamikaze veered off, crashing into *Leutze*'s fantail and exploding.

Now *Leutze* was in as much peril as *Newcomb*. The explosion holed her hull and jammed her rudder hard right. *Leutze*'s skipper,

Lt. Leon Grabowsky, who at age twenty-seven was one of the Navy's youngest destroyer captains, ordered every heavy object jettisoned—torpedoes, depth charges, topside weights—keeping the destroyer afloat so that it could be towed by a minesweeper back to Kerama Retto.

Both tin cans stayed afloat. Back in the Kerama Retto anchorage, astonished sailors gawked at the fire-blackened, shattered hulks. The wreck of a kamikaze plane still lay across *Leutze*'s fantail. *Newcomb*'s number two stack was gone, and her number one stack was bent at a garish angle to starboard. Her fantail was only six inches above the water.

Forty men from *Newcomb* were dead, as were eight aboard *Leutze*. Neither ship would see combat again.

Like swarms of locusts, they kept coming. Fresh waves of kamikazes threaded their way through the gauntlet of CAP fighters, headed for the ships of the amphibious force off the Hagushi beachhead.

The gunners on the transports lacked the discipline of those on the tin cans and the battlewagons. They were firing helter-skelter, without clear direction, shooting just as enthusiastically at friendly CAP fighters as they were the enemy. Shrapnel from their gunfire was raining back down on the task force, causing almost as much damage as the kamikazes.

Three Kawasaki Ki-45 twin-engine Nick fighters and a pair of Aichi Val dive-bombers made it through the CAP screen, then ran into the storm of fire from the transports. Four were shot down, and the fifth, apparently losing his nerve, retreated back to the north. More showed up to take their place, this time picking on destroyers of the antisubmarine screen.

The tin cans *Witter* and *Morris* each took kamikaze strikes but stayed afloat. Another, *Hyman*, was struck in the torpedo tubes, causing a violent explosion. Yet another destroyer, *Howorth*, rushing to assist *Hyman*, took a kamikaze in her main battery director.

Mullany, patrolling on the eastern side of Okinawa, also received a crippling kamikaze hit. The stricken destroyers were all dragged back to Kerama Retto, which was beginning to resemble a destroyer graveyard.

To the north, a minesweeper unit was clearing the channel between Iheya Retto and the eastern shore of Okinawa when they came under heavy kamikaze attack. Marine Corsairs from the Fast Carrier Task Force ripped into the attacking aircraft, shooting down twenty.

It wasn't enough. Five kamikazes singled out the destroyer *Emmons*. Two dove into the destroyer's fantail, taking out her rudder, and another crashed into the bow. Another flew directly into the destroyer's bridge, killing every man in the CIC. The fifth attacker crashed into the already blazing superstructure.

Emmons was finished. When the destroyer *Ellyson* came alongside two hours later to rescue survivors, *Emmons*'s hulk was still afire. Worried that the derelict would drift ashore to an enemy-held beach, Admiral Turner gave the order to sink her with gunfire. Of *Emmons*'s crew, eleven officers and fifty-three men had been killed.

As devastating as the attacks on the destroyers were, the kamikazes were still missing the bigger game. The anchorage at Kerama Retto where ammunition and fuel ships were clustered like ducks in a gallery came under only sporadic attack. A small landing ship filled with fuel oil was struck and blazed like a beacon through the night. Two thin-hulled Victory ships loaded with ammunition were hit. Their burning cargoes continued shooting tracers and explosions into the night sky until the ships were finally sunk by gunfire.

The real prize, the fast carriers of Mitscher's Task Force 58, made it through the day unscathed. They were operating far enough out in the Pacific that most of the ill-trained kamikaze pilots were unable to find them. Of those who did, most were shot down by CAP fighters or antiaircraft fire.

With nightfall came a break in the attacks. The day had been a sobering demonstration of Japan's most fearsome weapon. The kamikazes had sunk three destroyers—*Bush*, *Colhoun*, and *Emmons*. Three more—*Leutze*, *Newcomb*, and *Morris*—were damaged beyond salvage. Several other badly damaged destroyers would be repaired and return to service, but only *Howorth* and *Hyman* would see duty before the end of the war. Two ammunition ships and an LST went down at Kerama Retto. A destroyer escort, a light carrier, and seven minesweepers had taken damage.

The most sobering statistic was the toll of dead and wounded. In all, 367 U.S. Navy men died in *kikusui* No. 1, most in a gruesome fashion. For those who weren't killed outright by the attacks, death came from terrible burns, mostly from flaming gasoline and ruptured steam lines. Horribly wounded survivors often spent hours of agony in the water without medical attention.

Though American losses in the first *kikusui* operation were severe, they were far fewer than what the Japanese reported. Radio Tokyo claimed that sixty American ships, including two battleships and three cruisers, had been sunk, and sixty-one more heavily damaged. The attacks were "a blow from which the enemy will never recover."

While exaggerating the damage inflicted on the Americans, the Japanese high command withheld the facts about their own losses. In the first *kikusui* operation, seven hundred airplanes, half of them kamikazes, were thrown into battle. The lives of more than 350 *tokko* airmen had been snuffed out like expendable candles.

The Japanese public was not ready for the hard truth about the *tokko* warriors. Nor was the man who had sent them to their death.

At 1630 Ugaki roused himself from his command chair. The first wave of *tokko* aircraft had closed with the U.S. fleet, and reports were being relayed from the battle scene. Ugaki's spirits soared when he heard a scratchy transmission from one of the radio-equipped *tokko* aircraft: "I am crashing on a carrier."

This was exhilarating news. At the same time, the airwaves were filled with American radio transmissions about ships under attack and commanders requesting help. It meant that the *tokko* warriors were hitting their targets.

Admiral Ugaki's only disappointment was, as usual, with the army. General Ushijima's 32nd Army wasn't doing its share. Ushijima hadn't launched the promised counterattack on Okinawa in concert with the *kikusui* operation. "They didn't move at all," Ugaki complained, "saying that the general attack was to start in the night of the 8th."

Still, Ugaki was willing to believe in miracles. "The sea around Okinawa thus turned into a scene of carnage," he wrote, "and a reconnaissance plane reported that as many as 150 columns of black smoke were observed, while others described it as difficult to observe them."

The admiral needed no further proof. His *tokko* airmen had delivered a devastating blow to the American fleet. "It was almost certain that we destroyed four carriers," he wrote that evening.

Kikusui No. 1 was such a resounding success, Ugaki decided, that it would continue into the next day, supporting the historic mission of the *Yamato*.

18 ▸ BREAKOUT

I n the darkened space of *Yamato*'s upper radar compartment, Ens. Mitsuru Yoshida watched the slow, monotonous sweep of the radar. The room reeked of sweat, ozone, and cigarette smoke. Four off-duty sailors lay like bundles of laundry, asleep in a corner of the compartment. Four more were hunched over their direction finders, plotting bearings from what appeared to be radar emissions from two separate enemy submarines. When they directed *Yamato*'s own radar to the bearings, they received confirmation: two weak but telltale returns.

The task force had passed the midchannel point in the Bungo Strait. From here on they were in hostile waters. Vice Admiral Ito had redeployed his ships, putting them in the standard antisubmarine formation, destroyer screen in front, sonars pinging for enemy submarines. *Yamato* was in the center of the formation, the cruiser *Yahagi* bringing up the rear, each ship keeping a 2,700-yard separation from the others.

Enemy submarines were out there. It was no surprise. The exit of the Bungo Strait into the Pacific Ocean was a favorite hunting ground for American submarines. Thousands of tons of Japanese shipping had gone down here, and so had a fair number of U.S. submarines. It was a deadly cat-and-mouse game, matching the speed and agility of the screening destroyers against the nerve and skill of the submarine crews. American submarine captains liked to maneuver on the surface at night, both to recharge their batteries and to use their best speed to reach a firing position. They depended on radar to warn them of oncoming threats and also to pick up approaching targets.

The *Yamato* could hardly be missed on anyone's radar. Yoshida could imagine the size of the blip made by a 72,000-ton battleship. A U.S. submarine captain would be ecstatic at picking up such a contact.

Apparently, one just had.

In the fore of the destroyer screen, *Isokaze* went charging off in the direction of the nearest contact. After a hurried sweep, the destroyer lost the contact and came back to rejoin the formation. Minutes later, another contact. Again the destroyer went racing out toward the open sea.

On the southern side of the formation the destroyer *Asashimo* was doing the same thing, zigzagging over the blackened surface like a hound sniffing for rabbits. Each time the elusive contact would fade away. The game went on for nearly half an hour, thrusting and parrying, while the task force zigzagged and finally cleared the mouth of the Bungo Strait.

Their best defenses were speed and geography. The submarines couldn't match the speed of the task force, now moving at 22 knots. As the task force turned south and hugged the long coastline of Kyushu, it presented the submarines with only one side from which to attack. The task force was relatively safe—at least until dawn.

It was damned frustrating. Lt. Cmdr. John Foote, skipper of USS *Threadfin*, watched his target fade into the distance. His orders, which ran against the grain of any submarine commander, were not to attack until a contact report had been transmitted to Pearl Harbor. Pacific Fleet headquarters was expecting a breakout through the Bungo Strait by the battleship *Yamato*. It was critical that the movement of *Yamato* and her task force be reported *before* attempting an attack.

Despite his frustration, Foote knew the reason for the order. Two U.S. subs had been lost in these waters in the past two months.

If *Threadfin* were sunk before making the contact report, *Yamato*'s breakout might go undetected.

Foote's problem was that *Threadfin* had to remain on the surface while the report was transmitted. This time of night, the airwaves were jammed with military communications traffic. While the signalman tapped out the message, trying to break through the clutter of transmissions, a Japanese destroyer had been alerted to *Threadfin*'s presence. Now the destroyer was racing like a greyhound in their direction. Foote had the diesel engines screaming at full power, thrashing across the surface at *Threadfin*'s maximum speed of 19.5 knots. It wasn't enough. Judging by the radar blip, the Japanese destroyer was making a good 30 knots.

Foote was playing it down to the wire. In the near blackness of the overcast night, the Japanese gun crews wouldn't be able to fire on him until they were very close, probably inside a mile. If they had radar-controlled guns, of course, they could start firing any minute now, but Foote was betting that they didn't.

The signalman continued keying his transmitter, trying to get through. Foote kept trying to urge a few more knots from his already straining engines. The destroyer kept coming.

At 2000, after nearly half an hour of trying, the signalman was successful. At almost the same time, the Japanese destroyer gave up the chase. *Threadfin* was out of danger, at least for the moment. At 2020 came the acknowledgment that Pearl Harbor had received the report. But while *Threadfin* had been occupied with transmitting the report, her shot at glory—sinking the world's biggest battleship—had slipped away. The fast-moving Japanese task force had pulled out of range and *Threadfin* would not be able to catch up.

Another sub, USS *Hackleback*, was on station 20 miles to the south. Her skipper, Lt. Cmdr. Frederick Janney, was watching the oncoming task force on his radar from 11 miles away. Judging from the size and disposition of the blips, there could be no doubt. It had to be *Yamato* and her entourage. Janney's radio transmission at 2030 to Pearl Harbor would be a confirmation of *Threadfin's* earlier report.

Before *Hackleback* could set up a torpedo attack, she, too, drew the attention of the destroyer screen. The submarine was forced to turn her stern to the target and retreat from another onrushing destroyer. By the time the Japanese destroyer withdrew, *Hackleback* was also out of firing range.

As *Yamato* and her task group headed south, the news of their sortie was causing a hubbub in Pearl Harbor. The report was forwarded to Chester Nimitz's headquarters on Guam, to Fifth Fleet commander Raymond Spruance aboard *New Mexico*, and to Marc Mitscher on his flagship, the carrier *Bunker Hill*.

The flashed reports from the American submarines were also received in the communications room of *Yamato*. Staring at the intercepted message, the intelligence officer was perplexed. It was not encoded. The report had been sent in plain language, for all the world to read.

> *Enemy task force headed south. Course 190 degrees, speed 25 knots . . .*

To Mitsuru Yoshida, in the radar room in *Yamato*, it was an ominous sign. It meat that the Americans were tracking *Yamato's* every movement, and they didn't care whether the Japanese knew it.

Looking at the intercepted message, *Yamato's* navigation officer thought it was ironic. "I do believe we learn about our position faster from their side than from ours."

By dawn on April 7, *Yamato* was transiting Osumi Strait, the narrow and shoal-filled passage between southern Kyushu and the northernmost island of the Ryukyu archipelago. Admiral Ito was still hoping to deceive the Americans about *Yamato's* objective. On a tracking map, it would appear that *Yamato* was hugging the coast of Kyushu, making her way to the port of Sasebo on the northwestern tip of the island. Of course, the presence of such an escorting force—eight destroyers and a heavy cruiser—would be setting off alarms in every American intelligence office.

Ito's only advantage that morning, he decided, was the weather. Intermittent rain showers were peppering the decks of the task force. Dark clouds scudded low over the tossing sea. The white-caps provided ideal camouflage for the gray warships of the task force. Ito liked the forecast even better. The barometer was still falling, and the route to Okinawa was covered with squall lines and patches of heavy rain.

Since leaving the mouth of the Bungo Strait, there had been no more submarine contacts. Still, Ito knew the Americans were watching. All he had to do was gaze overhead. Enemy recon-naissance planes—fighters, long-range bombers, even lumbering Martin PBM flying boats—were flitting in and out of the clouds. Occasionally *Yamato*'s antiaircraft batteries would open up, but the gunfire was mostly a gesture of defiance. The planes were staying carefully out of range. They weren't there to fight, just to watch.

While they were still close to the Kyushu shoreline, Ito or-dered the two remaining floatplanes on *Yamato* to be catapulted and returned to land. *Yamato* normally carried a complement of seven "Pete" and "Jake" floatplanes. They were used for over-the-horizon reconnaissance and spotting to help direct *Yamato*'s big guns.

The two pilots, looking incongruous on *Yamato*'s bridge in their flight suits and leather helmets, dutifully asked permission to remain aboard the ship. The executive officer, Captain Nomura, waved them away. The floatplanes would be of no use in the com-ing battle, nor would the pilots, who would just get in the way. In any case, they should be spared for a future airborne mission.

Each of the floatplanes was hoisted to one of the two immense catapults. Minutes later, one after the other, they hurtled down the catapult track and wobbled into the sky. After a cursory search for submarines in the path of the task force, they turned north and vanished in the murk.

Ito ordered another course correction, heading the task force back to the east. He planned to continue the deception into the morning by returning to a westerly course, letting the American spotter planes report the zigzagging to their headquarters. At the right moment he would abruptly wheel to the south and race at flank speed toward Okinawa. Sometime after nightfall he would be closing with the American fleet, bombarding the enemy shore positions, spreading havoc with the U.S. invasion force.

Yamato's task force would have no air cover. That much had been decided even before the order for Ten-Go was written. Whatever airpower the Japanese Imperial Navy still possessed had already been allocated to the *kikusui* operation, the massed *tokko* attacks on the U.S. fleet.

The previous day, April 6, had been the first day of the first *kikusui*. The planners of Ten-Go, including Ugaki, Toyoda, and Ohnishi, were gambling that the American carrier-based warplanes would be too busy countering the waves of *tokko* raiders to mount a serious air attack on *Yamato*.

It was a pipe dream, Admiral Ito knew. *Yamato*'s fate was in the hands of the gods.

One of the screening destroyers, *Asashimo*, was having trouble. With the task force still steaming on the diversionary northwestward course, *Asashimo* was drifting slowly behind, unable to keep station. From the bridge of *Yamato*, Ens. Mitsuru Yoshida read the signal flags hoisted on the destroyer: "Engine trouble." A few minutes later came another message: "Repairs will take five hours."

It was bad news. Without the collective support of its task force, a lone destroyer in the waters south of Kyushu was as good as dead. If a submarine didn't pick it off, a flight of American warplanes would find it.

Aboard *Yamato*, Admiral Ito considered the situation. *Asashi-mo*'s problem seemed to be a damaged reduction gear in her power plant. Ito decided to give them time to repair the problem. The task force would reverse course, go back to gather up *Asashimo*, then steam at high speed for Okinawa. If *Asashimo* could maintain station, she would share in the glory of the coming battle. If not, she was on her own.

A buzz of excitement crackled in the flag plot compartment in *New Mexico*. Unlike similar spaces on other ships, the air on Raymond Spruance's bridge was not clouded with cigarette smoke. Spruance, a tobacco hater, had banned smoking in his flag spaces.

Spruance was studying the newly received reports about the Japanese task force. Seldom had his staff seen their boss's cold, gimlet eyes flash like this. The last of Japan's great battleships was coming out to fight.

Spruance was a black-shoe admiral—a surface sailor who had cut his teeth on battleships. In the Navy of 1945, he was something of an oddity—a nonaviator whose command now included the greatest naval air force ever deployed. But Spruance also commanded a task force of battleships and cruisers whose only duty until now had been the bombardment of enemy shore positions on Okinawa.

The last major engagement of surface forces had been the October 1944 night battle at Surigao Strait when a Japanese fleet of two battleships, one cruiser, and four destroyers, commanded by Adm. Shoji Nishimura, charged blindly into the waiting guns of the U.S. Seventh Fleet battleships. Nishimura himself went down with his flagship *Yamashiro*. For the Americans, it had been a sweet revenge. Five of the Seventh Fleet's six old battleships had been salvaged from the wreckage of Pearl Harbor.

Now, nearly six months later, the normally cool and analytical Raymond Spruance was hearing the siren song of a last epic sea battle. He signaled Rear Adm. Mort Deyo, who commanded

Task Force 54, to prepare his battle line to meet the *Yamato* task force. Spruance's own flagship, *New Mexico*, was one of Deyo's six battleships. It meant that Spruance himself was going to observe the great battle from a front-row seat.

In addition to his aging battleships, Deyo's task force included seven cruisers and thirty-one destroyers—enough firepower to counter anything the Japanese task force could mount. The prize of sinking the world's greatest dreadnought could go to the battleship admirals.

Maybe. On the eastern side of Okinawa, in his own flag plot aboard the carrier *Bunker Hill*, another admiral was eyeing the same prize.

19 ▸ RACE FOR GLORY

O ne of his code names was "Bald Eagle," and it fit him perfectly. The commander of Task Force 58, Vice Adm. Marc
"Pete" Mitscher, had the gaunt, wizened face of a bird of prey. His
eyes, according to one of his staffers, "could give an order with a
glance."

Mitscher looked older than his fifty-eight years. His lifestyle
was typical of his generation of flag officers, including Halsey and
McCain, who disdained exercise and smoked a pack and a half of
cigarettes a day. During flight operations Mitscher spent his time in
a four-foot-high, specially built swivel chair on the flag bridge. The
chair was invariably aimed aft, giving rise to speculation among his
sailors that the old man was more interested in where he'd been
than where he was going. The truth was that Mitscher didn't like
the wind in his face.

The chair was just one of Mitscher's foibles. Another was the
long-billed baseball cap, his standard shipboard headgear. The
"Mitscher cap" was so imitated that in 1946 the Navy authorized it
as a work uniform accessory.

Marc Mitscher was, above all else, a naval aviator. Unlike
Halsey, McCain, and chief of naval operations Ernest King, who,
at an advanced age and rank, had all undergone flight training in
order to wear wings and then command aviation units, Mitscher
was the real thing. He had been designated naval aviator number
33 back in 1916. While aviation was still an unwanted stepchild of
the Navy, Mitscher was catapulting off battleships, flying ungainly
patrol planes, and winning the Navy Cross for his role as pilot of

NC-1, one of a group of four Navy Curtiss flying boats to attempt the first transatlantic flight. Mitscher's plane was forced down in heavy seas near the Azores, but another of the flying boats, NC-4, became the first airplane to make it across the Atlantic.

Mitscher served in a succession of aeronautical staff and carrier-based assignments, and in 1941 became the first skipper of the newly built USS *Hornet*. It was from the deck of the *Hornet*, under Mitscher's command, that Lt. Col. Jimmy Doolittle and his sixteen B-25 bombers launched on the first strike against Japan on April 18, 1942.

As commander of the Fast Carrier Task Force at the Battle of the Philippine Sea in 1944, Mitscher won fame—and the everlasting gratitude of his pilots. When the planes of a strike were forced to return to the carriers after nightfall, Mitscher broke with standard operating procedure and ordered the flight deck lights and ships' searchlights turned on, exposing his carriers to Japanese subs and airplanes. The gamble paid off. Mitscher recovered most of his planes and pilots, and his precious carriers survived.

Like most senior brown-shoe commanders, Mitscher had spent a career battling the black shoes, especially the battleship admirals who had steered the navy's thinking for most of the current century. One of those was Raymond Spruance, and another was Chester Nimitz, both of whom were now Mitscher's bosses.

A decree had come down the previous year from the chief of naval operation, Ernest King, that carrier task force commanders would henceforth have surface officers assigned as chiefs of staff. The idea was that the mix of cultures would give the commander better coordination with his screening ships. Mitscher was assigned a highly decorated destroyer squadron commander, forty-three-year-old Capt. Arleigh Burke, as his chief of staff.

Mitscher had not been happy. Having a nonaviator so closely involved with the command of his carrier task force offended him, especially when it was one like Burke, who was already a celebrity for his exploits as a hard-charging destroyer division commander.

He had earned a nickname, "Thirty-one-Knot" Burke, for being a fast mover not only in a destroyer but in all things that involved guns and ordnance.

Burke, for his part, was just as unhappy. Without warning he'd been yanked from his Destroyer Squadron 23 at the Bismarck Archipelago and exiled to the most foreign of environments, the flag spaces of a 27,000-ton aircraft carrier. The two men were like dogs in a kennel, each warily sizing up the other.

It took a few weeks, but the crotchety Mitscher was eventually won over by Thirty-one-Knot Burke's obvious brilliance. By the time Task Force 58 arrived off Okinawa, the Bald Eagle and his black-shoe chief of staff had bonded into a formidable team.

Now Mitscher was seeing an opportunity he couldn't resist. Studying the sighting reports of the Japanese task force, he felt a stirring of the old battleship-versus-aircraft-carrier rivalry. Though the great battles of the Pacific had mostly been fought by the carriers, the matter of whether airpower alone could prevail over a surface force had not been proven beyond all doubt.

It had been Mitscher who sent carrier-based planes after *Yamato* and her sister ship *Musashi* at the Battle of Leyte Gulf. *Yamato* had escaped, and although *Musashi* eventually went down, the actual cause of her sinking was not certain. No one had ruled out the possibility that the coup de grace was delivered by a submarine. Here was a chance to end the debate forever.

But there was a problem. Mitscher's immediate superior, Admiral Spruance, had just transmitted an all-fleet order to allow the enemy task force to proceed southward, where it would be engaged by Admiral Deyo's surface task force. In the meantime, Mitscher's orders were "to concentrate the offensive effort of Task Force 58 in combat air patrols to meet enemy air attacks."

The battleships were going to get the *Yamato.*

Or maybe not. Like a team of sharp-eyed contract lawyers, Mitscher, Burke, and Cmdr. James Flatley, the fighter pilot who served as Mitscher's operations officer, pored over Spruance's order. It was a situation as old as warfare itself, officers trying to find the tiniest amount of slack in their orders.

Mitscher had served under Spruance long enough to know his style. Spruance believed in allowing his commanders discretion to act on opportunity, and Mitscher believed that he was looking at just such an opportunity. In any case, Spruance's order had not specifically *forbidden* Mitscher to go after the enemy task force. It was as much slack as Mitscher needed.

The problem, in Mitscher's mind, wasn't in complying with Spruance's order to maintain combat air patrols. With twenty-four carriers and air groups in his task force, he could provide plenty of combat air patrol coverage *and* still deploy a knockout blow against the enemy fleet. The trick was in knowing where the enemy fleet was headed and what their objective was.

Then came another order from Spruance. Deyo was to form his two battleship divisions, two cruiser divisions, and twenty destroyers into line of battle and head north. In his flag plot, Mitscher read his copy of the dispatch, then sent his own order to each of his carrier task groups. They were to steam northwestward, shortening the distance between them and the next day's likely position of the Japanese force. If Spruance had any objection, he would have to countermand Mitscher's order.

The race to get *Yamato* was on.

By now both Mitscher and Flatley were bleary-eyed after the arduous day. Each left to hit his bunk, leaving Burke to ruminate about the Japanese task force. Long ago Burke had learned how to ration his rest periods, catnapping during lulls in the action, seeming never to run out of alertness.

Alone in flag plot, Burke sucked on his pipe and thought about the Japanese task force. Spread out before him were charts of the seas off southern Japan and the Ryukyus. In his mind, he tried to insert himself into the Japanese commander's position. Where would *he* go? In which direction? After what objective?

The more he pondered the situation, the clearer it became to him. The Japanese commander intended to attack the amphibious force off the western shore of Okinawa. He wouldn't telegraph his intention by proceeding on a direct course, which would bring them into range of the carrier task force on the east side of Okinawa. He would ease westward, perhaps northward, feinting in the direction of Sasebo on the far coast of Kyushu, staying out of range of the carrier-based warplanes.

Burke was sure of it. Sometime the next morning, the Japanese commander would make his charge toward Okinawa.

In his flag bridge aboard *Yamato*, Ito ordered the task force into a turn to the southwest. They were at the spot where he had planned to pick up the lagging *Asashimo* and reintegrate her into the force. But *Asashimo* still couldn't keep up. She hadn't sorted out the reduction gear problem that had caused her to fall behind.

There was no time to wait. Ito gave the order to abandon the destroyer and proceed with only nine ships. As the fleet charged through the squally seas at a speed of 22 knots, the hapless destroyer disappeared from view.

There was only one prudent choice for *Asashimo*'s captain, Lt. Cmdr. Yoshiro Sugihara: to reverse course and return to Kyushu. The destroyer was no longer under the protective umbrella of the task force's air defense guns.

But this was not a day for prudence. Sugihara had no intention of missing what was surely the last stand of the Imperial Japanese Navy. *Asashimo* continued limping behind the task force, following the wake of the *Yamato*.

In the early hours of April 7, Mitscher became sick. Though the admiral's physician didn't have a diagnosis, he came to flag plot to inform Burke that Mitscher would have to stay in bed. The gaunt, heavy-smoking admiral was already in frail condition, and the doctor was worried that he might become incapacitated.

With Mitscher indisposed, the black-shoe chief of staff, Burke, became the de facto task force commander, with fighter pilot Cmdr. Jimmy Flatley as his air warfare expert. They ordered eight Hellcat fighters launched at dawn to comb a fan-shaped 90-degree sector from northeast to northwest. A division of four Marine Corsairs was stationed at 60-mile intervals to relay the message back to the task force flagship.

At 0830, a Hellcat pilot from *Essex* spotted the Japanese task force through the broken cloud deck. The ships were steaming on a northwest course of 300 degrees.

Northwest course? Receiving this information, Admiral Spruance ordered Deyo to go after the Japanese task force. Now he was worried that they might be slipping northward toward Sasebo. If so, they'd soon be out of range of both battleships and warplanes.

Aboard *Bunker Hill*, Burke reached a different conclusion. It was a head fake, he believed. The *Yamato* task force was making a zigzag turn, feinting northwestward. Sticking to his hunch, he deployed another sixteen-plane search group to a point *south* of the reported position. If he was right, the Japanese force would soon make a hard turn to port and be picked up by the search group.

And they did. Another *Essex* Hellcat radioed that the task force was now heading southwesterly, on a course of 240 degrees. Burke's hunch was right: the Japanese commander was making the course changes to confuse the trackers.

Burke sent the order to each of the carrier task groups: prepare their bombers, fighters, and torpedo planes for action.

Later that morning, Mitscher returned to the flag plot. Looking gaunter and more birdlike than ever, he settled himself into his chair and resumed command. "He looked like hell," Burke recalled. Later he surmised that Mitscher had suffered a small heart attack during the night.

The success of the attack would depend on the search planes keeping track of the Japanese task force and directing the warplanes toward it. The strike planes would be at the extreme end of their range, some nearly 300 miles from their carriers. They would have only minutes to locate the enemy and make the attack. Mitscher had no intention of running his airplanes out of gas before they made it home. He'd already had that experience the previous June in the Philippine Sea when nearly a hundred of his warplanes, returning from a maximum-range strike, were forced down in the ocean.

Another problem was communications. At this distance the planes would be out of contact with the task force command. Mitscher ordered more fighters to be stationed between the carriers and the estimated Japanese position to relay reports.

At 1000, the strike took off. The first to go were the planes from *Belleau Wood, Hornet, Bennington,* and *San Jacinto*. They were quickly followed by the warplanes from *Bunker Hill, Essex, Bataan, Cabot,* and *Hancock* — 283 airplanes of every type in the inventory, including Corsairs, Hellcats, Avengers, Helldivers, and even a few plodding Wildcat fighters.

Fifteen minutes later, *Hancock's* fifty-three-plane group took off. At 1045, 106 warplanes from *Intrepid, Langley,* and *Yorktown* — the carriers farthest from the target — headed off in search of the enemy task force.

From his swivel chair on *Bunker Hill's* bridge, Mitscher watched the warplanes depart, then he settled back to await the results. Either the Japanese would be where Burke had estimated, or they wouldn't be.

Not everyone in flag plot shared Burke's conviction. A Royal Navy observer, Cmdr. Charlie Owen, asked Burke if he actually *knew* where *Yamato* was going to be in two hours.

Burke shrugged off the question. "No."

"But you have launched before you can possibly be sure of their location."

"We are taking a chance," said Burke. He put his finger on a point on the chart. It was well south of *Yamato*'s most recent position. "We are launching against the spot where we would be if we were the *Yamato*."

Mitscher, for his part, seemed to have no doubts. He had gotten over his misgivings about having a destroyer sailor as his chief of staff. In fact, he'd become sufficiently impressed with Burke that he tried to have him promoted to rear admiral. Burke resisted, not wanting to be promoted over the heads of many senior captains, and settled for the rank of commodore, a wartime quasi-flag status with a one-star insignia.

Now that they had played their hand, it was time to open up with Spruance. But the Bald Eagle could still be disingenuous. He told Burke, "Inform Admiral Spruance that I propose to strike the *Yamato* sortie group at 1200 unless otherwise directed."

U*nless otherwise directed*. The words hung in the air while Mitscher, still feeling out of sorts, slumped in his padded chair. Fixed in his memory was the night during the Battle of the Philippine Sea when he had proposed to Spruance that his task force race toward the enemy carrier fleet in order to be in position for a dawn strike. After an agonizing delay, the cautious Spruance had denied Mitscher's request to attack.

Now Mitscher worried that Spruance might again hold back. It would take two hours for the strike groups to reach *Yamato*. If Spruance countermanded the air strike order, it would be at best a huge embarrassment for Mitscher. At worst it could be the end of his command.

The minutes ticked past without a reply. As noon approached, it began to make less and less sense to recall the warplanes. In any case, no gasoline would be saved and the bombs would have to be dumped, if not on the enemy, then into the sea.

Then came a relayed report from the search planes. The

Yamato task force had been sighted. Burke's hunch was correct. The first wave of warplanes was about to engage the enemy task force.

Mitscher still hadn't heard from Spruance. He sent a follow-up message: "Will you take them or shall I?"

More minutes ticked away. Then Mitscher received the reply he had been praying for. It was probably the shortest operational order of the war: "You take them."

20 ▸ FIRST WAVE

Erickson wondered what the hell was going on. It was 1030, and he had just been rattled out of his bunk. He'd been the duty officer for the 0600 launch. He was catching up on lost sleep when the squawk box in the Boys' Town bunkroom blared, "Ensign Erickson, report to the ready room."

He threaded his way through passageways and knee-knockers, across the hangar deck, and up the ladder to the ready room. He could sense the excitement in the smoke-filled compartment. Flight leaders were already briefing their pilots. Erickson had been yanked out of his bunk because they needed every available pilot. His buddy from flight training, Bill Ecker, had injured his hand and couldn't fly. Erickson was going in his place.

He wasn't flying with Hyland that day. The CAG was already airborne on another strike, and VBF-10 skipper Will Rawie was leading the mission. It was a massive strike, with planes from almost every carrier in the task force. *Intrepid*'s air group would be joined by planes from *Yorktown* and *Langley*, with Rawie leading the combined strike group.

They were going after something big. It was called the *Yamato*, and it was headed for Okinawa.

Erickson, now wide awake, pulled on his gear and headed for the flight deck. When he found his Corsair in the middle of the deck, he had to stop and stare. The fighter had a thousand-pound bomb fastened to its belly. So did all the others. Erickson had never dropped a bomb of this size before.

The plane captain, a chatty New Yorker named Felix Novelli, helped him strap in. Before he climbed down from the wing, Novelli handed Erickson a canteen of water and a chocolate bar. Plane captains didn't normally pass out candy bars, but today was special. It was Novelli's twentieth birthday, the plane captain told him. He wanted Erickson to sink the *Yamato* as a present for him.

Up and down the flight deck, clouds of gray smoke belched from exhaust stacks. Propellers kicked over. Big radial engines were chuffing to life, all resonating in a staccato growl.

The fighters at the front of the pack were already throttling up, following the deck officer's signals. The ship was steaming into a stiff northeasterly wind. Most of the fighters would be making deck launches — rolling down the deck under their own power — instead of catapulting.

Things were happening quickly. The deck officer was poised in front of the starboard wing, whirling his flag over his head. Erickson eased the throttle up. The deck officer swung his flag forward, pointing down the deck, and Erickson released the brakes. He shoved in the right rudder to counter the torque of the engine as he pushed the throttle to full power. The roar of the 2,000-horsepower Pratt & Whitney filled the cockpit, resonating through the airframe. The Corsair lumbered down the deck, its tail coming up as it gained speed, lifting off the bow and clawing its way into the sky.

Erickson joined the gaggle of dark blue warplanes circling beneath the clouds. His four-plane division was led by Lt. (jg) Wes Hays, a chuckling, round-faced Texan. The number two and three slots were filled by two more ensigns, Jim Hollister and Russ Carlisi. Erickson slid into his accustomed number four Tail End Charlie position.

When the strike force was assembled, "Red One" — Rawie's call sign — headed them to the northwest. Weaving through the ragged bottoms of the cloud layer, they crossed the Ryukyu island chain just south of the island called Amami Oshima.

Peering into the clouded skies, the spotters dutifully counted the planes. Never had they seen so many American warplanes in a single day. This was the third wave to pass over Amami Oshima in the past hour.

By noon the report had arrived on the bridge of the battleship *Yamato*: more than 250 American enemy airplanes had passed over Amami Oshima, all heading north. It appeared to be a massive air strike.

Seated in his commander's chair on the starboard wing of the flag bridge, Admiral Ito acknowledged the report with a silent nod. Since early that morning when they'd begun the southward dash for Okinawa, Ito had said almost nothing. He sat in his chair, arms folded, more an overseer than a director. Most of the tactical decisions he was leaving to Rear Admiral Ariga, captain of the *Yamato*.

Twenty minutes later, hovering over the screen of his air search radar, Ens. Mitsuru Yoshida saw them coming. They first appeared in the scope as three large blobs, one for each formation. Gradually the blobs dissolved into groups, then flights, then individual airplanes.

From the bridge came a flurry of orders. Each ship in the task force increased its speed to 25 knots. The entire formation swung together to an easterly heading. Every gun station was on alert.

The waiting was over, and so was the guessing. They knew the form the battle would take. *Yamato* would be fighting a sea-air engagement, not a surface action against other ships. The lookouts would focus on the incoming bearing of the enemy planes.

As if on signal a veil of light rain appeared, descending like a curtain from the clouds to the sea. It gave Yoshida a bad feeling. In weather like this, airplanes were harder to see than battleships.

As usual, no one in Spruance's flag plot aboard *New Mexico* could read the admiral's emotions. The Fifth Fleet commander was wearing his standard blank expression. Given the circumstances, he could rightly feel a mixture of disappointment and elation. One way or another, his forces were about to engage the Japanese task force.

Spruance, being Spruance, was taking nothing for granted. Maybe Mitscher's warbirds would destroy the *Yamato* task force. Maybe not. In any case, he had no intention of countermanding Deyo's orders. If by some fluke of war the Japanese eluded Mitscher's planes, Deyo's battlewagons, cruisers, and tin cans would be the last line of defense between *Yamato* and the beaches at Okinawa.

Spruance's own flagship, *New Mexico*, was now attached to Deyo's battle line. If there was the slightest chance of a historic shoot-out between battleships, the Fifth Fleet commander was going to be there.

A board his own flagship *Tennessee*, Admiral Deyo and his staff were still working up the battle plan. That morning they had steamed out of the roadstead at Kerama Retto to rendezvous with the other ships of the task force. *Idaho* was leading a battleship division that included Spruance's *New Mexico* and Deyo's *Tennessee*. The second battleship division would comprise *West Virginia*, *Maryland*, and *Colorado*. Their flanks were guarded by seven cruisers and ten destroyers.

Rear Adm. Mort Deyo, age fifty-seven, was a wiry, bushy-browed battleship sailor who had fought in both the Atlantic and Pacific. He had escorted convoys in the prewar days, then delivered naval gunfire at Utah Beach in the Normandy landings and again in the invasion of southern France. Like Spruance, Deyo could still dream. He clung to the vision of a last classic surface battle with the Japanese.

Deyo had just received a cheery send-off from his immediate boss, Vice Adm. Kelly Turner: "We hope you will bring back a nice fish for breakfast." Deyo was in the act of scribbling his reply,

"Many thanks, will try to . . ." when he was interrupted by an incoming report. Mitscher's planes had just found the Japanese fleet.

Deyo tried to swallow his disappointment. He finished the message with, ". . . if the pelicans haven't caught them all." Mort Deyo had been around the Navy long enough to know that some things never changed: given the chance, the damned airedales would steal all the glory.

Pelicans or not, Deyo was sticking to his orders. He was taking his battlewagons north. If nothing else, he was going to earn for himself a footnote in military history. Morton Deyo would be the last naval commander in World War II—perhaps in history—to form a battle line against an enemy fleet.

It was supposed to be a coordinated strike, with Task Force 58's carrier task groups supporting each other. The tactic had been used and refined since the first air battles of the South Pacific. In successive waves, strike groups from each carrier would bore down on the Japanese task force. The fighters were supposed to go first, strafing, rocketing, dropping their light ordnance, distracting the enemy gunners while the SB2C Helldivers plunged almost straight down with their heavy bombs. They would be closely followed by the Torpeckers—TBM Avenger torpedo planes—which needed all the distraction and diversion they could get when they made their dangerous low-altitude runs straight at the enemy ships.

At least, that was the plan.

The plan wasn't working that day. There was nothing coordinated about the frenzied, disjointed air strike on the *Yamato* force. Each carrier had launched its strike force without waiting for any other. Each strike leader was trying his best to be the first to hit the target.

The first to find the task force were the planes of Task Group 58.1, from the carriers *San Jacinto, Bennington, Hornet,* and *Belleau Wood.* Right behind them came the strike group from Task Group 58.3, the carriers *Essex, Bunker Hill, Bataan,* and *Cabot.*

Missing from the task group's complement were the planes from *Hancock*, which had gotten a late start, taking off behind the others. Now *Hancock*'s group was wandering in a fruitless search, trying to locate the Japanese task force.

At 1045, nearly an hour after the first warplanes had launched, another 106 planes of Rear Adm. Arthur Radford's Task Group 58.4 launched from *Intrepid*, *Yorktown*, and *Langley*, all led by Lt. Cmdr. Will Rawie.

As each flight of warplanes arrived over the target, they had to jockey for position in the narrow band of sky between the ocean and the lowest deck of clouds at about 1,500 feet. The risk of a midair collision was almost as great as the chance of being hit by the enemy gunners.

The SB2C Helldivers were plummeting down through whatever hole they could find in the overcast, sometimes having to share the hole with other airplanes. Some of the dive-bomber pilots lost sight of their targets in the clouds, then had to make frantic corrections as they broke clear and respotted their target.

Radio discipline had gone to hell. The tactical radio frequency was a bedlam of excited chatter, pilots yelling out target locations, calling bomb hits, reporting planes going down.

The Japanese ships were zigzagging across the water like rabbits evading hounds. The destroyers, more nimble than the big cruiser *Yahagi* and the dreadnought *Yamato*, were the hardest to hit. They were also the most vulnerable, sinking quickly when they took a bomb or torpedo.

Hamakaze went down within minutes of the first attack. Two more destroyers were trailing black smoke, moving at only half speed. They were maneuvering in a counterclockwise screening circle around *Yamato*, adding their guns to the collective antiaircraft fire.

For most of the pilots, it was their first look at the *san shiki* "Beehive" shells fired from the massive 18.1-inch guns. The shells were monsters, each weighing as much as an automobile and filled with incendiary tubes that burst in a cone toward incoming air-planes. The *san shiki* looked like a Fourth of July fireworks display, spewing out tendrils of phosphorus and dark shards of lead and shrapnel.

The pilots noticed something else peculiar. The antiaircraft fire was exploding in multiple colors. It was another Japanese tactic they'd heard about but not seen—each ship's gunfire a separate color to assist the gun directors in spotting their fire.

But the *san shiki* and the colored gunfire were a good sign. It meant the Japanese guns were probably not radar-directed. They were using visual aiming and ranging—and doing a bad job of it. Though they were putting up a storm of anti-aircraft fire, the gun-ners were missing with great consistency. A few unlucky warplanes had taken hits, but most were eluding the gunfire.

The best news was the absence of enemy fighters. It was almost too good to be true. For some unfathomable reason, the Japanese had deployed the task force with no air cover from the air bases on Kyushu. The Americans could concentrate on hitting the targets without constantly checking their six o'clock for enemy fighters.

It was Mitsuru Yoshida's first good look at enemy airplanes. There were at least a hundred of them, separating into groups of dive-bombers, torpedo planes, and fighters. They were taking their time, each group maneuvering into a different quadrant. While Yoshida peered upward, what looked to him like an entire squad-ron of airplanes emerged from a hole in the clouds. One after the other they peeled off in a dive.

Most were headed for *Yamato*.

"Commence firing!" The order came from *Yamato*'s captain, Rear Admiral Ariga, in the tower-top command post. In the next in-stant, twenty-four antiaircraft guns and 120 machine guns opened fire. Thunder reverberated through the steel decks of the battle-ship. From across the water came the echoing gunfire of the screen-ing ships. The gloomy sky turned crimson with the explosions of a thousand shells. The hellish concussion of antiaircraft fire, roaring engines, and rattling machine guns beat like a hammer on the flesh of every man aboard the ships.

Yoshida felt himself filled with a mix of terror and exhilaration. Tingling with excitement, he gritted his teeth and broke into an involuntary grin.

The long, gray shape of the battleship swelled in Lt. (jg) Bill Delaney's windshield. He could see the lines of the tracers arcing upward. Puffs of flak were bursting on either side of him. The airframe of the Avenger torpedo plane was rocking from the concussion of the gunfire.

Delaney was in the strike group from *Belleau Wood*, the first to arrive over the enemy task force. He'd become separated in the clouds from the other Avengers, and now he was on his own. While circling in the broken overcast, he'd spotted something through a break in the clouds. It was the big prize—the battleship *Yamato*. With more zeal than sense, Delaney rolled into a solo attack on the world's most heavily armed warship.

Too late, the thought struck him that it was a bad idea. Even when escorted by fighters and accompanied by other warplanes, the Avenger made a vulnerable dive-bomber. Designed as a torpedo plane, it was slow, even in a dive, and its fat shape made it a juicy target for shipboard gunners.

But Delaney was committed. Struggling to keep his gun sight pipper on the target, he released his bombs. He pulled out, skimming low over the bristling guns of the *Yamato*. Over his shoulder he glimpsed his bombs exploding in an impressive but harmless geyser off *Yamato*'s beam.

So far he'd been lucky. The Japanese gunners all missed him in his dive-bombing run. They kept missing as he bottomed out in his dive. As he was exiting the scene at low altitude and 250 knots, they stopped missing.

He sensed the tracers converging on him. He felt something

hit the belly of the Avenger like a hammer blow. He felt it again, and this time he saw his starboard wing tip disintegrate. The fuel tank in the right wing burst into flame. Seconds later the cockpit was filled with smoke.

The flames were spreading. Delaney pulled the nose up, trading airspeed for altitude. He yelled at his two crewmen, radio operator William Tilley and gunner Ed Mawhinney, to bail out.

The right sleeve of Delaney's flight suit was on fire, and he could feel something burning under his seat. Over his shoulder he saw Tilley and Mawhinney fling the aft cockpit canopy open. Seconds later, they were gone.

Delaney clambered out onto the port wing, faced aft, and dove off. His parachute canopy opened, and on his way to the water he caught sight of Tilley and Mawhinney descending in their chutes. Seconds later, Delaney was in the water, freeing himself from the entangling shroud lines and inflating his raft.

He realized he was close—too close—to the Japanese warships. When they spotted the bright yellow raft, they'd use it for target practice. To hell with the raft.

Bobbing in the freezing water, Delaney tried to get his bearings. Tilley and Mawhinney were nowhere in sight. He could hear gunfire, explosions, and the sound of airplanes. Even though he was out of the battle, Delaney knew one thing for sure: he was going to have one hell of a view.

Mitsuru Yoshida smelled blood. It was a peculiar smell, mixed with the heavy odor of gunpowder. Then came a sound, distinct from the overwhelming din of battle, an out-of-place smack. He realized that it was the sound of a skull hitting the bulkhead. The sailor next to him on the bridge had just been killed by a hunk of shrapnel.

Bombs and machine gun bullets were raining down on *Yamato*. Her thick armor plate was resisting most of the bombs, but shrapnel and bullets were mowing the deck crew down like a scythe.

VBF-10 Corsair over invasion fleet at Okinawa. (U.S. NAVY)

TOP ROW (*left to right*): Ens. Donald "Mighty Mouse" Croy, killed in a midair collision, April 7, 1945. Ens. Elmer "Al" Hasse, KIA over Amami Oshima, March 26, 1945. Ens. Ernest "Red" Bailey Jr., KIA over Kyushu, April 16, 1945. ABOVE LEFT: Ens. Loren Isley, KIA over Saeki, Kyushu, March 18, 1945. ABOVE RIGHT: Ens. Roy "Eric" Erickson, art student turned fighter pilot. (ALL U.S. NAVY)

ABOVE *(left to right)*: Cmdr. John Hyland, commander of Air Group 10, nearly missed the war. Lt. (jg) Phil Kirkwood, Air Group 10's highest-scoring ace at Okinawa. "Toni the Tease" entertains the Tail End Charlies in Atlantic City before they deployed aboard *Intrepid*. (ALL U.S. NAVY)

A VBF-10 Corsair on the catapult. (U.S. NAVY)

ABOVE *(left to right)*: Lt. (jg) Wes Hays won the Navy Cross for the attack on the *Yamato* task force. (U.S. NAVY/WESLEY HAYS COLLECTION) Lt. William "Country" Landreth became the air group's first POW, March 19, 1945. VBF-10 Executive Officer Lt. C. D. "Timmy" Gile. (BOTH U.S. NAVY)

Wreckage on the flight deck of USS *Bunker Hill* after kamikaze attack, May 11, 1945. (NMNA)

"The Bald Eagle," Vice Adm. Marc Mitscher, commanded the Fast Carrier Task Force. (NMNA)

Ernie Pyle hadn't wanted to come to the Pacific, but thought he owed it to the troops. (NHHC)

VBF-10 skipper Lt. Cmdr. Wilmer Rawie proposes a toast. (U.S. NAVY)

A Corsair fires rockets at target on Okinawa. (NHHC)

ABOVE LEFT: A Marine fires on a Japanese position with a Thompson submachine gun. (NHHC) ABOVE RIGHT: Air Group 10 airmen briefing before mission, April 1945. (U.S. NAVY

ABOVE: Destroyer/minelayer (DM-34) USS *Aaron Ward* after kamikaze attacks of May 3, 1945. (NARA) RIGHT: Ens. Alfred Lerch made history on April 16, 1945, when he shot down seven Japanese planes in one mission. (NMNA)

ABOVE: Hagushi beachhead four days after Love Day. (NHHC) RIGHT: Aft flight deck of USS *Bunker Hill.* (NMNA)

ABOVE LEFT: Ens. Chuck Schlag's mission briefing card from his last combat flight, April 16, 1945. (COURTESY CHARLES SCHLAG) ABOVE RIGHT: *Intrepid* crewmen working on a Corsair. (U.S. NAVY/WESLEY HAYS COLLECTION)

ABOVE LEFT: Kamikaze pilots about to depart on final missions. (NHHC)
ABOVE RIGHT: A Japanese Mitsubishi G4M "Betty" Bomber. (NHHC)

LEFT: War correspondent Ernie Pyle with a driver on Okinawa. (NARA) ABOVE (*left to right*): Lt. Gen. Simon Buckner, Vice Adm. Kelly Turner, Maj. Gen. Lemuel Shepherd. (NHHC)

ABOVE LEFT: An Ohka suicide bomber captured on Okinawa. (NARA)
ABOVE RIGHT: Okinawa invasion beach viewed from inland. (NHHC)

ABOVE LEFT: TBM Avengers over Okinawa. (NMNA) ABOVE RIGHT: The invasion beach at Okinawa. The first objective, the Japanese air base at Yontan, is at left. (NARA)

The superbattleship *Yamato* under way. (NARA)

ABOVE LEFT: The brass aboard USS *Eldorado* (*left to right*): Rear Adm. Forrest Sherman, Adm. Raymond Spruance, Adm. Chester Nimitz, Vice Adm. R. K. Turner. (NARA) ABOVE RIGHT: USS *Laffey* (DD-724) suffered more kamikaze attacks than any other ship without being sunk. (NHHC)

VB-10 SB-2C Helldiver approaching *Intrepid*. (U.S. NAVY)

VBF-10 Corsair in the barricade after a carrier landing mishap. (U.S. NAVY)

ABOVE: VBF-10 squadron insignia designed by Ens. Eric Erickson. (U.S. NAVY) RIGHT: The black shoe and the brown shoe: Cmdre. Arleigh Burke and Vice Adm. Marc Mitscher. (NARA)

Intrepid ablaze after kamikaze strike, April 16, 1945.
(*INTREPID* SEA, AIR & SPACE MUSEUM)

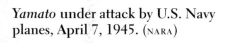

Yamato under attack by U.S. Navy
planes, April 7, 1945. (NARA)

ABOVE: Vice Adm. Matome Ugaki posing
without medals in front of the Judy dive-
bomber in which he flew on the last kamikaze
mission of the war. (CHIRAN KAMIKAZE PEACE
MUSEUM) RIGHT: Lt. Gen. Mitsuru Ushijima, commander of the IJA 32nd
Army, believed that if he prolonged the battle for Okinawa, Japan might still
be spared. (CHIRAN KAMIKAZE PEACE MUSEUM)

In one deafening explosion, a bomb from a Helldiver wiped out a 5-inch gun turret, shredding the bodies of all the gunners. Another bomb exploded into the radar room, killing everyone inside.

In his command post atop the bridge tower, *Yamato*'s captain, Rear Admiral Ariga, was standing out in the open barking commands. The navigation officer occupied Ariga's seat, coordinating the battleship's wild evasive turning and veering. At the helmsman's post in the wheelhouse, the chief quartermaster was spinning the small spoked wheel that sent electrical steering signals to *Yamato*'s massive hydraulic-powered rudder.

The dive-bombers were the hardest to defend against because they were attacking from almost straight overhead. The gunners were having trouble tracking them until they'd already released their bombs and were pulling out of their dives.

The fighters were attacking in shallow dives, mostly dropping lighter bombs, but their machine guns were raking the ship with deadly precision. Anyone caught on the exposed weather deck was turned into mincemeat.

The worst place to be was at the 25-millimeter machine gun mounts. By the second wave of air attacks, almost none of the original gunners was still alive. Replacements rushed to take their place, only to be killed themselves. Shattered bodies and hunks of scorched flesh littered the deck.

Ariga was peering into the sky, trying to judge the flight of the tiny wobbling objects hurtling toward him, yelling commands to the helmsman. He was able to evade many of the bombs, but not all. With terrible frequency they were crashing down on *Yamato*'s deck. Even more were exploding in the water close enough to buckle bulkheads and shear rivets, opening up compartments to flooding.

The battleship's gunnery officers were cursing the miserable results of their antiaircraft fire. Communications had been shattered early in the battle, ending all coordination of the air defense guns. Each gun director was picking his own targets, firing independently. Like most technical skills in the Imperial Japanese Navy, shipboard gunnery had fallen victim to poor training and backward technology. For the overwhelmed gunners, shooting at the swarming American warplanes was like trying to catch hornets with their bare hands.

Yamato's nine 18.1-inch main guns, designed for surface warfare, were ill-suited as air defense weapons. They were mounted in three turrets, and each took an interminable 40 seconds to reload between firings. Even though the gunners were firing the vaunted *san shiki* antiaircraft shells, the projectiles were exploding like harmless fireworks, hitting almost nothing. Even the secondary guns—the half-dozen 6-inchers and twenty-four 5-inch guns—were designed primarily to be used against other ships.

Yamato's most potent antiaircraft weapons were the two dozen 5-inch guns and her 150 machine guns. The machine guns could be deflected to fire straight up. Most of the machine guns fired at a rate of 220 rounds per minute, but some up on the tower bridge could fire at twice that rate. The trouble was, the machine gun crews were being mowed down as quickly as they could be replaced.

The worst was yet to come. Off *Yamato*'s port beam appeared the torpedo planes, looking dark and ominous in the gray murk. The Avengers were jinking to throw off the gunners but continuing straight through the hail of fire. *Yamato*'s gun directors were firing the big 18.1-inch guns directly into the water ahead of the oncoming warplanes, trying to throw up a wall of shrapnel-filled water. It didn't stop them.

As the Avengers bored in closer, the smaller guns on *Yamato* joined in the collective defense. One of the torpedo planes took a hit in the wing, pulled up in flames, then plunged into the sea.

The others kept coming. Torpedoes began dropping from the bellies. The gray shapes slashed through the water on converging courses toward *Yamato*.

Yamato's captain ordered a violent turn toward the incoming torpedoes, trying to "comb the wakes"—paralleling their path and steering between them. As Ariga barked the orders, two junior officers on the bridge plotted the tracks of the incoming torpedoes on a maneuvering board.

It worked, almost. The first bubbling white wake streaked past *Yamato*'s sides. Then another. It seemed that Ariga's luck was holding. Another passed close abeam.

Then one slammed into *Yamato*'s port bow. The impact knocked Captain Nomura, the executive officer, to the deck. Staggering back to his feet, Nomura, who also had the job of chief damage control officer, called for flooding reports. *Yamato* was still making 27 knots, he was told, and she wasn't listing.

Two more bombs exploded on the deck near the aft gunnery control tower. The explosions caused heavy casualties but didn't penetrate to a vital place belowdecks. *Yamato* was damaged but still fighting. The first wave of attackers seemed to be withdrawing, leaving *Yamato*'s crew to wonder when the next was coming.

They didn't have long to wonder. The next wave was almost there.

21 ▸ DUCKS IN A GALLERY

Leading the last division of *Intrepid*'s Corsairs, Lt. (jg) Wes Hays was having trouble keeping Rawie's flight in sight. They had launched from the carrier at 1045, two and a half hours before, flying at 1,500 feet beneath a solid overcast. Now the cloud cover was getting worse. Seeking better visibility, Rawie had led the formation up through the layers in the clouds. It was a game of blindman's bluff, each division leader trying to keep the preceding division in sight as they groped through the murk.

Somewhere between cloud layers, Hays lost sight of Rawie. In fact, he'd lost sight of everyone. Hays and his three wingmen—Hollister, Carlisi, and Erickson—were on their own.

Wes Hays's military career was typical of the wartime Navy. From newly winged naval aviator in February 1943, he'd gone through training as a photo reconnaissance pilot, then put in a tour instructing in Corsairs at Green Cove Springs, where Will Rawie handpicked him for his newly formed Grim Reaper squadron. Hays came from the western outback of Texas, a one-stop town called Novice, where his wife and baby son were living.

Hays was listening to the babble on the radio, and it didn't give him a good feeling. The weather was lousy and getting lousier. Everyone was having trouble finding the Jap task force, including Will Rawie. The lead Avenger in Rawie's group had gotten a radar contact from 30 miles out. The only problem was, it wasn't a Jap ship. It was a reef in the East China Sea.

Now the strike group was dispersed, some low over the water and others flying between the cloud layers, dodging rain squalls, using only their eyeballs to locate an enemy fleet. Fuel was becoming critical. They had only minutes left before they'd have to turn back to the ship.

According to the plotting board on Hays's lap, they *had* to be near where the Japanese force was last reported. A dark layer of cloud enveloped the whole area. Hays signaled his flight to come together so they wouldn't lose sight of each other, then he took them down through the clouds until they had only one broken deck between them and the water.

Hays was peering through the gloom, looking for something—*anything*—that resembled a Japanese ship, when he spotted the silhouette of an airplane off his left wing. Friend or foe? While he was still wondering, an anonymous voice crackled over the radio: "Corsairs, you're close. Stand by for my mark."

It was a plane from one of the other ships, he realized, probably *Yorktown*. Whoever the guy was, he knew the location of the enemy fleet. Hays snapped off a quick order to his wingmen: "Arm everything. Use your .50s." Besides dropping the 1,000-pounders, they'd be ready to strafe any target in sight.

Hays continued on his heading, waiting for the call. A minute later he heard, "Mark!" He shoved the Corsair's nose down through the cloud deck, praying that they were over water and not an island with a mountain on it. His wingmen stayed with him, descending through the thick cloud.

Hays peered through his windshield, straining to see something, anything. They were in a blind dive toward the ocean.

Abruptly they popped through the bottom of the cloud deck. To Hays's astonishment, directly ahead of his nose sprawled a great gray object. It was a Japanese cruiser, and the pipper of his gun sight, as if positioned by some mysterious power, was superimposed on the sweet spot—precisely between the cruiser's center stacks and fantail.

And then he noticed something else. Black, oily puffs were erupting like mushrooms around him. Then he felt the turbulence. The bastards were shooting at him.

Will Rawie, the strike leader, was approaching minimum fuel. He was about to turn back when he spotted a wake on the whitecapped surface below. When he dropped down to follow it, he saw the flash of gunfire. Then came more flashes, like twinkling lights in a fog.

Ahead Rawie made out the dark silhouettes of ships—three smaller vessels and one very large one that had the profile of a battleship. A sporadic barrage of gunfire was coming from the big ship. Rawie saw that it was slightly down at the stern, listing to starboard. It had to be the *Yamato*.

As strike leader, Rawie was supposed to coordinate the attacks of his warplanes. Now it seemed like a joke. His strike group was scattered, all dodging and weaving to avoid the antiaircraft fire, trying to get into position to attack. The only ones he could see besides his own flight of four Corsairs were the Torpeckers—the Avenger torpedo planes. He called for them to swing to the left, to set up for an attack from the north. Everybody else should take any target he could find.

Through the clouds Rawie spotted what looked like a cruiser. As he led his flight in a dive through a hole in the clouds, he nearly collided with a flight of Helldiver dive-bombers. They were all plunging through the same hole. Rawie pulled up in a tight circle, his wingmen in trail, then rolled back in for another try at the cruiser.

This time Rawie held his dive until the target filled his gun sight. He jabbed the release button, feeling the Corsair shed its thousand-pound load, and pulled out of the dive.

Grunting against the force of the pull out, Rawie peered back over his shoulder. Explosions were erupting from below the cruiser's decks. It looked like the cruiser was about to break up.

From his station on *Yamato*'s top deck, Lt. Naoyoshi Ishida saw how wrong they had been about the weather. They had thought that the rain squalls and low clouds would hide them. Instead, it was providing cover for the American warplanes. *Yamato*'s gunners were finding it almost impossible to track the blurred shapes as they came plummeting down from the cloud deck.

Despite the hatred Ishida had for the Americans, he couldn't help feeling a twinge of admiration. Unquestionably, they were brave. They were diving so low, firing their guns until the last moment, that Ishida could see their faces in the cockpits.

Watching the battle go against them, Ishida wrestled with his emotions. He hadn't expected that they would win this fight, but he also hadn't thought the *Yamato* could be so quickly damaged. Ishida was a product of the Meiji generation, the older class of professional naval officers imbued with an unquestioning willingness to die in battle.

Despite his *bushido* feelings, Ishida couldn't push from his mind the image of his wife and infant son. Without him, they would be alone to face an uncertain future. It was not the way a warrior was supposed to think in the midst of battle.

Things were happening too fast for Erickson. He'd barely had time to arm his bomb and guns. Now he was desperately trying to stay with Hays, who was diving on a cruiser beneath his nose. Erickson was hugging Hays's left wing while the second section— Hollister and Carlisi—hung on to Hays's right wing. Wherever Hays was going, they were going with him.

Erickson picked out the gray shape of the target. And he saw something else, a few hundred yards beyond the cruiser they were attacking—an even bigger ship, probably the *Yamato*. Every gun on every warship seemed to be firing at *him*. It didn't seem possible that they could all miss.

There was no time to think about it. With the airspeed building up, the target filling his gun sight, Erickson punched the release button. He felt the hard lurch of the half-ton bomb departing his airplane, and he saw the bombs dropping away from the other Corsairs.

Four thousand pounds of high explosives were plunging down on the enemy ship. Still in their dives, all four Corsairs opened fire with their .50-caliber machine guns. Erickson could see crewmen scurrying on the deck, their bodies being riddled by the hail of machine gun fire.

Pulling out of the dive, the Corsairs jinked and weaved, desperately trying to avoid the storm of fire coming at them. Erickson glimpsed the massive bow of *Yamato* swelling in front of him. The battleship seemed to be moving slowly, less than 10 knots, in a left turn. The ships of her screen were in a protective circle around her.

As he flashed past the battleship, Erickson saw what looked like brass wires extending upward from the ship. It took him a moment to realize what they were: tracers. For every tracer, there were five or more invisible bullets coming at him. More than 150 Japanese guns were shooting at him.

Black flak bursts were erupting on either side and directly ahead. Erickson felt the Corsair being slammed by the concussions. He could smell the sickly odor of the explosives. There seemed to be no chance he could avoid being hit.

An unwanted thought inserted itself in his mind. Aboard *Intrepid* he had watched the task force antiaircraft guns knocking kamikazes out of the sky like ducks in a gallery. Now the roles were reversed. He was one of the ducks.

Something caught Mitsuru Yoshida's eye as he stood on the bridge. Something red. One of *Yamato*'s screening destroyers on the port outer edge of the formation, *Hamakaze*, had just showed her crimson-painted belly. In the next moment her stern seemed to levitate straight out of the water.

Yoshida stared at the stricken destroyer. As in slow motion, *Hamakaze* dropped back into the sea and rolled over. In less than half a minute the destroyer was gone, leaving in her place a sheet of white foam.

It took Yoshida's brain several seconds to process what he had just seen. A torpedo had struck *Hamakaze*'s stern, blowing away the rudder. At almost the same time, a string of bombs landed one after the other on her deck. The combined effect was like smashing a beetle with a hammer.

A few of *Hamakaze*'s crew had been blown into the sea before the shattered hulk sank. Now Yoshida could see their heads bobbing in the bubbling foam where the destroyer had been. No one was stopping to pick them up.

A similar fate had already befallen the unlucky *Asashimo*. Just as Admiral Ito had feared, the straggling destroyer was an easy target. After falling behind the task force when it turned south, *Asashimo* was bringing up the rear. She was 5 miles behind the main force when the strike group from the carrier *San Jacinto* found her.

First went the fighters—six Hellcats and one older F4F Wildcat. All dropped 500-pound bombs, then came back to strafe with their machine guns. *Asashimo* fought back, putting up a stream of defensive fire and causing damage to some of the fighters. After several passes her deck was aflame and her hull was ruptured from bomb near misses. An ominous black oil slick surrounded the destroyer as she went nearly dead in the water.

Eight Avenger torpedo bombers swept in to finish the kill. As the torpedoes hit the water and headed in a perfect spread for the destroyer, her captain, Lt. Cmdr. Yoshiro Sugihara, turned the slow-moving destroyer to starboard, trying to parallel the wakes of the torpedoes. He dodged the first two, and several others swept by the stern.

Then a torpedo took her amidships, directly below the bridge. Seconds later, another exploded into the engine room.

It was the end of *Asashimo*. Her bow pitched upward, and she slid stern first into the sea. Another explosion under the surface blew the bow back above water, and it disintegrated. When the pieces had finished falling back onto the sea, nothing was left but an oil slick. None of *Asashimo*'s 326 crewmen survived the attack.

While Will Rawie was darting in and out of clouds, trying to pull his strike group together, the leader of *Yorktown*'s forty-three-plane strike group, Lt. Cmdr. Herb Houck, had a better view of the action. Houck was a thirty-year-old Minnesotan who had joined the Navy in 1936. He had already shot down six Japanese airplanes and won two Navy Crosses. That day he would add another.

Technically, Houck shouldn't have been there. The engine in his F6F-5 Hellcat had been cutting out during the long flight from *Yorktown* because of an air leak in the line from the fighter's auxiliary belly tank. Unwilling to turn back, Houck kept nursing the engine, switching the fuel feed from tank to tank, running his fuel boost pump to keep gas flowing to the big radial engine. He'd made it, finally managing to suck most of the fuel from the troublesome belly tank.

Now Houck was over the task group at 1,000 feet. His twenty Hellcat fighters each carried a single 500-pound bomb, which he knew would make hardly a dent in *Yamato*'s thick armor. He ordered the Hellcats to go in ahead of the torpedo planes, strafing with their six .50-calibers to deflect the Japanese guns from the vulnerable torpedo planes.

Houck still had his own 500-pound bomb, and he was saving it for the right target. He spotted it while the Torpeckers were still setting up their attack on *Yamato*. Ahead, trailing smoke but still very much alive, was a destroyer, the *Isokaze*. The Japanese tin can had just blown a *Yorktown* Helldiver out of the sky, killing Lt. Harry Worley and his gunner, Earl Ward.

Houck went after the destroyer. Placing the pipper of his gun sight on the midsection of the destroyer, he released the

500-pounder. As he pulled out of his dive, he saw over his shoulder a pillar of flame leaping from the destroyer's mid-deck. Within minutes she was sinking.

Houck wasn't finished. He could see *Isokaze*'s survivors flailing in the oil-slickened water. He dove again, this time blazing away with his .50-calibers. The other Hellcat pilots, bombs now expended, followed him, strafing the bobbing heads in the water.

It was the compassionless rationale of the Pacific war, and it was applied by both sides. The enemy deserved no mercy. The more you killed, the sooner the war would be over.

The Hellcats kept strafing, frothing the water with machine gun fire, until their ammunition was gone.

22 ▸ THERE SHE BLOWS

Yamato was listing to port. The system of pumps and valves that flooded the stabilizing compartments and had corrected the earlier list was no longer working. The all-important aft water control center had taken a torpedo strike and a direct bomb hit.

Watching the inclinometer go from 15 degrees to 20 degrees, Rear Admiral Ariga reached an agonizing decision. He would have to flood the starboard outer engine room. Flooding the space would help correct the list, but it would reduce *Yamato*'s available power. It would also mean certain death for the three hundred men in the starboard engine compartments.

In a choking voice, Ariga gave the order. The valves were opened. Seconds later the violent implosion of seawater snuffed out the life of every man in the flooded engineering rooms.

The desperate tactic worked, but only for a while. At 1410 Ariga felt another torpedo slam into *Yamato*'s stern, jamming her big main rudder hard to port.

Yamato's death was now certain. The ship was uncontrollable. The list to port worsened quickly, rolling toward 35 degrees. With her port rail nearly submerged, the ship was locked in a counter-clockwise turn. The lofty bridge tower was leaning so steeply over the water that the men in the uppermost decks had to cling to rails and stanchions for support.

Captain Nomura, the executive officer, clambered up the ladder to Ariga's command station. There was no chance of correcting *Yamato*'s list, he told the captain. Ariga seemed to be detached from what was happening. He appeared not to notice that the ship's public address system had already been destroyed. He kept repeating, as if his crew could hear him, "Don't lose heart!"

Nomura shouted at him, "The ship is sinking!" Nomura wanted Ariga's permission to give the abandon-ship order. Ariga stared back at him, seeming not to comprehend. Most of *Yamato*'s guns were silent now. There was only the isolated chatter of a few surviving machine guns.

Nomura kept shouting. Finally Ariga nodded his understanding. Yes, Nomura could give the abandon-ship order. And Nomura should join them, the captain added. Someone had to survive in order to tell the story.

There was no time to spare. Nomura sent messengers from the bridge to spread the word belowdecks: "Abandon ship!" *Yamato* was going fast.

Still in his command chair on the sixth deck of the bridge tower, the commander in chief, Vice Adm. Seiichi Ito, received the same report. *Yamato* was doomed. Until now the admiral had remained stiff and silent, aloof from the blow-by-blow events of the battle. From the beginning he had been opposed to what he thought was a senseless sacrifice. Now it was coming to the very end he had predicted.

Ito climbed out of his chair. For a moment he braced himself against the binocular stand, staring out ahead of the sinking ship. Then he issued his one and only direct command since the battle began. "Stop the operation," the admiral ordered. "Turn back after rescuing the men."

With that, Ito turned to salute the surviving members of his staff. Together they had endured nearly two hours of bombings, torpedoings, and relentless machine gun fire. Ito shook each man's hand, then descended the ladder to his sea cabin one deck below. It was the last anyone saw of Seiichi Ito.

On the top bridge deck at the captain's command station, a messenger was helping Ariga tie himself to the compass binnacle. Ariga intended to go with his ship, and he was taking no chances that his body would wash to the surface. He was having trouble because the linoleum deck was slippery with blood. As the ship shuddered from another internal blast, Ariga shouted that someone had to save the emperor's portrait.

The assistant gunnery officer, Lieutenant Hattori, carried out Ariga's order, after a fashion. Hattori made his way down to the wardroom, where the picture was mounted on the bulkhead. Instead of retrieving the portrait, he simply locked the door. At least the enemy would not recover it.

Yorktown air group commander Herb Houck was still on station, directing his strike group from his Hellcat fighter. He had already assigned his twelve Avenger torpedo planes, led by Lt. Cmdr. Tom Stetson, to finish off the cruiser *Yahagi*.

Stetson had just gotten a good look at the *Yamato*. She appeared to be listing badly, showing her belly. He told Houck he wanted to split his group and go after the *Yamato* with six of his Avengers.

Houck concurred, but he told Stetson to change the torpedo running depth from 10 feet to 20. The 10-foot depth had been preset to hit a cruiser's hull. Going to 20 feet would put the fish below *Yamato*'s thicker armor plate and right into her exposed lower hull.

It was easier said than done. In the back of his Avenger, tail gunner Charles Fries had the job of resetting the depth setting on their Mark 13 torpedo. It meant that he had to crawl into the bomb bay, pull wires inside the torpedo, and turn the indicator with a wrench. If Fries got it wrong, the airstream coming through the bomb bay could actually arm the torpedo.

The Torpeckers took their time getting into position. One of the pilots, Lt. (jg) John Carter, was in the last section. He watched Stetson's first four Avengers go in low and fast, dropping their torpedoes in a spread on *Yamato*'s beam. "As luck would have it," he recalled, "the big ship was turning to port, thereby exposing the full broadside expanse of her enormous hull to the converging torpedoes." Carter saw at least three of the torpedoes explode into

Yamato's hull from amidships to the bow. Two hit so close they looked like a single huge explosion.

The dreadnought was still fighting back. Her gunners were putting out a sporadic barrage of antiaircraft fire, frothing the water and hammering the Avengers with the concussion of the bursts. As Carter began his own run from aft of the battleship, he could see tracers arcing toward his Avenger. He launched his torpedo across *Yamato*'s curving wake. Pulling away from the target, he tried to shrink into the metal frame of his seat. He could feel the ping and clatter of shrapnel hitting the Avenger's skin. He saw that his torpedo had run true, cutting inside *Yamato*'s swerving turn and exploding into the battleship's port quarter.

Yamato's tower bridge was leaning at a precarious angle. Mitsuru Yoshida couldn't help thinking about the irony of the situation. It was the Imperial Japanese Navy who had taught the world how to destroy surface warships with airpower. They had done it at Pearl Harbor, and two days later they repeated the lesson off Malaya by sinking the British battleship *Prince of Wales* and the battle cruiser *Repulse*. The British commander, Admiral Sir Tom Phillips, had made the fatal mistake of taking his surface force into battle without air cover.

The Japanese had just made the same mistake.

Watching the American warplanes, Yoshida wondered about the men in the cockpits. They seemed undaunted by the wall of flak thrown up by the task force. Several had been hit, bursting into flame and crashing into the sea.

But none were emulating the Japanese *tokko* airmen. Not one American pilot had crashed his airplane into an enemy ship. To Yoshida, this single fact more than anything else revealed the chasm between their cultures.

The abandon-ship order was being yelled by messengers throughout the ship. It was time for Yoshida to leave the bridge. *Yamato*'s list was now 80 degrees. The ship was capsizing.

Kazuhiro Fukumoto heard the crash of the bombs and the booming of the guns. The sounds were coming from directly above him. He and the rest of his damage control unit beneath the middle section of the starboard weather deck were waiting to be sent to a stricken area of the ship. The suspense was nerve-wracking. Fukumoto envied the men up there shooting the guns. They were so busy they had no time to think about where the next bomb would hit.

At about 1400 Fukumoto's unit finally received orders. They were needed down on the lowest and second-lowest decks. They split up, with Fukumoto and three others going to the second-lowest deck, while two officers were to inspect damage on the lowest deck.

Just as they closed the hatch behind them, a torpedo exploded into the starboard hull. Within seconds every man on the lowest deck was killed by the avalanche of seawater. The lights extinguished in the space where Fukumoto stood, and water came surging up from below. In the pitch blackness, feeling the water closing around him, the young sailor fought against the panic that swelled up in him.

The air pressure in the rapidly filling compartment built up, blowing open an overhead hatch. A tiny stream of light burst into the flooded compartment, and the terrified sailors swam toward it. They were barely able to enter the compartment above before the flood of water came surging up behind them. They battened down the hatch, but the relentless pressure kept seawater gushing up through the cracks, threatening to blow the hatch.

More torpedoes slammed into *Yamato*. The battleship was listing severely to port. Fukumoto and his stranded shipmates swam through one compartment after another, making their way toward the stern. They finally arrived at a small hatch that opened to the aft deck.

Fukumoto was so exhausted from the effort he had to be pulled through the hatch by his division officer. Standing on the stern, he got his first look at the carnage topside. Dead gunners were sprawled across the deck next to their gun mounts. Fukumoto recognized one of his friends, a sailor named Yoshifuji who was no more than sixteen years old. Yoshifuji's head was split open, and blood pumped out each time he took a breath. The dying sailor moaned, "Long live the emperor."

The battle was almost over for *Yamato*. The ship was nearly capsized, listing so steeply that one of the main gun turrets was already submerged. The crew's *bushido* spirit had been replaced with the survival instinct. Fukumoto's division officer gave the order to toss into the sea everything that would float—wooden timbers, logs, judo mats, hammocks.

The sailors crawled up the nearly vertical deck to the starboard hull. It was wet and slick. With nothing to cling to, sailors were sliding and jumping into the sea.

Yoshida wriggled up through the lookout port and clung to the starboard bulkhead of the bridge tower, which was nearly submerged. Rear Admiral Ariga, lashed to his compass binnacle, had already vanished beneath the water. So had the navigation officer and his assistant, who also had tied themselves to their stations. Yoshida could see dozens of crewmen perched like stranded rats on the rust-colored belly of the battleship.

The sea rose from beneath them. As water engulfed the ship, men disappeared into the yawning eddies and whirlpools around the sinking hull. Yoshida drew a deep breath and rolled himself up in a ball. For what seemed an eternity, he churned inside the snarling whirlpool, unable to escape, feeling that each of his limbs was being torn from his body.

It was then that the *Yamato* exploded.

There she blows!" someone yelled over the tactical frequency. Every pilot saw it, including Herb Houck, who had positioned his Hellcat so that his aerial camera could record the battleship's last minutes. He'd been watching *Yamato* capsize, settling beneath the waves, with crewmen still clinging like ants to her red-bottomed hull. In the water around her he saw rafts, flotsam, floating bodies, and the heads of swimmers.

And then at 1423, she blew up. The fireball looked like a volcanic eruption, soaring a thousand feet above the surface. As the fireball dissipated, a black, mushroom-shaped cloud took its place, billowing a mile into the sky. The smoke column was seen by coast watchers more than a hundred miles away on the shore of Kyushu.

Later it would be theorized that *Yamato*'s 90-degree list caused the shells for her main batteries to slide in their magazine, hitting their fuses and exploding. The explosion sent thousands of pieces of shrapnel into the air, and the rain of debris killed most of the unlucky sailors swimming on the surface. The underwater concussion killed those near the submerged main deck. The swimmers unlucky enough to be near *Yamato*'s raked smokestack were caught in the massive suction created by the huge open funnel as the ship went under.

Kazuhiro Fukumoto's timing was perfect. *Yamato* exploded precisely in the tiny sliver of time while he was dropping to the sea. Many who had just splashed into the water were killed, their internal organs crushed by the concussion. Those close to the side of the ship died in the blast. Fukumoto hit the water, stunned but alive.

He had no time to rejoice. The sunken ship was moving slowly forward, and he was sucked into the whirlpool created by the still-revolving 16-foot-long bronze propeller blades.

Fukumoto couldn't free himself from the tug of the whirlpool. For the second time in ten minutes, he was about to drown. He tried to take a breath, but sucked in a lungful of seawater. With darkness closing around him, Fukumoto knew he was doomed.

M itsuru Yoshida was clawing his way up from the depths. Because he'd gone into the water from the bridge, he had been shielded from the worst of the blast. The bodies of the men on the surface absorbed most of the falling debris, but Yoshida received a gash in his head from underwater shrapnel. In shock, his lungs nearly bursting, he clawed his way to the surface.

Naoyoshi Ishida leaped from the starboard rails as *Yamato* was capsizing. He was sucked into one of the whirlpools, struggling to breathe, unable to claw his way to the surface. As he was suffocating, knowing that he was being dragged to the bottom along with the battleship, he had a vision. He saw the face of his newborn son, whom he had cradled for the first and last time during his visit before the *Yamato* left Kure. Ishida had been unable to say farewell to his wife and child. Now it was too late.

The vision gave him new strength. Clawing madly, he fought his way up through the debris and gushing whirlpool and popped to the surface. The underwater explosion had burst an eardrum, and a piece of shrapnel had snapped a tendon in Ishida's hip. Floating in the oil slick, he dodged machine gun bullets and clung to floating objects, all the while keeping the image of his newborn son firmly fixed in his mind.

Another one still alive was Kazuhiro Fukumoto. Somehow the eighteen-year-old sailor had been spat out of the whirlpool around *Yamato*'s giant propeller blade. Submerged and barely conscious, he had sensed light and air above him and thrashed his way to the surface. In a daze, he found that he could breathe and still swim. He spotted a wooden timber floating nearby, and he clung to it while he gathered his senses.

The *Yamato* was gone. There was nothing in sight except an immense column of smoke. As far as Fukumoto could tell, he was the only one still alive in the tossing sea. Then a wave raised him up, and he saw other heads bobbing on the surface. For nearly two more hours Fukumoto clung to his timber until he heard an officer calling for the survivors to come together. Fukumoto was able to climb onto an emergency raft with a couple dozen others. With the overloaded raft nearly submerged, the exhausted survivors had to turn away other struggling swimmers.

As an officer, Mitsuru Yoshida took charge of a party of ten swimmers, ordering them to gather pieces of flotsam to fashion a raft. The oil-slicked water stung their eyes and clogged their throats and windpipes. Many had used all their strength to escape the whirlpools and explosions. Now they were unable to hang on to the floating objects. They gave up and slipped beneath the waves.

The *Yamato* might be gone, but the enemy was still there. The sprawling oil slick served as a marker on the ocean for where the ship had sunk—and where her surviving crewmen were floating. The warplanes came swooping back down, one after the other, leaving long white tracks of .50-caliber machine gun fire spurting across the water. For twenty minutes they raked the survivors of *Yamato* and *Yahagi* and the sunken destroyers.

Ducking bullets, watching the heads of their comrades splattering like melons, the swimmers felt a mixture of terror and hatred. It was not a surprise that the enemy would shoot them in the water. Given the chance, they would do the same. For some, the hail of bullets had an energizing effect. Hating the Americans gave them the spark to stay alive.

The destroyer *Fuyutsuki* hove into view, signaling with a flag that the men in the water should hold out just a little while longer. The enemy airplanes were still in the area. Finally the destroyer slid up to them and put down rope ladders. The men in the water were black with oil, barely able to maintain a grip on the ropes. Several made it to the top, only to lose consciousness, fall back into the water, and drown.

Mitsuru Yoshida was one of the last to climb aboard *Fuyutsuki*.

Smeared with blood and oil, he summoned his last ounce of strength to haul himself up the rope ladder.

With darkness coming, another still-intact destroyer, *Yukikaze*, joined the search for survivors. One of those hauled aboard was Lt. Naoyoshi Ishida, nearly delirious from his injuries. Another was the young sailor Kazuhiro Fukumoto. Faltering at the top of the rope ladder, Fukumoto was slapped on both cheeks by an officer to keep him conscious long enough to climb over the side. The sailor stumbled belowdecks, where the crew gave him blankets and warm wine.

Four hours had passed since *Yamato* blew up. Nearly 4,000 men who had sailed aboard the battleship and her escorts were dead. Of *Yamato*'s crew, only 269 had been saved, and Kazuhiro Fukumoto was one of them. He would spend the rest of his life wondering why.

Of the ten warships that had set out with the Second Fleet task force, six were still afloat, but barely. The destroyers *Isokaze* and *Kasumi* were shattered hulks, dead in the water and awash with blood.

At 1655, after removing 15 officers and 270 men from *Kasumi*, *Fuyutsuki* put two torpedoes into the destroyer and sent her to the bottom. Later that evening, *Yukikaze* came alongside the wreck of *Isokaze*. After off-loading the still-living crew members, she tried to scuttle the destroyer with a torpedo, but it passed beneath the hull without exploding. *Isokaze* finally pumped shells at point-blank range, leaving the derelict with her dead crewmen blazing like a torch on the darkened ocean.

Meanwhile, another destroyer, *Suzutsuki*, had gone missing during the aerial attack and was presumed sunk. Not until the next morning did the shattered destroyer appear off the coast of Kyushu, laboriously steaming backward to protect her destroyed bow.

The search for survivors ended, and the remaining warships

of the task force threaded their way back through the picket line of American submarines to the base at Sasebo. *Yukikaze* suffered the indignity of two more torpedo hits from lurking American submarines. Neither torpedo exploded, but the thunk of the weapons slamming into the ship only further twanged the nerves of the traumatized survivors.

That night the message reached the Combined Fleet Headquarters: Operation Ten-Go was officially ended.

23 ▸ DUMBO AND MIGHTY MOUSE

Their call signs were "Dog Eight" and "Dog Ten." Lieutenants Dick Simms and Jim Young were the pilots of the two Martin PBM Mariners of VPB-21 that had been shadowing the Japanese task force. Since early morning the big flying boats had flitted in and out of the clouds, radioing position reports, staying just out of range of the antiaircraft guns on the ships below. When the strike planes showed up to hit the task force, the PBMs remained on station as "Dumbos"—search and rescue aircraft—so named from the Walt Disney cartoon featuring a baby flying elephant.

The Mariner was a gull-winged, two-engine flying boat with a crew of seven and an on-station time of fourteen hours. It was both a lethal weapons platform—it could carry 8,000 pounds of bombs and torpedoes and had eight .50-caliber guns—and a sitting duck. Like all flying boats, the lumbering PBM was slow and easy to hit.

In the hierarchy of military aviation, being a Dumbo pilot didn't carry the same cachet as flying a fighter. Dumbo duty was tedious and often dangerous. When the PBM crew located an aircrewman in the water, they would keep a vigil overhead, dropping a float light or a raft, flying cover until a destroyer or submarine showed up. When necessary, they made an open ocean landing, a high-risk maneuver in heavy seas. After hauling the airman aboard, the Dumbo pilot would coax the flying boat back into the air, slamming through waves and troughs, praying that the hull didn't split apart.

Dog Eight and Dog Ten were ringside witnesses to the epic sea battle playing out beneath them. Their greatest danger was collision with the strike planes buzzing in and out of clouds and rain showers. They had watched the grand finale—the pulsing fireball that leaped up from the dying *Yamato*. The cruiser *Yahagi* was already gone, and so were several of the destroyers. The Mariner crews could see Japanese survivors in the oil-slicked water clinging to pieces of flotsam.

As the strike planes withdrew, a *Yorktown* Helldiver pilot radioed that he had spotted a yellow life raft—the kind used by American airmen. He didn't know if anyone was in it or not.

Simms and Young, the Dumbo pilots, went down to take a look. At first they saw only the heads of Japanese sailors. Nearby were three enemy destroyers, still afloat and presumably able to fire their guns. Crewmen inside each Dumbo scanned the water with binoculars.

Then someone spotted it. There *was* a yellow raft, and a lone figure was in it, waving like crazy. While Dick Simms, flying Dog Eight, made a decoy pass by the nearest destroyer, drawing fire but taking no hits, Young set up for the water landing in Dog Ten.

The sea conditions were on the ragged edge of what the PBM could handle—wave crests 25 feet apart, with a heaving swell. If the PBM smacked directly into a wave, the hull could be crushed or a wing would snap. There would be eight men in the water instead of one.

Young leveled out over the waves, floated for a moment while he looked for the right place between crests, then settled the flying boat into the churning sea. Still in one piece, Dog Ten wallowed through the water toward the tiny figure in the yellow raft.

Bill Delaney had been afraid they were going to leave him. Numb from the frigid water, he kept waving until, to his immense relief, he saw one of the Dumbos turn back and land. Now it was plowing like a great seabird toward him, rising into view on the tops of the swells, disappearing between them. Delaney had broken open a second dye marker. Now the stuff was spread around his raft like fluorescent goo. Nobody could miss it, including the Japanese.

The Dumbo made two passes at the raft. Each time the wind and waves caused the pilot to miss. On the third try, the pilot cut the engines and let the seaplane drift toward the raft. When the PBM had floated to within twenty yards, Delaney took matters into his own hands. He dived off the raft and tried to paddle the rest of the way.

He couldn't make it. Before he drowned, two Dumbo crewmen managed to snag the floundering pilot with a boat hook and drag him aboard.

Meanwhile, the closest Japanese destroyer was taking a renewed interest in the operation. Plumes of shellfire were working their way toward the Dumbo.

Firing up Dog Ten's engines, Jim Young swung the Mariner into the wind. Normally, an open-sea takeoff in a heavily loaded Mariner was a close contest between machine and nature. But Dog Ten had just been equipped with a new device called JATO—jet-assisted takeoff. Two pairs of solid-fuel rocket bottles were installed on either side of the aft fuselage.

Young shoved up the throttles and ignited the JATO bottles. Spewing a comet's tail of fire and smoke, the big seaplane surged through the swells, slamming into each wave, finally skipping off the top of a swell and rocketing into the air.

Bill Delaney was one of the lucky ones. Several parachutes had been observed descending in the battle zone, but only a few airmen had been found alive. Tilley and Mawhinney, the crewmen Delaney had last seen bailing out of his Avenger, were never found.

The warbirds headed back to their carriers! The only ones to miss the party were the airmen from *Hancock*. Delayed in getting airborne, they hadn't joined the massed force from *Essex*, *Bunker Hill*, *Bataan*, and *Cabot*. Heading off on their own, they milled around the East China Sea, never finding the *Yamato* task force.

The strike group from *Intrepid* didn't bother trying to rejoin in a mass formation. The Corsairs, Helldivers, and Avengers segregated themselves into separate flocks, each flying at its best fuel-conserving speed for the long trip home.

Droning southward over the gray ocean, the pilots had time for reflection. By some miracle, *Intrepid*'s group had made it through the strike without a single loss. And each of them had been a witness to history: they had watched the great battleship *Yamato* go to her grave.

For Ens. Jim Clifford, Will Rawie's wingman, there was no chance to savor the moment. Thirty feet away, his skipper was giving him urgent hand signals. Rawie's radio had failed. He was signaling that he wanted Clifford to lead them back to the carrier.

The twenty-four-year-old ensign's heart sank. Bombing battleships was one thing; leading a formation back to the ship was another. In the rush to launch for the *Yamato* mission, Clifford hadn't paid any attention to the navigational details of the briefing. Hell, he was a wingman, not a leader. Clifford had no idea where the *Intrepid* was.

Neither, as it turned out, did the other flight leaders. Clifford could hear them on the tactical frequency asking for a heading back to the carrier. Then through the chatter came the voice of someone who sounded like he knew what he was doing. A good heading would be about 165 degrees.

It was good enough for Clifford. Off he went, his commanding officer on his wing, the rest of *Intrepid*'s Corsairs in trail. Weaving through the clouds, peering down at the vastness of the Pacific, Jim Clifford prayed that the heading would get them close enough to spot the fleet. If not, they were all screwed. They would run out of gas and ditch in the ocean.

Two hours passed. Clifford's butt hurt. His arms and legs were stiff. There was no sign of the sprawling task force that they had left behind nearly five hours ago. Clifford sweated and prayed while the fuel gauge continued a relentless decline toward zero. He could feel Rawie's silent gaze from the cockpit thirty feet away.

After what seemed an eternity, he heard something in his head-phones—a faint dash-dot signal. It was the ship's YE homing trans-mitter. The signal couldn't be picked up at a range of more than about sixty miles. It was the most glorious sound Jim Clifford had ever heard in his life. *Intrepid* was dead ahead, ten minutes' flying time away.

Each of the Corsairs plunked safely back down on *Intrepid*'s deck. Minutes later, the fatigued but adrenaline-charged pilots were jabbering and gesturing with their hands in the ready room, reliving the dramatic mission. They had been airborne five hours and fifty minutes, longer than most had ever flown in a single sor-tie. Will Rawie was telling everyone who would listen how his wingman, a lowly ensign, had led them back to the ship with such uncanny skill. It was amazing.

Jim Clifford had the sense to smile and shut up. It *was* amaz-ing. He wasn't about to tell them that it was pure blind luck.

While the battle for *Yamato* was playing out in the East China Sea, the skies around Okinawa were filled with kamikazes. It was the second wave of Admiral Ugaki's initial *kikusui*, but on a diminished scale.

Like their brethren of the day before, the *tokko* warriors of the second wave were drawn to the same targets—the destroyers on the picket stations. And as they had before, the carrier-based CAP fighters pounced on them, splashing five before they could reach the picket ships.

One kamikaze managed to slip through the gunfire and crash into the destroyer *Bennett*, killing three men and wounding eigh-teen. Another slammed into the destroyer escort *Wesson* on her screening station north of Ie Shima.

To the northwest of Okinawa, another handful of kamikazes

found Task Force 58's fast carriers. Only one, an Aichi D4Y Judy dive-bomber, survived the CAP fighter screen and then the anti-aircraft fire from the surface. Spotting the great gray shape of the carrier *Hancock*, the kamikaze swept in on the carrier's bow at such a low angle that the propeller chewed through the port catapult before the crash. The Judy's 250-kilogram bomb detached, smashing into the flight deck just aft of the forward mid-deck elevator.

What happened next was becoming a familiar scenario. The bomb punched straight through *Hancock*'s wooden flight deck, exploding in the forward hangar bay, killing every man in the space. Fueled and armed warplanes in the bay burst into flame and exploded. Topside, the hulk of the shattered dive-bomber caromed down the flight deck and slammed into a pack of nineteen parked airplanes, setting three ablaze and starting an inferno on the wind-swept deck.

Hancock was engulfed in flames belowdecks and topside. Her skipper, Capt. Robert F. Hickey, ordered a hard turn to starboard in a desperate attempt to slide the burning airplanes over the side. The fires on the hangar bay extinguished all the carrier's lights and filled the darkened compartments with deadly smoke.

By 1345—a little more than an hour after the attack—*Hancock*'s crews had the blazing airplanes shoved overboard and the fires extinguished. It was eloquent testimony to how the U.S. Navy's damage control skills had evolved in the past three years.

The kamikaze strike wasn't the only indignity that *Hancock* would endure that day. While the ship's crew was fighting the blazes, her air group was groping through the clouds over the East China Sea, searching for the *Yamato*. They never found her. At the end of their fuel, they were forced to jettison their bombs and torpedoes and return to *Hancock*.

But instead of a ready deck for landing, the airmen were greeted with a gaping hole in the flight deck and an ominous cloud of smoke. They orbited overhead, conserving their last gallons of fuel, praying that the damage control crews could patch the hole.

They did. At 1630, after a down-to-the-wire feat of damage repair, *Hancock* was bringing her aircraft back aboard.

There was no celebrating aboard *Hancock* that evening. Smoke and the smell of death wafted through the passageways. Sixty-three crewmen were dead and eighty-two more wounded, mostly from burns.

Hancock was able to continue operations for another day, but the port catapult was demolished and the forward elevator inoperable. The damage could not be repaired on station. *Hancock* was detached from her task group and sent to Ulithi, then further eastward to Pearl Harbor.

One more carrier was out of the fight. By the time *Hancock* returned, the battle for Okinawa would be history.

I t was a bitter pill for *Intrepid*'s ambitious air group commander, Johnny Hyland, to miss the historic *Yamato* strike. That morning when the mission was being hurriedly put together, Hyland was already airborne on a fighter sweep over Tokuno, in the north Ryukyus. By default, group command of the *Yamato* attack had fallen to Will Rawie.

But the day wasn't a complete loss for Hyland. While he was covering the Corsairs strafing the Japanese airfield, he glimpsed the silhouette of a low-flying Val dive-bomber headed south. Pouncing like a hawk, Hyland gunned the Val down with a single burst from his .50-calibers, chalking up his second air-to-air victory of the campaign.

The CAG wasn't the only one in the group to score. Ens. Raymond "Freddie" Lanthier, while strafing a target at Tokuno, spotted an incoming Nakajima Tojo fighter. The Tojo was a fast mover, nearly as capable at climbing and diving as the Corsair. Attacking from below, Lanthier put enough rounds into the Tojo's engine to send the fighter flaming into the sea.

Another senior officer who missed the *Yamato* battle was Lt. Cmdr. Wally Clarke, skipper of the VF-10 Grim Reapers. Clarke had led another twelve-plane strike on the airfields in the northern Ryukyus. Despite heavy antiaircraft fire, Clarke's fighters strafed the field, destroyed eight parked airplanes, and withdrew to the south without losing an airplane—until they were en route home.

Clarke's wingman was one of the Tail End Charlies, a short, youngish-looking ensign named Don Croy, whom the squadron nicknamed "Mighty Mouse." A few days earlier, Mighty Mouse had had a close call. On a strike over Minami, he'd taken a hit and ditched his Corsair dangerously close to the enemy island. After several hours in his raft, he had been rescued by a daring OS2U floatplane pilot.

Now Croy was flying close formation on Clarke's wing while the skipper weaved through the towering cumulus that obscured most of the East China Sea. In a moment of inattention, Croy didn't see Clarke's Corsair banking into him.

What happened next was never clear. Clarke's propeller chewed into Croy's wing. An instant later Mighty Mouse was spinning uncontrollably toward the sea. Clarke's broken propeller was shaking his airplane so violently he had to shut the engine down. He glided to a water landing 4,000 yards behind a destroyer. Minutes later, the tin can crew was hauling him aboard.

But not his wingman. The destroyer sailors told Clarke they had witnessed the whole thing—the collision, the Corsairs dropping to the ocean—but no one saw a parachute. Mighty Mouse had disappeared without a trace.

Still slumped in his padded chair in *Bunker Hill*'s flag plot, Mitscher received the reports from the strike groups. When the strike was finished and the last warplanes had landed safely aboard their carriers, the Bald Eagle scribbled a message of congratulations to all the air groups. They had achieved a glorious victory, he wrote. He was proud of them.

Each strike group had brought back rolls of film documenting the attack. As quickly as the film could be processed, prints

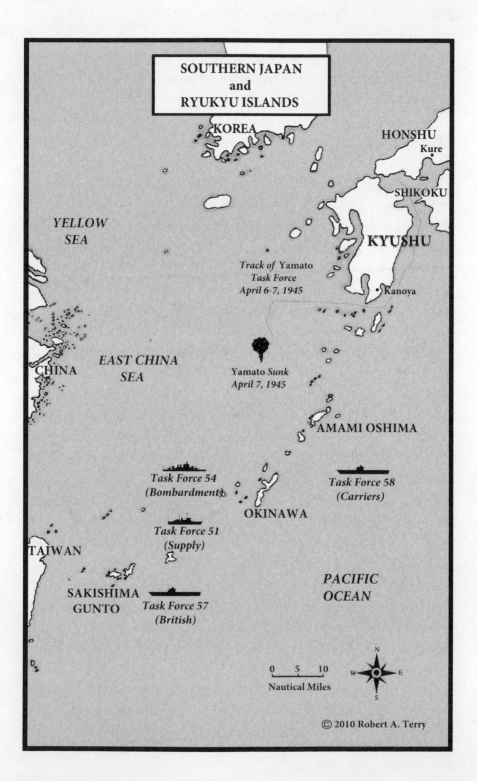

SOUTHERN JAPAN
and
RYUKYU ISLANDS

KOREA

HONSHU

Kure

SHIKOKU

YELLOW
SEA

KYUSHU

Track of Yamato
Task Force
April 6-7, 1945

Kanoya

EAST CHINA
SEA

CHINA

Yamato *Sunk*
April 7, 1945

AMAMI OSHIMA

Task Force 54
(Bombardment)

Task Force 58
(Carriers)

OKINAWA

Task Force 51
(Supply)

TAIWAN

PACIFIC
OCEAN

SAKISHIMA
GUNTO

Task Force 57
(British)

0   5   10
Nautical Miles

N
W   E
S

© 2010 Robert A. Terry

were being rushed to the flag bridge on *Bunker Hill*. With his ever-present cigarette dangling from his mouth, the admiral peered at the still-wet black-and-white images.

It was all there in the photos. Mitscher's gamble had paid off. The grainy images provided the ultimate proof of the airplane's dominance not only of the sky but of the sea. The age of the battleship was over. Mitscher should have been reveling in his moment of triumph.

But he wasn't. The Bald Eagle was not his old self. His face was more haggard than ever, his eyes red-rimmed from the undiagnosed medical event of the night before. Mitscher took one more look at the photos, then rose from his chair. Without comment, he returned to his cabin and went back to bed.

Aboard *New Mexico*, Adm. Raymond Spruance was also digesting the reports. Although he'd gotten over the disappointment at missing out on a last great sea battle, he wasn't ready to recall Deyo's surface force, which was still steaming northward to engage the enemy. Four destroyers from the Japanese task force were still afloat, leaving the remote possibility that there might still be a surface action.

Rear Adm. Mort Deyo, on his flagship *Tennessee*, was accepting the fact that the damned airedales had again stolen the glory. That night, when the recall order finally came from Spruance, he sent off a jovial note to Mitscher. It was too bad, he wrote, that the surface sailors wouldn't have "Japanese scrambled eggs for breakfast."

A battle with the *Yamato* task force would have been a glorious last hurrah for Deyo and his beloved battlewagons. The next day they would go back to their shore bombardment duties off Okinawa.

For Mitscher's airedales, the destruction of the *Yamato* and five of her screening ships had not come without a price. Ten warplanes—four Helldivers, three Avengers, and three Hellcats—had been lost. Four pilots and eight aircrewmen were missing and presumed dead. Several, including eyewitness Bill Delaney, had been snatched from the enemy's midst by daring Dumbo crews. Still, the losses were minuscule when measured against those of the previous great air-sea battles. Mitscher's airmen had won a spectacular victory.

Now Spruance could return his attention to the bigger picture. The *Yamato* encounter was dramatic, satisfying, perhaps even historically significant. But the pragmatic admiral knew the truth: it was a side show. The real battle for Okinawa was just beginning.

Aboard *Eldorado*, Kelly Turner was in an ebullient mood. A week had passed since the landings on Okinawa, and as far as the Alligator was concerned, things were going exceedingly well. The *Yamato* and five of her entourage lay at the bottom of the East China Sea. The greatest wave of kamikazes ever seen had been gunned down like coveys of quail. Buckner's Tenth Army was meeting only sporadic resistance in its march across Okinawa.

Turner couldn't resist sending a jocular message to his boss, the Pacific Fleet commander in chief. "I may be crazy," he signaled Nimitz, "but it looks like the Japanese have quit the war, at least in this sector."

Nimitz wasn't buying it. From his Guam headquarters, he signaled back, "Delete all after 'crazy.' "

As it turned out, Nimitz's instincts were correct.

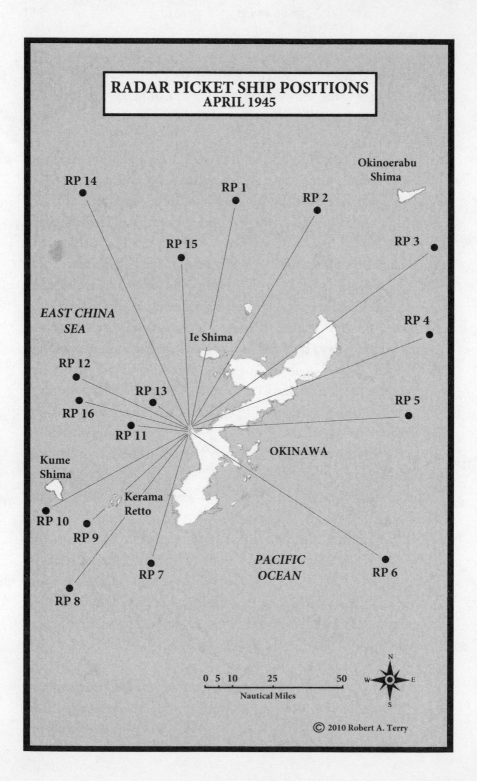

RADAR PICKET SHIP POSITIONS
APRIL 1945

PART THREE

FLOATING CHRYSANTHEMUMS

▼

DEAR PARENTS:

    PLEASE CONGRATULATE ME. I HAVE BEEN GIVEN A SPLENDID OPPORTUNITY TO DIE. THIS IS MY LAST DAY. THE DESTINY OF OUR HOMELAND HINGES ON THE DECISIVE BATTLE IN THE SEAS TO THE SOUTH WHERE I SHALL FALL LIKE A BLOSSOM FROM A RADIANT CHERRY TREE.

    —LETTER FROM FLYING PETTY OFFICER FIRST CLASS
      ISAO MATSUO ON THE EVE OF HIS *TOKKO* MISSION

WE WATCHED EACH PLUNGING KAMIKAZE WITH THE DETACHED HORROR OF ONE WITNESSING A TERRIBLE SPECTACLE RATHER THAN AS THE INTENDED VICTIM. WE FORGOT SELF FOR THE MOMENT AS WE GROPED HELPLESSLY FOR THE THOUGHTS OF THAT OTHER MAN UP THERE.

    —VICE ADM. C. R. BROWN

24 ► A RIDGE CALLED KAKAZU

The honeymoon was over.

To Lt. Gen. Simon Buckner, the report came as no surprise. It was the news he'd been expecting since Love Day. He no longer had to wonder where the Japanese were. His Tenth Army had found them, and they were putting up a hell of a fight.

In the south of the island, XXIV Corps had slammed into the enemy line drawn across the narrow isthmus leading to the southern peninsula of Chinen. The heavily fortified line was protected by pillboxes with steel doors impervious to the new weapon introduced at Iwo Jima, flamethrowers.

Meanwhile in the north, the 6th Marine Division had moved so fast up the isthmus that their supporting artillery had trouble keeping up. Eight days after the Love Day amphibious landings, Marines were standing on the rocky outcropping of Hedo Misaki, the northern tip of Okinawa. Their last objective was Motobu Peninsula, a knob-shaped protuberance on the northwest coast of Okinawa where the Japanese had constructed a fortified line of defense.

Though Buckner still kept his command post aboard Turner's flagship *Eldorado*, he spent most of each day ashore conferring with his commanders, Marine major general Roy Geiger and Army major general John Hodge. The *Eldorado* still afforded the best communications with Spruance and Mitscher, as well as with the units driving in opposite directions on the island.

What *did* surprise Buckner and his division commanders was the Japanese artillery. Effective artillery support had been an Achilles' heel of the Japanese army during most of the previous island battles.

Here at Okinawa, the Japanese 32nd Army had the heaviest concentration of field guns of any battle in the Pacific war, and it was clear that they had learned how to use them. A steady barrage of shells was descending on the U.S. XXIV Corps as they approached the high ground near Shuri. In a single twenty-four-hour session, fourteen thousand Japanese shells rained down on the Americans.

Though casualties were light, the barrage had the effect of halting the U.S. advance. The Japanese guns were well enough concealed that even the big shipboard batteries offshore hadn't been able to silence them.

The soldiers and Marines in the front line were finding Okinawa to be a strange and disconcerting battleground. No other island battle had been fought in the presence of so many civilians. Most of the population was crammed into the south, and their villages were now combat zones. Most young Okinawan men had been conscripted into the local Japanese defense force. The remaining elders, women, and children were terrified of the Americans, having been told by the Japanese that the invaders would murder and rape.

Wary GIs, for their part, were unsure whether the Okinawans were hostile or not. Mistakes were made, and tragedies happened with numbing suddenness. Civilians were mowed down in deadly cross fire. Mortar shells were lobbed onto huts and other dwellings occupied by natives. Soldiers hurled grenades into caves and tunnels only to find inside the shattered bodies of women and children.

One of the men slogging across the island was war correspondent Ernie Pyle. Pyle had spent the first two days of the invasion with the headquarters of a Marine regiment, then joined an infantry company, moving with the grunts into the shattered countryside of Okinawa.

This was where Pyle was most comfortable, in the company of the foot soldiers, young GIs from the heartland of America with whom he shared foxholes, rations, and the danger of combat.

When they called him "sir" or "Mr. Pyle," he corrected them: the name was Ernie.

Pyle listened to their stories and wrote about what happened to them. "I was back again at the kind of life I had known so long," he wrote in a dispatch. "It was the old familiar pattern, unchanged by distance or time . . .a pattern so imbedded in my soul that it seemed I'd never known anything else in my life."

Lt. Gen. Mitsuru Ushijima peered through his field glasses at the oncoming Americans. From Ushijima's observation point at Shuri Castle, the enemy looked like ants, moving in long columns, pausing every few hundred yards to reconnoiter and await their support vehicles.

Ushijima's staff had come up with a battle slogan to bolster the spirits of the Japanese 32nd Army at Okinawa:

One plane for one warship.
One boat for one ship.
One man for ten of the enemy or one tank.

For sure, the Americans would be protected by tanks. The trick was to separate the troops from their tanks, first with artillery, then at close range with special teams of tank-killers who would throw satchel charges and bundles of flaming rags beneath the armored vehicles. As tank crewmen tried to escape their burning vehicles, they would be shot or bayoneted. Without the covering fire of the tanks, the troops assaulting the slopes would be exposed and annihilated.

Ushijima knew that his garrison ultimately could not prevail over the Americans, but he didn't intend to waste the lives of his soldiers for nothing. He counseled his soldiers, "Do your utmost. The victory of the century lies in this battle."

In preparation for the massive bombardment that was surely coming, Ushijima had ordered the construction of a labyrinth of tunnels and underground spaces, some large enough to contain an entire company of infantry. For his own headquarters, a 150-foot-long tunnel was burrowed beneath Shuri Castle. This subterranean network allowed Ushijima to move troops where they were most urgently needed, and it afforded protection from the incessant pounding of ship and field gunfire.

The approaches to the hills were seeded with land mines and tank traps. At the foot of the slopes were trenches for machine gunners and mortar batteries. Further up were heavier machine gun nests, and on the reverse slopes more mortars and light artillery. Spotters were positioned on the high ground to call in artillery fire from Ushijima's big guns to the south of the lines.

At least that was the plan. Not until April 9 would Ushijima's plan be put to a test. That was the day the U.S. 96th Infantry Division arrived at a 1,000-yard-long outcropping on the western flank called Kakazu Ridge.

Col. Ed May, commander of the 383rd Regiment, studied the features of the pocked terrain 1,200 yards away. Kakazu Ridge didn't look all that formidable. It rose only about 300 feet and wasn't particularly steep. May's regiment was part of the 96th Division, which had just come to a grinding halt against the Japanese line. Taking the ridge would put the division in position to assault the more formidable objective, the Urasoe-Mura escarpment, about a thousand yards further south of Kakazu.

It looked to May as if he could take it with no more than four rifle companies. He'd keep two more in reserve and back them up with another full battalion. The only obstacle would be the deep gorge that ran the full length of the base of the ridge. The gorge was a natural tank trap, filled with trees and brush, which meant that May's troops would make the assault without covering armor.

Still not a problem, May concluded. Attacking before first light, they'd have the advantage of surprise, particularly if they went without preliminary artillery bombardment or air strikes. It would be a classic frontal assault, quick and efficient. May wasn't worried.

He should have been. Even through the lenses of his high-resolution binoculars, May wasn't seeing the true picture. What neither he nor the XXIV Corps commander, Maj. Gen. John Hodge, realized was that Kakazu Ridge and the adjoining hill, called Kakazu West, were honeycombed with tunnels and fortifications. An intricate network of overlapping mortar and artillery was buried in concrete-fortified positions, all part of the extensive underground defenses the 32nd Army commander, Lt. Gen. Ushijima, had ordered to be constructed weeks before the invasion. The reverse slopes of Kakazu Ridge were festooned with gun emplacements and tunnels that concealed the battle-toughened Japanese 13th Independent Infantry Battalion.

But Ed May was an optimistic—and ambitious—soldier. With the American advance halted against the Japanese line, May and his regiment would be the first to crack a key sector in the line. It was an opportunity he couldn't resist.

May launched the assault before dawn on April 9. Still in darkness, two rifle companies stormed up the slope of Kakazu Ridge, and two more ascended Kakazu West. Their only opposition was a few sentries, who were quickly bayoneted. As the first light of dawn hit the slope, May's troops were on both crests.

There was no time to celebrate. Almost immediately the length of the ridge erupted in a thunderous artillery barrage. A wave of Japanese soldiers emerged from tunnels and spider holes, charging directly through their own artillery fire. The newly arrived Americans found themselves in desperate hand-to-hand combat. Falling back to pockets, saddlebacks, and gullies, they tried to fight off the Japanese. Reinforcements headed up the hill but were pinned down by enfilading Japanese fire. Company commanders radioed urgent requests for covering fire so they could withdraw.

Colonel May wasn't ready to give up the high ground he had just won. Worried that he'd lose more men in a withdrawal, he gave the order to "hold the ridge at all costs." The fight dragged on into the afternoon. One by one, May's company officers were killed or wounded. Finally, beneath an artillery barrage and the smoke from a chemical-mortar battery, the battered soldiers made an agonizing retreat from Kakazu Ridge.

It was during the withdrawal that a twenty-three-year-old private first class named Ed Moskala earned the regiment's first Medal of Honor—posthumously. Moskala wiped out two enemy machine gun nests on the crest of the ridge. Fighting a rearguard action while his unit withdrew, the young soldier mowed down two dozen Japanese attackers. He returned to the crest of the ridge to drag wounded men back, then went back for more. On his second trip, he was cut down by machine gun fire.

The failed mission cost the 383rd Regiment 326 casualties. The next day, April 10, the unit was joined by the 381st Regiment in another assault on the ridge. This attack was preceded by heavy air strikes, an artillery barrage, and a bombardment by the heavy guns of the battleship *New York*.

None of it dislodged the Japanese. From the reverse slope of Kakazu Ridge, mortar shells continued to rain down on the advancing Americans, sometimes at the rate of one a second. The American commanders were perplexed. None had ever before seen the Japanese employ mortar and artillery with such deadly accuracy. The bitter battle lasted all that day and into the next until, once again, the bloodied American troops were forced to withdraw.

It was the same story up and down the line. The 96th Division was stalemated on the western end of Kakazu Ridge, and the Army 7th Division was making no better progress to the east. The Japanese defensive positions seemed impregnable to the heaviest naval bombardment or to the bombs and rockets of the close air support aircraft from the carriers.

One of the *kikusui* No. 1 pilots was an enlisted flight petty officer named Sata Omaichi. Before Omaichi had reached his target, his Mitsubishi JM2 "Jack" fighter was intercepted and shot down by a Hellcat fighter from the *Hornet*.

Omaichi, however, was not bent on suicide. After he ditched his stricken fighter, he was taken prisoner aboard the destroyer *Taussig*. Interrogators learned from the garrulous pilot that the next massed attack—*kikusui* No. 2—was set for April 11. This one, Omaichi boasted, would be the most intense attack ever and would wipe out the American fleet.

It was valuable information. Combined with intercepted messages from Admiral Ugaki's headquarters at Kanoya, it was enough to persuade Mitscher and Spruance to suspend ground attack missions over Okinawa on April 11. Mitscher ordered all his dive-bombers and torpedo planes defueled, disarmed, and parked on hangar decks. CAP coverage would be increased over the picket ships and the carrier task groups.

Then came the rain. Squalls and low visibility shut down air operations for both the Japanese and Americans. As the weather cleared on April 11, the kamikazes came out, but not in great numbers. It seemed to be a patchwork attack, with the apparent purpose of keeping pressure on the American fleet. Of the swarm of *tokko* aircraft sent southward, only a few reached their targets.

One was a Zero that threaded its way through the storm of fire thrown up by the carriers and escorts of Task Group 58.4. Skimming low on the water, the Zero swept in on the stern of the *Missouri*, aiming for what was considered the battleship's most vulnerable spot—the bridge. Instead, the kamikaze plowed into the rail of the starboard gun deck, shearing off the port wing and cart wheeling forward to crash behind a gun mount. Flames and debris showered *Missouri*'s deck, but the fires were quickly extinguished.

The *Missouri* had been lucky. The kamikaze's bomb didn't explode. The only real damage to the heavily armored battleship was a dented rail and scorched paint, and the only casualty was the kamikaze pilot, whose remains were found among the wreckage. He appeared to be a young man of eighteen or nineteen years of age.

The next morning Chaplain Roland Faulk conducted a funeral service for the dead Japanese. The service angered several of *Missouri*'s crew, who didn't think he ought to be rendering military honors to a deceased enemy.

Faulk went ahead with the funeral. "A dead Jap," the chaplain declared, "is no longer an enemy."

25 ▸ OHKA

Vice Adm. Matome Ugaki was frustrated. *Kikusui* No. 2 was behind schedule. He had been stymied first by the dismal weather, then by the lack of success his search planes had in locating the enemy carriers.

By dawn on April 12, Ugaki thought he had a clear picture of the enemy's disposition. Reconnaissance planes had located the American carrier force 60 to 80 miles east of the northern tip of Okinawa.

Ugaki had a special hatred for the American aircraft carriers. In one battle after another since the war began, he had seen the balance of the war tilting against Japan. He blamed it on the carriers. "I want to wipe them out by any means," he wrote in his diary.

Though his *tokko* warriors hadn't scored great successes yet against the enemy carriers, Ugaki believed they had caused significant damage to the enemy's heavy surface ships. According to the action reports, the attacks of April 6–8—*kikusui* No. 1—had sunk or seriously damaged sixty-nine American ships. These supposedly included two battleships, three cruisers, and three destroyers.

The Japanese estimates were wildly off the mark. In total, twenty-eight American ships had been hit, eight of them sunk. Two were the destroyers *Bush* and *Colhoun*, and five others—*Leutze*, *Morris*, *Mullany*, *Newcomb*, and *Bennett*—had taken such damage that they were out of the war. They were serious losses, but of no real consequence to the operating strength of the Fifth Fleet.

What worried Ugaki now was a recent report from Okinawa. Spotters had counted as many as 130 enemy fighters, mostly F4U Corsairs, based at the two captured airfields, Yontan and Kadena.

Being so close to the anchorages at Okinawa, the shore-based fighters posed an even more serious threat to the *tokko* raiders than the American carrier-based planes. Ugaki ordered that the two airfields on Okinawa receive special attention from the next wave of *tokkotai*.

Kikusui No. 2 finally took to the air in the late morning of April 12. For this massed attack, Ugaki had assembled 185 *tokko* aircraft, 150 fighters, and 45 torpedo planes.

First went the fighters, taking off in twenty-four-plane waves throughout the morning. Their mission would be to engage the enemy air patrols guarding the carriers and the anchorages at Okinawa. At midday, 129 more warplanes roared down the runway at Kanoya. Eight were Mitsubishi Betty bombers carrying *Ohka* rocket-boosted, human-guided missiles.

As wave after wave of warplanes headed toward their targets, Ugaki again settled himself in his command post to await the reports. As usual, he entered his trancelike state while the excited voices of men in the last minutes of their lives crackled over the speaker: "Stand by for the release of *Ohka*." Then, "Release—hit a battleship." Finally, "One battleship sunk."

Battleship? Listening to the terse radio transmissions, Matome Ugaki could barely contain his excitement. Could the reports be true?

The reports weren't true. Of the three battleships under attack by kamikazes—*New Mexico, Idaho,* and *Tennessee*—none had been sunk. On Turner's order, Rear Adm. Mort Deyo had moved his entire beach gunfire force—ten battlewagons, seven cruisers, and twelve destroyers—out to what was being called "Kamikaze Gulch," the open triangle of ocean bounded by Ie Shima, the Kerama Retto, and the shore of Okinawa. Once on station, Deyo arranged his ships in air defense formation to await the kamikazes.

The first wave showed up in the early afternoon. Once

again, they homed in on the northern picket station, RP1. The veteran picket destroyer *Cassin Young*'s luck ran out when a Val dive-bomber slithered through the hail of gunfire and slammed into her, knocking out the vital radar, damaging the fire room, and causing sixty casualties.

More kamikazes sank one of *Cassin Young*'s supporting gunboats, LCS-33, and knocked another out of action. Yet another kamikaze, chased by three CAP fighters, crashed alongside USS *Purdy*, a picket destroyer, knocking out her steering.

In the space of a few fiery minutes, the kamikazes had put every ship on RP1 out of action. Not for long, however. Two more destroyers, *Stanly* and *Lang*, were already racing across Kamikaze Gulch to take up duty at the critical RP1.

They, too, would be met by kamikazes. Among them were the Thunder Gods—the *Ohka* pilots from Kanoya's *Jinrai Butai*.

Lt. (jg) Saburo Dohi, like the other young Thunder Gods, had lived with the knowledge that he could be called to sortie at any moment. Dohi was from Osaka and was a graduate of the public school system. For the previous two weeks, the young officer had kept himself occupied improving the living quarters of his fellow *Ohka* pilots. They were billeted in an ancient primary school building with holes in the roof and windows broken out from air raids. Dohi and a group of junior pilots mopped floors, patched holes, and acquired straw mats and bamboo beds for the incoming airmen. Until the day came when they departed on their missions, they would have decent beds and quarters to sleep in.

For Saburo Dohi, that day, April 12, had come. He had been assigned as one of the eight Thunder Gods making *Ohka* human-guided bomb attacks against the U.S. fleet.

As the *Ohka*-carrying Betty bombers lumbered through the sky toward Okinawa, they spread out, each taking a different route to the targets. The bitter lesson from the sixteen-ship *Ohka* attack of

March 21 had been that, in a massed formation, the overloaded Bettys were like a flock of geese: easy to find, easy to kill. Every one of the bombers had been gunned down by American fighters.

If Dohi had any trepidation about that day's mission, it didn't show. While the bomber droned southward, the young pilot dozed on a makeshift cot until they were within range of American ships. Then, with great formality, Dohi tied his ceremonial white *hachi-maki* over his forehead. He shook hands with the aircraft commander, then climbed down through the bomb bay to the cockpit of the *Ohka*. Over the voice tube connection to the Betty crew, he announced that he was ready.

The explosive charge that was supposed to release the *Ohka* failed. The *Ohka* was still fastened to the mother ship. For another perilous minute, while the bomber flew into the jaws of the enemy fleet, Dohi waited in the cockpit of his rocket ship.

Finally a crewman yanked the manual release. The *Ohka* dropped away from the mother ship. Suspended by its tiny wings, the craft plunged earthward from 19,000 feet.

Peering through the flat front glass of his windshield, Saburo Dohi selected his target—a gray object four miles in the distance. The enemy warship appeared to be dead in the water. Nearing the target, Dohi ignited the three rocket boosters. The *Ohka* shot ahead, accelerating to nearly 600 miles per hour.

The destroyer *Mannert L. Abele* was already in trouble. On station at RP14, she had just been crashed by a Zero kamikaze plane. The explosion destroyed the engine room, broke both propeller shafts, and broke the ship's keel. Now, while *Abele*'s crew was struggling to save the ship, antiaircraft gunners picked up another incoming object.

It wasn't another Zero. This was something tiny, moving at high speed, slanting down toward the stationary destroyer. It didn't look like anything they'd ever seen before. Before *Abele*'s gunners could track the kamikaze—or whatever the thing was—it was too late. The object crashed into *Abele*'s hull just below her number one stack.

For the *Mannert L. Abele*, it was instant death. The explosion blew the destroyer in half. Within seconds both pieces of the shattered destroyer sank, taking eighty men to their deaths.

Abele had just earned a singular distinction: she was the first warship to be sunk by the mysterious new *Ohka* human-guided bomb. And Saburo Dohi had also earned a place in history: he was the first of the Thunder Gods to sink a major enemy warship.

Dohi would not be alone. In the sky over the other picket stations, his fellow Thunder Gods were making their own final flights.

*W*hat the hell is that?

None of the gunners on the picket destroyer USS *Stanly* had ever seen such a thing. The low-flying object looked like an aerial torpedo, hurtling at bullet speed across the water. *Stanly*'s gunners weren't able to touch it.

Before anyone could react, the object slammed into *Stanly*'s hull, hitting with such velocity that it passed completely through the destroyer's thin steel hull, not exploding until it had exited on the other side. The destroyer's bow was punctured and wrinkled, but the ship was still operational.

Before *Stanly*'s crew had recovered from the shock of the first attack, another of the weird objects appeared. This one was coming just as fast, low on the water, and it looked as if the pilot couldn't control it. Porpoising up and down, the craft skimmed over the destroyer's bow without making contact. The tiny craft went into a hard left turn and was trying to set up for another pass at the destroyer when the gunners finally found the mark. The object exploded into the water slightly more than a mile off *Stanly*'s port side.

Stanly had been lucky, but the destroyer *Lang*, which had joined *Stanly* for mutual fire support, was even luckier. *Lang*'s gunners had been busy blazing away at incoming enemy planes, flaming a Val that had attempted a bombing run, when they saw a blur of motion 500 yards to their port. Before they could react, the sleek, fast-moving object crashed into the ocean.

Minutes later, it happened again. Another blurry object just like the first one came zooming in. The high-speed craft went into a violent porpoising movement and crashed into the ocean off the port bow.

The tin can crews were mystified. Whatever the strange new aircraft were, they were apparently difficult to control at such speed. Both pilots had missed their targets.

Another lucky ship was the destroyer *Jeffers*, which had been ordered to RP14 to assist the stricken *Abele*. Unlike the previous crews, the men aboard *Jeffers* spotted the peculiar, stubby-winged aircraft while it was being launched from a Betty bomber high overhead. Watching the tiny craft gaining speed, they realized that *Jeffers* was its target.

Every antiaircraft gun on the destroyer opened as the guided bomb came at them, trailing a plume of smoke. Some of the gunfire appeared to hit the rocket ship, but it kept coming. At the last moment, *Jeffers*'s skipper gave the tin can hard left rudder.

It was enough to throw off the *Ohka* pilot's aim. The missile smacked the water fifty yards off *Jeffers*'s port rail, then ricocheted into the destroyer's starboard quarter without exploding. By a miracle *Jeffers* escaped with only slight damage.

It was the Americans' first close encounter with the *Ohka*. Stanly's skipper, Cmdr. R. S. Harlan, reported, "From the scraps of the jet-propelled plane that were left on board, we observed that they are constructed largely of plywood and balsa, with a very small amount of metal, most of that being extremely light aluminum."

Intelligence officers were already piecing together the parts of the puzzle. An example of the piloted bomb had been captured intact a few days ago at Yontan airfield on Okinawa, with a cherry blossom emblem on its nose. Intercepted Japanese message traffic referred to an operation involving bombers "equipped for cherry blossom attacks."

The *Ohka* quickly received an American code name—*baka*. In Japanese it meant "idiot."

L ate that afternoon, April 12, the Betty bomber that had carried Saburo Dohi's *Ohka* thumped back down on the runway at Kanoya after a nearly six-hour round trip. The Betty was the only survivor of the eight *Ohka*-carrying mother ships that had departed at midday. One never made it to the target area. The other six were shot down after launching their *Ohka* rocket planes.

The crew of the lone Betty bomber brought with them the electrifying news of Dohi's success. They had watched his *Ohka* streak downward toward a battleship, six miles in the distance. Minutes later, a column of black smoke belched 500 meters from the ocean where the enemy battleship had been. It was glorious!

What the bomber crew identified as a battleship was, in fact, the destroyer *Mannert L. Abele*. But it didn't matter. After all the discouraging failures, Dohi's success was a hugely symbolic victory. The Thunder Gods had sunk their first ship.

What none of them knew was that it was also their last.

Saburo Dohi's place was quickly taken by a new arrival. Since the beginning of the *kikusui* operations, there was a constant flow of new faces at Kanoya. Those who had departed on one-way *tokko* missions now numbered in the hundreds.

The mood among the pilots waiting for their final flights was a mixture of melancholy and pride. With the arrival of spring, some volunteered to help the local population, who were mostly farmers, with their harvesting. The villagers reciprocated by bringing them gifts—eggs, chickens, even a cow.

One day a mother and daughter came to Kanoya to visit the young woman's fiancé. They hadn't heard from him recently and they were concerned. What they didn't know was that he was a *tokko* volunteer. He had made his last flight a few days before. The pilot's best friend was at a loss what to tell the two women, so he sought the advice of Cmdr. Tadashi Nakajima.

The senior officer thought it would be too cruel to tell the truth. The women were informed that the young man had left a few days before to go to an advance island base. They were showed the room that had recently been occupied by the departed pilot. The young woman touched the bamboo bed on which her fiancé had recently slept. "No further questions were asked," recalled Commander Nakajima, "but they seemed instinctively to understand what had happened."

26 ▸ GUNSLINGERS

Lt. Mark Orr peered into the blackness beyond the Hellcat's nose, trying to pick up the bogey. It was like staring into an inkwell. The visibility was down to four miles, the sea and the night sky blending into a horizonless void. Orr and his wingman, Ens. Tom Stixrud, had been on station over the carrier task force when the FIDO sent them on a hot vector after the bogey.

It was nerve-wracking. Even with precise radar vectoring to within close range of the bogey, the night fighter pilots still had to get close enough to actually *see* the target before they could shoot him. Night air-to-air intercepts were a dangerous and demanding form of combat, wholly different from the swirling dogfights of the daytime. Night fighter pilots trusted their lives to their instruments, constantly fighting the vertigo induced by the lack of visual references. Every pinpoint of light—star, gunfire, ship's light, aircraft engine exhaust—provided a false clue that could lure them into the black ocean.

Someone had to do it. More and more the Japanese were turning to night attacks. Under cover of darkness, raiders slipped past CAP pilots and destroyer lookouts. Radar was the only means of detection, and shipboard fighter directors vectored the night CAP airplanes to intercept the incoming bogeys. The night fighters used their own onboard radar for the final intercept of the mostly invisible enemy. On most nights the system worked splendidly. Sometimes it didn't work at all.

The men who flew the night fighters were segregated from the air group by the clock and by culture. The other pilots—the day fliers—viewed them with awe and suspicion. Anyone who actually *volunteered* for night carrier duty was, by definition, certifiably weird. The night fighters went by various names—"Gloomies," "Bat-CAPs," and "red goggle gang," so called because of the goggles they wore to protect their night vision.

The Gloomies aboard *Intrepid* were led by Orr, a thirty-year-old Texan who formerly had been an instrument instructor in the training command. Orr and his pilots lived like nocturnal animals, sleeping by day, hunting bogeys by night.

Orr and Stixrud were 40 miles east of the task force, closing on the bogey, when Orr picked him up on his onboard radar. The shadowy silhouette of a Betty bomber loomed out of the darkness ahead of them. Like a pair of disciplined hunting dogs, the Hellcat pilots went after him, alternating firing passes. Stixrud attacked from behind, then pulled away as Orr came in on a 45-degree flat run from the starboard side. When Orr broke off, Stixrud came back in to blaze away at the Betty's left side.

It was a cold and efficient exercise, lasting less than three minutes. Stixrud delivered the final burst of machine gun fire. An orange ball of fire punctuated the night sky. Sheathed in flame, the Betty rolled onto its left side and plunged into the ocean.

Twenty-five minutes later, Orr was chasing another bogey while Stixrud remained at the CAP station. Orr again slid in close behind the bogey—another low-flying Betty bomber—and opened fire. He could see his bullets converging like tentacles on the Betty, but the Japanese plane somehow kept flying.

As Orr kept shooting, his .50-caliber gun barrels overheated. Now half of them were no longer firing. Exasperated, he kicked the Hellcat's rudder left and right, trying to spray the reduced machine gun fire across the Japanese bomber.

Then came a warning from the FIDO. The two airplanes—Orr's Hellcat and the Japanese Betty—were flying directly into the fleet's antiaircraft screen. Orr had to break it off before he was hit by the ships' gunners.

In the next second, as if on signal, gunfire from the fleet escort ships erupted around both airplanes.

By now Mark Orr was a driven man. Ignoring the flak, he pulled in close enough to the Japanese bomber to see the orange flickers from the engine exhausts. Before he could fire again, a destroyer fired an antiaircraft burst directly in front of him. Orr zoomed over the top of the destroyer, still chasing the Betty, which was now headed directly for the carrier *Yorktown*.

Orr stayed on the Betty's tail, spraying bullets with his three still-firing guns. By now both the bomber's engines were ablaze. Just as it seemed inevitable that it would crash into *Yorktown*, the Betty abruptly nosed over and hit the ocean.

Now Orr was the only target left, and the ships' gunners kept blazing away. Flying at 50 feet off the water, Orr zoomed through the hail of antiaircraft fire, somehow exiting the area without taking a hit.

It had been a hell of a mission, but it wasn't over. The climax of a night fighter mission was the night carrier landing. With his eyes fixed on the tiny illuminated stick figure of the landing signal officer on the edge of the flight deck, Orr landed the Hellcat back down on the darkened *Intrepid*. With adrenaline still surging in his veins, he made his way down to the Grim Reapers' ready room, eager to tell someone what it was like out there.

Nobody cared. The day fighter pilots were busy watching a movie in the ready room. They weren't interested in the exploits of the weird Gloomies.

As much as any man on the Grim Reaper roster, Lt. Wally Schub flew, talked, and looked like the Hollywood version of a fighter pilot. He had a dark mustache and wore the practiced gaze of a hard-eyed gunslinger. As one of Tommy Blackburn's "irregulars" in the VF-17 days in the Solomons, Schub had gunned down two Japanese aircraft. Since then, he had been waiting for the day when he could add three more and be an official "ace"—a fighter pilot with five enemy kills to his credit.

Now it was a few minutes past noon on April 12, 1945, and Schub was leading one of the three VF-10 Grim Reaper CAP divisions over the radar picket stations. On the most dangerous of the stations, RP1, was the destroyer *Cassin Young*, whose fighter directors were frantically vectoring the CAP fighters toward the incoming blips on their radars. The raiders were coming directly for the picket ships, flying down the corridor of airspace from Kyushu to Okinawa that the tin can sailors were calling "Kamikaze Alley."

Schub was the first to spot the bogeys. There were fifteen of them, Val and Kate dive-bombers, spread out in a loose gaggle low on the water. Directly behind Schub's division came another Grim Reaper division, this one led by a Marine, 1st Lt. W. A. "Nick" Nickerson. Nickerson was one of four Marine Corsair pilots, formerly deployed aboard *Wasp*, who had volunteered to augment *Intrepid*'s Corsair fighter squadron.

The lumbering Japanese dive-bombers were fat targets. On his first pass, Schub flamed two of the hapless Vals. On Schub's wing, twenty-one-year-old Ens. John "Barney" Godwin shot down another, and Schub's second two-plane section—Lt. (jg) Whit Wharton, another VF-17 Jolly Roger veteran, and Ens. Walt Brauer—sent three more down in flames.

Right behind them came Nickerson, shooting down two Vals while his Marine wingman, 2nd Lt. H. O. Taylor, knocked down another. Ens. Fred Meyer, leading the second section, turned his guns on a Val dive-bomber and a Nakajima fixed-gear "Nate" fighter, sending both down in flames. Another Tail End Charlie, Ens. Ed Deutschman, added one more Val to the tally.

The one-sided dogfight was over in minutes. Of the fifteen kamikazes in the formation, twelve had been blown out of the sky, and the three lucky survivors had disappeared. None of the Corsairs had taken any hits, but the two divisions were now scattered.

As Nickerson was making his way back to the *Intrepid*, he spotted another swarm of ten Japanese planes—a mix of Jill torpedo bombers and Judy and Val dive-bombers. They were circling at 5,000 feet, about to pounce on the picket destroyer *Purdy* and her gunboat escorts. With Ed Deutschman on his wing, Nickerson swept down from directly overhead, splashing one of the Jill torpedo bombers, then going for the Judy dive-bombers.

Too late, Nickerson realized that these Judys were different. Unlike most of the kamikaze-configured planes, these had tail gunners. Nickerson saw the winking orange flashes of the 7.7-millimeter machine guns. An instant later he felt the bullets thudding into his engine. A sheet of oil blacked out his windshield.

With no forward visibility, Nickerson dove through the enemy formation, praying he wouldn't hit one of them or take more bullets. Directly behind him came his Tail End Charlie, Walt Brauer, who flamed one of the Judys in passing.

Nickerson's engine, punctured by the tail gunners' bullets, was out of oil. One way or the other, he was going into the water. He had only one decision left to make: ditch or bail out?

Despite the oil-smeared windshield, he opted for ditching. Flying on instruments, his only view out the side of the canopy, Nickerson glided the Corsair down to the wave tops. The fighter hit, skipped once, then lurched to a halt, still upright. The Marine scrambled out and, minutes later, was hauled aboard one of the LCS gunboats escorting *Purdy*.

The leader of the third Grim Reaper division was a heavy-set lieutenant named Frank Jackson. Jackson's division had been vectored to intercept another wave of kamikazes, but as they closed on the bogeys at 20,000 feet, Jackson realized that they weren't slow-moving dive-bombers and torpedo planes. They were

238 FLOATING CHRYSANTHEMUMS

sleek Oscar and Zero fighters, and they were flying cover for the kamikazes.

The fight was on. As Jackson and his wingmen, Lt. (jg) Tommy Tucker, 1st Lt. G. A. Krumm, and 2nd Lt. H. F. Newell, the last two both Marines, swung in behind the Japanese planes, they realized that these weren't the usual unskilled kamikaze airmen. Three tight-turning Zeroes whipped into a pursuit curve on Jackson's tail, their cannons blazing. Jackson was saved by his wingman Tucker, who flamed one of the Zeroes and put enough rounds into the other two to drive them off Jackson's tail.

Seconds later, Jackson was locked on to the tail of another Zero, but before he could open fire, the Zero pitched up in a steep climb. With Jackson in pursuit, the Zero executed a sharp wingover turn to the left, while Jackson mirrored the maneuver, turning to the right. The two fighters swung back toward each other in a head-on pass, guns firing.

Jackson saw the ominous orange flashes from the Zero's machine guns and wing-mounted cannons. He could also see his tracers pouring into the Zero's blunt nose and its wing roots. Smoke belched from the Zero.

The Zero pilot had had enough. He dove for the ocean with Jackson still in pursuit. With the East China Sea rising to meet him, Jackson hauled the Corsair's nose out of the dive just in time to see the Zero exploding into the water.

Minutes later, Jackson had rejoined the melee above and was on the tail of another Zero. His guns had overheated during the mano a mano with the first Zero, and now only one of the six .50-calibers was firing. He was popping away at the hard-turning Zero when, too late, he glimpsed something dark blue in his peripheral vision. It was a stubby FM-2 Wildcat fighter, one of a four-plane division that was chasing the same Zero.

In the next instant Jackson felt the sickening crunch of the two fighters' wings coming together. With his airplane out of control, Jackson flung the canopy open and clambered over the side.

Seconds later, he was descending to the sea beneath his parachute canopy.

After floating for a while in his life raft, Jackson was picked up uninjured by the destroyer *Hudson*. The pilot of the Wildcat, a young ensign named C. J. Jansen from the escort carrier *Petrof Bay*, wasn't as lucky. His fighter had tumbled out of the sky like a broken toy, and Jansen was never found.

While the air battle swirled above the radar picket ships, another division of Grim Reaper Corsairs was flying TCAP—target combat air patrol—over Tokuno. The VF-10 executive officer, Lt. Cmdr. John Sweeny, had spotted a formation of Zeroes headed south at 17,000 feet. Sweeny led his division in a climbing 360-degree turn, swinging onto the Zeroes' tails.

It should have been John Sweeny's moment of glory. Sweeny's pursuit curve led him into a perfect firing position. With the shape of a Japanese fighter fixed in his gun sight, he squeezed the trigger.

Nothing happened. Sweeny rechecked his armament switch, making sure it was in the on position, and squeezed again. Nothing.

Sweeny kept trying. He engaged another Zero with the same result. The damned guns wouldn't fire. Seething with frustration, Sweeny wouldn't quit. He locked on to the tails of five different Zeroes without firing a shot.

Sweeny's wingman, Ens. Jack Twedell, was having no such problem. Chasing a Zero through a wide right turn, Twedell hammered it with his machine guns until it burst into flames.

Meanwhile, the leader of Sweeny's second two-plane section, Lt. (jg) Les Gray, was entering the record books. Gray was a veteran of the old Grim Reaper Hellcat squadron and already had four kills to his credit.

With the fierce determination of a man about to become an ace, Gray followed a Zero through a split-S—rolling inverted and pulling through the bottom half of a loop. Bottoming out, he put another burst into the Zero. The Japanese pilot did another split-S, pulling out at wave-top height, then abruptly crashing into the water.

With his status as ace now official, Gray wasn't finished. He spotted a lone Zero exiting to the north. With the Corsair's superior speed, Gray finally caught up with him over the Japanese island of Amami Oshima, shooting the Zero down with a two-second burst into the cockpit.

The sky was clear of enemy fighters. Sweeny, filled with disgust over his nonfiring machine guns, was calling it a day. With his wingman in tow he headed back to *Intrepid*, leaving Les Gray and Ens. Jack Halbe on the CAP station over Tokuno.

For Gray and Halbe, it was almost a welcome respite after the heart-pounding engagement with the Zeroes. CAP duty again became what it was most of the time—an exercise in tedium.

The tedium lasted exactly thirty minutes. Then it was interrupted by a burst of gunfire.

N either Gray nor Halbe saw it coming. From out of the sun a solitary enemy fighter—an elliptical-winged Mitsubishi JM2 Jack fighter—came swooping down on them.

Halbe's first clue was the impact of the 7.7-millimeter machine gun rounds. Bullets thunked into the cockpit, and he felt a searing pain in his leg. The forward fuel tank shattered, spewing raw gasoline into his face. Halbe was saved from instant death by the armor plate around his seat. By some miracle the streaming fuel didn't light off and burn him alive.

Les Gray was already turning hard into the Japanese fighter, trying to throw him off Halbe's tail. Halbe's Corsair had gone into a spin. A bullet had gone through his knee, and another had torn through his parachute. Bailing out wasn't a good option, but neither was ditching.

It didn't matter. The out-of-control fighter was flopping through the sky like a shotgunned pigeon. Halbe struggled against the rotation of the spin, which was pressing him into the seat. Finally he was able to jettison the canopy, then haul himself over the edge of the cockpit and into the slipstream.

Tumbling through the air, Halbe yanked the rip cord. The canopy fluttered, then popped open, and Halbe saw that one entire panel of the chute had been shot away. The rest of the chute held together. Halbe made a larger-than-normal splash, coming down in the ocean close to the shoreline of Japanese-owned Amami Oshima.

Les Gray was trying to even the score, but the Jack pilot who'd shot Halbe down wasn't sticking around. The Japanese fighter was fast, nearly as fast as the Corsair, and the pilot's diving pass on Halbe left him with plenty of excess speed. Gray watched the Jack continue its dive down to treetop level and streak over Amami Oshima at high speed, heading north. Gray squeezed off a few rounds at his tail, mostly for the hell of it, then turned back to look for his wingman, who by now was crawling into his life raft.

Gray flew low cover over Halbe's raft, ready to strafe any Japanese boats that might be tempted to come after him. After an hour, a Dumbo rescue seaplane splashed down and hauled the wounded pilot aboard.

L t. (jg) Phil Kirkwood, a calm, cold-eyed young man from New Jersey, was another VF-10 veteran who had four enemy kills to his credit. Since arriving at Okinawa aboard *Intrepid*, he'd scored again, officially joining the list of aces. Kirkwood had a special incentive: a businessman back in his hometown had offered to pay $100 for each enemy plane Kirkwood shot down.

At midafternoon on April 12, Kirkwood was leading another CAP flight over the embattled picket ships. His wingman, Ens. Norwald "Dick" Quiel, was a Tail End Charlie who had already figured out that flying on Kirkwood's wing was a good deal. Not only did Kirkwood have a knack for finding bandits, but sometimes he even shared them with his wingmen. Today was one of those days.

They were at 16,000 feet when Kirkwood called out a bogey 10 miles on their nose, 3,000 feet below them. Closing rapidly, they tagged the bogey as a bandit—a two-engine Betty bomber. Kirkwood fired first, getting hits on the right engine, but his excess speed carried him past the Betty.

It was Quiel's turn. Making a flat run on the bomber's starboard side, he put another long burst into the right engine, setting it ablaze. The doomed Betty rolled into a spiraling dive to the ocean.

Quiel's kill was the last in what had been a day of spectacular air-to-air engagements. The Corsair pilots landed back aboard *Intrepid* flushed with victory and full of themselves. The atmosphere in the smoke-filled, low-ceilinged ready room crackled with excitement as the pilots jabbered and gestured, reliving moments of death and near-death.

April 12 was a day for the record books. In a single sortie, three *Intrepid* CAP flights had gunned down thirteen Vals, one Judy, one Nate fighter, one Jill, and six Zeroes—a total of twenty-two confirmed kills, with one more probable. Every one of the twelve pilots had scored at least one victory.

Then came the divisions led by Gray and Kirkwood, who contributed four more kills, giving the Grim Reapers a total of twenty-six enemy planes downed for the day. And any doubts anyone had had about the Marines who recently joined the squadron were put to rest. Nine of the day's kills were shared by four Marine pilots.

A more sobering statistic was that three Corsairs were lost. Nickerson had been gunned down by a Judy tail gunner, and Jackson bailed out after a collision with a friendly fighter. Jack Halbe had been ambushed in a high-side attack out of the sun. The good news was that all three pilots were okay. Each was now a guest aboard the tin can that had plucked him out of the water.

The Japanese pilot who shot down Jack Halbe, they figured,

was not one of the amateurs they had been fighting. He had pulled off a perfectly executed hit-and-run, picking Halbe off with one quick burst, then exiting without ever taking a hit. On some level beyond their gut hatred of the Japanese, the Americans could almost feel admiration for the enemy pilot's skill.

Almost, but not quite. What they felt most of all was a desire for a rematch. Next time they'd shoot the little bastard out of the sky.

One pilot in the ready room didn't feel like celebrating. Grim Reaper executive officer John Sweeny would not forget the day he *should* have become an ace. Fixed in Sweeny's memory were the dark shapes of five Zeroes, one after another, superimposed on his gun sight, his finger squeezing the trigger, hearing only the silence of his nonfiring .50-caliber guns.

A bitter pill, but it was the nature of aerial warfare. Sweeny had been around long enough to know that fate treated fighter pilots capriciously. Your shot at glory came and went in the space of a heartbeat. Sweeny had missed his shot.

27 ▸ BLACK FRIDAY

In his headquarters beneath Shuri Castle, General Ushijima could hear the steady pounding of the heavy artillery. The great excavated space was deep enough that it was virtually impregnable to any shellfire the Americans could deliver. Still, the thunder of the shellfire was rattling every fixture in the space.

Ushijima could also hear the sounds of combat around his conference table. The two senior officers on his staff, Lieutenant General Cho and Colonel Yahara, were at it again. Cho had consumed more than his usual ration of sake, and his voice was more strident than ever. They should stop this defensive campaign, Cho insisted. It was time to launch a massive counterattack.

During the past two weeks, Yahara had become increasingly isolated in his views. Almost to a man, the other staff officers were leaning toward Cho's side. Japanese warriors shouldn't be allowing the enemy to advance on his own terms, dictating the time and place of battle. It was an echo of the same argument the hard-liners were making in Tokyo.

In his usual manner Ushijima nodded, listening to both sides. Until recently he had sided with the calm and rational arguments of Yahara. But the battle was taking its toll on Ushijima. He was losing men and ground at an unsustainable rate.

In the fiery rhetoric of General Cho, Ushijima was hearing the seductive call of the samurai: *Repel the invaders. Hurl them back into the sea. Better to die while attacking than to be hunted down like fleeing animals.*

Ushijima let himself be persuaded. Over Colonel Yahara's

vehement protests, the general gave the order: prepare the 32nd Army for a counterattack.

General Cho would be the architect of the operation. It would be a night assault, the kind of engagement at which Japanese infantry excelled. Success would hinge on quickly infiltrating the American lines, mixing positions, preventing the enemy from using his heavy artillery.

According to Cho's plan, six battalions of infantry—three of the Imperial Japanese Army's 62nd Division and three of the 24th—would penetrate the American line, hitting the U.S. 7th Division on the eastern front and the 96th Division on the west. The Japanese troops would slice through the American line, advance to within four miles of Kadena airfield, then take cover in the hundreds of tombs. By daylight they would emerge to attack the rearguard American units.

Like General Cho himself, the plan was wildly optimistic. At the last minute, Colonel Yahara was able to reduce the assault forces to four battalions. Even the commanders of the advance battalions, sensing the inevitable extermination of their units, held back some of their forces.

General Cho's plan was complete. The counterattack would launch after nightfall on April 12.

I t began with a thirty-minute artillery barrage. The shelling was the heaviest single Japanese artillery bombardment of the war—over 3,000 rounds raining down on the American units clinging to their positions on the western flank.

Following the artillery barrage, Cho's troops surged from their concealed positions. It was a reversal of roles—the Japanese now charging into the lines of the entrenched Americans. Japanese troops swarmed over Kakazu Ridge and Kakazu West, attacking the same U.S. units—the infantry regiments of the 96th Division—that they had been repulsing the previous days.

Alerted by the Japanese artillery barrage, U.S. fire control batteries called in the big guns of the warships offshore—*Colorado*, *Nevada, San Francisco, Biloxi*, and two destroyers. The barrage from the warships rained down on the exposed Japanese units. Caught in the open and illuminated by star shells fired from offshore destroyers, the first wave of Japanese attackers was mowed down.

One of the American heroes of the night battle was a twenty-two-year-old army technical sergeant named Beauford Anderson. With Japanese troops overrunning their position, Anderson and his mortar squad were trapped in the saddle between Kakazu Ridge and Kakazu West.

Anderson ordered his men to take cover in a tomb while he fought off the advancing enemy troops. With his carbine out of ammunition, he grabbed an unexploded Japanese mortar round and hurled it back at the oncoming enemy. To Anderson's astonishment, the shell exploded, killing several Japanese and halting their charge.

But only for a short while. With the Japanese again advancing toward him, Anderson broke out a case of his own mortar shells. Yanking the safety pin of a shell, he banged it on a rock to arm it, then threw the shell at the charging Japanese. He threw another, then reloaded his carbine. Alternately firing the weapon and hurling mortar shells, he forced the enemy to withdraw.

When daylight came, twenty-five Japanese soldiers lay dead outside the tomb. Anderson himself was wounded by shrapnel. For his actions, he would receive the Medal of Honor.

The fighting subsided during the day as each side took shelter beneath artillery barrages. At nightfall on April 13, the battle resumed. Again Japanese squads tried infiltrating the American lines. Again the battlefield was illuminated by ship-fired star shells, and the Japanese were repulsed in savage, close-quarters fighting.

By dawn on April 14, it was clear that the counterattack was a failure. The impermeability of the Shuri Line extended in both directions. The Japanese were even less successful attacking from the south than the Americans had been from the north. In the gathering daylight, the survivors of the decimated Japanese battalions crept back to their defensive line. The bodies of hundreds of their fellow soldiers littered the northern slopes of the line, a net loss of almost four entire battalions. Fewer than a hundred Americans had been killed.

Colonel Yahara, whose initial assessment had been proven correct, was disgusted. The architect of the failed assault, General Cho, remained unhumbled. He continued to insist that offensive actions, even if they failed, were preferable to a slow defeat.

No one was willing to argue. In the gloomy atmosphere of the Japanese underground headquarters, the ancient code of *bushido* still had a romantic appeal.

While the battle in the south of Okinawa was stalemated at the Shuri Line, it was a different story in the north. The 6th Marine Division had encountered only sporadic resistance as they raced to the northern tip of Okinawa.

Still to be taken was the bulbous Motobu Peninsula, jutting from the upper west coast of the island. The 10-mile-long, 8-mile-wide peninsula was densely forested, with a 1,200-foot-high pinnacle in the southwest quadrant called Yae-dake. It was here that the Japanese defenders, led by veteran commander Col. Take-hido Udo, would make their stand.

Udo was a shrewd tactician. His defensive network on Motobu Peninsula was even more intricate than the tunnels and rabbit warrens of the Shuri Line in the south. As the Marines advanced across the peninsula, Udo's troops waited in ambush, firing from concealed positions, then vanished like ethereal ghosts back into the dense foliage.

Japanese snipers became adept at identifying the officers of American units. Maj. Bernard Green, a battalion commander of the 4th Regiment, was talking to his operations and intelligence officers when he was picked off by an unseen shooter. It was a lesson the Marines learned quickly: anyone carrying a pistol instead of a carbine, waving a map, or pointing with his finger as if giving directions was a sniper's target.

By April 15, the Marines were closing in on the summit of Yae-dake. The fighting grew more intense as they neared the crest. As the XXIV Corps had already discovered in the south of the island, the Japanese on the Motobu Peninsula had made the most of the terrain, concealing their positions in a honeycomb of tunnels and caves.

Company A of the 1st Battalion was the first to gain the summit but was pushed back by a fierce Japanese mortar and small-arms attack. After calling in a heavy artillery barrage, they again assaulted the crest of Yae-dake, taking heavy casualties. Nearly out of ammunition, they were forced to hunker down while Marines below organized a frantic hand-to-hand resupply chain.

The resupply came just in time. At nightfall, the Japanese launched a screaming, suicidal *banzai* counterattack. With the help of artillery, the Marines stopped the attackers, killing seventy-five of them at close quarters.

Finally Yae-dake was secure. For the next two days, the Marines mopped up the rest of the peninsula. In a ravine on the slope of Yae-dake they stumbled upon Colonel Udo's exquisitely concealed headquarters, outfitted with radio and telephone communications and connected to a network of caves.

But Udo was gone. Instead of sacrificing himself *bushido*-style, the colonel had slipped away to fight as a guerrilla. Like a mythical Japanese warrior, Udo faded into legend, never to be found.

The battle for Okinawa wasn't front-page news back home. The Pacific war was being upstaged by the historic events in Europe. The Red Army was at the gates of Berlin. American and Soviet troops had linked up on the banks of the Elbe River. The end of the Third Reich was at hand. Okinawa was just another island in the Pacific war.

On Friday, April 13, a day later than in Washington, came a

flash that eclipsed all the war news. Everyone aboard the ships of the Fifth Fleet—sailors, officers, gunners, aviators—stopped in midstride.

The announcement blared over every loudspeaker: "Attention, all hands! President Roosevelt is dead. Repeat, our supreme commander, President Roosevelt, is dead."

The news had the same impact as losing a parent. Roosevelt had been elected an unprecedented four times. For teenage GIs still not old enough to vote, he was the only president most could remember. He was a larger-than-life father figure whom they credited with lifting the nation from the Depression and guiding it through the crisis of war. In the minds of many servicemen, it seemed that the country was leaderless. Who was the bespectacled little man with the twangy voice, Harry Truman? How could he fill the shoes of a giant like Franklin Roosevelt?

Of all the services, the Navy was most closely identified with Roosevelt. Appointed assistant secretary of the Navy by President Woodrow Wilson in 1913, Roosevelt worked to expand the Navy and founded the U.S. Naval Reserve. Roosevelt had sent the Navy and Marines to intervene during skirmishes in Central America and the Caribbean. Roosevelt had steered the Navy through World War I, and it was Roosevelt who had fought against plans to dismantle it after that war.

To the Japanese high command, the death of Roosevelt meant something else: it was a direct result of the war. The next day propaganda leaflets were scattered around U.S. positions at Okinawa.

American Officers and Men:
We must express our deep regret over the death of President Roosevelt. The "American Tragedy" is now raised here at Okinawa with his death. You must have seen 70% of your carriers and 735 of your B's [presumably

*surface warfare ships] sink or be damaged causing
150,000 casualties. Not only the late president but anyone
else would die in the excess of worry to hear such an
annihilative damage. The dreadful loss that led your late
leader to death will make you orphans on this island. The
Japanese special attack corps will sink your vessels to the
last destroyer. You will witness it realized in the near future.*

The weary Marines and soldiers on Okinawa got a good laugh
from the leaflets. *Orphans on this island?* It was a rare moment of
comic relief. Reading Japanese propaganda leaflets was almost as
much fun as listening to Tokyo Rose.

Most fighter pilots weren't superstitious. To Lt. Mark Orr, the
night of Friday, April 13 was no different from any other
night off Okinawa—black, horizonless, vertigo-inducing. He was
doing what he usually did on such nights—chasing another bogey
through the darkness.

This one was low, skimming the wave tops. More and more,
the Japanese night attackers were coming in on the deck. By now
they'd figured out that the ships' radars wouldn't pick them up
until they were almost close enough to make their attack. The
night fighters were reluctant to engage them that low because they
risked flying into the water.

Orr radioed that he had spotted his bogey. It was at low altitude,
heading directly for the carrier task group. Orr eased the Hellcat
down to the bogey's altitude, close to the water, and slid in behind
him.

In the red-lighted CIC compartment aboard the screening destroyer, the FIDO was following the intercept on his radar. The
two blips on the screen looked like glowworms in a column. With
each sweep of the cursor, they came closer together. The Hellcat
was gaining on the bogey, almost close enough to fire. Any minute
now, he'd report that the bogey was dead.

The FIDO waited for the call. Nothing came over the radio. In the next sweep on the radar, the blips had merged. On the next sweep, they were gone.

The bogey *and* the Hellcat had vanished from the radar screen.

The director radioed the night fighter pilot. There was no reply. Perplexed, he stared at the empty scope. What the hell had happened? It was if the blackened ocean had swallowed up both aircraft. Did Orr shoot down the bogey before inadvertently hitting the water? Did the airplanes collide?

The answer was never learned. No trace was ever found of Mark Orr or the bogey.

The next morning, April 14, Lt. Gen. Simon Buckner stomped onto the hard-packed beach at Hagushi, bringing most of his staff with him. His new command post ashore was nearly finished. He would no longer be sharing space aboard Kelly Turner's flagship, *Eldorado*.

Buckner's patience was running out. His infantry divisions had ground to a halt in the south. No amount of sea, land, or air bombardment seemed able to dislodge the Japanese from their burrowed positions. In his booming, resonant voice, the white-haired general made it clear to everyone within earshot that he wanted this campaign to start moving again.

Buckner gave the order that every available infantry unit was to be assembled for an all-out frontal assault, to begin on April 19. To back up the 7th and 96th Divisions, he would bring a third division, the 27th Infantry, out of reserve. Ironically, it had been the 27th Division commander who was fired by the Marine general, Howlin' Mad Smith, at Saipan because Smith didn't think the 27th was carrying its weight. It was the incident that had ignited the most recent feud between the Army and the Marine Corps, and, like a persistent headache, it was affecting decisions at Okinawa.

Now the 27th Division was taking over from the 96th on the

western flank, which included the bloody Kakazu Ridge. The 96th would take the center of the front, and the 7th Division would attack the eastern end of the line.

The plan was straightforward. By sheer force of firepower and numbers, Buckner intended to break the enemy line. No flanking maneuvers, no amphibious landings behind enemy positions, no pincer attacks. Such tactics weren't the style of the son of a Confederate general. Simon Buckner's offensive would be an all-out frontal assault.

The offensive began with the heaviest land-based artillery barrage of the Pacific war. Nineteen thousand shells rained onto the Japanese positions along the Shuri Line. While the cloud of smoke and dust was still rising, a bombardment from six battleships, six cruisers, and six destroyers pounded the same positions. Then came strikes by 650 carrier-based aircraft dropping bombs, firing rockets into cave entrances, and hammering the line with machine guns.

The three assault divisions moved out. Their progress was mostly unopposed—at first. While the line was still partly obscured by the dust from the bombardment, the Japanese slipped back into the positions they had temporarily evacuated. With machine gun fire, mortars, and artillery, they began mowing down the Americans.

The offensive faltered. On the eastern flank, units of the 7th Division, led by flame-throwing tanks, made it to the crest of a knife-edged feature called Skyline Ridge. Minutes later, they were hurled back by Japanese counterattacking from the reverse slope. Other units of the 7th Division were pinned down by murderous mortar and artillery fire in a swale called Rocky Crags.

Not even the flame-throwing tanks were able to root out the Japanese defenders. They kept popping out from spider holes, hurling satchel charges and grenades into the faces of the Americans.

In the middle of the line, the advance of the 96th Division

ground to a halt. The only success came from the much-maligned 27th Division, which succeeded in making an end run around the deadly Kakazu Ridge and reaching the next objective, the Urasoe-Mura escarpment. But the simultaneous frontal attack on Kakazu Ridge was again repulsed, and the entire division's gains were lost.

A force of armored vehicles—thirty M4A3 Sherman tanks, flame-throwing tanks, and self-propelled howitzers—was hurled into the fray. Rumbling through Kakazu Gorge and onto the reverse slope of the ridge, they ran into a firestorm. Japanese popped out of spider holes to blind the tank crews with smoke charges and fling satchel charges under the vehicles. Others ran up to attach magnetic demolition charges. Antitank guns blasted them from concealed positions.

It was a disaster. Separated from their protecting infantry units, the armored vehicles were picked off one by one. Only eight tanks escaped the massacre, making it the worst loss of armored vehicles in the entire campaign.

By afternoon, heavy thunderstorms were drenching the battle zone, making the barren ground slippery and adding to the difficulties of the assault.

Grim-faced, Simon Buckner received the reports. Each of his divisions had run into a wall of resistance. By evening the American line had advanced only about 1,000 yards on either end, with a heavily fortified enemy salient in the center of the line.

With darkness falling, it was apparent to Buckner that the assault had failed. "Progress not quite satisfactory," he wrote that night in his diary.

From inside his fortified shelter at Kanoya, Admiral Ugaki listened to the explosions on the airfield. The American fighter-bombers were back. About eighty of them had slipped in through the cloud cover without being detected. The air raid alert hadn't sounded until a few minutes before the enemy bombers arrived.

Now they were bombing the base at Kanoya.

Ugaki felt a deepening sense of frustration. The next "float-ing chrysanthemum" operation—*kikusui* No. 3—was supposed to have begun that morning, but the operation was delayed by the weather. Clouds and rain again covered the East China Sea. This afternoon, just as the cloud cover was opening, the enemy war-planes appeared.

Ugaki was perplexed. Why did the enemy always seem to antic-ipate his next move? Where had the American planes come from? Most still had long-range belly tanks attached, reinforcing Ugaki's belief that they must be coming from Kadena and Yontan, the re-cently captured airfields on Okinawa. The air raids went on for an hour. The American warplanes swarmed over the airfields on Kyu-shu, seeming to devote special attention to Ugaki's headquarters at Kanoya.

When the raiders finally withdrew to the south, a few Japanese Zero and George fighters took off to nip at their heels. It was mostly a symbolic gesture. The damage had already been done.

Darkness was falling when Ugaki emerged from his shelter. In all, fifty-one aircraft had been destroyed on the ground, and another twenty-nine shot down. Despite the setback, he gave the order to proceed with *kikusui* No. 3. As an afterthought, he included the enemy-occupied airfields of Kadena and Yontan in their list of targets.

In the waning daylight, Admiral Ugaki watched the first wave of *kikusui* No. 3 finally rumble into the sky. The next day at dawn, the attacks would resume.

28 ▸ KEEP MOVING AND KEEP SHOOTING

One thing they would all agree on later: April 16 was a hell of a day. For the tin can sailors as well as the fighter pilots sent to protect them, it was the wildest day of combat most of them would ever experience.

The day began with another massed kamikaze attack, the second phase of *kikusui* No. 3. Three divisions of Grim Reaper Corsairs were on CAP stations over the radar picket ships.

One of the divisions was led by Lt. (jg) Phil Kirkwood. Still on his wing was Ens. Dick Quiel, who knew that staying close to Kirkwood meant you had a good chance of seeing action. Their second two-plane section was led by Ens. Horace "Tuck" Heath, whose wingman was a baby-faced ensign named Alfred Lerch.

Photographs of Al Lerch showed a skinny, grinning kid who looked barely old enough to borrow his father's roadster. Lerch was from Coopersburg, Pennsylvania, and he had become a Grim Reaper by accident. He was supposed to have joined VF-87 aboard USS *Ticonderoga*, but a broken leg caused him to miss their deployment. In January 1945 he was reassigned to the re-formed VF-10 on *Intrepid*.

Al Lerch was still looking for his first air-to-air victory. As he had already discovered, being the Tail End Charlie in a division meant that you got the leftovers. Two days earlier he had flown on Tuck Heath's wing while Heath methodically shot up an incoming Betty bomber and sent it smoking into the ocean. Lerch, the Tail End Charlie, never got to fire his guns.

But this was another day, and things were looking up for Lerch. En route to the CAP station, Heath developed radio trouble. It meant that Lerch was now the section leader. It also meant that *he* would get first crack at the bogeys.

The action started twenty minutes after they reached the CAP station. Bogeys were reported inbound, passing the island of Amami Oshima. Lerch and Heath headed north, while Kirkwood and Quiel took a station a few miles behind them. Kirkwood stayed low, beneath the cloud deck, where he could pick off any wave-skimming kamikazes, and sent Quiel to a high perch at 8,000 feet. The assignment suited Dick Quiel, who was happy to be on his own. Any target he spotted was all his — if he was lucky.

Minutes later, Quiel got lucky. He spotted the bogeys. They were high, heading south, and Quiel could tell by the fixed landing gear and the peculiar straight leading edges of the wings that they were Nakajima Ki-27 Nate fighters. The Nate was an obsolete warplane that had seen its heyday in the China battles of the 1930s. Now they were relegated to kamikaze missions.

The Nates were spread out in a loose gaggle, two flights of three each. In a wide pursuit curve, Quiel swung in on their tails. He selected the furthest aft Nate fighter and opened fire. The unarmored Japanese fighter burned almost instantly.

Quiel nudged the Corsair's nose over to the next Nate and repeated the process. That Nate burned almost as quickly as the first. Both were leaving blazing trails down to the sea.

But now Quiel was overtaking the rest of the slow-flying Nates. The Japanese pilots were all flying straight ahead, seemingly unaware that two of them had just been shot down.

Quiel pulled up to the right, then swung back in a pursuit curve on the four remaining Japanese fighters. He shot down another one. Then another. But with the Corsair's speed advantage of nearly a hundred knots he was again overrunning the two surviving fighters.

As Quiel bore down on them, one of the Nates abruptly rolled inverted and did a split-S — the bottom half of a loop, disappearing into the clouds. Quiel guessed that he would impact the water before pulling out.

The single remaining Nate continued boring straight ahead, apparently fixated on one of the picket destroyers in the ocean. Quiel was overtaking him too fast to get a shot. He tried to slow the Corsair, snatching the throttle back, putting the propeller into full low pitch, extending several degrees of landing flap.

It wasn't enough. Seconds later, Quiel found himself alongside the Nate fighter, wing tip to wing tip. Time seemed to freeze while Quiel stared at the enemy pilot 30 feet away. The Nate's cockpit canopy was open. Quiel could see the young man's face, the leather helmet with white fur trim. The Japanese pilot refused to look at him. As in a trance, he had his eyes riveted on his target—the destroyer straight ahead.

Quiel opened his canopy and yanked out his .38 revolver. There was almost no relative motion between the airplanes. He'd shoot the son of a bitch the old-fashioned way. At this range he couldn't miss.

Quiel was aiming the pistol, about to squeeze off a round, when an explosion erupted just ahead of him. Then another. Antiaircraft fire was erupting all around him. *Damn.* The gunners on the destroyer were shooting at both airplanes, not bothering to distinguish between them.

In the next instant, the Nate was gone, diving almost straight down at the destroyer. Quiel dove after him, trying to get into firing position again. Antiaircraft fire was bursting around both airplanes.

Quiel couldn't get another shot. Helplessly he watched the Japanese plane crash into the destroyer's forward gun turret. He thought it was the end of the destroyer.

It wasn't. To Quiel's amazement, the tin can emerged from the smoke and debris of the crash, seemingly unfazed. Still steaming at full speed, the destroyer had shrugged off the kamikaze hit as if it were a mosquito bite.

Phil Kirkwood, true to form, had tangled with a flock of twenty kamikazes that were bearing down on another destroyer. In less than a minute Kirkwood shot down a Val dive-bomber as it was beginning its run. Seconds later he flamed a Nate fighter, also bearing down on the destroyer.

Kirkwood kept shooting, chasing each kamikaze down through bursts of antiaircraft fire. He splashed three more before they could reach the destroyer.

When the enemy airplanes had finally stopped showing up, he rejoined with Quiel. They were on their way back to the CAP station when Kirkwood spotted the silhouettes of kamikazes attacking yet another destroyer. In the space of a few minutes, Kirkwood shot down yet one more Nate, exploding it into the water a hundred yards short of the destroyer.

For Kirkwood and Quiel, the melee over the picket stations was over. Together the pair had accounted for ten enemy airplanes. The day's action put Quiel on the roster of aces and elevated Kirkwood to double ace status. By downing six in a single mission, Phil Kirkwood had accomplished a feat almost unmatched by anyone else in his squadron.

Almost. What he didn't know was that twenty miles to the north, his Tail End Charlie, Al Lerch, was making history.

The radarman in the picket destroyer *Laffey* stared at his scope. There were at least fifty bogeys, more than he'd ever seen in a single cluster. They looked like fast-multiplying amoebas spreading over the fluorescent screen.

The bogeys were headed straight for *Laffey*.

Escorting *Laffey* at the lonely radar picket station were a pair of support gunboats, LCS-51 and LCS-116. The gunboats had been on station for two days without firing a shot. There'd been several nerve-jangling late-night calls to battle stations but no kamikaze attacks. Their luck seemed to be holding.

Laffey's skipper, Cmdr. Julian Becton, had already seen his share of action. He'd been the executive officer of the destroyer *Aaron Ward* when it was sunk off Guadalcanal in April 1943. After fighting in several more surface actions in the South Pacific, he took command of a new destroyer, USS *Laffey*, in February 1944. The 2,200-ton *Laffey* was the second destroyer to bear the name. Her predecessor, DD-459, had also gone down off Guadalcanal in 1942.

Becton and his new ship joined the bombardment force at the D-day landings at Normandy, firing more shells than any other destroyer in the invasion. By the end of 1944, *Laffey* had transferred to the Pacific, joining the fight in the Philippines, then at Iwo Jima, and now at Okinawa.

Two days ago *Laffey* had been in the Kerama Retto anchorage taking on ammunition and supplies. As they were leaving, Becton exchanged greetings with the skipper of the destroyer *Cassin Young*, which had taken a kamikaze hit a few days earlier. *Young*'s captain was a friend and Naval Academy classmate of Becton's. "Keep moving and keep shooting," yelled out *Cassin Young*'s skipper. "Steam as fast as you can, and shoot as fast as you can."

It was good advice, Becton thought. So were the parting words from a gun captain on another destroyer, *Purdy*: "You guys have a fighting chance, but they'll keep on coming till they get you. You'll knock a lot of them down, and you'll think you're doing fine. But in the end there'll be this one bastard with your name on his ticket."

Now it was the morning of April 16, and *Laffey* was on station at RP1, which had become the kamikazes' favorite hunting ground. The crew's chow line had been interrupted once already by a call to general quarters. A snooper had come close enough for the forward 5-inch gun batteries to open fire. The snooper fled, but in his place came the swarm of bogeys. Now they were circling overhead, staying just out of range of the antiaircraft guns.

The first to peel off were four fixed-gear D3A Val dive bombers. Swooping down like vultures, they split into pairs, two on the starboard bow, the other pair coming from astern.

Becton ordered *Laffey* into a hard turn to port. The destroyer's forward 5-inchers opened up, splashing both Vals attacking at the bow. The pair from astern were coming in low—so low that one inadvertently caught his landing gear in the wave tops and pitched over into the sea. The second disintegrated in the torrent of combined gunfire from *Laffey* and one of her escorting gunboats.

Four up, four down, but there was no break in the action. Two D4Y Judy dive-bombers were coming in from either side. The Judys were sleeker and faster than the obsolescent Vals—and harder to hit. The 40-millimeter and 20-millimeter gunners chopped up the Judy attacking on the starboard side, but the one from the port side slipped through the fire. As he drew closer, the pilot opened up with his machine guns. Bullets raked the deck, killing gunners and pinging into *Laffey*'s superstructure.

Just as the antiaircraft fire converged on the Judy, the pilot released his bomb. The bomb detonated on the water, but the explosion sent shrapnel slashing across *Laffey*'s deck, mowing down more crewmen and knocking out the critical surface search radar.

Keep moving and keep shooting. The words from *Cassin Young*'s skipper were fresh in Becton's mind. He was swinging *Laffey*'s bow in vicious turns from port to starboard and back again, keeping her guns broadside to the attackers.

Another pair of kamikazes, a Val and a Judy dive-bomber, came swooping in from opposite sides in a coordinated attack. *Laffey*'s gunners splashed them both, but the shattered Val grazed the destroyer's aft 5-inch mount, killing one of the gunners, before crashing into the sea on the far side of the ship.

Laffey had been under attack for twelve minutes, but it seemed like a year. The destroyer had fought off eight kamikazes without taking a single direct hit. The combined firepower of the destroyer and her two LCS gunboat escorts had taken down every attacking plane. *Laffey*'s luck seemed to be holding.

For three minutes there was a break in the attacks. Then another Val came roaring in from the port bow. Even as the streams of gunfire from the destroyer and the gunboats poured into the kamikaze, it somehow held its course. The Val slammed into *Laffey*'s port side, exploding into the amidships 20-millimeter gun station before caroming off the starboard side into the sea.

Three more gunners were killed instantly, and the entire aft half of the destroyer was torched in flaming gasoline. *Laffey*'s streak of luck had ended.

A few miles to the north, Tail End Charlie Al Lerch was making the most of his new role—section leader. On his wing was Tuck Heath, whose dead radio, at least according to standard procedure, should have excluded him from the mission. But Heath's guns still worked, and he was sticking with Lerch.

Then Lerch spotted the most tantalizing sight he'd ever seen—a flock of thirty Nate fighters, droning toward them like ducks to a blind. The Nates were in loose three-plane formations. Each was carrying an external bomb intended for a U.S. ship.

With Heath in trail, Lerch swept down on the Nates. On the first pass, each pilot gunned down one Nate. The panicky survivors scattered, diving for the water, with Lerch and Heath hard on their tails. The inept Japanese pilots were clearly untrained in air-to-air combat, milling around close to the water, making themselves easy targets for the Corsairs.

Lerch slid in behind three slow-moving Nates. Firing from dead astern, he poured .50-caliber bullets into each of the hapless Nates. In the space of three minutes, Lerch had sent all three flaming into the ocean.

Climbing back to altitude, Lerch looked around for Heath, who had gone missing. Then Lerch spotted three more Nates cutting across the northern tip of Okinawa, a few miles away. He was sweeping in behind one of them, about to squeeze his trigger, when he sensed a dark blue object swelling in his peripheral vision.

It was Heath. He was still radioless, but he was fixated on the same target that Lerch had in his sights. At the last instant, Lerch swerved out of the way, barely avoiding a collision, while Heath blazed away at the hapless Nate fighter.

There was no shortage of targets. Minutes later, Lerch was behind another Nate. At close range, he opened fire from directly astern.

The next thing Al Lerch saw was a fireball in front of his nose. Instinctively he ducked in the cockpit, feeling pieces of the exploding Nate thunking into his wings and cowling.

Emerging from the cloud of debris, he peered around. There was nothing left of the Nate. Lerch's Corsair was damaged—he could see dents and rips in the leading edges—but the engine was still running.

And his guns still worked. Minutes later, Lerch found himself in yet another nose-to-nose contest with Heath, both of them chasing another Nate. This time Lerch got to it first, setting it afire, with Heath delivering the coup de grace.

It was another day for the record books. Phil Kirkwood's four-plane division had gunned down twenty enemy airplanes, with Kirkwood and Quiel accounting for half the total. The second pair, Tail End Charlies Heath and Lerch, did just as well. Tuck Heath, who by strict interpretation of the rules shouldn't have been in the fight, was credited with three kills.

But it was Al Lerch who won the greatest share of the glory. In a single mission, the baby-faced ensign shot down seven enemy airplanes, a feat of arms matched by only four other Americans in history.

29 ▸ AS LONG AS A GUN WILL FIRE

The fires on the *Laffey* weren't going out. Skipper Julian Becton was forced to slow the destroyer's speed to keep from fanning the flames. An ominous column of black smoke was billowing into the sky, a beacon for more kamikazes.

In quick succession, two more Val dive-bombers swept down on *Laffey*. The first attacked from astern, close to the water and partly obscured by the cloud of smoke trailing the destroyer. Despite taking repeated hits, the Val plowed into *Laffey*'s aft gun mounts. Gun captain Larry Delewski was blown over the side by the explosion. Amazingly, Delewski was unhurt, and so were two other crewmen who went into the water and were later picked up by one of the gunboats.

Flames were leaping from *Laffey*'s fantail, and the black smoke thickened over the ship. Firefighters worked desperately to keep the fires from reaching the ammunition magazines. Just when it seemed that *Laffey*'s condition could get no worse, an eleventh attacker crashed into the stern in almost the same spot as the one before. Another gun crew was killed instantly.

Yet another Val came diving from astern. Unlike the committed kamikazes, this one planted his bomb directly into *Laffey*'s stern, then pulled up and soared back into the sky. The explosion of the bomb severed the cables and hydraulic lines to the destroyer's steering gear, jamming the rudder at 26 degrees to port.

Keep moving and keep shooting. The advice Becton had received now seemed like a bad joke. He had no choice except to steam in a leftward circle. He couldn't straighten the ship's rudder, and he had only a few remaining guns.

For the kamikazes still circling, the crippled destroyer was an easy target. Two more Vals came boring in from the port quarter. The first exploded into the aft deckhouse, sending up a cascade of fire and shrapnel. Right behind it came the second, crashing in almost the same spot. Flaming gasoline covered the aft half of the destroyer.

Belowdecks, the crew was fighting to save the ship—and their lives. Two machinist's mates, George Logan and Stephen Waite, were trapped in the emergency diesel room. With no light and no ventilation, they signaled the engine room of their predicament. Their fellow machinist's mates John Michel and Buford Thompson managed to chisel a hole in the bulkhead large enough to thread an air hose into the compartment. Two more machinist's mates, Art Hogan and Elton Peeler, went to work with cutting torches, finally opening a hole large enough to haul the trapped men to safety.

Overhead, a dozen Corsairs had showed up to engage the attacking kamikazes. As Becton watched from his bridge, a Nakajima Ki-43 Oscar fighter came streaking toward *Laffey*'s port bow, flying through a hail of 40-millimeter and 20-millimeter fire. Directly behind it, flying through the same fire, came a Marine Corsair, blazing away at the Oscar that was aimed at *Laffey*'s bridge.

The Oscar missed the bridge, but his wing ripped through the port yardarm of the mast. With a spectacular crash, the yardarm crashed to the deck, carrying the American flag with it. A half second later, the pursuing Corsair hit the same mast, tearing off the air-search radar antenna.

Astonished, Becton watched the crippled planes flounder back over the water. Each was struggling to stay airborne. The fatally damaged Oscar wobbled, then dropped its nose and crashed into the sea. The Corsair clawed its way up for a few hundred feet more, then a tiny figure tumbled from the cockpit. Moments later, Becton saw a parachute canopy blossom, and the pilot descended to the water.

On *Laffey*'s bridge, nineteen-year-old Ari Phoutrides, the quartermaster of the watch, was supposed to be writing down everything that happened. "I couldn't even hold a pencil," Phoutrides recalled, "let alone write."

With all other communications lines severed, Phoutrides was the captain's lookout and messenger. Phoutrides spotted a kamikaze coming in low on the port beam. "I had to practically beat the OOD [officer of the deck] over the head with my fist before he paid any attention to me. This was the only time I've hit an officer and gotten away with it." Alerted to the danger, the gunners splashed the kamikaze just in time.

The Corsairs were taking down some of the kamikazes, but not all. A Judy dive-bomber came roaring in on the port beam with a Corsair nipping at his tail. *Laffey*'s gunners opened up on the Judy, trying to keep from hitting the American fighter, finally exploding the kamikaze 50 yards short of *Laffey*. The shrapnel slammed into the destroyer, slicing the communications lines to the 5-inch guns and wounding most of the gunners.

That made seventeen attackers so far, and there seemed to be no end in sight. With the electrical controls of their gun mounts gone, *Laffey*'s gunners were down to old-fashioned manual control.

Two more kamikazes, both Oscar fighters, were converging from the starboard side. The first exploded from a direct hit in the nose by a manually controlled 5-inch gun mount. The second, boring in on the starboard bow, also went down from 5-inch fire.

Laffey was almost finished. The assistant communications officer, Lt. Frank Manson, asked Becton if he thought they'd have to abandon ship. "No," snapped the captain. "I'll never abandon ship as long as a gun will fire."

Luckily, Becton didn't hear the lookout next to him, who added in a low voice, "And if I can find one man to fire it."

On his CAP station over the northern picket ships, Grim Reapers skipper Lt. Cmdr. Wally Clarke was finally getting into the action. He had just received a vector to intercept bogeys coming from the northwest.

Clarke's number three, Lt. (jg) Charles "Bo" Farmer, was the first to spot them: twelve o'clock high, at 20,000 feet. Bo Farmer had the same score as Clarke—four kills—from his earlier combat tour. Like Clarke, he was one tantalizing number away from being an ace.

Climbing through 16,000 feet, they got a good look at the bogeys. These weren't the sitting-duck Nates and Val kamikazes like Kirkwood's flight had just finished blowing out of the sky. These were Tony and Zero fighters—*real* fighters—and they were there to cover the kamikazes.

As the Corsairs approached, the Japanese fighters peeled off, swooping down to meet them. Instead of a turkey shoot, this was going to be a classic, no-holds-barred dogfight.

Clarke's Tail End Charlie, Ens. Ray James, saw the distinctive shapes of three Tony fighters swooping down toward him in a perfect pursuit curve. The Tony was unique, the only Japanese fighter powered by an in-line, liquid-cooled engine. When the Tony made its first appearance in the Pacific, it was mistaken for a German Messerschmitt Bf 109.

James winced as he saw the tracers of the first Tony's 12.7-millimeter machine guns searing past him. But the Japanese pilot had been too eager. The bullets missed James's Corsair, and now Wally Clarke was whipping in behind the Tony. Seconds later, Clarke had him in his sights, gunning the Japanese fighter out of the air.

Behind the Tonys came four Zeroes. One made the mistake of overshooting his high-side run on Tail End Charlie Ray James. James took advantage of the mistake, maneuvering behind the Zero's tail. He stayed there, all six machine guns firing, until the Japanese fighter went into the water.

Up above, the other three Corsair pilots were mixing it up with the remaining Japanese fighters. Bo Farmer was having a field day, splashing three Zeroes and a Tony fighter. Clarke climbed up after an escaping Zero, catching the fighter and blowing it to pieces.

The fight was over as quickly as it had begun. The surviving Japanese fighters scattered like quail. Clarke's flight was returning to the orbit point when another call for help crackled on the tactical frequency. A destroyer—USS *Laffey*—was in trouble.

When they arrived over the radar picket ship, they found a swirling tableau of antiaircraft fire, swarming kamikazes, and friendly fighters, including Wildcats and Hellcats from other carriers and a contingent of Marine Corsairs from the Okinawa airfields.

Clarke and his wingman, Ens. Jack Ehrhard, went after a pair of Vals that were positioning for a run on the *Laffey*. Clarke flamed one, and Ehrhard put enough rounds into the second to send it smoking toward the water.

Minutes later, they spotted a Japanese Betty bomber low on the water, racing at top speed from a pair of pursuing F6F Hellcats. Sportsmanship between fighter pilots, especially those from different carriers, was virtually nonexistent. Clarke and Ehrhard rolled in on the Betty, neatly cutting out the Hellcats.

In his eagerness to nail the Betty, however, Clarke overran the bomber before he could get it in his sights. That left his wingman, Ehrhard, to claim the prize, while the disgruntled Hellcat pilots watched from astern.

But the Betty didn't crash, even after Ehrhard poured a hail of lead into it. The bomber skipped off the water, pulled up, then splashed down in a semicontrolled ditching. As the Corsair pilots swept overhead, they saw three figures clamber out of the wreck of the bomber. The Japanese crewmen were bobbing like otters in the water, within paddling distance of a nearby enemy-occupied island.

This was not a day—nor an era—for compassion. None of the American pilots had charitable feelings for the enemy who had been killing American sailors all morning. One after the other, .50-calibers firing, they strafed the water around the downed Betty until nothing was left but a dark froth.

L*affey*'s gunners were being killed or wounded as fast as they could be replaced. Even though the CAP fighters were engaging the kamikazes, shooting down or chasing away most of them, *Laffey* was still a target.

A bomb struck her just below the bridge, wiping out the two 20-millimeter mounts and killing both gun crews as well as several already wounded men being treated below in the main-deck-level wardroom being used as a dressing station.

Then came a Judy dive-bomber, hurtling in from the port quarter. *Laffey*'s gunners blazed away with their remaining 40-millimeter and 20-millimeter guns, but the blunt-nosed shape of the Judy continued to swell in size. At the last moment before impact, a Corsair caught the kamikaze from behind. The Judy crashed into the water close aboard. The blazing hulk skidded into the destroyer's hull, causing a dent but no serious damage.

For the moment, no more enemy planes seemed to be targeting *Laffey*. Peering into the sky, Ari Phoutrides had the feeling that it was over. He could see more than a dozen fighters—Corsairs and Hellcats—chasing the few remaining kamikazes.

For the wounded *Laffey*, it was almost too late. Fires in the aft half of the ship were still burning out of control. The destroyer was slowly flooding. Her shattered fantail was nearly submerged. Though her engines were running, the rudder was still jammed hard to port. Captain Becton was trying every combination of engine thrust to steer the destroyer southward, away from the kamikaze hunting ground. Nothing worked.

The destroyer-minesweeper *Macomb* steamed up to assist with the frantic damage control efforts and to take the destroyer under tow. With her flooded stern and jammed rudder, *Laffey* was untowable by a single vessel. In the early afternoon, a pair of fleet tugs arrived. After using pumps to control the flooding, they managed to haul the destroyer back to the Hagushi anchorage at Okinawa.

Laffey wasn't the only casualty that day on RP1. Both her gunboat escorts had taken heavy damage. LCS-116 was struck topside, suffering seventeen dead and twelve wounded. LCS-51 had a gaping hole in her hull, with three men wounded.

In the fading light at the anchorage that evening, sailors from other ships gawked at the mangled USS *Laffey*. It was hard to believe any ship could take that much punishment and keep fighting. Several ships of *Laffey*'s size had been sunk from a single kamikaze.

No other vessel in the war would take as many kamikaze hits and remain afloat. In twenty-two separate attacks *Laffey* endured six kamikaze crashes and two bomb strikes. Thirty-two of her crew were dead, and seventy-one were wounded. In exchange, her gunners took down nine kamikazes. In seventy-nine minutes of hellish combat, USS *Laffey* had earned herself a niche in naval history.

30 ▸ GLORY DAY

Lt. George "Bee" Weems gazed into the morning sky, trying to spot the dark specks coming from the north. The bogeys were reported flying at low altitude, not in their usual loose formation but singly, strung out in a line. Weems guessed that they were coming from an island in the northern Ryukyus.

Like many fighter pilots, Bee Weems had a quirk. His was the pair of binoculars he carried in the cockpit, earning him the moniker "Eyes of the Fleet," though no one had actually seen him use the glasses in flight. The binoculars were a carryover from his days as a destroyer man. Weems was a Naval Academy grad and the son of a naval officer, Capt. Philip Weems, who was a renowned pioneer of sea and air navigation.

Weems's wingman, Ens. Charlie Schlag, nicknamed "Curly," was a balding young man from West Virginia who had trained in dive-bombers before being switched to fighters. Schlag had his own quirk. He carried two canteens in his emergency equipment. One was aluminum, for water. The other was plastic, and it contained whisky. Schlag had heard somewhere that whisky had enough nutritional value to keep you alive for a week in your life raft. He had no idea whether it was true or not, but what the hell—he was willing to give it a try.

They spotted the first bogey a few minutes before 0900. It was a Zero at low altitude and climbing, confirming Weems's suspicion that the kamikazes had begun staging from one of the nearby islands, probably Kikai. Weems and Schlag rolled in on the Zero, coordinating their firing passes, each getting solid hits, sending the Zero down in flames. It was a coldly efficient team attack, for which the pilots would share the credit.

Seconds later, they spotted another Zero, also low and climbing. This one Weems promptly shot down. Then a third showed up, and Schlag took his turn. He was still putting bullets into the Zero, making it smoke, when the Japanese fighter abruptly rolled inverted and dove for the ocean. Weems was there, guns firing, and the Zero joined its two predecessors in the ocean. Another shared kill.

The action wasn't over. Five minutes later, yet another solo Zero showed up. Like the others, it was in a climb, and Weems wasted no time blasting it out of the sky.

The sky was cleared of enemy planes, at least for the moment. The Zeroes had all carried external bombs, which meant to Weems that they were kamikazes and not fighters. He requested permission to reconnoiter the enemy island of Kikai, only 10 miles away.

Minutes later, permission received, Weems and Schlag, now joined by their second two-plane section, were sweeping over the Japanese airfield. They caught one Betty bomber out in the open, which they exploded with their guns. They found a Zero in a revetment and set it afire.

And that was it. If there were more kamikazes based on Kikai, they were well concealed. Or, as Bee Weems suspected, they were already airborne and attacking American ships.

W eems was right. On the northern picket stations, the kamikazes were again pouncing on the tin cans. The destroyer *Bryant*, which had been steaming to *Laffey*'s assistance from nearby RP2, came under attack by six kamikazes. One crashed into the base of her bridge, wiping out the CIC compartment and the plotting rooms, killing thirty-four sailors.

At the same time on RP14, three more picket ships, the destroyer *Pringle*, the destroyer/minesweeper *Hobson*, and their escorting gunboat, LCS-191, were all slugging it out with kamikazes.

Pringle's gunners had already splashed one attacking Zero and were now fighting off three Vals.

Pringle's skipper, Lt. Cmdr. John Kelley, was following the "keep moving, keep shooting" doctrine, turning hard in each direction to give his main batteries a full field of fire. It wasn't enough. A Val wove its way through the smoke and flak, smashing into *Pringle* just behind her forward stack. *Pringle* didn't have *Laffey*'s toughness—or her luck. The impact of the kamikaze buckled the destroyer's keel. *Pringle* broke in half, and in less than five minutes she went to the bottom, taking sixty-two men with her.

April 16 was turning into one of the deadliest days ever for kamikaze attacks. In *kikusui* No. 3 the Japanese had sent fewer airplanes than in the two previous massed attacks—only 165 airplanes instead of the initial wave of 355—but the tactics had become more deadly. The kamikazes had learned to coordinate their attacks and hit from opposite sides, relentlessly stalking ships that were already wounded and smoking.

But a question still puzzled American commanders: why were the kamikazes throwing themselves at the picket destroyers instead of at the higher-value warships farther south? One explanation was that the Japanese considered the radar picket ships to be vital targets. Another was that the picket ships were birds in hand—the first targets the anxious kamikaze pilots spotted on the route to Okinawa.

And then there was an even simpler possibility: the kamikaze pilots didn't know the difference between warships. Several had been heard excitedly transmitting that they were "diving on a battleship" when their target was a destroyer.

But on the afternoon of April 16, the *tokko* pilots stalking the ships of Task Force 58 northeast of Okinawa knew exactly what class of warship they were hunting. Their targets were big, fast, and unmistakable. One of them was the aircraft carrier *Intrepid*.

While the Grim Reapers of VF-10 were lighting up the sky over the picket ships, their sister squadron, VBF-10, was doing what the air-to-mud fighters had always done—diving through fire and flak to hit targets on the ground.

It was a dirty, dangerous job. As he usually did, air group commander Johnny Hyland had assigned himself to lead the twelve-plane strike on Kokubu, a Japanese airfield on the southern tip of Kyushu. Intelligence reports indicated that Kokubu had become a nest for the kamikazes that were savaging the picket ships.

Six of the fighter-bombers were carrying 500-pound general-purpose bombs, while the others carried clusters of the new 5-inch Holy Moses rockets. As expected, the Japanese put up a curtain of antiaircraft fire. The familiar roiling black puffs were already blossoming around each Corsair as they rolled into their dives. Also as expected, the enemy airplanes were well concealed beneath camouflage or in sheltered revetments.

Not well enough. By the time the Corsairs expended their bombs and rockets, a trio of two-engine Mitsubishi Ki-57 "Topsy" transports had been destroyed, and nine other warplanes, mostly Zeroes, had been transformed into flaming hulks. Ten more single-engine airplanes were damaged enough that they wouldn't soon be used as kamikazes.

Pulling off the target, Hyland gathered his fighter-bombers for the trip back home. But when he counted planes, he was one short. One of his Tail End Charlies, Ens. Ernest "Red" Bailey, was missing.

No one had seen Bailey go down. No one had heard a distress call. Gazing back in the direction of Kokubu, they could see the columns of black smoke rising from the airfield. One of them, in all likelihood, was coming from the wreckage of Red Bailey's Corsair.

Hyland turned his flight to the south, leaving Japan behind them. While the Corsairs droned back to the south, a heavy silence settled over the tactical frequency, each pilot alone with his thoughts. It was a somber end to what was otherwise a perfectly executed strike. Red Bailey was another of the Texas contingent, a newlywed who had gone to Rice University before leaving early to join the Navy. He had become the fifth VBF-10 pilot lost in combat since the squadron arrived off Okinawa.

When they were still five miles east of Kikai, Lt. Paul Cordray's voice broke the silence. He had spotted two Zeroes dead ahead. Someone else called out eight more, 3,000 feet above them.

The Corsairs still had ammunition left. Splitting his divisions, Hyland led the attack from one side while Cordray took the other. Another fight was on.

P aul Cordray was already an ace. He was a tall, broad-shouldered Texan, another of the VF-17 veterans of the Solomons campaign who had been drafted by Will Rawie for his new squadron. Cordray was also considered by most of the Tail End Charlies to be the best fighter pilot in the squadron.

Now he proved why. Slashing into one of the Zeroes, Cordray put his first burst into the fuselage and wing roots. It was enough. The Japanese fighter burst into flame and did a wingover straight into the water.

Another division leader, Lt. Ralph "Go" Goetter, was chasing an Oscar fighter through a hard left turn. Firing a long burst well ahead of the Oscar's nose, he watched his tracers arc back into the Japanese fighter. Seconds later, trailing flame and smoke, the Oscar plunged into the ocean.

It was clear that these Japanese airmen hadn't been trained as fighter pilots. "They used very little evasive action," Goetter wrote in his action report, "and didn't return our fire."

Eager to add another kill to his own record, Johnny Hyland tailed in behind one of the Zeroes. He fired several bursts directly into the Zero's tail. To his amazement, the bullets seemed to have no effect. Hyland fired again. Still nothing. It was mystifying. The Japanese fighter kept flying straight ahead as if he were bulletproof.

Abruptly the Zero made a left turn. Hyland's wingman, Ens.

Eldon Brooks, saw his chance. Like a dog after a rabbit, he cut inside the Zero's turn, firing one short burst into the Japanese fighter's fuselage.

The Zero burst into flame.

Watching the Zero go into the ocean, Hyland couldn't believe it. Not that he begrudged his wingman getting the kill—that's what air-to-air combat was all about—but why hadn't the damned Zero gone down when *he* shot it?

He was still in a fit of pique when he wrote his after-action report. "There is in this attack some evidence that this plane, apparently a kamikaze, was especially well armored and protected," he wrote. "From previous experience, this plane was expected to burn much sooner than it did."

An especially well-armored Zero? It didn't seem likely, but no one in the strike group, least of all a Tail End Charlie like Eldon Brooks, was foolish enough to say so.

Brooks wasn't the only Tail End Charlie to draw blood. Ensigns Paul Pavlovich and Tom Boucher also seized the moment, picking off a Zero and a Tony from the wave of southbound kamikazes.

With their ammunition spent and the kamikazes scattered, Hyland again turned his group southward. The hour-and-a-half flight back to the *Intrepid* gave everyone time to think. The same silence fell over the eleven remaining Corsairs.

For Hyland, it was a time of mixed emotions. He had a special relationship with his young pilots. Losing a kid like Red Bailey over Kokubu was painful. But he also had reason to feel gratified. He had been one of the early advocates of using the Corsair in the dual roles of fighter and ground attack.

Today's mission was the ultimate proof that he was right. His strike group had destroyed a dozen enemy airplanes on the ground. Minutes later they'd shot five more out of the air. The age of the fighter-bomber had arrived.

For the Tail End Charlies, the morning of April 16 held one more moment of glory. A four-plane flight of the most junior officers in VBF-10—each one an ensign, the lowest officer's rank in the Navy—had intercepted a wave of kamikazes headed directly for *Intrepid*'s task group.

Led by Ens. Freddie Lanthier, the Corsairs pounced on the low-flying kamikazes. Lanthier brought down the first one, a bomb-carrying Zero, with a short burst. Less than a minute later, he repeated the feat, shooting down a second with another quick burst.

His fellow Tail End Charlies were doing just as well. Loren McDonald caught a Zero at 5,000 feet and put a single long burst into him from behind. As the Zero went into a shallow glide, McDonald eased alongside. He could see the dead pilot lying against the instrument panel. McDonald escorted the Zero until it smacked into the ocean.

Ens. Robert "Pappy" Sweet pulled behind a bogey that was clearly not a kamikaze. It was a snooper—a Nakajima C6N1 "Myrt" reconnaissance plane—and it was there to provide guidance for the incoming kamikazes.

And then Sweet discovered something else different about the Myrt: it carried a tail gunner. For several seconds Sweet and the gunner exchanged fire, both missing, until Sweet pulled up and to the side, out of the gunner's range. Then he swept back down in a pursuit curve, making himself a hard target while he blasted the snooper out of the sky.

With fuel and ammunition nearly expended, the exhilarated fighter pilots landed back aboard *Intrepid*. Safely back in their low-ceilinged, smoky ready rooms, they relived the life-and-death moments of combat, doing their usual nonstop gesturing and jabbering. It had been a history-making day—and it was only half over. The two Corsair squadrons had gunned down forty-two Japanese airplanes, with one more probable.

The list of aces—pilots with five or more kills—was growing.

And they weren't just the veterans like Kirkwood and Cordray and Clarke. Several of the Tail End Charlies—guys including Lerch, Quiel, and Heath—had become aces, some, including Lerch, achieving fame in one spectacular mission.

But not all aces were equal, at least in the opinion of some. A few pilots groused that it was one thing to slide in behind a flock of slow-moving Nates or Vals and blast them out of the sky. It was quite another matter to go head-to-head with the escorting Zeke and George fighters, which were often flown by combat-hardened Japanese fighter pilots. Winning a one-on-one dogfight was in a different class from exterminating a clueless suicider.

Most had the sense to keep their mouths shut, at least in the ready room. By now they all knew the hard truth: aerial combat was a fickle business. The type of enemy airplane that happened to fill your gunsight was the luck of the draw. When the war was over and the roster of aces was published, no one would care what kind of airplanes you'd shot down. Only the numbers counted.

At 1327, the chatter in the ready rooms abruptly ceased. The klaxon was sounding. Over the bullhorn came the order for *Intrepid*'s crew to man their battle stations.

Kamikazes were inbound. Five had already slipped through the CAP and antiaircraft screens.

31 ▸ TARGET *INTREPID*

Intrepid's guns were firing. By now, everyone knew the sequence. When you heard the rumbling blast of the 5-inchers, it meant that the kamikaze was still at long range. He hadn't yet zeroed in on a target, and every ship in the task group was tracking him. Then came the stuttering *pom-pom-pom* of the shorter-range 40-millimeter Bofors guns. That was worrisome. The kamikaze was coming closer. He was headed for *Intrepid*.

When you heard the staccato rattle of the 20-millimeters, you stopped in your tracks and stared up at the gray steel overhead. The kamikaze was *very* close. "Close enough to hit with a beer can," observed radarman Ray Stone, whose battle station was in the ship's combat information center.

Stone was 19, a high school graduate who had gone directly from Navy boot camp to Fleet Radar School at Virginia Beach, Virginia. He had been aboard *Intrepid* since her commissioning in August 1943. Forever embedded in Stone's memory was what had happened off the Philippines the previous November. Two kamikazes, six minutes apart, had crashed through the flight deck and exploded on the hangar deck below. Thirty-two men, mostly radarmen on standby duty, were killed instantly in Ready Room 4 on the gallery deck.

Stone was worried about a repeat performance. His duty station in CIC was on that same gallery deck. "If the flight deck had a target painted on it," he recalled, "the meatball in the center would be right over CIC. The wooden flight deck and thin steel ceiling above us wouldn't stop much. One day, I thought, one of these bastards is going to hit the bull's eye and that will be it."

On the flight deck, plane captain Felix Novelli was having the same morbid thoughts. He'd been aboard *Intrepid* since the carrier left Alameda in February. This morning Novelli had watched his assigned Corsair lumber off the deck on another mission. Now, as he always did, he was waiting for it to return.

Like everyone above deck, Novelli was wearing his steel gray battle helmet. The steady din of the antiaircraft guns was beating against his eardrums. Out there over the water, surrounded by the black antiaircraft bursts, he could see the ominous specks. *Kamikazes*. While Novelli watched, the specks came closer. They were threading their way through the web of gunfire.

The first was a pointy-nosed Ki-61 Tony fighter. The Tony was in a 20-degree glide directly toward *Intrepid*'s bow. The carrier's forward 5-inch batteries were firing, having no apparent effect. At 3,000 yards range, the 40-millimeters opened up. Still nothing. Just in time, the 20-millimeters rattled, tracers closing around the kamikaze, splashing it close off *Intrepid*'s starboard bow.

Then came the second. This one was a round-nosed Zero fighter, also zooming in from dead ahead. The combined fire of all the ships in *Intrepid*'s task group took him apart, cartwheeling him into the sea off the carrier's port quarter.

There was no break in the action. From astern came another Zero in a 40-degree dive through the maelstrom of fire. Still in his dive, the pilot switched targets, going for the battleship *Missouri*, which was steaming on a course parallel to *Intrepid*. The guns on both ships hammered away at the kamikaze. The Zero made it to within a thousand feet of *Missouri* before losing a wing and plunging into the ocean.

The attacks were unrelenting. Like a scene from Dante's *Inferno*, the deep-throated thunder filled the air. The sky roiled with smoke. Explosions seemed to come from everywhere.

Eighteen-year-old Seaman 1st Class Ed Coyne was watching from his battle station. "How did they get this close?" he recalled wondering. "There were other ships out there. Why didn't they get them?" To the young sailor, it didn't seem possible that any airplane could get through so much gunfire.

But they did. Two more were sweeping in from astern. Ens. Fred Meyer of VF-10 had just returned from a CAP mission. He was standing in the catwalk watching the action. He saw the kamikaze erupt in flame a thousand feet from the *Missouri* before making a wingover into the ocean. Then he saw the next one, right behind. While the task group's guns had been trained on the closest kamikaze, the second managed to slip through most of the air defense fire. By the time Meyer's eyes fixed on the kamikaze, it was already in its dive. The Zero was hit but still flying. Trailing smoke and debris, it was aimed at *Intrepid*'s stern.

Meyer was getting a bad feeling. He whirled and headed for the nearest ladder to a lower deck.

Felix Novelli, watching from the flight deck, had the same feeling. He sprinted for the island—the carrier's superstructure—where the plane captains normally stood watch. As he ducked into the compartment, he glanced up and caught an image that would stay fixed in his memory for another half century. "There was Old Glory, stiff as a board in the 30-knot wind, with tracers flying all around it. I couldn't help thinking of 'The Star Spangled Banner.' "

For the gunners squinting through their sights at the smoking kamikaze, time slowed to a crawl. The dusky-colored shape swelled in size. The features of the Zero fighter became clearly visible—the round, blunt nose, greenhouse canopy over the cockpit, oblong-shaped bomb fixed to its belly. It felt like a replay of the nightmare they'd lived off the Philippines the previous November.

The Zero didn't waver from its death dive. Like an unstoppable comet, it kept coming, shedding parts and trailing flame. The Zero plunged into *Intrepid*'s aft flight deck next to the number three elevator. It was almost the same spot where the kamikaze had struck five months before.

A geyser of flame and debris leaped from the deck. The heaviest components of the Zero—the engine, part of the fuselage, and its 250-kilogram bomb—punched straight through the flight deck and ricocheted off the armored hangar deck. The bomb exploded three feet above the deck, sending a cascade of fire and shrapnel the entire length of the hangar bay. Nearly every airplane stowed in the forward hangar bay instantly burst into flame.

The explosion punched a 5-by-5-foot hole in the thick armor plate of the hangar deck. Above the explosion, the flight deck was shoved upward a foot. The gallery deck, as in the previous kamikaze strikes, was engulfed in smoke and salt water from the extinguishing system. The number three elevator, which had been rebuilt during *Intrepid*'s last stay at the Hunters Point shipyard in San Francisco, was ruined again.

A 12-by-14-foot gash had been ripped in the flight deck. The imprint of the Zero's wings was still embedded in the wood like a fossilized skeleton. The cockpit and upper fuselage had skidded all the way to the forward flight deck, where the remains of the Japanese pilot were found in the wreckage. After being searched for items of intelligence value, the body was unceremoniously heaved overboard.

Intrepid wasn't out of danger. Radar screens showed the blips of more incoming bogeys. Like vultures drawn to wounded prey, the kamikazes were homing in on the plume of smoke cascading from *Intrepid*'s deck. Gunners fired at the attackers while firefighters battled the blazes in the hangar bay.

A pair of Zeroes came sweeping in low on the water. Neither, apparently, was a committed suicider. The first dropped his 550-pound bomb, missing *Intrepid*'s starboard quarter by 75 yards. As he pulled up to escape, a direct hit from a 40-millimeter gun blew him out of the sky. The second Zero's bomb came closer, exploding near the carrier's port bow. He too flew into the web of gunfire and tumbled flaming into the sea.

Through it all, *Intrepid's* damage control crews kept working. The intensive training they'd received plus the newly installed fire extinguishing nozzles and foam generators were paying off. In fifty-one minutes, they had the raging fires in the hangar bay put out. Forty of *Intrepid's* warplanes had been torched by the fires. After removing vital instruments, cameras, and hardware, deck crewmen shoved the charred hulks over the side.

The telltale beacon of black smoke had stopped, but *Intrepid's* flight deck had a gaping cavity. A dozen planes were still airborne, returning from CAP duty and low on gas. They needed a deck to land on. Capt. Giles Short, *Intrepid's* skipper, gave the order: *Patch the deck—now!*

And they did. With guns still firing over their heads, *Intrepid's* carpenters and welders labored to install a massive steel plate over the hole in the landing deck. In a classic display of grace under pressure, they completed the task less than three hours after the kamikaze had crashed through the deck.

At 1615, Commander Geisser, *Intrepid's* air boss, signaled the orbiting airplanes: *Intrepid* had a ready deck. One after the other, the exhausted pilots landed back aboard their ship.

I ntrepid was operational but crippled. Her number three aircraft elevator was wrecked. Most of the compartments on the gallery deck were charred or damaged from smoke and salt water. The worst damage was in the hangar bay, where gasoline servicing outlets, water sprinkling systems, and most of the electrical controls for the elevators, lights, and some of the gun mounts were wiped out.

The flight deck was serviceable, but barely. The newly installed steel patch was not flush with the deck, and the explosion itself had raised the wooden planking as much as 12 inches in places. Several of the vital arresting cables were gone. Forty valuable warplanes now lay at the bottom of the Pacific.

The next day, April 17, *Intrepid* was detached and ordered to the fueling area, several miles east of the task group's operating area, where her damage could be accurately assessed. A naval damage assessment group came aboard to inspect the ship. To no one's surprise, they determined that *Intrepid* was too badly wounded to continue combat operations. In company with a pair of screening destroyers, she headed for the anchorage at Ulithi for repairs.

That afternoon, *Intrepid*'s crew assembled at elevator number 2, on the port side of the ship, for a now-familiar ritual. Eight flag-covered canvas bags lay in pairs at the deck edge. On either side of the body bags stood a row of the fallen sailors' shipmates. At one edge of the elevator was the Marine honor guard, heads bowed, at parade rest. The adjoining hangar bay, still smelling of smoke and carnage from the previous day's battle, was filled with the officers and men of *Intrepid*, assembled in formation to honor the dead.

Intrepid's losses from the kamikaze attack—8 dead and 21 wounded—were light compared to the kamikaze strikes of the November before, when 69 were killed and 150 wounded. For many of those standing on the hangar deck, this was their first close-up look at the results of war. "Up until now," recalled Eric Erickson, "my pilot friends who had perished in combat were just not there. There was no funeral, no eulogy, and no ceremony. It was just like they never existed."

This was different. Each of the eight canvas bags contained the body of a shipmate. The chaplain recited the Twenty-third Psalm, then commended the souls of the fallen men to the Almighty. The bugler played taps. As each mournful note echoed through the steel bulkheads of the hangar bay, many men wept openly. Together they flinched at each volley fired by the Marine honor guard. As each name was read, a board was tilted and a canvas body bag, weighted by a 5-inch shell, slipped from beneath the Stars and Stripes and disappeared into the sea.

The ritual was complete. In silence the men left the hangar

bay and went back to work. The next day, one of the wounded died from his injuries. The crew mustered on the lowered elevator and repeated the ceremony.

Not all *Intrepid*'s airplanes made it back to the carrier. A three-plane flight led by Lt. (jg) Wes Hays had launched shortly after noon on the day of the attack. Their mission was to fly cover for a PBM Dumbo seaplane while it rescued downed airmen from the Inland Sea in Japan. With Hays were his two wingmen, Ensigns Jim Hollister and Bill Ecker.

It was a long and tedious day. They encountered no Japanese fighters while the Dumbo rescued the crew. Then, for what seemed an eternity, the Corsairs escorted the lumbering PBM seaplane all the way back to Okinawa, throttled back and flying as slowly as they could. Darkness was falling by the time the Dumbo finally plopped into its sheltered seaway in the Kerama Retto near Okinawa. As they turned toward *Intrepid*, Hays received a terse order over the tactical frequency: "Red One, do not return to base." No explanation was given, but Hays knew that something had happened to their ship.

With night coming and no other good options, he and his flight diverted to Yontan airfield on Okinawa. The runways on the newly captured airfield were cratered and crudely patched. The fatigued pilots were still climbing from their cockpits when Japanese warplanes roared in from the north, strafing and bombing the airfield. The pilots spent the night huddled in a bunker, sharing Spam and crackers with the Marines, while around them the guns boomed and bombs exploded.

A day passed, and then another. By now they knew that *Intrepid* had taken a kamikaze hit and had been detached from the task force. Hays finally managed to wheedle from the Marines three 55-gallon barrels of aviation gasoline, one for each Corsair. It was barely enough to get them to the closest carrier, but they didn't care. Anyplace was better than Yontan. They'd had enough of tents, Spam, and grunt warfare.

Bumping and lurching on the same cratered runway on which they'd arrived, they roared back into the sky. They flew east until they found the USS *Essex*.

As Hays climbed out of his cockpit, he saw the deck crewmen on *Essex* rubbing their hands on the Corsair's wing-fold mechanism. The fighter was still covered with dried mud from Yontan. To the sailors on *Essex*, who had been at sea for nearly two months, the dirt was almost sacred. It was the closest thing to real earth that they'd seen.

The task group commander aboard *Essex*, Rear Adm. Fred Sherman, gave them a choice: they could stay there and join the *Essex* air group, or they could make their way back to wherever they'd come from. In either case they were losing their airplanes. The Corsairs were staying right there on *Essex*, where they were needed.

The *Intrepid* pilots made an instant collective decision. To hell with joining somebody else's air group. Wearing the same salt-stiffened clothes in which they'd begun their odyssey, they high-lined over to an oiler, then to a destroyer escort, then to an escort carrier, which eventually deposited them on Guam. There they threw themselves on the mercy of fellow aviators, who lent them clean khakis and enough cash to buy booze at the bar.

More days passed. Nearly two weeks after they'd launched from *Intrepid* on the Dumbo escort mission, they finally got a ride home. Wearing borrowed khakis and feeling like refugees, Hays, Hollister, and Ecker climbed onto a camouflage-painted Marine R5C Commando transport for the trip to Ulithi, where *Intrepid* was undergoing repairs.

As he was boarding the transport, Hays glanced into the cockpit. One of the pilots looked familiar. He had a flashy grin and movie-star good looks. Hays did a double take. Hell, the guy *was* a movie star. Their pilot was none other than Tyrone Power, now an aviator and first lieutenant in the Marine Corps.

Wes Hays had to shake his head. It was just another bizarre

scene in what seemed like an endlessly weird movie. The folks back in Novice, Texas, weren't going to believe this one.

Lt. Harold "Bitz" Bitzegaio limped into the Grim Reapers ready room, dreading the ceremony that awaited him. The squadron skipper, Wally Clarke, was going to pin a medal on him.

Bitzegaio was the only pilot injured in the kamikaze attack on *Intrepid*. He had been standing on the flight deck when the flaming Zero was diving on the ship. Seeing what was coming, he had already turned and was headed for cover, getting the hell out of the way, when he felt something tap him in the rear. It took several seconds before he realized that he'd been nailed with shrapnel.

Bitzegaio wasn't badly wounded, but while he was walking down to sick bay under his own power, the sickening realization hit him: he was going to get a Purple Heart out of this. And he'd been around Navy squadrons long enough to know where they were going to pin it.

And they did. He didn't mind so much getting the Purple Heart pinned to the seat of his pants by the skipper. The worst part for Bitzegaio was knowing that years from now, when they were all recounting their war exploits, he'd still be explaining how he got hit in the butt running from the enemy.

32 ▸ CALL ME ERNIE

Lt. Gen. Simon Buckner was spending most of the daylight hours in his new command post ashore. In two more days he intended to move his entire staff and all their gear off the *Eldorado*.

Buckner had reason to be optimistic. Even if the campaign wasn't progressing as quickly as he wanted in the south, the battle in the north was almost wrapped up. The 6th Marine Division had the Motobu Peninsula nearly secured.

Now Buckner was anxious to seize Ie Shima, the oval-shaped island three miles off the tip of Motobu. Ie Shima was five miles long and two miles wide, a flat plateau covered in scrub brush and a patchwork of vegetable and sugarcane fields. The island's main value lay in its airfield, which had three runways long enough to accommodate heavy bombers.

For the capture of Ie Shima, Buckner intended to use the crack 77th Division, led by Maj. Gen. Andrew Bruce. Buckner was impressed with Bruce's aggressive spirit. "I much prefer a bird dog that you have to whistle in to one that you have to urge out," Buckner wrote. "He is of the former variety."

It had been Bruce's 77th Division that seized the Kerama Retto in the days before the Love Day landings. The islands of the Retto were taken with surprising ease, and intelligence reports indicated that Ie Shima would be the same. Aerial reconnaissance and advance scouting teams revealed no sign of enemy activity. The base appeared to be abandoned and the runways ripped up. Fighter sweeps over the island had drawn no return fire. Ie Shima, it seemed, had been abandoned.

It was a deadly deception. Hidden on the island were 3,000

Japanese troops, commanded by a tough army major named Masashi Igawa. With time to prepare his defenses, Igawa had constructed a classic beehive of interconnecting tunnels and fortified gun positions dug into the limestone rock. Igawa augmented his garrison with local conscripts and several hundred support personnel and armed them with every available weapon—mortars, antiaircraft guns, aircraft machine guns, even bamboo spears.

The Japanese defenses were centered near the village of Ie, on the eastern end of the island. Overlooking the village was the pyramid-shaped Mt. Iegusugu, an extinct volcano that the Americans would call "the Pinnacle." Rising like a monolith on the east of the island, the Pinnacle had the same deadly features as Mt. Suribachi on Iwo Jima. With its expanse of flat plateau, three long runways, and 578-foot-high promontory at one end, Ie Shima had the appearance of a giant, unmoving aircraft carrier.

The assault began at dawn on April 16 with a massive naval bombardment. Two battleships, four cruisers, and seven destroyers pounded the island. The landing beaches on the south and southwest shores were blanketed with rockets, mortar shells, and close air support from carrier-based fighter-bombers. The covering fire was so intense that most of Ie Shima was obscured in smoke and billowing dust. A Japanese soldier wrote in his journal: "After a fierce air and naval bombardment, the enemy began his landing in front of the 4th Company, using amphibian tractors. Their firepower is so great we dared not show our heads."

Not until the Americans had charged several hundred yards inland did the truth become apparent: the enemy had not conceded Ie Shima. From concealed machine gun nests and mortar sites and cave openings, the Japanese opened fire. The resistance grew steadily more vicious as the soldiers of the 77th advanced to the eastern part of the island.

On the second day of the battle for Ie Shima, America's most famous war correspondent came ashore to see the action for himself.

E rnie Pyle was tired. He was glad to be riding in a Jeep instead of slogging up another damned hill with the foot soldiers. Pyle was three weeks short of his forty-fifth birthday, but he looked older. Three years of sleeping in foxholes, riding troop transports, and witnessing the carnage in Europe had taken a toll on him. He was gray-haired, balding on top, with a haggard, war-weary expression. Pyle was beginning to look more and more like one of the "GI Joe" caricatures drawn by his friend, artist Bill Mauldin.

Pyle arrived on Ie Shima April 17. That afternoon he watched the fighting from an observation post. The heaviest action was in the east of the island, where the Japanese were making a stand on a stretch of high ground the GIs were calling Bloody Ridge. The next morning he dutifully signed autographs for the troops, then had a meeting with General Bruce.

What Pyle really wanted, though, was to see the fighting. That's what he'd come for, not to sign autographs and get briefed by generals. Lt. Col. Joe Coolidge, who commanded the 305th Infantry Regiment, had a Jeep and was headed for the front. Pyle could come along.

Pyle, Coolidge, and three soldiers were bumping along a dirt road that paralleled the southern shore. Their Jeep had joined a procession of three trucks and a military police Jeep. In the distance, from Bloody Ridge and the town of Ie, they could hear the crackle of gunfire and mortars.

The convoy was nearing a road junction when they heard the sharp rattle of a machine gun. On either side of the Jeep, puffs of dirt kicked up. The front tires were hit, and steam gushed from a hit in the radiator. The machine gun fire was coming from a coral ridge ahead of them.

The Jeep lurched to a halt, and all five men dove into a ditch. The machine gun went silent. Pyle let several seconds go by, then he looked around. Coolidge was next to him in the ditch. The two men raised their heads to look for the other three. Pyle saw that they were all safe. He smiled and said to Coolidge, "Are you all right?"

He had barely uttered the words when the machine gun opened up again. Coolidge ducked as a round kicked up dust in his face and whizzed over his head. At the same time he saw Pyle drop back into the ditch. It took him a moment to realize what had happened.

Pyle was lying on his back, clutching the knitted cap he always had with him. Coolidge didn't notice any blood, but then he saw the purplish hole in the left temple. He yelled for a medic while a an infantry squad from the 305th went after the machine gunner. For Ernie Pyle it was too late. The bullet had killed him instantly.

There was no time to mourn. The battle for Ie Shima was still raging. They buried the war correspondent, still wearing his helmet, in a long row of fresh graves on Ie Shima. A private lay on one side of him, an engineer on the other. Someone erected a wooden marker: "On this spot, the 77th Division lost a buddy, Ernie Pyle, 18 April, 1945."

In the reporter's pocket they found the rough draft of a piece he'd written in anticipation of the war ending in Europe.

There are many of the living who have had burned into their brains forever the unnatural sight of cold dead men scattered over the hillsides and in the ditches along the high rows of hedge throughout the world.

Dead men by mass production—in one country after another—month after month and year after year. Dead men in winter and dead men in summer.

Dead men in such familiar promiscuity that they become monotonous. Dead men in such monstrous infinity that you come almost to hate them...

It was a final touch of irony. Ernie Pyle might have been writing his own epitaph.

I t took three more days to close the ring around the Pinnacle. Again and again the Japanese defenders made suicidal counterattacks, rushing the American lines, hurling satchel charges, and blowing themselves up with live mortar rounds.

Even the old warrior General Bruce was shocked at the ferocity of the enemy defenses. After four and a half days of bloody fighting, as his troops were closing in on the last remaining stronghold, Bruce reported to General Buckner, "Base of Pinnacle completely surrounded despite bitterest fight I have ever witnessed against a veritable fortress."

And it still wasn't over. Reaching the summit was an even more bitter fight. By the time the 77th had captured the Pinnacle and Ie Shima was declared secure, 218 American soldiers were dead and nearly 1,000 wounded. The Japanese had lost 4,700, and 409 were taken prisoner.

A t noon the next day, April 19, *Intrepid* pulled into the heart-shaped lagoon at Ulithi in the western Caroline Islands. Ulithi looked different than when *Intrepid* had been there in March. Gone were the long rows of gray warships assembling for the invasion of Okinawa. The only big ships in the anchorage were the battleship *Iowa*, the carrier *Enterprise*, which was undergoing repairs from her own kamikaze hit on April 11, and the fast carrier *Shangri-La*, on her way to join the task force off Okinawa.

And Ulithi had become swelteringly hot. At 10 degrees above the equator, the atoll baked in the tropical sun and humidity. While crews labored to repair *Intrepid*'s combat damage, sailors sought relief from the heat on the recreation island of Mog Mog.

Mog Mog was one of many islets nestled inside Ulithi's coral reef. The Navy had persuaded the local chieftain, King Ueg, to move Mog Mog's three hundred inhabitants to another island in the atoll. Now Mog Mog had a movie theater, a chapel, and an array of refreshment stands.

When the anchorage was filled with warships, as many as fifteen thousand sailors a day swarmed over the 60-acre island of Mog Mog. They were given coupons for two beers apiece, but enterprising sailors always found ways to exceed the limit. Separate areas were fenced off for officers, whose booze limits were less restricted. There was nothing much to do on the atoll except drink the rations of beer, try to cadge more from nondrinking buddies, and comb the beach for exotic shells. Mog Mog, someone cracked, had "no wine atoll, no women atoll, no nothing atoll."

Sailors being sailors, some managed to get drunk. The nightly trip on the LCVP (landing craft vehicle personnel) ferry boat to the ship was a classic return from shore liberty: fights, men falling overboard, sailors unaccustomed to alcohol heaving their guts out.

Unlike most of the other Tail End Charlies, Erickson wasn't interested in hanging out at the makeshift officers' bar at Mog Mog. Instead, he finagled permission to visit the island of Fassari, which was off-limits to everyone except Navy photographers and journalists. Bartering cigarettes in exchange for posing, Erickson toured Fassari with his sketchbook in hand, filling pages with drawings of native life.

Meanwhile, crews from the repair ship *Ajax* struggled to get *Intrepid* back in fighting shape. It had already been determined that the carrier's number three elevator was beyond fixing. Still, they figured that after repairing the damage to her hangar bays and electrical systems, the carrier would be 80 percent combat capable. There was a war on, and that was good enough.

On April 24 came more bad news. They found that the number two elevator—the deck edge elevator on the ship's port side—had been knocked out of alignment, probably from the effect of rolling forty damaged airplanes over its edge on the day of the kamikaze attack. The elevator didn't work, and it couldn't be fixed.

Which meant that *Intrepid* couldn't operate as a fighting carrier. With only one working elevator, she couldn't move airplanes between the hangar and flight decks fast enough to support combat operations. Nimitz himself made the decision: *Intrepid* would return to the Hunters Point shipyard in San Francisco for permanent repairs.

Most of *Intrepid*'s planes, however, were staying where they were needed. While still at anchor in Ulithi, pilots catapulted off the stationary carrier, then landed on the nearby runway at Ulithi. Each pilot gritted his teeth against the jolt of the catapult shot, which was harder than normal to compensate for the lack of wind over the deck.

Now that *Intrepid* was leaving, no longer functioning as an aircraft carrier, she would become a transport. Instead of airplanes, the ship was hauling U.S.-bound passengers, including the pilots from the carrier *San Jacinto*.

In the crew spaces there was jubilation. Going home, even for the brief time it would take to repair the ship, was an unexpected gift. For the Tail End Charlies in Boys' Town, the news had a bittersweet flavor. The Battle of Okinawa wasn't over, but the end was in sight. They were going to miss the finale of the show they had started.

Or maybe not. Rumors were flying like missiles around the ship. The normal time for an air group to be deployed in a combat zone was six months. If a carrier was taken off the line, her air group was usually off-loaded to await another carrier headed back to the war. The time you spent waiting for the next carrier didn't count.

To the Tail End Charlies it meant they might have to hang around in the Pacific for months before they went back aboard a carrier. They might even miss the rest of the war.

33 ▸ COUNTEROFFENSIVE

Stepping onto the tarmac at Yontan, Adm. Chester Nimitz surveyed the scene around him. Yontan still had the look of a base under siege. The place was covered with tents, sandbagged trenches, and fortified sentry posts. Marine Corps Corsairs were dispersed all over the field to make them less vulnerable to the nightly air attacks and artillery shellings.

But the commander in chief of the Pacific Fleet hadn't come to Okinawa to inspect the facilities. He was there on urgent business. Normally a patient and even-tempered commander, Nimitz had lost his patience.

The Navy's ship losses at Okinawa had become unacceptable. Between April 1 and April 22, sixty vessels had been sunk or nearly destroyed by Japanese warplanes. More than eleven hundred Navy men had been killed and twice as many wounded.

In Nimitz's view, there was one overwhelming reason for these losses: the battle for Okinawa was dragging on too long. As long as the Tenth Army was bogged down on the island, the kamikazes would continue to savage Nimitz's ships offshore.

Waiting on the ramp to meet the admiral was the white-haired, fit-looking commander of the Tenth Army, Lt. Gen. Simon Buckner. Nimitz had brought with him an entourage: Fifth Fleet commander Adm. Raymond Spruance, Lt. Gen. Alexander Vandergrift, the Commandant of the Marine Corps, and Nimitz's chief of staff, Vice Adm. Forrest Sherman.

The meeting started off amicably enough. Buckner took his guests on a tour of the captured sectors of Okinawa. The mood was still jovial and relaxed when Nimitz presented Buckner with a bottle of liquor, remembering his traditional toast, "May you walk in the ashes of Tokyo." Buckner joked that he would keep the bottle in reserve until Okinawa had been secured.

Then they sat down in Buckner's headquarters, and the mood changed. Nimitz got right to the point. It was time to break the impasse, he told Buckner. If it took another amphibious landing behind the Japanese lines, then Buckner should do it. Whatever it took, he *had* to speed up the advance.

It was a tense moment. That a Navy admiral had overall command of a land campaign had always been a sensitive issue with Army brass. Bristling, Buckner informed Nimitz that the ground assault was the Army's job. He would take care of it.

Nimitz's eyes flashed, and his temper rose to the surface. "I'm losing a ship and a half a day," he snapped. "If this line isn't moving within five days, we'll get someone here to move it so we can all get out from under these damn air attacks."

Buckner held his ground. What this son of a Confederate general might have lacked in imagination, he made up for in stubbornness. Supporting another front, in his opinion, didn't make sense. He'd already lost two ammunition ships at Kerama Retto. Opening another front would overstretch his supply system.

Vandergrift, the Marine commandant, sided with Nimitz. He told Buckner he ought to "play the amphib card." Vandergrift's 2nd Marine Division, which had played a diversionary role in the initial landings, was now on Saipan and available. They could make a landing on the southeast coast of Okinawa, just north of Minatoga, turn the Japanese right flank, and end the stalemate.

Even Buckner's division commanders, including his favorite, Maj. Gen. Andrew Bruce, were on record as favoring an amphibious end run. Bruce himself had executed such a move behind Japanese lines during the Leyte invasion with brilliant success. Here was the perfect opportunity to do it again.

Buckner wasn't having any of it. If he erred, it was damned well going be on the side of caution. The proposed landing beaches were directly beneath a set of treacherous steep cliffs. Buckner thought the landings could turn into "another Anzio [the disastrous 1944 landing in Italy] but worse."

The argument, like the battle itself, dragged to a stalemate. Buckner would not be swayed. As long as he was in command, he intended to continue the classic frontal assault. In the long run, he insisted, it would save lives.

Spruance, for one, didn't think so. "I doubt if the Army's slow, methodical method of fighting really saves any lives in the long run," Spruance wrote to a friend. "It merely spreads the casualties over a longer period. The longer period greatly increases the naval casualties when Jap air attacks on ships is a continuing factor. . . . There are times when I get impatient for some of Holland [Howlin' Mad] Smith's drive."

Nothing had been resolved. At the end of the historic meeting, it was Nimitz who backed down. The last thing Nimitz wanted at Okinawa was another Army-Navy brawl over a fired general.

The next day they were again standing on the ramp at Yontan. Nimitz shook hands with Buckner and climbed back aboard his plane. Buckner was still in command of the Tenth Army. He would continue to run the campaign his way. No surprises, no amphibious landing, no flanking maneuvers. Everyone expected that the battle would drag on.

And then that night, the enemy did something no one expected.

It began soon after dusk. An intense artillery barrage, more than a thousand rounds, poured down on the front-line American units. Directly behind the bombardment, almost as if summoned by the Japanese, came a dense fog that enshrouded the entire battle zone. Beneath the fog and the artillery cover, the Japanese defenders slipped away in the darkness, withdrawing to the second defense line on the Urasoe-Mura escarpment.

At first, the American troops on the front line didn't believe it. It had to be another Japanese deception. The pockmarked ground for which they had fought so bitterly was unoccupied. After days of sacrifice and failure the first Japanese line of defense, including the bloody Kakazu Ridge, was theirs for the taking.

The withdrawal, in fact, had gone exactly according to the plan proposed by Colonel Yahara and approved by General Ushijima. Despite their success at holding off the American assault, the Japanese had lost ground over the past few days on Skyline Ridge, Nishibaru Ridge, and the Tanabaru escarpment. Rather than stand their ground and be annihilated, the Japanese had executed a strategic withdrawal so they could continue fighting.

Still, the fire-eaters on Ushijima's staff, led by General Cho, were belligerent. That night in the headquarters under Shuri Castle, the same old debate raged on about defensive versus offensive tactics. Cho continued urging a counterattack, throwing the Americans back to the beach. As usual, Ushijima listened, nodding respectfully, letting all his officers weigh in. He wasn't inclined to change the strategy, at least not after the failed night attack of April 12. For now, he was sticking with Yahara's campaign of slow, measured attrition.

Yahara, for his part, had reason to be pleased. His strategy was working. Already the 32nd Army had held out longer and with greater success than in any other Pacific island campaign. From their fallback line on Urasoe-Mura escarpment General Ushijima would continue Yahara's carefully constructed holding strategy.

Then came the night of April 29. It was the emperor's birthday, and General Ushijima convened his staff officers in the underground headquarters. Fueled by larger-than-usual quantities of sake, General Cho was in his most strident *bushido*-obsessed voice. By now the divide between the conservatives, led by Colonel Yahara, and the fire-eaters, championed by Cho, had widened to a chasm.

Cho was again demanding a counteroffensive. It was a matter of honor, he insisted. The 32nd Army should be revered in history as an army of warriors, not failed defenders. By the next night, April 30, a majority of Ushijima's staff officers were recommending that he launch an all-out counteroffensive against the American line.

To American officers—and to those of most other countries— it would seem a peculiar command style, a general taking a vote of his subordinates before making a crucial decision. It was not uncommon in the Imperial Japanese Army, and it was General Ushijima's style. Without further deliberation, Ushijima signed the order. The counteroffensive would launch on May 4. It would be coordinated with *kikusui* No. 5, another massed *tokko* attack on the American fleet.

Col. Hiromichi Yahara had again been outvoted and overruled. Dismayed, he watched his carefully constructed strategy for a holding action come apart. Yahara was a loyal soldier. He hoped that Cho's counteroffensive would work. In his secret heart he knew that it was doomed.

Like most Japanese battle plans, Cho's counteroffensive was ambitious and overly complicated. It envisioned the 24th Division seizing the eastern flank of the Maeda escarpment, taking control of the center of the line. Two engineering/shipping regiments were to make amphibious landings behind the American lines on both the east and west coasts.

The 44th Brigade would cut off the two U.S. Marine divisions holding the western end of the line. Two Japanese regiments would dislodge the U.S. 7th Division from its positions on Conical Hill on the eastern flank while the 44th and 62nd Divisions wiped out the trapped U.S. Marine units. Tanks and heavy artillery would concentrate on the critical Maeda escarpment, where the breakthrough would take place.

The counteroffensive began in the rainy predawn darkness of May 4. The flash and thunder of the massive artillery barrage reflected from the low overcast. For half an hour more than twelve thousand rounds of artillery exploded on the American lines.

Then the Japanese assault troops moved out, making their way across the mud-slickened no-man's-land to the American lines.

They were moving too slowly. As the first rays of sunlight illuminated the battlefield, not all the units of the 24th Division had reached their jumping-off point. Caught in the open, they became targets for U.S. artillery and mortars. The advancing Japanese infantrymen ran into a wall of machine gun and mortar fire from the entrenched Americans.

Instead of a coordinated frontal assault against the U.S. lines, the counteroffensive quickly turned into a tableau of disconnected firefights, with Japanese infantry units being cut off and decimated one after the other. The attempt by the engineering/shipping regiments to make amphibious landings behind the lines was intercepted, and a thousand troops were mowed down.

The 27th Tank Regiment—the only Japanese armor to be employed offensively at Okinawa—ran into trouble before most had neared their objective on Maeda hill. Only two tanks managed to reach the American perimeter, and both were destroyed by a single American soldier, Private 1st Class James Poore, who took each out with a round from his bazooka.

General Ushijima was appalled. From his vantage point at Shuri Castle, he watched the attack on the Maeda escarpment falter. The counteroffensive was turning into an even greater disaster than the failed night assault of April 12.

But neither Ushijima nor Cho was willing to concede failure. The battle raged on for the rest of the day, with Japanese troops closing in on a sector held by the U.S. 306th Infantry Regiment. After hours of combat, the Japanese were finally beaten back with heavy losses.

The only notable Japanese success was by the 1st Battalion of the 24th Division, led by a resourceful army captain named Koichi

Ito. Concluding that a daylight attack was suicidal, Koichi came up with his own plan. After nightfall his battalion infiltrated the American lines, penetrating half a mile and seizing a stronghold on the Tanabaru escarpment.

Then they were stuck. Surrounded by the enemy and cut off from the rest of the division, which was stalled back at the main line, Ito and his men dug in. They held their perimeter all day and into the night against vigorous American attacks while they waited for the 24th Division to make a breakthrough.

The breakthrough never came. Despite the agonizing lack of progress, the Japanese counteroffensive continued into another rainy day, May 5.

By late afternoon, General Ushijima had seen enough. He gave the order for all units to withdraw, ignoring for a change the protests of his junior staff officers. Under cover of darkness, the surviving Japanese troops crept back through the mud and smoldering remains of tanks to their lines.

Not until the next night, May 6, did Captain Ito's battalion, still holding out behind the American lines, manage to exfiltrate with 230 surviving troops back through the enemy positions to their own lines.

The counteroffensive was a catastrophe from which the 32nd Army would never recover. Nearly 7,000 of the unit's original 76,000 soldiers had been lost. Almost all their tanks were destroyed. The few surviving tanks would be buried to be used as immobile pillboxes. The once-formidable Japanese artillery on Okinawa had been reduced by half.

But the worst loss to General Ushijima's army was its morale. The fighting spirit of the Japanese soldiers on Okinawa would never be the same. Though none yet knew it, they had just conducted the last Japanese ground offensive of the war.

As ordered, Col. Hiromichi Yahara appeared at the commanding general's office. Standing at attention, he rendered a silent salute. He had no idea why Ushijima had summoned him. It was the evening of May 5, and the disastrous offensive was finished. Was the general planning to sacrifice the rest of the 32nd Army in a final fight-to-the-death offensive? Was this the end?

General Ushijima was in his usual pose, sitting cross-legged on the worn *tatami* floor. He wore a pensive expression. "Colonel Yahara," the general said in a soft voice, "as you predicted, this offensive has been a total failure. Your judgment was correct." Ushijima told Yahara that meaningless suicide would no longer be their strategy. With what strength they had left, the 32nd Army would fight for every last inch of the island. "I am ready to fight," said the general, "but from now on I leave everything up to you."

Yahara was speechless. Such an admission from a high-ranking commander was unheard of in the Imperial Japanese Army. Then, thinking about it, Yahara became furious. Now that the army had been beaten to exhaustion, Ushijima was ready to do what Yahara had been advocating since the beginning.

The trouble was, it was too late. Yahara calculated that if the army's strength had not been squandered in the stupid offensive, they could have held out for at least a month longer. It might have made a difference in the outcome of the war. Thousands of lives might have been saved.

There was only one possible benefit from the disaster that Yahara could see. The offensive would make the enemy more cautious about any Japanese course of action.

As it turned out, it was just another false hope.

34 ► BOTTOM OF THE BARREL

Matome Ugaki had a bad case of diarrhea. The problem only worsened the admiral's foul mood, which was caused by the news from Europe. Mussolini had been captured and executed by his own people. The Russians were in the streets of Berlin. Hitler had committed suicide.

Ugaki thought the Fuehrer's death was a tragedy. "But his spirit will remain long with the German nation," he wrote in his diary, "while the United States and Britain will suffer from communism some day and regret that their powerful supporter, Hitler, was killed."

Another floating chrysanthemum operation—*kikusui* No. 5—was supposed to be coordinated with the counteroffensive by Ushijima's 32nd Army on Okinawa. Ugaki was skeptical of the army's chances. "This attempt does not have much prospect of success," he wrote, "but better to be venturesome, hoping to put up a fight while they have enough guts, than to be knocked while idle."

Ugaki was sending every plane he could muster into this next *kikusui*. It wasn't enough—only 125 dedicated *tokko* aircraft, along with an equal number of conventional warplanes—but the admiral retained his high hopes. He was sure that with improved tactics they would cause even more destruction to the Americans than in the first days when the *tokkotai* were at full strength. The trouble was, American B-29s were showing up almost every night, cratering runways and making it risky to assemble the waves of *tokko* airplanes.

In the waning light of May 3, during a break from the bombers, Ugaki's first wave of *kikusui* No. 5 rumbled into the sky.

To the tin can sailors on RP10, 73 miles west of Okinawa, it was the same old story—blips on the radar, klaxons blaring, bullhorns ordering the crews to battle stations. CAP fighters roared overhead, heading northward to intercept incoming bogeys. Nervous gunners aboard the tin cans peered into the pale gray sky.

A sailor with a dark sense of humor put up a sign on his destroyer with an arrow pointing eastward: "Carriers That Way."

Radarmen aboard the destroyer-minelayer *Aaron Ward* and destroyer *Little* were tracking a swarm of incoming bogeys. The fighter CAP—four F6F Hellcats—had already engaged the attackers, but they were overwhelmed by sheer numbers. Two dozen kamikazes swept over the destroyers and their four accompanying gunboats.

Within minutes, the picket ships were fighting for their lives. *Ward*'s gunners splashed the first two attackers, both Vals. Then came a faster-moving Zero fighter on the port side. Just before impact, the Zero released its 550-pound bomb. The explosion killed more than a dozen crewmen, jamming her rudder to port and slowing the ship to a crawl.

It seemed a replay of the *Laffey* ordeal two weeks ago. Sensing blood, more kamikazes appeared, but *Ward*'s gunners turned them away. She was out of danger, but only for the moment.

The nearby *Little* was in just as much trouble. Her gunners downed one kamikaze, then another, but it wasn't enough. Four more, one after another, crashed into *Little*, wrecking the destroyer's superstructure and breaking her keel. With the ship listing severely to starboard, her rails nearly submerged, *Little*'s skipper, Cmdr. Madison Hall, gave the order to abandon ship.

The order didn't come too soon. Four minutes later, *Little* sank in 850 fathoms of water, taking thirty of her crew with her.

The carnage on RP10 continued. LSM(R)-195, a rocket-firing amphibious support craft, was at full speed to assist the destroyers when she came under attack by a pair of kamikazes. The 203-foot-long gunboat lacked both the firepower and the speed to fight off the kamikazes. One crashed into her port side, exploding her rocket magazines, flinging fire and shrapnel around the decks. In fifteen minutes, the amphibious craft was gone.

Meanwhile, more kamikazes were pouncing on the damaged and smoking *Aaron Ward*. *Ward*'s gunners fought back, shooting down three attackers. Then, in quick succession, the destroyer took five more kamikaze strikes and bombs on her main deck, her hull on the port side, her superstructure aft, and her number two stack. Her engines were dead. *Ward* lay adrift, burning in the gathering darkness.

Incredibly, the destroyer stayed afloat. Through the long night *Ward*'s crew, aided by the destroyer *Shannon* and two gunboats, fought to save the ship. Early the next morning, the shattered but still defiant *Aaron Ward* arrived under tow in Kerama Retto.

For its opening day, *kikusui* No. 5 had been impressive. Two U.S. ships had gone to the bottom of the East China Sea. Several others were damaged, including *Aaron Ward*, so badly mangled she was out of the war. In the brief action of May 3, the picket ships had suffered 248 casualties. To the sailors on the tin cans, it didn't seem that it could get much worse.

They were wrong.

Biplanes? The gunners on the destroyer *Morrison* the next morning couldn't believe what they were seeing. They peered through the pall of smoke at the apparitions coming toward them. There were seven of them—old-fashioned biplanes, equipped with floats. They were lumbering toward *Morrison* at the approximate speed of a Jeep. Each of the ancient floatplanes had a 250-kilogram bomb strapped beneath it.

It was the latest twist in the battle at RP1. Since dawn *Morrison*, her accompanying destroyer, *Ingraham*, and their four gunboats had been under siege by a continuous wave of kamikazes.

CAP Corsairs had already taken down four at close range to *Morrison*, and two more were splashed by the destroyer's guns. One of the bogeys, chased by a Corsair, glanced off *Morrison*'s bridge and crashed close astern. Another sheared a wing on the destroyer's bridge.

Then *Morrison*'s luck had run out. Two Zeroes, pursued by Corsairs and hammered with antiaircraft fire, exploded into the destroyer's topside, opening her hull and setting the ship ablaze. It was then, while the crew was battling the fire, straining to pick out the next wave of kamikazes through the smoke, that they saw the biplanes.

Code-named "Dave," the antiquated aircraft were, in fact, highly effective kamikazes. Their wood-and-fabric structure made them nearly invisible on search radars. The proximity fuses of anti-aircraft shells failed to detonate when they whizzed past the flimsy craft. Pilots of high-speed CAP fighters were having a devilishly hard time shooting the twisting, slow-moving biplanes.

On they came. Looming out of the smoke, one of the biplanes crashed into *Morrison*'s aft 5-inch mount, lighting off the magazine and causing a cataclysmic explosion. A second biplane, in no hurry, landed in the water behind the destroyer long enough to elude a pursuing Corsair, then took off again. The kamikaze continued straight into *Morrison*'s stern, touching off another magazine explosion.

It was the final blow for *Morrison*. Ripped apart, the destroyer rolled to starboard and sank stern first. One hundred fifty-two men—nearly half *Morrison*'s crew—went down with her.

The battle wasn't going any better for *Morrison*'s escorts. One of the gunboats, LSM(R)-194, was caught in the stern by a diving Val. Within minutes her bow tilted up and she joined *Morrison* at the bottom of the sea. Thirteen men aboard the rocket-firing LSM went down with her.

It was a sobering sight for the crew of the nearby destroyer *Ingraham*, who had watched *Morrison*'s death throes while they fought off their own attackers. Now the kamikazes were turning their full attention to *Ingraham*. *Ingraham*'s gunners and the CAP fighters shot down a succession of attackers, but it wasn't enough. *Ingraham* had two near misses before a Zero crashed near her number two 5-inch mount, flooding the forward fire room and killing fourteen men.

The CAP fighter pilots overhead were astonished at the variety of kamikaze warplanes—everything from Betty bombers and Zero fighters to training planes and museum-piece biplanes. The Japanese were scraping the bottom of the barrel. Did they have anything left to throw at the Americans?

They did. In the murky sky over RP14, Sub-Lt. Susumu Ohashi was lowering himself through the bomb bay of the twin-engine Mitsubishi Ki-46 "Dinah" bomber, settling into the cockpit of his *Ohka* guided bomb. Ohashi was one of seven Thunder Gods of the 7th Cherry Blossom Unit who had launched that morning from Kanoya airfield.

The Dinah bombers were an improvement over the slower G4M Bettys that carried the first *Ohka* guided bombs. Originally designed as reconnaissance aircraft, the Dinah was faster than the Betty, but it was more lightly armored. Now the pilot of Ohashi's Dinah was becoming anxious. Enemy fighters had just spotted them. They were already swooping in a pursuit curve onto the bomber's tail. Machine gun tracers were converging on the Dinah.

The Dinah pilot wasn't waiting any longer. He gave the signal to Susumu Ohashi, who had just strapped himself into the cockpit of the *Ohka*: ready or not, he was going to be released *now*.

The gunners on the minelayer *Shea* were cursing the smoke. The visibility around them and their escorts was now less than three miles, and it was because of the damned smoke screen someone had laid down back at the Hagushi anchorage. The smoke had drifted northward until it covered *Shea* and her escorts on their picket station. *Shea*'s nervous gunners were squinting through the murk, trying to pick out the first ominous silhouettes of incoming bogeys.

At 0857, they spotted one. It was a twin-engine bomber, still high, at the upper edge of the haze blanket. A pair of FM-2 Wildcat fighters was already after it, guns blazing. The bomber would be splashed before it came close enough to threaten *Shea* and her entourage. There was nothing to worry about.

High above, the Wildcat pilots were pouring machine gun fire into the Dinah bomber when they glimpsed something peculiar. An odd-shaped object dropped from the bomber's belly. Not until a few seconds later, when they saw fire spit from the object's tail, did they know what it was. Then it was too late.

The *Ohka* was accelerating like a bullet. One of the Wildcats dove after the weird-looking aircraft, but it was no contest. The rocket-boosted guided bomb was already moving at 350 knots, becoming a distant speck in the Wildcat pilot's gun sight.

Down below, the startled gunners on the *Shea* had almost no warning. The gnatlike object came screaming out of the hazy murk, aimed like a meteor for the bridge of their ship. Gun captains were yelling commands, trying to track the object, but it was unstoppable.

The *Ohka* slammed like a battering ram into the starboard side of *Shea*'s bridge superstructure—and kept going. A millisecond later, the *Ohka* emerged on the other side, leaving a large exit hole in *Shea*'s port hull. Not until the warhead of the *Ohka* was 15 feet past the ship's hull did it explode.

Shea rocked from the external blast. Several frames were buckled and plates were ruptured. Twenty-seven men were killed in the attack, and 130 were wounded. *Shea* had been punctured from one side to the other, but the minelayer could still make her own way and was in no danger of sinking.

Shea had been saved by a miracle—and by the ballistics of the *Ohka*, which was designed to penetrate heavy armor, not the thin skin of a minelayer such as USS *Shea*.

At Hagushi anchorage, the gunners aboard the heavy cruiser *Birmingham* were busy. *Birmingham* was the flagship of surface force commander Rear Adm. Mort Deyo, and it had been under attack most of the morning by kamikazes coming from the sea. While the gunners were preoccupied, a lone Oscar was sneaking in from over the island of Okinawa, undetected on radar.

No one spotted the kamikaze until he was just a mile out. The close-in 20-millimeter guns opened fire, but it was too late. The bomb-carrying Oscar plunged into *Birmingham*'s number two 6-inch forward turret, exploding downward into the spaces below.

For half an hour flames poured from the cruiser. Fifty-one men were killed, including most of the ship's medical corpsmen, who were concentrated in the ship's wardroom and main casualty center. Eighty-one more were wounded. *Birmingham* was so badly damaged she had to retire to Guam for repairs.

The Americans weren't the only targets that morning. Operating off the Sakishima Gunto, the southern island group between Okinawa and Formosa, British Task Force 57 was bombarding the Japanese airfields of Nobara and Sukuma.

The Royal Navy task force had joined the U.S. Fifth Fleet in March 1945, with the responsibility of covering the southern approaches to Okinawa. Now the commander, Vice Adm. Sir Bernard Rawlings, had split off his battleships and cruisers from his carriers, sending the heavy surface ships in close to use their heavy guns.

Which, as it turned out, was a tactical mistake. The screen around the British carriers had been weakened. It was an opening the kamikazes quickly exploited.

At 1131 on May 4, a Zero wound its way through the British CAP fighters and the antiaircraft barrage and crashed into the flight deck of the carrier HMS *Formidable*. There was a fireball, a number of casualties, and damage to parked airplanes and deck equipment. The kamikaze had splattered on *Formidable*'s armored flight deck like a scrambled egg.

And that was it. No raging fires or cataclysmic explosions. The carrier shrugged off the hit and continued operating.

The incident revealed a crucial design difference between British and American aircraft carriers. All the U.S. flattops, including the newest *Essex*-class fast carriers such as *Intrepid*, had wooden flight decks. With deadly frequency kamikazes were punching through the wooden decks like knives through cardboard, exploding into the packed hangar bays.

The wooden decks were a carryover from 1930s aircraft carrier design. Wood could be more easily repaired than steel and, in theory, the lighter wooden decks allowed the ships to carry more airplanes.

No one had foreseen the specter of suicide planes crashing through the wooden planking. Now U.S. carrier skippers, watching the kamikazes ricochet off the British steel decks, were already thinking about the future. Postwar U.S. Navy aircraft carriers would not have wooden decks.

35 ▸ GONE WITH THE SPRING

L t. (jg) Windy Hill's loathing of submarines had reached a new intensity. After what seemed like years but was only a few weeks, the *Sea Dog* finished her war patrol and pulled into Guam. With his flight gear in a pillowcase over his shoulder, wearing sandals and a borrowed shirt and trousers, Hill stepped ashore. It was his first time on dry land since the day in March when he flew his last combat mission from *Intrepid*.

Hill's cruise aboard the *Sea Dog* had revealed to him the vast culture gap between airedales and submariners. Submarine officers, he discovered, didn't gather in a stateroom at night to sip Coon Range and swap stories. As far as he could tell, they didn't sip anything, and in any case, there were no staterooms.

Sea Dog's officers had invited him to join them at their rest-and-recreation camp. Hill politely declined. He'd seen enough of submarines and submariners. Thank you and goodbye.

Hill headed across the naval base, looking for the fleet aviation headquarters, where he would report his return. He didn't make it. En route he spotted a Quonset hut atop a hill that had the unmistakable look of an officers' club. "It took me about one-half of a second to decide where to re-direct my feet," Hill recalled. "I figured the war could get along without me for a while."

It *was* an officers' club, and it had a bar. The bartender asked if he wanted a beer. No, Hill said. He wanted *six* beers, and he wanted them opened and lined up in front of him. "When I start inhaling these, I don't want to waste time reordering."

He drank the beers. The bartender lined up six more. And so passed the afternoon while Hill put the weeks of submarine tedium behind him. Finally he gathered up his pillowcase full of gear and wobbled down the hill to the fleet aviation headquarters. He marched into the headquarters office and announced that he was ready to return to the *Intrepid*.

The duty officer looked at him quizzically. *Intrepid?* Hill might as well relax and wait awhile. The *Intrepid* had taken a kamikaze hit off Okinawa. She was on her way back to Pearl Harbor.

Further up the hill at the naval base on Guam, in the complex of Quonset huts that served as the advance Pacific Ocean Area Headquarters, Adm. Chester Nimitz and his staff were pondering the action reports of the past two days. The Japanese had thrown 350 planes into the latest massed kamikaze attack—*kikusui* No. 5. Based on the claims of CAP pilots and air defense gunners, 249 had been shot down.

Even though *kikusui* No. 5 was on a smaller scale than most of the previous attacks, the tactics were becoming more deadly. Six U.S. ships—three destroyers and three gunboats—had been sunk. Ten more had taken extensive damage, most of them finished for the duration of the war. Nearly five hundred Navy men had lost their lives, and an equal number were wounded.

The losses only added to Nimitz's frustration over the land battle on Okinawa. As long as the stalemate continued, Nimitz's ships would be targets for the kamikazes.

In his sheltered command post at Kanoya, the man responsible for *kikusui* No. 5 mulled over the same statistics. As usual, Matome Ugaki was inclined to accept the inflated damage reports. "Explosions and the burning of two battleships, three cruisers, and five unidentified ships were seen from shore," Ugaki wrote. "Besides the sinking of several cruisers or destroyers and the burning of a battleship were also seen off Kadena. Thus we achieved a great deal of success."

The fact that the *tokko* airmen were still misidentifying

destroyers as battleships hadn't registered with Ugaki. Nor had the hopelessness of the land battle on Okinawa. More and more, Ugaki was becoming a victim of his fantasies. In his diary he reported that the "32nd Army sent its appreciation" for the navy's efforts. He was sure that "when our troops can see enemy vessels sunk and set on fire in front of their very eyes and observe planes with the Rising Sun mark fly overhead, their morale will soar."

Ugaki was undaunted by the deteriorating situation at Okinawa. He was already preparing his next floating chrysanthemum attack, *kikusui* No. 6.

On May 8, there was a lull in the action, as if both sides were absorbing the momentous news: Germany had surrendered. The war in Europe was over.

In the United States, jubilant Americans were in the streets, honking horns, cheering, embracing each other. In Japan, the significance of losing their main ally was minimized by government spokesmen. The new premier, Admiral Kantaro Suzuki, insisted that he was "determined to fight through this war with all I have."

There was little jubilation on Okinawa. To the American soldiers and Marines in the mud-filled trenches of the front line, the end of the war in Europe had as much relevance as a tremor on Mars. Their own war had no foreseeable end. It was clear that the Japs on this miserable island weren't quitting until the last one was dead. Then would come the *real* battle. They were going to have to fight for every inch of ground in Japan.

Nor did the sailors on the tin cans or the pilots on the carriers have much to celebrate. Sure, the end of the conflict in Europe meant that more military assets would eventually be sent to the Pacific. In the meantime, there seemed to be no end to the kamikazes.

Vice Adm. Kelly Turner, however, thought that this historic occasion should receive special recognition. From his flagship *Eldorado* he sent an order: precisely at noon on May 8, every big gun ashore on Okinawa would fire one round. The barrage would be accompanied by full gun salvoes from the fire support ships offshore. It would be a dramatic, boisterous salute to the victorious troops in Europe.

And so the guns fired. The earth reverberated, and the concussion sent ripples across the mud puddles along the front lines. No one ashore or on the ships was especially impressed. When it was over and the dust and thunder had subsided, the grunts and the sailors went back to what they'd been doing—trying to get this damned island secured.

At age twenty-eight, 1st Lt. Robert Klingman was the old man of his group of Tail End Charlies. Klingman had already served as an enlisted man in both the Navy and the Marine Corps. Now he was a Marine Corsair pilot in the VMF-312 Checkerboard squadron at Kadena air base on Okinawa. With the two captured airfields, Yontan and Kadena, up and running, the Marines were flying a greater share of the CAP missions over the picket stations, as well as delivering close air support for Buckner's ground forces.

On the morning of May 10, Klingman was Capt. Ken Reusser's wingman in a four-plane CAP mission over Ie Shima. They'd gone after a high-flying Japanese reconnaissance plane, a twin-engine Kawasaki Ki-45 Nick fighter. The high-altitude planes had been making daily overflights, photographing the disposition of the fleet for the next kamikaze attacks.

The Marines dropped their belly tanks and firewalled the engines of the Corsairs, clawing their way up to the Nick's contrails. They caught up with him at 38,000 feet, a barely sustainable altitude for the Corsairs. To lighten the Corsairs so they could climb higher, they had expended much of their heavy .50-caliber ammunition.

Reusser opened fire first, getting hits in the Nick's left wing and engine. Then his guns ran out of ammunition. Klingman gave it a try, then his guns stopped firing. In the subzero temperature they had frozen. He could see the Japanese tail gunner in the rear cockpit glowering at him. The gunner was banging on his own frozen machine gun.

Klingman was determined to bring down the Nick. He climbed slightly above the Nick's slipstream, then eased back down on the aft fuselage. In full view of the horrified tail gunner, Klingman's propeller sawed into the aft fuselage. Pieces of canopy, machine gun, and gore from the decapitated gunner spewed into the slipstream. A hunk of the rudder tore away.

It wasn't enough. Somehow the Nick kept flying. Ignoring the ominous vibration from his damaged propeller, Klingman took another whack at the Nick. This time he chopped off the Nick's rudder and part of the horizontal stabilizer.

Still, as if defying all laws of aerodynamics, the Nick kept flying.

The chase had taken them out to sea, north of Okinawa. The thought crossed Klingman's mind that he might not have enough fuel to make it back to Kadena. He pushed the thought away as he went for a third chopping session on the Nick's tail. This time he lopped off most of the right elevator.

The Nick was finished. Streaming debris, the Japanese fighter fell away in a spin. And so did Klingman, his Corsair having stalled out in the thin air. When he recovered a few thousand feet below, he could see the Nick still spinning. The Japanese fighter shed both its wings and dove like a stiletto straight into the ocean.

Now Klingman was in trouble. His Corsair was rattling like a farm tractor from its shattered propeller. At 10,000 feet, still well north of Kadena, the engine coughed and quit, out of fuel. With no power and the propeller slowly windmilling, the Corsair descended like a brick toward the airfield.

He almost made it. Klingman landed in the dirt overrun short of the runway, then bounced up to the hard surface and rolled to a stop. The Corsair was a mess. Six inches were missing from each of the three propeller blades. Shrapnel from the chopped-up Nick was embedded in the wings, cowling, and propeller.

Two days later, on another mission, Klingman ran into trouble again. His hydraulic system failed, and he elected to bail out instead of making a crash landing on one wheel. He was picked up by a destroyer escort, which deposited him on Admiral Turner's flagship *Eldorado*.

Klingman didn't know that he was a celebrity. Admiral Turner had heard about Klingman and insisted that he stay aboard and have dinner. The Alligator loved a good war story, and he wanted to hear the one about the Marine who had chopped off a Jap's tail.

E rickson couldn't believe his eyes. He was standing on the flight deck of *Intrepid* as the carrier slid up to her berth in Pearl Harbor on May 11. There on the dock to greet them were a twenty-piece band, hula girls, and a women's glee club.

And something else. Erickson thought he recognized a face in the crowd, not one of the musicians or singers, but a guy in a gaudy Hawaiian shirt. He was grinning like a baboon, mixing it up with the hula dancers, waving at the men on the flight deck. Erickson stared at the apparition. The guy looked exactly like Windy Hill, whom he'd last seen floating without a life raft off the coast of Kyushu.

It *was* Windy Hill, alive and apparently in the pink of health. In fact, judging by the suntan and relaxed expression, Hill appeared to be in better shape than most of the pasty-faced men staring at him from the deck of the *Intrepid*. Hill was eager to get back aboard *Intrepid*, he told his buddies, because he needed a rest from all this tiresome shore duty.

But when Hill returned to the stateroom he had shared with Lt. Hal Jackson, he received a shock. Most of his stuff was gone from his locker. Jackson had given away most of his clothes, thinking that Hill was dead.

That wasn't the worst part. He had also disposed of Hill's stash of whisky. It had been for a good cause, Jackson explained, because when they heard that Hill had been rescued by a submarine, they decided to celebrate. It had been a terrific party, Jackson told him. Windy should feel honored that he had so many friends.

As he did for every floating chrysanthemum operation, Admiral Ugaki stood on the tarmac watching the *tokko* planes and the Thunder Gods of the *Jinrai Butai* take off. It was May 11, the day of the sixth massed *kikusui* attack.

With his dwindling inventory of airplanes, Ugaki could muster less than half the number he'd launched on the first *kikusui*. *Kikusui* No. 6 totaled only 150 warplanes.

When the last of the *tokko* planes had lifted from the runway at Kanoya, the admiral returned to his shelter, where he was moved to write a melancholy poem.

> *Flowers of the special attack are falling,*
> *When the spring is leaving.*
> *Gone with the spring*
> *Are young boys like cherry blossoms.*
> *Gone are the blossoms,*
> *Leaving cherry trees only with leaves.*

Most of the *tokko* warriors would attack the usual targets—the picket station destroyers and the gunboats to the north of Okinawa.

But not all. Some were hunting bigger game. They were headed for the eastern side of the Ryukyus, where the American carrier force had last been sighted.

36 ▸ CHANGE OF COMMAND

Mitscher hated the steel battle helmet. Almost as much as he despised wearing the helmet, he hated the kapok life preserver. The bulky life preserver and the tublike helmet made the skinny admiral look even more emaciated. It had taken the nagging of Arleigh Burke, Mitscher's chief of staff, to finally get him to wear the battle gear when he stood out on the exposed bridge wing of the carrier *Bunker Hill*. Burke was concerned not only about Mitscher's safety but also about the example the admiral set for *Bunker Hill*'s crewmen.

The Bald Eagle had a routine. During combat operations, he would exchange his baseball cap for the helmet and life preserver and observe the action from the exposed bridge wing. If the kamikazes were getting uncomfortably close, he'd duck back into the heavily shielded flag plot, one level below the captain's bridge, and watch the battle through the bulletproof glass windows.

Mitscher looked wrung out these days. So did Burke, the rest of the flag staff, and, for that matter, most of the men on *Bunker Hill*. May 11 was their fifty-ninth straight day at sea. They'd been in almost daily action since two weeks before the invasion of Okinawa.

Mitscher and Burke were both called into flag plot a few minutes after 1000. CIC had picked up incoming bogeys. An enemy formation appeared to have sneaked in behind a returning flight of *Bunker Hill*'s strike planes. A broken cloud layer was helping to hide them from the CAP fighters.

In the next two minutes, the radio speaker on the fighter frequency confirmed it: "Alert! Alert! Two planes diving on the *Bunker Hill*!" Mitscher recognized the voice. It was Maj. Jim Swett,

whom Mitscher knew from the Guadalcanal campaign, where the
Marine had shot down seven enemy planes on one sortie and was
recommended by Mitscher for the Medal of Honor.

Swett's warning came just as the antiaircraft guns in *Bunker
Hill's* task group opened up. For many of the crew on deck—plane
handlers, ordnancemen, pilots still in their cockpits—there was no
other warning, just the sound of the guns, then the blurred glimpse
of a dusky shape hurtling toward them from astern. A trail of machine gun fire spattered across the deck, chewing up wood and
pinging into airplanes.

Still in his dive, the Zero pilot, a Japanese navy ensign named
Yasunori Seizo, released his bomb. The bomb hit a millisecond
before the Zero, plunging through the wooden deck, through the
gallery deck directly below, then into the hangar deck and piercing a hole in the portside bulkhead. With its delayed fuse, the
250-kilogram bomb didn't explode until it was 20 feet outside the
carrier's hull.

The effect was almost as disastrous as if it had detonated inside
the ship. The explosion mowed down gunners and crewmen along
the carrier's port side. Shrapnel sliced into the hangar bay, setting
fueled airplanes ablaze. The inferno leaped from airplane to airplane through the hangar bay.

Meanwhile, the wreckage of the Zero fighter glanced off the aft
flight deck and skidded through the pack of airplanes waiting to be
launched. Airplanes were hurled in every direction, bursting into
flame, exploding like firecrackers. The blazing fuselage of the kamikaze snagged a Corsair and part of the catwalk filled with sailors
and yanked them all over the side.

With *Bunker Hill's* aft flight deck ablaze and sending up a
dense cloud of black smoke, a second kamikaze appeared. The
Zero was flown by an ensign named Kiyoshi Ogawa, a former student and the wingman of the kamikaze who had just crashed into
Bunker Hill.

This time the gunners had warning. For nearly half a minute, every available gun on *Bunker Hill* and her escorts poured fire at the onrushing Zero.

It wasn't enough. Even as shrapnel and 20-millimeter bullets shredded Ogawa's Zero and set it ablaze, he kept his aim straight and true. Like the first kamikaze, he released his bomb just before impact.

The effect was even more horrific than the strike of a few minutes before. The bomb hit amidships, drilling through the wooden flight deck and exploding in the gallery deck immediately below. An entire ready room full of fighter pilots was immolated. So were almost all the spaces on the fragile gallery deck. Many on the gallery deck who weren't killed by the blast died soon after from burns or smoke inhalation.

The shattered kamikaze plane careened into the base of the island—the carrier's superstructure—sending a tower of flame leaping high above the ship. Deadly smoke, laden with poison and soot, gushed through the ship. The smoke poured into Mitscher's flag plot through the ventilators, forcing the admiral and his staff to evacuate. Standing outside, Mitscher paused to take in the scene around him. As he watched, a third kamikaze came diving toward *Bunker Hill*. At the last moment, gunners sent him cartwheeling into the ocean.

Bunker Hill's agony went on for the rest of the afternoon. As flames and smoke continued to billow from the carrier, the cruiser *Wilkes-Barre* and several destroyers came alongside to help fight the raging fires. Not until nightfall were most of the blazes extinguished.

Though still under her own power, *Bunker Hill* was out of the war. The attack cost 396 men aboard *Bunker Hill* their lives, making it the single most deadly kamikaze strike of the war. Only *Franklin*, which lost 724 men to a Japanese dive-bomber, suffered greater damage and casualties and still remained afloat.

At 1630 Mitscher and his staff gathered up their gear and transferred the task force commander's flag to the carrier *Enterprise*.

Mitscher seemed unfazed by what had happened. The fact that a kamikaze had come within 20 yards of obliterating him didn't show in the old Bald Eagle's piercing gaze. After three and a half years of war, it was his first close-up encounter with a kamikaze. Such a thing didn't seem likely to happen again.

But it did, three days later.

M itscher resumed tactical command of Task Force 58 the next day, May 12. The situation on *Enterprise* was far from ideal. His flag plot was stuck atop the captain's bridge instead of below it, as on *Bunker Hill*. *Enterprise* had been designated a night carrier, which meant that aircraft engines and catapults roared and hammered through the hours of darkness while the ship spent much of the daytime at general quarters.

The disaster on *Bunker Hill* made one thing abundantly clear: *something* had to be done about the kamikazes. At the urging of his staffers, Burke and Flatley, Mitscher ordered his carriers north to carry out two days of strikes on the Kyushu airfields.

As usual, the results of the strikes were hard to measure. How many kamikaze airplanes had been destroyed on the ground? No one knew for sure. But the airfields had been shot up and the runways damaged, even if only temporarily. If nothing else, the presence of the strike planes had the effect of delaying the next *kikusui* offensive.

But the strikes also put the carriers dangerously close to the kamikazes' bases. Soon after dawn on May 14, Mitscher was in his padded chair in flag plot when CIC reported twenty-six incoming bogeys on the radar screen.

By now it was a familiar ritual: the crew running to general quarters, anxious lookouts squinting into the sky, CAP fighters racing to intercept the raiders. Picking off the kamikazes one by one, the fighters managed to take down nineteen. Antiaircraft gunners accounted for another six.

Which left one. The lone remaining Zero was flown by a

twenty-three-year-old lieutenant (jg) named Shunsuke Tomiyasu. He had been the leader of the group that took off from Kanoya at dawn, and he was the only still alive. Now Tomiyasu was dodging in and out of the cloud cover, looking for an opening.

Down below, gunners were straining to catch a glimpse of the single kamikaze. At 0656 they spotted him, breaking out of the cloud cover. Every gun aboard *Enterprise* and her escorts opened up. *Enterprise*'s captain had the carrier heeled hard over in an emergency turn.

Cmdr. Jimmy Flatley, Mitscher's operations officer, was standing out on the exposed bridge wing when he saw the kamikaze diving from the clouds. Knowing what was about to happen, Flatley darted back through the steel door to flag plot and slammed it behind him. He yelled for everyone to hit the deck. Seconds later came the concussion, followed by the clatter of metal pinging into the light armor of the flag bridge.

Then it subsided. Flatley raised his head from the deck and peered around. Mitscher was standing among the prone bodies on the deck, arms folded, a frown covering his face. "Flatley," said the admiral, "tell my task group commanders that if the Japs keep this up they're going to grow hair on my head yet."

Then came the smoke. It was a replay of the scene three days earlier aboard *Bunker Hill*. A cloud of noxious smoke came gushing in through the ventilators. Again the flag staff had to evacuate their compartment.

Down on the flight deck, flames were leaping from the hole where the bomb had penetrated. The concussion of the blast had hurled *Enterprise*'s forward elevator 400 feet in the air. Damage control crews had the fires extinguished in half an hour, but *Enterprise* was too severely wounded to continue operations.

The next day they held a burial at sea for the twelve crewmen killed in the attack. Then they held another, from the stern of the ship, for the remains of Lt. (jg) Shunsuke Tomiyasu. His name and rank they had learned from the business cards they found in his pocket. One of the cards was given to Mitscher as a parting memento.

For the second time in four days, the Bald Eagle and his staff packed up their smoke-permeated belongings and transferred Mitscher's flag to yet another carrier, USS *Randolph*. Like *Bunker Hill*, the "Big E" had been knocked out of the war. It was her third kamikaze hit, earning her a footnote in history: she would be the last carrier of the war to be struck by a kamikaze.

W earing his starched khakis and metal-rimmed spectacles, Kelly Turner exchanged salutes with his successor, Vice Adm. Harry Hill. It was May 17, and for the Alligator it was a day of mixed emotions. The job he'd begun back in March—the capture of Okinawa—was still not finished.

It was the Navy way, this periodic rotation of commanders, even in the midst of battle. Harry Hill had already taken charge of the 5th Amphibious Force, and today's ceremony completed the turnover, relieving Turner as commander, Task Force 51. In ten days, similar change-of-command rituals would be conducted on the flagships of the Fifth Fleet and the Fast Carrier Task Force when Raymond Spruance and Marc Mitscher turned over their commands to Bull Halsey and Slew McCain.

The disputatious Turner wouldn't be missed, at least by the officers who served directly under him. Turner's subordinates would not forget the tongue-lashings, the egotism, the peremptory rudeness of the man. They would long retain the image of those bushy eyebrows descending like a hood over the icy blue eyes, the signal that another volcanic eruption of temper was on the way.

But even those who most disliked Turner had to acknowledge his brilliance. Working for the Alligator amounted to a graduate-level course in meticulously detailed operational planning. It was hard to imagine a massive amphibious operation without the masterful guidance of Kelly Turner.

Which, in fact, was why Turner was on his way back to Pearl

Harbor. With the invasion of Okinawa now a fait accompli, the Alligator's specialized skills were needed for the greatest amphibious landing yet conceived—Operation Olympic, the invasion of Kyushu, the southern island of Japan, which was scheduled for November 1, 1945. Turner would be the point man in the critical landings. To go with his new duties, he was pinning on a fourth star.

For the officers who had served under "Terrible" Turner, the change of command brought an abrupt lifestyle change. Their new boss, Harry Hill, was the opposite of Turner, a genial, mild-mannered officer who seldom raised his voice. Serving in Hill's flag plot on the *Eldorado* felt almost like a vacation. For some, after the challenge of working for the Alligator, it even seemed boring.

On the day Kelly Turner was turning over command of his task force, his fire support ships were busy doing what they'd done since the invasion began: bombarding enemy positions on southern Okinawa. One of the destroyers, USS *Longshaw*, spent that night firing star shells to thwart Japanese infiltrators creeping through the lines in southern Okinawa.

It was tiring, tedious duty, and like the rest of his crew, *Longshaw*'s skipper, Lt. Cmdr. C. W. Becker, was exhausted. On the morning of the 18th, during a bombardment mission along the coast, *Longshaw* ran aground. She was stuck on Ose Reef, just off the Naha airstrip on the western shoreline.

Becker didn't need to be told he was in a dangerous place. He was dead in the sights of the very guns he had come to destroy. The only good news was that so far the Japanese had shown no inclination to fire their coastal defense guns at offshore targets. They didn't want to reveal their positions, saving their big guns to use against the American ground forces.

Now Becker just wanted to get the hell out of there. He tried backing off, churning the water to a muddy froth with his propellers. The destroyer didn't budge. Then he ordered the crew to jettison everything that wasn't bolted down, to lighten the ship. They were still stuck. The destroyer *Picking* arrived to give them a tow. The line was too light, and it parted.

The fleet tug *Arikara* showed up to pass them a heavier line. Becker could see *Arikara* taking up strain on the line. In a few minutes, *Longshaw* would be out of danger.

It was then that the first shell exploded. Geysers of water began erupting around *Longshaw*. A Japanese battery commander, observing the scene, had decided the destroyer was too tempting a target to pass up. *Longshaw*'s gunners fired back, more out of defiance than anything else. Tin can sailors knew their main defenses were speed and agility. Now they were trapped like a fox in a snare.

A salvo landed just short of *Longshaw*, another a few yards long. The Japanese gunners had them bracketed. In rapid succession four shells crashed down right on target. *Longshaw*'s gun mounts were shattered. The superstructure was ripped apart. A round detonated on the forward deck, touching off an ammunition magazine. In the explosion, the forward half of the destroyer was blown away.

Amid the chaos, the mortally wounded Becker shouted the order to abandon ship. Some men did, some didn't. With shell-fire exploding all around them, going into the sea seemed as bad a choice as staying with the ship.

By the time the guns had stopped firing, eighty-six *Longshaw* crewmen were dead, including the captain. Ninety-seven more were wounded. The ruined *Longshaw*, still trapped on the reef, had to be destroyed by gunfire and torpedoes.

The massed kamikaze attacks resumed on May 23. Instead of concentrating on the northern picket stations this time, most of the 165 planes of *kikusui* No. 7 tried an end run around the pickets and CAPs and went after the fire support ships.

Most of the *tokko* planes arrived over their targets after dark, flying in the glow of a full moon. They managed to crash a destroyer-transport, *Barry*, damaging her badly enough that her abandoned hulk would be towed out to sea to serve as a decoy for further kamikazes. A minesweeper, *Spectacle*, was knocked out of action, as well as the destroyer *Stormes* and an LSM fire support ship. The destroyer-transport *Bates*, after taking two kamikaze strikes, made it under tow back to Hagushi, only to capsize and sink the same day.

The *tokko* pilots weren't the only night raiders. At the Japanese base at Kumamoto, in central Kyushu, a daring mission called Operation *Giretsu* (Operation Faith) lifted into the sky after nightfall on May 24. Each of the twelve specially equipped Mitsubishi Ki-21 twin-engine "Sally" bombers carried ten special attack commandos. Their mission was to assault the Marine bases at Kadena and Yontan.

Admiral Ugaki, who was still convinced that the Okinawa airfields were being used for attacks on his bases in Kyushu, had ordered the *Giretsu* operation. The truth was, the first strikes on Japan from Kadena and Yontan weren't flown until June 10, 1945.

A wave of conventional bombers went ahead of the commando-carrying *Giretsu* aircraft, attacking Kadena and Yontan as well as the newly captured air base on Ie Shima. But like most tightly coordinated Japanese missions, this one unraveled early. Several of the *Giretsu* aircraft became lost in the darkness. Several more developed engine trouble.

By 2230, when the commando-carrying Sally bombers arrived over the northern tip of Okinawa, they were down to only four airplanes. Directly ahead of them, illuminated in the pale moonlight, was the runway at Yontan.

And then they were spotted. The antiaircraft guns opened up, and within a minute three of the Sallys had gone down in flames. The lone survivor made it through the gunfire unscathed, lined up on a runway at Yontan, and belly-landed. While the twin-engine bomber was still scraping along the concrete surface, sending up a shower of sparks, pieces, and propeller blades, the hatch flew open and ten *Giretsu* commandos tumbled out.

For several minutes they had the advantage of surprise. Sprinting down the darkened flight line, the *Giretsu* commandos threw hand grenades and phosphorous bombs into the rows of parked warplanes. Flames from burning Corsairs and transports billowed into the night sky. The surprised Marines on the base's perimeter defense reacted quickly, chasing down the raiders one by one.

It took most of the night. As dawn came to Yontan, the charred remains of seven warplanes were still smoking. Twenty-six other airplanes had been damaged, some irreparably. Two fuel dumps had gone up in flames, torching 70,000 gallons of precious aviation gasoline. The body of each *Giretsu* commando lay on the tarmac where he had been shot.

Two Americans had been killed in the action and eighteen wounded. Fifty-six Japanese commandos and bomber crewmen had been sacrificed. The audacious *Giretsu* raid, if nothing else, was a graphic reminder that the spirit of *bushido* was still very much alive.

Admiral Ugaki was running out of airplanes. For his next *tokko* attack, *kikusui* No. 8 on May 27, Ugaki could muster only 110 aircraft. It was the smallest number of airplanes so far in any of the floating chrysanthemum attacks.

Some of the *tokko* aircraft were antiques, including flimsy Kyushu KIIW *Shiragiku* trainers, with a top speed of only 100 mph. Even in a dive, they reached a maximum speed of no more than about 200 mph.

Ugaki had no illusions about their chances. "Apart from their use at night," wrote Ugaki in his diary, "they couldn't stand even one second against enemy fighter attacks."

Despite the decrepitude of the airplanes and their small numbers, *kikusui* No. 8 was deadly. Two Val dive bombers set the destroyer *Braine* afire, killing 67 men and wounding 103. Many of the tin can sailors died gruesome deaths in the water, devoured by sharks after they abandoned the burning ship.

The next dawn, May 28, a twin-engine bomber, probably a Nick, managed to slip past two Corsair CAP planes and a wall of flak from the destroyer *Drexler*. The Nick was carrying a larger-than-normal kamikaze payload. When the kamikaze crashed the *Drexler* amidships, the cataclysmic explosion blew the sides of the destroyer out. She was gone in less than a minute, taking 158 crewmen with her.

The bloody month of May was drawing to a close. Ninety U.S. ships had been sunk or damaged to the extent that they were out of the war. More than a thousand Navy men were dead, with hundreds more injured, many from horrible burns. The Battle of Okinawa had become the costliest naval engagement in U.S. history. And it wasn't over.

These grim facts were hanging like a pall over the deck of the cruiser USS *New Mexico* on the cloudy morning of May 27. Raymond Spruance, wearing his standard expressionless countenance, greeted his old friend Bill Halsey. In the space of a salute and brief verbal exchange, Spruance turned over command of the world's mightiest naval armada. Once again the Fifth Fleet was the Third Fleet. Task Force 58 became Task Force 38, and every task group and unit changed its prefix accordingly.

Spruance had been a pillar of tenacity throughout the ordeal of Okinawa. Historian Samuel Eliot Morison observed, "A less serene and courageous man might, before reaching this point, have asked, 'Is this island worth the cost? Is there no better way to defeat Japan?' But no such doubts or questions ever even occurred to Raymond A. Spruance."

On the same day that Spruance was relieved by Halsey, Marc Mitscher handed over Task Force 58—the Fast Carrier Task

Force—to his counterpart, Vice Adm. John "Slew" McCain. As the two grizzled admirals met on the deck of *Randolph*, the years of nonstop combat operations showed in their haggard looks. Mitscher was fifty-eight, McCain not yet sixty-one, but each had the face of a man two decades older. Though McCain was just beginning another tour of duty, he looked as beat-up as Mitscher. Neither man weighed much over a hundred pounds, their khaki uniforms hanging like shrouds over their skinny frames.

Everyone was tired, including the flag staff officers. Several days later, when Mitscher and Burke and their staff lined up back in Pearl Harbor for an awards ceremony, they looked "like a parade of scarecrows," according to Mitscher's biographer. Of all the senior commanders, Spruance seemed to be holding up the best, his smooth face never showing signs of strain. Like everything about Spruance, though, it was hard to tell.

For the three commanders—Spruance, Mitscher, Turner—it was an unfulfilling end to the task they had begun back in March. None of them would have predicted then that two months later their forces would still be fighting for the last few square miles of Okinawa.

I n the last week of May, the rain arrived. It came in torrents, dumping inches of water every day, turning gullies into rushing streams, making the landscape a sodden quagmire. Tanks mushed to a stop, their tracks clogged with mud. With no vehicles able to navigate the terrain, logistics ground to a halt. Not even amphibious tractors could shuttle supplies through the swampy terrain. Everything—ammunition, food, litters of wounded soldiers—had to be carried on the backs of weary troops through ankle-deep muck. The pelting rain and boot-sucking mud compounded the melancholy of the grunts in the foxholes.

The battle was still stalemated at the Shuri Line. Shuri had been pounded incessantly with naval gunfire, close air strikes, and artillery bombardment. The Japanese still showed no inclination to yield the ground. Simon Buckner and his division commanders were convinced that Shuri was where the Japanese would make their last stand.

They were wrong. In the bunker beneath the shattered ruins of Shuri Castle, their adversary was already making his next move.

37 ▸ RITUAL OF DEATH

Carrying his folding fan, General Ushijima led his soldiers into the darkness outside his headquarters. Flashes of artillery fire were glimmering off the low clouds, illuminating the landscape with a strobing yellow light.

The withdrawal from the Shuri Line had begun. Ushijima could only hope that the foul weather would last long enough for his army to reach its new positions on the southern end of the island before the enemy could cut them off

On the winding path to the south, they stumbled across bodies of fallen Japanese soldiers. Shattered field guns and vehicles were strewn like discarded junk. Every few yards they had to take shelter from incoming artillery or mortar rounds. Star shells from offshore destroyers burst over their heads, making them feel like rats caught in a spotlight. Mercifully, the low visibility prevented enemy airplanes from coming to strafe them, bomb them, and incinerate them with napalm, the deadliest new weapon in the Americans' arsenal.

Leading the next group out of the headquarters was Lt. Gen. Isamu Cho, Ushijima's second in command. Cho had stopped his strident talk about offensives or even of holding the Shuri Line. Both flanks were crumbling. It was just a matter of hours before the redoubt at Shuri Castle was surrounded and cut off. If Ushijima's force were trapped there, the Battle of Okinawa would be over.

With Ushijima on the darkened trail was Col. Hiromichi Yahara, who had given the withdrawal a quaint label: "offensive retreat." Ushijima liked the euphemism. In some small measure it dulled the bitter taste of defeat. In the nearly two months since the Americans landed at Hagushi, Ushijima had lost over 60,000 men, more than half his fighting force. His once formidable artillery group had been pounded into a small portion of its original strength. Ushijima knew that they were retreating into what would be a final trap for them all.

So be it. Ushijima was buying time. His life and career were now distilled to a single unwavering duty: to prolong the battle for Okinawa. If he succeeded, Japan might still be spared.

The withdrawal succeeded. On the morning of May 28, when Marines of A Company, 1st Battalion, 5th Marine Regiment, stormed into the courtyard of Shuri Castle, they met almost no resistance. The town of Shuri, at the base of the ancient castle and once the home of 17,500 Okinawans, was obliterated. So was the castle, and so was every man-made object in view. The labyrinth beneath the castle that had been the headquarters of General Ushijima's 32nd Army was deserted.

The enemy had gotten away.

It was the same story on each flank, skeleton Japanese units fighting holding actions while the bulk of the army slipped southward. Realizing what was happening, Buckner ordered his forces to converge to the south of Shuri to isolate whatever remained of the Japanese 32nd Army around Shuri Castle.

He was too late. The same mud that had slowed the Americans' advance up the Shuri Line now hindered their pursuit of the retreating Japanese. Most of Ushijima's forces were already settling into their new positions four miles to the south where a pair of hill masses called Yuza-Dake and Yaeju-Dake formed a jagged wall across the southern tip of Okinawa.

Buckner tried to put a positive spin on the situation. "Ushijima missed the boat on his withdrawal from the Shuri Line," he told his subordinates on May 31. "It's all over now but cleaning pockets of resistance. This doesn't mean there won't be stiff fighting but the Japs won't be able to organize another line."

No one believed it, of course, especially the weary soldiers and Marines who were mad as hell that the enemy had been allowed to slip away from the Shuri Line. It meant that all the suffering and sacrifice they'd endured trying to dislodge the Japanese from Shuri would have to be repeated on the next ridge to the south.

Criticism of Simon Buckner's generalship was swelling both on Okinawa and on the home front. Now that the war was over in Europe, military reporters in the United States were turning their attention to Okinawa. The appalling casualty figures were getting front-page coverage. Journalists and armchair generals were comparing Buckner's strategy to the attritional battles of World War I, where generals flung entire armies at each other in frontal assaults.

One of the noisiest critics was Homer Bigart of the *New York Herald Tribune*, who had been at the Anzio and Salerno landings. Bigart was scathing about Buckner's refusal to conduct amphibious landings behind the Japanese line. "Our tactics were ultra-conservative," Bigart wrote. "Instead of an end-run, we persisted in frontal attacks. It was hey-diddle-diddle straight down the middle. Our intention to commit the entire force in a general assault was apparently so obvious that the Japanese quickly disposed their troops in such a way as most effectively to block our advance."

In his syndicated column, "Today in Washington," David Lawrence took an even harsher line. "Why is the truth about the military fiasco at Okinawa being hushed up?" Lawrence postulated that the stalemate was due to an Army–Marine Corps dispute over strategy, implying that Buckner and his Army generals didn't "understand the dynamics of island warfare."

Even the imperious MacArthur weighed in. Without naming names, he accused the Okinawa commanders of "sacrificing thousands of American soldiers." Instead of the frontal assault, MacArthur thought they should have done as he did in the southwestern Pacific, leapfrogging Japanese strongholds, isolating them from the rest of the war. With most of Okinawa already in American hands, the Japanese could have been contained on their southern

tip of land while the United States had free use of the airfields and
harbors for the coming invasion of Japan. The saving in American
lives would have been immense.

MacArthur, of course, was biased. Buckner had become a
"Navy general" by virtue of serving under MacArthur's chief rival
in the Pacific, Adm. Chester Nimitz. In a Manila meeting with Lt.
Gen. Joseph Stilwell, MacArthur let it be known that in the coming invasion of Japan, he would see to it that Buckner would not
play a role.

Nimitz, who had already invested his own credibility in Buckner's leadership, defended the general against Lawrence's accusa-
tions. "The article, which has been widely reprinted, shows that
the author has been badly misinformed, so badly as to give the im-
pression that he has been made use of for purposes which are not
in the best interest of the United States."

For the diplomatic Nimitz, it was a blunt statement. No one
could be sure, though, whether he was defending his designated
ground commander or just heading off another Army-Navy turf war.

Simon Buckner, for his part, wasn't a general who took fire
without firing back. He called a special press conference at his
Okinawa headquarters on June 15. "If we'd scattered our forces,"
he told reporters, "we might have got licked, or it might have un-
duly prolonged the campaign; or we might have been forced to call
on additional troops, which we did not want to do."

The journalists dutifully reported Buckner's statement, but it
didn't stop the criticism. The controversy, like the battle itself, continued to fester like an open wound. The end was in sight, and
at this point no one in Washington or in Pacific Fleet headquarters was willing to change strategies or commanders on Okinawa.
Buckner would stay until the end. Or so everyone thought.

By the morning of June 18, Simon Buckner had every reason to
be upbeat. The heady scent of victory was in the air. The general flashed his confident, white-toothed grin for the photographers

as he made his way up to the observation post at the Kunishi ridge-line. Against the advice of his staff, he was headed for the front line to observe an assault by the 2nd Marine Division against an enemy holdout. It would be one of the last actions of the long battle, and he was determined to observe it close up. As was his habit, he carried his own compact camera to capture the moment for his personal archives.

Escorting Buckner was the regimental commander, Col. Clarence Wallace, whose Marines were making the assault. Buckner settled himself into the observation post, which was sheltered on either side by boulders. He focused his attention on the battle unfolding in front of him, unaware of the events on the adjoining ridge.

From the concealed entrance of their cave, the Japanese gunners observed the scene. The men in the American observation post appeared to be high-ranking officers, judging by the deference being shown them. The gunners' artillery battery had been reduced to one remaining 47-millimeter mobile gun. They had been waiting for an opportunity to use the gun before it was destroyed or captured.

Here was such an opportunity. They hurried to ready the weapon. They knew they would have one tiny window in which to fire before the fury of a hundred American artillery shells came crashing down on them.

They fired the first round. The loaders crammed fresh shells into the breech, and in quick succession they pumped out four more rounds. Then they whirled and retreated back inside their cave.

Buckner was pleased. He'd gotten what he came for—a look at what might be the last assault of the Okinawa campaign, some shots on film, and some goodwill points with the Marines. It was 1315, time to move on to the next outpost. Buckner was shaking hands all around, saying goodbye to his hosts, when the first shell exploded.

It wasn't a direct hit. Nor were the next rounds, which landed so close, one behind the other, that they seemed almost to arrive in salvo. One of the rounds exploded into the massive coral boulder that protected the observation post. Debris slashed like a cleaver across the narrow space, missing all the men standing in the observation post.

All except Simon Buckner.

Before anyone could fathom what had happened, Buckner was down. His chest and abdomen were punctured by the pieces of shrapnel. Corpsmen rushed to his side, trying to stanch the flow of blood. Semiconscious, the general lay on the ground while the life ebbed from him. Despite the efforts of the corpsmen, his wounds were too severe. Buckner was dead in ten minutes.

The news stunned both sides. To the Americans in the foxholes and on the sprawling, muddy landscape of Okinawa, it was incomprehensible that the man who had led them to within two miles and a few hours of final victory was no longer with them. To Buckner's critics in the press and in the military establishment, it seemed a profound irony. The general they accused of needlessly expending American lives had just joined the twelve thousand men lost at Okinawa.

To Buckner's enemies still clinging to the southern tip of Okinawa, it meant something else.

H uddled in their cave beneath Hill 89 near the village of Mabuni, the staff officers of the Japanese 32nd Army could hardly believe their good fortune. They had killed the American commander! Their army was almost annihilated, but even as they approached their own deaths, they had won this symbolic victory. Gen. Isamu Cho, the fire-eating samurai who had argued against this slow battle of attrition, was beside himself with joy. So were most of the other headquarters officers.

There was one exception. Mitsuru Ushijima, the courtly general who had been Buckner's chief antagonist these past three months, was not rejoicing. "He looked grim," recalled Colonel Yahara, "as if mourning Buckner's death. Ushijima never spoke ill of others. I had always felt he was a great man, and now I admired him more than ever."

The day before, Ushijima had received a message from Buckner. "I believe that you understand as clearly as I," wrote Buckner, "that the destruction of all Japanese resistance on the island is merely a matter of days." Buckner urged Ushijima to surrender to avoid "the necessity of my destroying the vast majority of your remaining troops."

Ushijima's only reaction had been to smile. Surrendering to Buckner was never a consideration. Now, with the battle of Okinawa nearing its conclusion, Ushijima intended to exercise his final option. He would join the American general in eternity.

In accordance with Buckner's orders in the event he was killed, Maj. Gen. Roy Geiger, USMC, took command of the Tenth Army, making him the only Marine ever to command a field army. It was a distinction that wouldn't last. The assignment immediately ignited memories of the old Army-Marine blood feud. Five days later Geiger was relieved by Army Lt. General Joseph "Vinegar Joe" Stilwell, who was a MacArthur ally and one of Buckner's most vocal critics. As far as the Army was concerned, order had been restored.

It no longer mattered. The campaign was over. By the time Stilwell took charge, the American flag had been raised on the southern tip of Okinawa. After the mop-up, the new commander's primary task was to preside over the occupation.

On June 21, while the remainder of Ushijima's 32nd Army was being exterminated on Okinawa, a gloomy Admiral Ugaki gave the order to launch *kikusui* No. 10. The calamity unfolding at Okinawa only convinced the admiral more than ever that Japan's survival depended on destroying the enemy at sea.

The problem, of course, was that his *tokko* assets—airplanes and airmen—were becoming scarce. For what would be the last of the floating chrysanthemum attacks, only forty-five airplanes could be mustered. Six of these would be *Ohka*-carrying bombers, and for the first time they would receive an umbrella of fighter protection.

At dawn on June 22, Ugaki watched the bombers and fighters rumble into the pinkening sky. As usual, he assumed his trancelike solitude in the underground shelter to await reports. Also as usual, the scratchy, blurted radio messages led him to the same erroneous conclusion: the attacks were a brilliant success.

In truth, one American ship took a direct kamikaze hit. A Nakajima Ki-84 "Frank," a high-performance Japanese fighter, managed to penetrate the air defense screens around Kerama Retto and crash the seaplane tender USS *Curtiss* on the starboard side forward. The ship blazed like a torch all night, and forty-one of her crew were dead.

Of the six *Ohka*-carrying bombers, only two released their human-guided bombs in the target area. Both missed. Two others failed to release, and two were forced to turn back. Despite Ugaki's high hopes, the exotic *Ohka* guided bomb had turned out to be a dismal failure.

Kikusui No. 10 was the last major *tokko* mission. Not only Admiral Ugaki but most of his airmen sensed that Okinawa was a lost cause, not worth the expenditure of lives and airplanes. From now on, Ugaki would hoard his resources for the fiery final battle on Japanese soil.

U shijima was cut off. It was the night of June 21, and inside the rabbit warren of caves and tunnels beneath Hill 89, Ushijima and his chief of staff, General Cho, were delivering their final orders. Ushijima had already received an urgent message from his 24th Division, fighting a battle to the death a mile away. The situation was hopeless, reported the commander.

Ushijima didn't need to be told. From directly over his head he could hear the thump of enemy grenades, the chatter of their machine guns. That evening Ushijima and Cho held a farewell party for their staff, complete with fish cakes, cabbage, rice, and plenty of sake. For the occasion Cho broke out his remaining stock of captured Scotch whisky.

Soon after midnight, most of the 32nd Army's remaining staff officers and men took up their weapons and went outside. In the glow of a full moon, they made a final *banzai* charge to the hilltop. The frenetic chattering of enemy machine guns lasted for less than ten minutes, then it was over.

A few minutes before 0400, Ushijima and Cho, in full dress uniform, went out to a ledge overlooking the ocean. Each opened his tunic to expose his abdomen for the ritual. Standing behind them was the *hara-kiri* assistant, Captain Sakaguchi, a master swordsman.

Ushijima, being senior, went first. He thrust the short dagger into his belly. An instant later Sakaguchi, wielding his sword in both hands, swung the razor-sharp blade downward, beheading the general. A minute later, General Cho followed suit. Again Sakaguchi's unerring sword flashed in the moonlight.

The ritual was finished. The few remaining soldiers in the headquarters broke ranks and ran down the cliff to meet the enemy in their own fashion. The death of their commander was also the death of the 32nd Army—and the end of organized resistance on Okinawa.

38 ▶ SETTING SUN

The sign said it all. Someone stuck it on the dock alongside *Intrepid* at the Hunters Point shipyard: "This Fighting Lady has a date in Tokyo. DON'T MAKE HER LATE!"

The carrier's voyage from Pearl Harbor had taken five days. Now everyone was in a hurry. The airedales of the air group and most of the ship's crew headed off for two weeks' leave while the workers at the shipyard labored nonstop to repair *Intrepid*'s battle damage.

The Tail End Charlies scattered like Gypsies across the continent. Maurie Dubinsky headed straight for Kansas City to see his family and sweetheart. Wes Hays jumped on a train for Texas to rejoin his wife and infant son. Charlie Schlag was on his way to meet his family in West Virginia. Phil Kirkwood, the Grim Reapers' leading ace with twelve kills, had an appointment in New Jersey to collect on the promise of $100 for every Japanese airplane he shot down. Eric Erickson headed for his home town of Lincoln, Nebraska, to become acquainted with the fiancée he still knew mainly through letters.

In late June, while the pilots were returning to the *Intrepid* for the long voyage back to the war, they heard the reports. The battle for Okinawa was over. The longest and bloodiest campaign of the Pacific war had finally ground to a halt.

To the Tail End Charlies it was good and bad news. It meant that this time they really *were* catching the tail end of the war. But what they were catching was going to make Okinawa look like a picnic.

It was a now-familiar passage. Erickson, Hill, Dubinsky, and most of the rest of the squadron were lined up on *Intrepid*'s flight deck. Gliding past them were the gray hump of Alcatraz, the stark skyline of San Francisco, the Golden Gate Bridge bearing another contingent of underwear-waving girls. Then came the barely perceptible rolling motion as the great ship entered the open ocean.

There were few hangovers this time and almost no seasickness. It occurred to Erickson that since his previous departure for the Pacific, heaving his guts out, he'd changed. Technically he was still a Tail End Charlie, but he was no longer one of the new guys. They had a fresh batch of new guys, replacements for the pilots lost during *Intrepid*'s previous combat cruise. Now he understood why the veterans had been cool to him and the other Tail End Charlies.

Erickson had been tested. He'd been fired on by enemy planes, ships, and shore-based heavy guns. And he'd fired back. He'd been credited with shooting down one and a half enemy fighters, bombing and strafing bases in Japan, and helping to destroy the *Yamato* task force, and he had two Distinguished Flying Crosses to show for it. He'd seen half a dozen friends plummet to their deaths.

None of this had the new guys yet experienced. Until they had, they would be segregated from the veterans by a subtle wall of formality.

Erickson now enjoyed another privilege: he no longer had to live in Boys' Town. The new guys would take up residence there. Though he missed the rowdy camaraderie of the bunkroom, Erickson liked the privacy of his new two-man stateroom. He had good light and a quiet place to work on his paintings and sketches.

On July 30, 1945, *Intrepid* steamed out of Pearl Harbor, headed for Eniwetok, where she would prepare to join Halsey's armada off Japan. En route the carrier and her air group would pause long enough to bombard Japanese-occupied Wake Island.

The island itself no longer had any strategic importance. Since its capture by the Japanese in the weeks after the Pearl Harbor attack, Wake had been bypassed by American forces. Cut off by U.S. submarines from all resupply lines, the Japanese garrison had slowly starved, surviving mainly on the island's abundant rat population.

But shooting up Wake Island had become a rite of passage. No self-respecting task force or carrier group commander passed Wake without giving the place a token bombing, mainly for the hell of it, but also for the purpose of warming up the air group on a real enemy. Like trapped animals, the Japanese could be expected to fight back, but not with great lethality.

Not everyone thought it was a good idea. Johnny Hyland complained that "if there is anything that sounds unreasonable to a pilot, it is the idea that he should practice encountering fire from an anti-aircraft gun."

They did it anyway. Both Corsair squadrons were equipped with new airplanes, the latest model of the Corsair, the F4U-4. This one had a massive four-bladed propeller, a full bubble canopy, and a more powerful Pratt & Whitney R-2800-18W, and it was nearly 30 knots faster than the F4U-1D the squadrons had taken to Okinawa.

On the morning of August 6, thirty-eight of the new Corsairs, each loaded with 5-inch rockets, swept over the Wake atoll. They were followed by twenty-eight bomb-loaded Avengers and Helldivers. For most of the day, the *Intrepid* warplanes bombed and strafed Wake while enemy gunners obligingly fired back with their few remaining guns. There was no air opposition; the last Japanese fighter at Wake had been destroyed long ago, and the airfield once used by the U.S. Marines was now a bomb-holed moonscape.

No *Intrepid* planes were shot down, and the worst threat of the day came from a towering afternoon cumulonimbus. By nightfall, all *Intrepid*'s airmen were safely back aboard, and the carrier was steaming at 15 knots for Eniwetok.

What no one aboard *Intrepid* knew was that while their bombers were hitting the Japanese on Wake, another bomber—a solitary

B-29 named *Enola Gay*—was releasing a single weapon over the Japanese city of Hiroshima.

And then three days later, while *Intrepid* lay at anchor in the coral-reef-enclosed lagoon at Eniwetok, it happened again, this time over a place called Nagasaki.

It was a confusing, frustrating time for the men aboard *Intrepid*. Atomic bomb? Few aboard the carrier had ever heard of such a thing. Most had never seen a B-29 up close. The notion that one bomb could devastate an entire city stretched the limits of their imaginations. Rumors spread like wildfire. Where were they headed? Would Japan surrender? Would there be an invasion?

On the morning of August 15, while *Intrepid* was taking on fresh ammunition and provisions, the answer was crackling over the radio in Japan.

Matome Ugaki leaned forward, straining to understand the thin, reedy voice. The static made the emperor's words hard to understand. Hirohito was carefully avoiding the word *surrender*, but his meaning was clear. The war situation, he told his countrymen, "has developed not necessarily to Japan's advantage." The Japanese people would have to "bear the unbearable" and "endure the unendurable." The Japanese would have to lay down their arms.

Listening to the broadcast, Ugaki was filled with an excruciating torment. While sending hundreds of *tokko* warriors to their deaths in the floating chrysanthemum attacks, he had always consoled himself with the promise that someday he would join them. Now, as a dutiful subject of the emperor, he was bound to obey a direct order to surrender. But he was also a warrior steeped in the *bushido* ethos. Death in battle was the only acceptable way for him to end the war.

Ugaki would take the path of the warrior. He rationalized that because he had not yet received an official cease-fire order from navy general headquarters, he was not constrained from carrying out a final *tokko* mission. In his last diary entry he wrote, "I'm going to follow in the footsteps of those many loyal officers and men who devoted themselves to the country, and I want to live in the noble spirit of the special attack."

At 1600 that afternoon, he drank a farewell sake toast with his staff at the Fifth Air Fleet headquarters. Then he removed all badges and emblems of rank from his dark green uniform. By auto he rode to Oita airfield, carrying with him the short ceremonial sword given him by Admiral Yamamoto.

Waiting on the ramp at Oita were eleven Asahi D4Y Judy dive-bombers—the same type he had dispatched by the hundreds on *tokko* missions against the Americans. Their two-man crews were waiting, all wearing the ceremonial *hachimaki* headband with the emblem of the rising sun.

Ugaki protested. He had asked for only five airplanes for his mission. The commander of the detachment, Lt. Tatsuo Nakatsuru, insisted that the admiral not conduct such a mission with only five airplanes. "My unit is going to accompany him with full strength!"

Ugaki was touched. He climbed onto a stand and addressed the pilots. "Will all of you go with me?"

"Yes, sir!" they replied, raising their right hands. Ugaki was at first taken aback, then his face brightened. The prospect of adding more lives to the thousands already sacrificed didn't seem to trouble him. Nor did the pointlessness of the mission.

The admiral shook hands with each of his staff, then he boarded Lt. Nakatsuru's plane, taking the rearmost seat in the dive-bomber. In the gathering dusk, the flight of bombers roared off the runway at Kanoya and turned south.

By the time the news of Ugaki's mission reached navy general headquarters, it was too late to stop them. The commander in chief, Adm. Jisaburo Ozawa, was furious. "It was wrong of him to take his men with him as companions to the other world, knowing the Imperial mandate through the emperor's broadcast. If he wanted to commit suicide, he should have done it alone."

By the time Ugaki's flight neared Okinawa, three of the eleven dive-bombers had already turned back with "engine trouble." At 1924, Ugaki radioed a message. He intended to "ram into the arrogant American ships, displaying the real spirit of a Japanese warrior."

No one saw Matome Ugaki again. None of his planes made it through the U.S. air defense screen, and no U.S. ships were struck by kamikazes. The mission of the last kamikaze had ended in failure.

The war is over. The news spread at the speed of sound through the passageways, compartments, and decks of USS *Intrepid*. The chorus of yelling and cheering swelled over the ship, spilling across the surface of the Eniwetok anchorage, becoming a collective din of sirens and horns and cheering men. The sound was an echo of the same jubilation going on in every city and town of America.

It was 1100 on August 15 in Eniwetok. The new president, Harry Truman, had announced the surrender of Japan. Minutes later the order from Admiral Nimitz's headquarters flashed to all units of the U.S. Navy in the Pacific: "Cease offensive operations against Japanese forces."

For the young men on the ships, it was too soon to comprehend the full meaning of what had happened. Fifty million human beings had perished in the costliest war in history. The political geography of the planet had been changed forever. Weapons of unthinkable destructive power had been unleashed. Their own lives had been transformed in ways that would not be apparent until years from now.

None of this was clear to them on this August day in the sweltering heat of the South Pacific. But the Tail End Charlies knew that they had the best reason in the world to celebrate. The war they'd almost missed had ended. The enemy they had hated with a cold, unreasoning fury was defeated, and they had helped win the victory. Now it was time to go home. At least for some of them.

Erickson sprawled in the leather-padded ready room chair, waiting for his name to be called. The squadron skipper, Will Rawie, was reading the list of the pilots who were eligible to leave the Navy immediately.

Erickson fidgeted in the chair, agonizing over his decision. Stay in or get out? He had come to love the Navy. He especially loved flying fighters like the Corsair. He knew in his gut that he would never again be bonded as strongly to any group as he was to his squadronmates here in this ready room.

Rawie was going down the list, stopping at each name to see if the pilot raised his hand. He came to Erickson's name. After a moment's hesitation, the young pilot's hand, as if disconnected from his body, shot straight into the air.

And that was it. Decision made. Erickson would return to civilian life to pursue his dream of becoming an artist.

That evening he packed his seabag, then stopped off to have a farewell martini with Windy Hill, who had restocked his private booze stash after his absence on the submarine *Sea Dog*. The next morning Erickson and eight of his squadronmates rode a boat to Okinawa, where they would await transportation to the United States.

For most of them, it was the first time they had ever actually set foot on the island. They gazed around the rocky landscape with almost reverential awe. Looking at the rutted, pockmarked terrain, it was impossible not to reflect on the battle that had changed their lives.

The human cost for capturing Okinawa had been staggeringly high—12,520 Americans killed or missing, another 36,631 wounded. Among the dead were 4,907 Navy men, with nearly as many wounded, 4,824. Thirty-four Allied ships and other craft had been sunk and 368 damaged, with 763 aircraft lost, making Okinawa the costliest naval engagement in U.S. history.

For the Japanese who defended Okinawa, the price had been exponentially higher, with 110,000 sons of Nippon killed and 7,400 taken prisoner. In the air and sea fighting for Okinawa, Japan lost 16 ships and more than 4,000 airplanes. But the greatest suffering had been among Okinawa's civilian population. Most studies estimated that more than 100,000 noncombatants died in the fighting.

The rationale for seizing Okinawa—that the island would be a springboard for the Allied invasion of Japan—had been obviated by the surrender in August. The objective of Admiral Ugaki's massed *tokko* attacks and General Ushijima's defense of the island was to prove that the Japanese would fight to the death not just for an outpost such as Okinawa but for their homeland. Faced with such resistance, the Japanese believed, American commanders would decide *not* to invade Japan's home islands.

And so they did—but not for the reason the Japanese expected. Appalled at the casualties suffered at Okinawa, the new president, Harry Truman, concluded that invading Japan would be "an Okinawa from one end of Japan to the other."

To Truman and his commanders, the lesson of Okinawa was that the use of *any* weapon, even one as horrendous as the atomic bomb, was preferable to an invasion.

Eric Erickson would finish art school and become a successful artist and interior designer in California. Wes Hays would return to Novice, Texas, and start a thriving hardware business. Grim Reapers top ace Phil Kirkwood would leave the Navy to become a dentist, and so would his Tail End Charlie, Ray James. Ziggy South would go back to Kansas to become a chiropractor.

Not all the Tail End Charlies would leave the Navy. Some, such as Dick Quiel and Windy Hill and Bill Ecker, had found their calling. They would stay in uniform, fight another war in Korea, and eventually rise to senior rank.

Another was Country Landreth, who had languished in a Japanese prison since his first mission over Japan in March. On September 2, 1945, the newly repatriated Landreth had a splendid
view from his hospital ship of the great gray battleship *Missouri*,
anchored in Tokyo Bay, while Japanese emissaries formally surrendered to the United States. The next time Landreth came to Japan,
it would be as skipper of his own carrier-based squadron.

Air Group 10 commander John Hyland would also stay in
the Navy. During the years of the Cold War, Hyland would rise
steadily in rank, eventually wearing four stars and commanding all
U.S. naval forces in the Pacific.

Few of the Japanese combatants at Okinawa would return
to their homeland. The architects of the *tokko* attacks, Admiral
Ohnishi and Admiral Ugaki, as well as the two senior army officers
on Okinawa, General Ushijima and General Cho, chose a samurai's death. An exception was Col. Hiromichi Yahara, chief strategist of the battle of attrition on Okinawa, who ended the war as a
prisoner. In the postwar years Yahara's bitterness at what he considered the ineptitude of Japan's wartime leadership would spill out
in his 1972 book, *The Battle for Okinawa*.

Another survivor was Ens. Mitsuru Yoshida, the young radar
officer on the battleship *Yamato*. In later life Yoshida would become a successful banker in Japan, retiring in 1979. Like many of
his countrymen, he would never stop questioning his actions in the
last battle of the war. In the closing pages of his book *Requiem for
Battleship* Yamato, he would ask:

> *Did I really do my part? Did I look death in the face in
> the line of duty?*
>   No.
>   *Didn't I submit to death quite willingly? Didn't I
> cloak myself in the proud name of special attack and find
> rapture in the hollow of death's hand?*
>   Yes.

For the rest of his life Erickson would be able to close his eyes and summon with perfect clarity the events of that first day. It was March 18, 1945, and his Corsair had been poised on *Intrepid*'s No. 1 catapult. He was peering out into the blackness of the predawn Pacific, hearing only the deep-throated rumble of his Pratt & Whitney radial engine.

Seconds later Erickson had been hurled into the night sky. For the next hour he and his squadronmates flew northwestward toward Japan. Their target—the naval base at Saeki—finally appeared through the morning mist on the coast of Kyushu. At the first angry black puffs of antiaircraft fire, Erickson had felt a jolt of adrenaline coursing through him.

One after another they had dived on the row of enemy airplanes parked on the airfield below. Through his gun sight Erickson had seen the distinctive red meatballs on their wings. He had squeezed the trigger, feeling the hard rattle of the six .50-caliber machine guns. He saw one of the enemy airplanes explode. Then another.

And that's when it happened. In the space of a few seconds—two bursts of machine gun fire—Erickson understood that his life—and the lives of his fellow Tail End Charlies—had changed forever. Nearly two years of waiting and training and worrying that the war would end before they got there were behind them. The moment would remain fixed in their memories for the next half century.

It had been the first day of the ninety-five-day-long air, sea, and land battle for Okinawa. For the Tail End Charlies, it was the day they became warriors.

ACKNOWLEDGMENTS

At the heart of this story are the real-life heroes of Carrier Air Group 10. Their generosity in sharing with me their recollections, mementoes, letters, and photographs helped bridge the sixty-five-year chasm between the events at Okinawa and today. Special thanks are owed to pilots Wesley Hays, William "Country" Landreth, Charles Schlag, Ray James, James South, Les Gray, Dick Quiel, Maurie Dubinsky, Jack Anderson, Orlo Wilmeth, Ed Deutschman, Jim Hollister, Don Oglevee, Frank Stolfa, Jim Clifford, and Dave Anderson, who gave me their perspective of the air and sea battle for Okinawa and whose friendship I will always cherish. Hanging in a place of honor on my office wall is the plaque they presented making me an honorary member of their illustrious air group.

My thanks again go to sailors Felix Novelli, Ray Stone, and Ed Coyne for sharing their wartime experiences aboard USS *Intrepid*.

For his help with research and in finessing the finer points of military nomenclature, I am indebted to submarine officer, historian, and stickler for accuracy Julian K. "Joe" Morrison III. His brother, Capt. Vance Morrison, USN (ret.), receives big thanks for threading the labyrinths of Washington's archives to retrieve many of the photographs. Cdr. Robert "Boom" Powell, USN (ret), offered valuable comments on the early drafts. Researcher John Bowen helped track down some of the more elusive photographs needed for the book.

Another round of thanks to my editor at Broadway Books, Charlie Conrad, for his belief in this project and for his expert guidance with the structure and tone of this story. Thanks to Jenna Ciongoli of Broadway Books for her cheerful and efficient help with assembling the parts of the book.

As he did for *Intrepid*, Robert A. Terry created the splendidly detailed maps. Dr. Harry Ohanian, master modeler, shared with me his incredibly real vision of the mighty *Yamato*. Artist Robert Bailey gave permission to use his dramatic painting, *Imperial Sacrifice*. Jason McDonald, of MFA Productions LLC, donated transcripts from www.dayofthekamikaze.com. Turner Publishing Company kindly gave permission to quote from Roy D. Erickson's memoir, *Tail End Charlies*.

For their generous support for this book, I thank my friend and co-author of *Intrepid*, Bill White, president of the *Intrepid* Sea, Air & Space Museum, and executive vice president Dave Winters.

My gratitude again goes to my agent Alice Martell, of the Martell Agency, for her cheerleading and wise counsel, and to her efficient assistant, Stephanie Finman. As always, my ultimate thanks and a full measure of love to Anne Busse-Gandt, my wife and staunchest supporter.

THE HONORED DEAD OF
CARRIER AIR GROUP 10

Ens. Bailey Badgley

Ens. Ernest M. Bailey Jr.

Lt. Alvin DeMaine Blackman

Ens. William Pearson Brede Jr.

Ens. Donald H. Croy

ARM3c Thomas S. Dally

ARM3c Charles E. Ford

Ens. Arthur Fulton

Ens. Robinson W. Harris

Ens. Elmer H. Hasse

Ens. Horace W. Heath

ARM3c Cecil B. Hollinhead

Lt. Oliver W. Hubbard

ARM1c Lee B. Hurst

Ens. Loren F. Isley

Ens. Charles W. Jensen

AOM2c Bernard A. Konitzer

AOM3c Charles M. Lowell Jr.

Lt. (jg) Richard W. Mason

Lt. (jg) Lawrence B. Mead

2nd Lt. Carl R. Miller, USMC

Lt. (jg) Willard J. Miller

Lt. (jg) Spence P. Mitchell

Ens. Willard E. Norgren

Lt. Mark L. Orr

Lt. (jg) Stanley Powell

Ens. Arthur H. Rogers

ARM1c Theodore Schevon

ARM3c Harry D. Weiner

Ens. William L. York

NOTES

Prologue

PAGE 1 ▸ The predeployment party at Alameda is drawn from Roy D. Erickson's memoir *Tail End Charlies!* 69–71, and from interviews of VBF-10 and VF-10 pilots.

2 ▸ Descriptions of Rawie and Hyland are based on official biographies in the CAG-10 1945 cruise book, *The History of Bomber Fighting Squadron Ten*, and from multiple VBF-10/VF-10 interviews October 31, 2008.

1 ▸ The Next Island

7 ▸ Spruance, Nimitz, King aboard *Indianapolis*: Thomas B. Buell, *The Quiet Warrior: A Biography of Admiral Raymond A. Spruance*, 321.

8 ▸ "You did a damn good job": Buell, *Master of Sea Power: A Biography of Fleet Admiral Ernest J. King*, 466.

9 ▸ The Japanese would fight back with every weapon: ibid., 441.

10 ▸ Vice Adm. Ohnishi and the *tokko* warriors at Mabalacat drawn from Rikihei Inoguchi and Tadashi Nakajima, *The Divine Wind: Japan's Kamikaze Force in World War II*, 3–11.

2 ▸ Tail End Charlies

13 ▸ Erickson profile and the descriptions of flight training at Pasco, Washington, Corpus Christi, Texas, and Atlantic City, New Jersey, are from Erickson's *Tail End Charlies!* 19–40 and 49–63.

20 ▸ Details of carrier qualification aboard USS *Core* are from interviews with James South, Charles Schlag, and Wesley Hays, and Erickson recollections in *Tail End Charlies!* 54–61.

22 ▸ Partying was as much a part of squadron life as flying: interviews with VBF-10/VF-10 pilots, and Erickson's *Tail End Charlies!* 51.

3 ▸ You Are Already Gods

24 ▸ "You are already gods without earthly desires": Inoguchi and Nakajima, *The Divine Wind*, 19.

26 ▸ Lieutenant Seki's unconventional weapons: ibid., 57–60.

29 ▸ The kamikaze attacks of November 25, 1944, are drawn in part from the excellent online study at www.dayofthekamikaze.com.

33 ▸ *Intrepid*'s hangar deck is a scene of horror: Ray Stone, *My Ship!* 167–79; White and Gandt, *Intrepid,* 113–20.

33 ▸ *Intrepid* is headed back to San Francisco: USS Intrepid *War Diary,* November–December, 1944.

4 ▸ Tiny Tim

39 ▸ *Holy shit:* Interviews with VBF-10 pilots.

40 ▸ The war news [for Japan] is all bad: Vice Adm. Matome Ugaki, *Fading Victory: The Diary of Admiral Matome Ugaki 1941–1945,* 536.

40 ▸ the "Golden Mask," label for Ugaki, from Evan Thomas, *Sea of Thunder,* 9.

41 ▸ "My thoughts ran wild seeking ways to save the empire": Ugaki, *Fading Victory,* 531.

5 ▸ Your Favorite Enemy

43 ▸ From the lavatories come a steady litany of gagging and retching: Erickson, *Tail End Charlies!* 71–72.

46 ▸ Description of kamikaze attack on USS *Randolph*: interview with Radioman 2/c V. J. Verdolini, *Randolph* crewman.

47 ▸ The Frances bomber plunges straight into the uninhabited islet: David Sears, *At War with the Wind,* 284.

49 ▸ Halsey: "It was hard on the horses, but it was effective": E. B. Potter, *Nimitz,* 294.

49 ▸ "We welcome *Intrepid* to the Okinawa area": Erickson, *Tail End Charlies!* 76.

51 ▸ "he [R. K. Turner] is known as a 'mean son of a bitch' ": *Time,* February 7, 1944.

52 ▸ "whose head could conceive more new ideas . . . than any flag officer in the Navy": Samuel Eliot Morison describing Turner in *Victory in the Pacific: 1945,* 89.

6 ▸ First Blooding

53 ▸ Scenes of first strike, March 18, 1945, based on interviews with William Landreth, Felix Novelli, and Wesley Hays, and recollections of Roy Erickson in *Tail End Charlies!*

55 ▸ "Erickson, turn off those goddamn lights": Erickson, *Tail End Charlies!* 80–81.

58 ▸ "From horizon to horizon the ocean was covered with the might of the United States Navy": interview with Landreth.

60 ▸ Within seconds the Corsair vanishes, and so does Rob Harris: *Air Group Ten Action Report,* March 18, 1945.

7 ▸ The Mood in Boys' Town

62 ▸ Frances bomber hits the water 50 feet from *Intrepid*'s starboard bow: *USS* Intrepid *War Diary*, March 18, 1945.

63 ▸ A few minutes past 1300, it is *Yorktown*'s turn: Morison, *Victory in the Pacific: 1945*, 94.

64 ▸ Incident of ships' gunners firing on Japanese airmen in parachutes recalled by Lt. (jg) Fred Meyer in Erickson's *Tail End Charlies!* 83–84.

67 ▸ "we were no longer virgins": ibid., 85.

8 ▸ Shoot the Son of a Bitch

69 ▸ Landreth still adrift in his raft: interview with William Landreth.

71 ▸ Encounter with the elite IJN 343rd Kokutai described in Henry Sakaida and Koji Takaki, *Genda's Blade*, 42–45.

73 ▸ "I heard it might not be a good thing to do, as it didn't help the treatment given to our POWs below": Erickson, *Tail End Charlies!* 88.

73 ▸ "Shoot the son of a bitch, Eric!": Erickson's *Tail End Charlies!* 87.

75 ▸ The thirty-four-year-old Hyland gets his first air-to-air kill: *Air Group Ten Action Report*, March 19, 1945.

9 ▸ We Will Save the Ship

78 ▸ "If you save us from the Japanese, we will save the ship": David H. Lippman, article in *World War II* magazine, March 1995.

78 ▸ *Franklin* suffers the greatest damage inflicted on any aircraft carrier without being sunk: Morison, *Victory in the Pacific*, 95–98.

81 ▸ Japanese high command detached from reality: ibid., 100.

10 ▸ Thunder Gods

83 ▸ The *Ohka* carries enough explosive power to devastate virtually any warship: Bernard Millot, *Divine Thunder*, 140.

84 ▸ "Bees die after they have stung": Albert Axell and Hideaki Kase, *Kamikaze: Japan's Suicide Gods*, 35.

86 ▸ "We are ready to launch the attack, sir": Millot, *Divine Thunder*, 142–43.

86 ▸ "All right, you little gods, you've had the balls to come this far": Hatsuho Naito, *Thunder Gods: The Kamikaze Pilots Tell Their Story*, 44.

87 ▸ "Is it, sir, that you lack confidence in me?": Inoguchi and Nakajima, *The Divine Wind*, 144.

90 ▸ Dick Mason disappears after air-to-air action: *Air Group Ten Action Report*, March 21, 1945.

92 ▸ "I am going to ram a carrier": Ugaki, *Fading Victory*, 559–60.

11 ▸ Three Seconds to Die

94 ▸ Loss of Al Hasse recalled by Erickson in *Tail End Charlies!* 101.

95 ▸ Ziggy South ditches after midair collision: interview with James "Ziggy" South.

97 ▸ Silently they toss Al Hasse's love letters into the Pacific: recalled by Lt. (jg) Fred Meyer in Erickson's *Tail End Charlies!* 101.

98 ▸ Windy Hill goes down off Kyushu: ibid., 106.

12 ▸ And Where Is the Navy?

101 ▸ Hirohito description, his reign called "Showa": Max Hastings, *Retribution*, 39.

103 ▸ Adm. Oikawa and his staff have only a few days to decide: Russell Spurr, *A Glorious Way to Die*, 86–87.

104 ▸ Adm. Toyoda signs off on his last operational order of the war: ibid., 97.

107 ▸ "Preparations for getting under way completed": Mitsuru Yoshida, *Requiem for Battleship* Yamato, 5.

108 ▸ "Kamikaze *Yamato*, be truly a divine wind!" ibid., 8.

13 ▸ Gimlet Eyes and the Alligator

110 ▸ "His fame may not have gone to his head": Spruance's nuanced observation of Halsey, quoted in William Tuohy's *America's Fighting Admirals*, 345.

110 ▸ "I wish that Spruance had been with Mitscher at Leyte Gulf": Adm. William Halsey, in Theodore Taylor's *The Magnificent Mitscher*, 165.

111 ▸ "I am lazy, and I never have done things myself that I could get someone to do for me": attributed to Spruance, Buell, *The Quiet Warrior*, xxxi.

112 ▸ Loss of USS *Indianapolis* as described in *Dictionary of American Fighting Ships*.

113 ▸ Windy Hill rescued by USS *Sea Dog*: Erickson, *Tail End Charlies!* 106.

14 ▸ Love Day

120 ▸ "I felt miserable, and an awful weight was on my heart": Ernie Pyle, *Last Chapter*, 99.

120 ▸ "And yet we couldn't see a bit of firing ahead. We hoped it was true": ibid., 102.

122 ▸ " 'This is the finest Easter present we could have received' ": *Time*, April 9, 1945.

123 ▸ Zeke fighter pilot lands at Yontan, jumps from the cockpit with his gun drawn: Morison, *Victory in the Pacific*, 171.

123 ▸ "Please send us a dead Jap. A lot of my men have never seen one": "Buck's Battle," *Time*, April 16, 1945.

125 ▸ Nimitz vetoes choice of Lt. Gen. Holland Smith and picks Buckner to command at Okinawa: Hastings, *Retribution*, 376.

15 ▸ Bourbon and Puddle Water

127 ▸ "May you walk in the ashes of Tokyo": Buckner quote in *Time*, April 16, 1945.

130 ▸ Col. Yahara clashes with Lt. Gen. Cho. Keith Wheeler, *The Road to Tokyo*.

130 ▸ "They were obviously scared to death . . .": Ernie Pyle describing Okinawa natives in *Last Chapter*, 108–9.

132 ▸ Windy Hill learns that he will be aboard *Sea Dog* another five weeks. Hill recollection in *Tail End Charlies!* 107–8.

16 ▸ Ten-Go

134 ▸ "*Yamato* and the Second Destroyer Squadron will sally forth": *Yamato*'s orders and the preparations for her last sortie are drawn from Yoshida's *Requiem for Battleship* Yamato, 3–17, and Spurr's *A Glorious Way to Die*.

135 ▸ Impressions of *Yamato* crewmen are drawn, in part, from the *Nova* PBS series "Sinking the Supership."

138 ▸ "We are fine. Please do put your best effort into your duties": Kunai Nakatami, quoted in Yoshida's *Requiem for Battleship* Yamato.

138 ▸ "It is a great opportunity as well as a great honor to be skipper of a ship in this sortie to Okinawa": Capt. Tameichi Hara, *Japanese Destroyer Captain*, 268.

17 ▸ Divine Wind

142 ▸ Ugaki is opposed to the *Yamato* mission: Ugaki, *Fading Victory*, 575.

145 ▸ *Bush* and *Colhoun* under kamikaze attack: Morison, *Victory in the Pacific*, 187.

147 ▸ Ordeal of survivors from *Bush*: Spurr, *A Glorious Way to Die*, 146.

149 ▸ *Leutze* and *Newcomb* heavily damaged but still afloat: Morison, *Victory in the Pacific*, 185, and article by John B. Penfold, *Our Navy* magazine, January 1, 1946.

150 ▸ *Emmons* ordered sunk by friendly gunfire: Morison, *Victory in the Pacific*, 195.

151 ▸ U.S. losses in *kikusui* No. 1 and ordeal of survivors: Sears, *At War with the Wind*, 326.

152 ▸ *Kikusui* No. 1 regarded as a resounding success: Ugaki, *Fading Victory*, 573–74.

18 ▸ Breakout

153 ▸ Scenes of *Yamato* under way: http://www.pbs.org/wgbh/novasupership.

153 ▸ *Yamato's* passage through the Bungo Strait: Yoshida, *Requiem for Battleship* Yamato, 45–47.

154 ▸ *Threadfin* and *Hackleback* tracking *Yamato* task force: Spurr, *A Glorious Way to Die*, 185.

156 ▸ "I do believe we learn about our position faster from their side than from ours": *Yamato's* navigation officer, quoted in Yoshida's *Requiem for Battleship* Yamato, 43.

157 ▸ Floatplanes catapult from *Yamato*: Spurr, *A Glorious Way to Die*, 203.

19 ▸ Race for Glory

161 ▸ Mitscher profile: Taylor, *The Magnificent Mitscher*, 189; Tuohy, *America's Fighting Admirals*.

165 ▸ *Asashimo* falls behind task force: Yoshida, *Requiem for Battleship* Yamato, 54.

166 ▸ "He looked like hell": Burke's appraisal of Mitscher's condition drawn from Potter, *Admiral Arleigh Burke*, 250.

169 ▸ "You take them": ibid., 250.

20 ▸ First Wave

170 ▸ Scenes of preparation for *Yamato* strike based on interviews with Felix Novelli and Wesley Hays, and recollections of Roy Erickson in *Tail End Charlies!*

172 ▸ More than 250 American warplanes spotted heading north: Yoshida, *Requiem for Battleship* Yamato, 61.

173 ▸ "We hope you will bring back a nice fish for breakfast": Turner to Deyo, as quoted by Morison in *Victory in the Pacific*, 204.

176 ▸ "Commence firing!" Yoshida, *Requiem for Battleship* Yamato, 64.

177 ▸ Downing of Bill Delaney from http://www.ussbelleauwood.com/air_group_30.htm, and Spurr, *A Glorious Way to Die*, 249–51.

21 ▸ Ducks in a Gallery

183 ▸ "Corsairs, you're close. Stand by for my mark": Description of VBF-10 attacks on *Yahagi* from interview with Wesley Hays and Erickson recollections in *Tail End Charlies!* 110–12.

184 ▶ Rawie impressions from his own account in *Air Group Ten Action Report*, April 7, 1945.

188 ▶ Herbert Houck's role in the *Yamato* operation drawn from his postwar recollection in http://www.yorktownsailor.com/yorktown/battleship.htm.

189 ▶ American warplanes strafe *Yamato* task force survivors: Spurr, *A Glorious Way to Die*, 285.

22 ▶ There She Blows

190 ▶ Flooding *Yamato*'s engineering rooms: Yoshida, *Requiem for Battleship Yamato*, 82.

191 ▶ Seiichi Ito, "Stop the operation": ibid., 108.

192 ▶ Resetting torpedo running depth: http://www.yorktownsailor.com/yorktown/fries.htm.

193 ▶ *Yamato* fighting back at torpedo planes: http://www.yorktownsailor.com/yorktown/battleship.htm.

193 ▶ Yoshida marvels that not a single American pilot had crashed into an enemy ship: Yoshida, *Requiem for Battleship Yamato*, 83.

196 ▶ Experiences of escaping *Yamato* crewmen were vividly described in the *Nova* series "Sinking the Supership."

23 ▶ Dumbo and Mighty Mouse

202 ▶ Rescue of Bill Delaney: Morison, *Victory in the Pacific*, 208.

204 ▶ Return of *Intrepid* strike group: Jim Clifford correspondence, interview with VBF-10 pilot Wesley Hays, and *Air Group Ten Action Report*, April 7, 1945.

206 ▶ Kamikaze strikes *Hancock*: http://www.usshancockcv19.com/gallery.htm.

208 ▶ Loss of Don Croy and recovery of Clarke: *Air Group Ten Cruise Book 1945*, and Robin Rielly, *Kamikazes, Corsairs, and Picket Ships*, 124.

210 ▶ Mitscher not his old self: Taylor, *The Magnificent Mitscher*, 285, and Spurr, *A Glorious Way to Die*, 312.

211 ▶ Nimitz to Turner, "Delete all after 'crazy' ": Morison, *Victory in the Pacific*, 215.

24 ▶ A Ridge Called Kakazu

217 ▶ Buckner and commanders are surprised by Japanese artillery: Hastings, *Retribution*, 377.

219 ▶ "I was back again at the kind of life I had known so long": Pyle, *Last Chapter*, 112.

219 ▶ "One man for ten of the enemy or one tank": James H. Hallas, *Killing Ground on Okinawa: The Battle for Sugar Loaf Hill*, 6.

222 ▸ Sata Omaichi captured and interrogated: Rielly, *Kamikazes, Corsairs, and Picket Ships*, 129.

224 ▸ "A dead Jap is no longer an enemy": http://www.ussmissouri.com/sea-stories-kamikaze.

25 ▸ Ohka

225 ▸ Ugaki misled by *kikusui* No. 1 reports: Rielly, *Kamikazes, Corsairs, and Picket Ships*, 128.

227 ▸ Attack on *Cassin Young*: Sears, *At War with the Wind*, 340.

227 ▸ Saburo Dohi profile, flies a Thunder God mission: Inoguchi and Nakajima, *The Divine Wind*.

227 ▸ *Ohka* attacks described in Rielly's *Kamikazes, Corsairs, and Picket Ships*, 142, 145.

232 ▸ "No further questions were asked": recollection by Nakajima in *The Divine Wind*, 158.

26 ▸ Gunslingers

233 ▸ Mark Orr profile and night mission tactics based on *Air Group Ten Cruise Book 1945* and *Air Group Ten Action Report*, April 11, 1945, and correspondence with VF-10 night fighter pilot Frank Stolfa.

235 ▸ Schub and Nickerson actions taken from *Air Group Ten Action Report*, April 12, 1945.

238 ▸ Frank Jackson collision with FM-2 Wildcat: Rielly, *Kamikazes, Corsairs, and Picket Ships*, 132.

239 ▸ Gray, Halbe, and Sweeny actions in *Air Group Ten Action Report*, April 12, 1945, and *Air Group Ten Cruise Book 1945*.

27 ▸ Black Friday

246 ▸ Beauford Anderson earns Medal of Honor during Japanese counterattack: Roy E. Appleman et al., *Okinawa: The Last Battle*, 134–35.

249 ▸ "Attention all hands! President Roosevelt is dead": Morison, *Victory in the Pacific*, 231.

250 ▸ "The dreadful loss . . . will make you orphans on this island": Appleman, *Okinawa: The Last Battle*, 125.

250 ▸ Loss of Mark Orr in night action: *Air Group Ten Cruise Book 1945*.

251 ▸ Feuding between Army and Marine Corps over Howlin' Mad Smith: Keith Wheeler, *The Road to Tokyo*, 109.

253 ▸ Worst loss of U.S. armored vehicles in the campaign: Appleman, *Okinawa: The Last Battle*, 203–4.

253 ▸ Buckner realizes assault has failed, "Progress not quite satisfactory":

Simon B. Buckner and Joseph Stilwell, *Seven Stars: The Okinawa Battle Diaries of Simon Bolivar Buckner Jr. and Joseph Stilwell*, 42.

254 ▸ Ugaki believes air attacks on Kyushu come from Okinawa: Ugaki, *Fading Victory*, 586–87.

28 ▸ Keep Moving and Keep Shooting

256 ▸ Lerch, Kirkwood, and Quiel actions described in Norwald Quiel letter to author and in *Air Group Ten Action Report*, April 16, 1945.

259 ▸ "Keep moving and keep shooting": *Purdy* skipper to *Laffey* captain Becton, quoted by Dale Harper in *World War II*, March 1998.

29 ▸ As Long as a Gun Will Fire

263 ▸ Ordeal of *Laffey* described by her skipper, Julian Becton, in his *The Ship That Would Not Die*.

265 ▸ "I couldn't even hold a pencil": interview with *Laffey* quartermaster Ari Phoutrides.

265 ▸ "I'll never abandon ship as long as a gun will fire": *Laffey* skipper Becton quoted in *Time*, June 4, 1945, and from Phoutrides interview.

265 ▸ Clarke, James, Farmer, Ehrhard actions from Ray James interview and from *Air Group Ten Action Report*, April 16, 1945.

269 ▸ *Laffey* endures more kamikaze attacks than any other and stays afloat: Harper, *World War II*, March 1998.

30 ▸ Glory Day

270 ▸ Weems and Schlag actions from Charles Schlag interview and *Air Group Ten Action Report*, April 16, 1945.

271 ▸ *Pringle* and *Bryant* under kamikaze attack described in Morison, *Victory in the Pacific*, 237–38, and Rielly, *Kamikazes, Corsairs, and Picket Ships*, 174–76.

273 ▸ Loss of Red Bailey at Kokubu, and actions of Hyland, Cordray, and flight drawn from *Air Group Ten Action Report*, April 16, 1945, and interviews of VBF-10 pilots.

31 ▸ Target *Intrepid*

279 ▸ "One day . . . one of these bastards is going to hit the bull's eye": Radarman Ray Stone in his memoir, *My Ship!*

280 ▸ Fred Meyer watches the Zeke aiming at *Intrepid*'s stern: Erickson, *Tail End Charlies!* 121.

280 ▸ "There was Old Glory, stiff as a board": interview with plane captain Felix Novelli.

282 ▸ *Intrepid* repaired, lands her aircraft aboard: USS Intrepid *War Diary*, April 16, 1945.

283 ▸ "It was just like they never existed": Erickson laments his lost squadronmates in *Tail End Charlies!* 124.

284 ▸ Hays and wingmen, unable to return to *Intrepid*, make odyssey around Pacific: interview with Wesley Hays.

286 ▸ Bitzegaio wounded in seat of pants related in Ed Deutschman correspondence and *Air Group Ten Cruise Book 1945*.

32 ▸ Call Me Ernie

287 ▸ "I much prefer a bird dog that you have to whistle in": Buckner on Maj. Gen. Andrew Bruce, Buckner and Stilwell, *Seven Stars*, 24.

288 ▸ Comparing Ie Shima terrain to Iwo Jima: Appleman, *Okinawa: The Last Battle*, 150. Another enemy-held feature called "the Pinnacle" confronted the 24th Corps in the south of Okinawa.

288 ▸ "Their firepower is so great we dared not show our heads": Japanese soldier's diary entry on Ie Shima landings, ibid., 157.

289 ▸ Ernie Pyle's death on Ie Shima is drawn from various accounts including David Nichols's *Ernie's War: The Best of Ernie Pyle's World War II Dispatches*, 32, and Lee Miller, *The Story of Ernie Pyle*, 419–26.

291 ▸ "Base of Pinnacle completely surrounded despite bitterest fight I have ever witnessed": Andrew Bruce quoted by Appleman, *Okinawa: The Last Battle*, 177.

291 ▸ Japanese lose 4,700 dead on Ie Shima: Gordon Rottman, *Okinawa, 1945*, 69.

291 ▸ Sailors go ashore on Mog Mog: Wheeler, *The Road to Tokyo*, 88.

33 ▸ Counteroffensive

294 ▸ Nimitz worries that the Okinawa battle is dragging on too long: Hallas, *Killing Ground on Okinawa*, 10.

295 ▸ "If this line isn't moving within five days, we'll get someone here to move it so we can all get out from under these damn air attacks": Nimitz to Buckner, ibid., 10.

296 ▸ Buckner concerned that the proposed amphibious landing could turn into "another Anzio": ibid., 11.

296 ▸ Spruance is "impatient for some of Holland Smith's drive": Buell, *The Quiet Warrior*, 356–47.

298 ▸ Col. Yahara believes Lt. Gen. Cho's counteroffensive is doomed: Hiromichi Yahara, *The Battle for Okinawa*, 196.

300 ▸ Counteroffensive is a disaster from which the 32nd Army will not recover: Rottman, *Okinawa 1945*, 73–75.

301 ▸ "from now on I leave everything up to you": Lt. Gen. Ushijima to Col. Yahara, in Yahara, *The Battle for Okinawa*, 41.

34 ▸ Bottom of the Barrel

302 ▸ Hitler's death lamented by Ugaki: Ugaki, *Fading Victory*, 603.

303 ▸ "Carriers That Way" sign, cited by Vice Adm. C. R. Brown in foreword to Inoguchi and Nakajima, *The Divine Wind*, vii.

304 ▸ *Morrison* attacked by biplanes: Rielly, *Kamikazes, Corsairs, and Picket Ships*, 213.

306 ▸ *Ingraham* receives full attention of kamikazes: Morison, *Victory in the Pacific*, 255.

308 ▸ Actions of the British Task Force 57 and effects of kamikazes on armored flight decks described ibid., 264–66.

35 ▸ Gone with the Spring

310 ▸ "When I start inhaling these, I don't want to waste time reordering": Windy Hill in Guam, quoted in Erickson's *Tail End Charlies!* 126–27.

311 ▸ Nimitz is frustrated by the continuing losses to radar pickets. He asks Adm. Forrest Sherman whether he didn't think the kamikazes would lay off the pickets in search of bigger game. Sherman didn't think so. "You could get a man down quicker by hitting him on the same tooth than by punching him all over." Morison, *Victory in the Pacific*, 256.

312 ▸ Ugaki is sure that "when our troops can see enemy vessels sunk and set on fire in front of their very eyes and observe planes with the Rising Sun mark fly overhead, their morale will soar." Ugaki, *Fading Victory*, 604–5.

312 ▸ Reaction in Japan to the surrender of Germany: Robert Sherrod, *History of Marine Corps Aviation in World War II*, 389.

312 ▸ Turner orders full gun salvoes to salute the troops in Europe: Morison, *Victory in the Pacific*, 268.

314 ▸ Robert Klingman chops off the Japanese Nick's tail: "Strangest Dogfight Ever," *Leatherneck*, January 2007, and http://www.f4ucorsair.com/vmf312/312.html.

316 ▸ "Flowers of the special attack are falling": poem by Ugaki lamenting the loss of *tokko* airmen, *Fading Victory*, 610.

36 ▸ Change of Command

317 ▸ "Alert! Alert! Two planes diving on the *Bunker Hill*!": Taylor, *The Magnificent Mitscher*, 290–91.

319 ▸ Mitscher evacuates flag plot, observes a third kamikaze diving on *Bunker Hill*: ibid., 291.

319 ▸ *Bunker Hill*'s agony continues: Morison, *Victory in the Pacific*, 263.

321 ▸ "Flatley, tell my task group commanders that if the Japs keep this up they're going to grow hair on my head yet": Taylor, *The Magnificent Mitscher*, 297.

321 ▸ The service for Shunsuke Tomiyasu was one of the rare occasions when the remains of a kamikaze were given a dignified burial. For years after the war, Tomiyasu's name was incorrectly reported as "Tomi Zae"; http://wgordon.web.wesleyan.edu/kamikaze/stories/tomiyasu/index.htm.

322 ▸ *Enterprise* becomes last carrier of the war to be struck by a kamikaze: http://www.cv6.org/1945/1945.htm.

324 ▸ *Longshaw* is lost with eighty-six crew: Theodore Roscoe, *U.S. Destroyer Operations in World War II*, 480–81.

324 ▸ *Kikusui* No. 7 details: Morison, *Victory in the Pacific*, 279.

326 ▸ USS *Braine* crewmen lost in *kikusui* No. 8: Rielly, *Kamikazes, Corsairs, and Picket Ships*, 279.

327 ▸ Okinawa now the costliest naval engagement in U.S. history: Morison, *Victory in the Pacific*, 272.

327 ▸ "A less serene man and courageous man might, before reaching this point, have asked, 'Is this island worth the cost?' ": Morison describing Spruance's tenacity, ibid., 272.

328 ▸ Mitscher and his staff look "like a parade of scarecrows": Taylor, *The Magnificent Mitscher*, 300.

37 ▸ Ritual of Death

330 ▸ Ushijima buys time with the "offensive retreat": Yahara, *The Battle for Okinawa*, 88–89.

331 ▸ "It's all over now but cleaning up pockets of resistance": Buckner quote in Appleman, *Okinawa: The Last Battle*, 422.

332 ▸ Journalists Bigart and Lawrence criticisms of Buckner from Bill Sloan, *The Ultimate Battle: Okinawa 1945*, 312.

332 ▸ MacArthur accuses Okinawa commanders of "sacrificing thousands of American soldiers": "The Trouble I've Seen: The Nils Andersen Story," http://notorc.blogspot.com/2007/07/lest-we-forget-sacred-grove-at-montrose.html.

333 ▸ MacArthur will see to it that Buckner does not play a role in the invasion of Japan: Cole C. Kingseed, *Old Glory Stories*, 73.

333 ▸ "If we'd scattered our forces, we might have got licked": Buckner quote from *Seven Stars*, 80.

334 ▸ Japanese gunners fire five rounds from their concealed position: George Feifer, *The Battle of Okinawa: The Blood and the Bomb*, 378–79.

334 ▸ The circumstances of Simon Buckner's death are covered in multiple sources, including Appleman's *Okinawa: The Last Battle*, Sloan's *The Ultimate Battle*, and Feifer's *The Battle of Okinawa*.

336 ▸ Ushijima rejects Buckner's urging to surrender: Yahara, *The Battle for Okinawa*, 136.

338 ▸ Ushijima and Cho commit ritual suicide: ibid., 156.

38 ▸ Setting Sun

339 ▸ Thoughts and impressions of the Tail End Charlies aboard *Intrepid* returning to the Pacific are drawn from multiple interviews and correspondence with pilots of VBF-10 and VF-10, including James South, Wesley Hays, Ray James, and Charles Schlag, and the published memoir of Roy D. Erickson.

341 ▸ "if there is anything that sounds unreasonable to a pilot, it is the idea that he should practice encountering fire from an anti-aircraft gun": Hyland, *Air Group Ten Action Report*, August 6, 1945.

343 ▸ Ugaki will "follow in the footsteps of those many loyal officers and men": Ugaki, *Fading Victory*, 664–65.

344 ▸ Ugaki intends to "ram into the arrogant American ships, displaying the real spirit of a Japanese warrior": ibid., 666.

346 ▸ Truman dreads "an Okinawa from one end of Japan to the other": Feifer, *The Battle of Okinawa*, 413.

347 ▸ "Did I really do my part?" Yoshida, *Requiem for Battleship* Yamato, 150.

REFERENCES

Books

Appleman, Roy E., James Burns, Russell Gugeler, and John Stevens. *Okinawa: The Last Battle*. Center for Military History, 1948.

Astor, Gerald. *Operation Iceberg*. Dell, 1998.

Axell, Albert, and Hideaki Kase. *Kamikaze: Japan's Suicide Gods*. Longman, 2002.

Becton, Julian F. *The Ship That Would Not Die*. Pictorial Histories Publishing Company, 1980.

Blackburn, Tom. *The Jolly Rogers: The Story of Tom Blackburn and Navy Fighting Squadron VF-17*. Zenith Press, 2006.

Buckner, Simon B., and Joseph Stilwell. *Seven Stars: The Okinawa Battle Diaries of Simon Bolivar Buckner Jr. and Joseph Stilwell*. Texas A&M University Press, 2004.

Buell, Thomas B. *The Quiet Warrior: A Biography of Admiral Raymond A. Spruance*. Little, Brown, 1974.

———. *Master of Sea Power: A Biography of Fleet Admiral Ernest J. King*. Little, Brown, 1980.

Burrell, Robert S. *The Ghosts of Iwo Jima*. Texas A&M University Press, 2006.

Dyer, George C. *The Amphibians Came to Conquer: The Story of Admiral Richmond Kelly Turner*. U.S. Government Printing Office, 1973.

Erickson, Roy D. *Tail End Charlies!* Turner Publishing Company, 1995.

Feifer, George. *The Battle of Okinawa: The Blood and the Bomb*. Lyons Press, 2001.

Hallas, James H. *Killing Ground on Okinawa: The Battle for Sugar Loaf Hill*. Greenwood Publishing Group, 1996.

Hara, Tameichi. *Japanese Destroyer Captain*. Naval Institute Press, 2007.

Hastings, Max. *Retribution*. Alfred A. Knopf, 2008.

Hornfischer, James D. *The Last Stand of the Tin Can Sailors*. Bantam, 2004.

Huber, T. M. *Okinawa 1945*. Military Press, 2001.

———. *Japan's Battle of Okinawa April–June 1945*. University Press of the Pacific, 2005.

Inoguchi, Rikihei, and Tadashi Nakajima. *The Divine Wind: Japan's Kamikaze Force in World War II*. Naval Institute Press, 1958.

Jablonski, Edward. *Airwar*. Doubleday, 1971.

Kingseed, Cole C. *Old Glory Stories*. Naval Institute Press, 2006.

Leckie, Robert. *Okinawa: The Last Battle of World War Two*. Penguin Books, 1996.

Manchester, William. *American Caesar*. Little, Brown, 1978.

Miller, Lee G. *The Story of Ernie Pyle*. Viking Press, 1950.

Millot, Bernard. *Divine Thunder*. Pinnacle Books, 1971.

Morison, Samuel Eliot. *Leyte, June 1944–January 1945*. Castle, 2001.

——. *The Two-Ocean War: A Short History of the United States Navy in the Second World War*. Little, Brown, 1963.

——. *Victory in the Pacific: 1945*. Little, Brown, 1960.

Naito, Hatsuho. *Thunder Gods: The Kamikaze Pilots Tell Their Story*. Dell, 1989.

Nichols, David. *Ernie's War: The Best of Ernie Pyle's World War II Dispatches*. Random House, 1986.

Parrish, Thomas. *The Simon and Schuster Encyclopedia of World War II*, 1978.

Potter, E. B. *Nimitz*. Naval Institute Press, 1976.

Pyle, Ernie. *Last Chapter*. Henry Holt, 1946.

Reynolds, Clark G. *The Carrier War*. Time-Life Books, 1983.

Rielly, Robin L. *Kamikazes, Corsairs, and Picket Ships*. Casemate, 2008.

Roberts, John. *The Aircraft Carrier* Intrepid. Naval Institute Press, 1982.

Roscoe, Theodore. *U.S. Destroyer Operations in World War II*. Naval Institute Press, 1953.

Rottman, Gordon. *Okinawa, 1945*. Osprey Publishing, 2002.

Sakaida, Henry, and Koji Takaki. *Genda's Blade: Japan's Squadron of Aces: 343 Kokutai*. Classic Publications, 2003.

Sarantakes, Nicholas Evan. *Keystone: The American Occupation of Okinawa and U.S.-Japanese Relations*. Texas A&M University Press, 2001.

Sears, David. *At War with the Wind*. Citadel Press, 2008.

Sherrod, Robert. *History of Marine Corps Aviation in World War II*. Combat Forces Press, 1952.

Sloan, Bill. *The Ultimate Battle: Okinawa 1945*. Simon & Schuster, 2007.

Spector, Ronald H. *Eagle Against the Sun*. Vintage Books, 1985.

Spurr, Russell. *A Glorious Way to Die: The Kamikaze Mission of the Battleship* Yamato, *April 1945*. Newmarket Press, 1981.

Stone, Raymond T. *My Ship!* G. P. Books, 2003.

Styling, Mark. *Corsair Aces of World War 2*. Osprey Publishing, 1995.

Taylor, Theodore. *The Magnificent Mitscher*. Naval Institute Press, 1951.

Thomas, Evan. *Sea of Thunder*. Simon & Schuster, 2006.

Tillman, Barrett. *Corsair: The F4U in World War II and Korea*. Naval Institute Press, 1979.

Toland, John. *Rising Sun: The Decline and Fall of the Japanese Empire, 1936–1945*. Bantam, 1970.

Toliver, Raymond, and Trevor Constable. *Fighter Aces of the U.S.A.* Schiffer Press, 1997.

Tuohy, William. *America's Fighting Admirals*. Zenith Press, 2007.

Ugaki, Matome. *Fading Victory: The Diary of Admiral Matome Ugaki 1941–1945*. Trans. Masataka Chithaya. University of Pittsburgh Press, 1991.

Wheeler, Keith. *The Road to Tokyo*. Time-Life Books, 1979.

Yahara, Hiromichi. *The Battle for Okinawa*. John Wiley and Sons, 1995.

Yoshida, Mitsuru. *Requiem for Battleship* Yamato. University of Washington Press, 1985.

Zollo, Anthony F. *USS* Intrepid *CV-11 CVA-11 CVS-11*. Turner, 1993.

Interviews and Correspondence

Anderson, Dave (VBF-10), October 31, 2008.
Clifford, James (VBF-10), February 25, 1945.
Davis, William (VBF-10), February 28, 2009.
Deutschman, Edward (VF-10), May 18, 2009.
Dubinsky, Maurice (VBF-10), March 22, 2009.
Gray, Les (VF-10), October 9, 2009.
Hays, Wesley B. (VBF-10), July 15, 2009.
Hollister, James O. (VBF-10), March 3, 2009.
James, Ray (VF-10), May 14, 2009.
Novelli, Felix (USS *Intrepid*), March 3, 2008.
Oglevee, Don (VF-10), October 9, 2009.
Phoutrides, Ari (USS *Laffey*), August 17, 2009.
Quiel, Norwald R. (VF-10), June 16, 2009.
Schlag, Charles (VF-10), September 1, 2009.
South, James (VF-10), October 31, 2008.
Stolfa, Frank (VF-10 night fighters), June 2, 2009.
Verdolini, V. J. (USS *Randolph*), June 10, 2009.
Wilmeth, Orlo (VF-10), May 26, 2009.

Internet

History of USS *Cabot*. http://www.mcallen.lib.tx.us/books/cabot/cab00_02.htm (accessed January 15, 2009).

Kamikaze images. http://wgordon.web.wesleyan.edu/kamikaze/stories/tomi
     yasu/index.htm (on kamikaze who struck *Enterprise* May 14, 1945; ac-
     cessed April 1, 2009).
Nova. "Sinking the Supership," http://www.pbs.org/wgbh/nova/supership/
     (accessed March 1, 2009).
USS *Yorktown* at Okinawa. http://www.yorktownsailor.com/yorktown (ac-
     cessed May 5, 2009).
World War II database. http://ww2db.com.

Articles
"Year of Attack," *Time*, February 7, 1944.
"Mechanical Man," *Time*, June 26, 1944.
"For Once, Men Could Laugh," Robert Sherrod, *Time*, April 9, 1945.
"Buck's Battle," *Time*, April 16, 1945.
"World: Becton's Word," *Time*, June 4, 1945.
"Two Teams, One Goal," *Time*, June 11, 1945.
"Seven Kamikazes Were Not Enough to Send This DD Down," John B.
     Penfold, *Our Navy*, January 1, 1946.
"USS *Franklin*: Struck by a Japanese Dive Bomber During World War II,"
     David H. Lippman, *World War II*, March 1995.
"Thriller at 38,000 Feet," *Leatherneck Magazine*, May 1995.
"*Laffey* Attacked off Okinawa, World War II," Dale Harper, *World War II*,
     March 1998.
"1945: The Deadliest Duty," *Mission: History* (from the Naval Order of the
     United States), April 3, 2000.
"Strangest Dogfight Ever," *Leatherneck Magazine*, January 2007.
"Terrible Turner: The Man Who Gave the Navy Webbed Feet," Owen
     Gault, *Sea Classics*, August 2008.
"The Trouble I've Seen: The Nils Andersen Story," *Postscripts* online maga-
     zine, May 21, 2009, http://notorc.blogspot.com/2007/07/lest-we-forget
     -sacred-grove-at-montrose.html.

Other
The History of Bomber Fighting Squadron Ten, 2 January 1945–15 Novem-
     ber 1945; VBF-10/A12, Serial No. 109.
Air Group Ten Cruise Book 1945.
Air Group Ten Action Reports. 1–12, March 21, 1945.
———. 13–39, April 27, 1945.

——. 40–56, April 27, 1945.

——. 57–85, April 28, 1945.

USS *Intrepid* (CV11) *War Diaries*, September 1, 1944–December 4, 1944, and March 3, 1945–August 21, 1945.

Letter from Adm. John Hyland to Air Group Ten airmen on the occasion of their reunion, November 1997.

U.S. ORDER OF BATTLE

OKINAWA, APRIL 1945

C in C Pacific Fleet: Adm. Chester Nimitz
C in C Fifth Fleet: Adm. Raymond Spruance

Task Force 58 (FAST CARRIER TASK FORCE) ▸ Vice Adm. Marc Mitscher
   Task Group 58.1 (CARRIER TASK GROUP) ▸ Rear Adm. J. J. Clark
     Hornet, Bennington, San Jacinto, Belleau Wood
   Task Group 58.2 (CARRIER TASK GROUP) ▸ Rear Adm. Ralph Davison
     Enterprise, Randolph, Independence
   Task Group 58.3 (CARRIER TASK GROUP) ▸ Rear Adm. F. C. Sherman
     Essex, Bunker Hill, Bataan, Cabot, Hancock
   Task Group 58.4 (CARRIER TASK GROUP) ▸ Rear Adm. Arthur Radford
     Intrepid, Yorktown, Langley

Task Force 51 (JOINT EXPEDITIONARY FORCE) ▸ Vice Adm. R. K. Turner
Task Force 54 (GUNFIRE AND COVERING FORCE) ▸ Rear Adm. Morton Deyo
Task Force 57 (BRITISH CARRIER FORCE) ▸ Vice Adm. Sir H. B. Rawlings

U.S. Tenth Army (JOINT EXPEDITIONARY TROOPS) ▸ Lt. Gen. Simon Buckner
   XXIV Corps ▸ Maj. Gen. John Hodge
     7th and 96th Infantry Divisions
   77th Infantry Division ▸ Maj. Gen. Andrew Bruce
   27th Infantry Division ▸ Maj. Gen. George Griner
   III Amphibious Corps ▸ Maj. Gen. Roy Geiger USMC
     1st and 6th Marine Divisions

JAPANESE ORDER OF BATTLE

OKINAWA, APRIL 1945

Imperial Joint Staff—Emperor Hirohito—Imperial War Council

Imperial Japanese Navy ▸ Combined Fleet C in C ▸ Adm. Soemu Toyoda
    Land-Based Air Fleets ▸ Vice Adm. Takijiro Ohnishi
    Fifth Air Fleet (Kamikaze) ▸ Vice Adm. Matome Ugaki
    Second Fleet (flagship *Yamato*) ▸ Vice Adm. Seiichi Ito
        ***Yamato* Task Force**
        BB *Yamato* / CL *Yahagi* / DD *Fuyutsuki* / DD *Suzutsuki* /
        DD *Yukikaze* / DD *Isokaze* / DD *Hamakaze* / DD *Hatsushimo* /
        DD *Asashimo* / DD *Kasumi*

Imperial Japanese Army
    32nd Army (Okinawa) ▸ Lt. General Mitsuru Ushijima
        24th Division, 62nd Division
        44th Independent Mixed Brigade
        2nd Tank Regiment
        Okinawan Labor Unit (Boeitai)
        5th Artillery Group

GLOSSARY

Angels ▸ altitude in thousands of feet

APA ▸ attack transport ship

Bandit ▸ aircraft identified as hostile

BB ▸ battleship

Betty ▸ Mitsubishi G4M medium bomber, also mother ship for the *Ohka*

Bogey ▸ Unidentified aircraft

Buster ▸ Order to fighter aircraft or flight to proceed at maximum sustained speed

CA ▸ Heavy cruiser

CAG ▸ carrier air group commander

CAP ▸ combat air patrol

Carrier Air Group ▸ unit of two or more squadrons under one commander for operations from a carrier

CIC ▸ combat information center

CL ▸ light cruiser

CNO ▸ chief of naval operations

ComInCh ▸ commander in chief (of the U.S. Navy)

CV ▸ large aircraft carrier

CVE ▸ escort carrier

CVL ▸ light aircraft carrier

DD ▸ destroyer

DE ▸ destroyer escort

Division ▸ formation of four airplanes

Dukw ▸ six-wheeled amphibious truck

F4U-1D ▸ Corsair model assigned to VF-10/VBF-10 during Okinawa campaign (3-bladed propeller)

F4U-4 ▸ Corsair model assigned to VF-10/VBF-10 on redeployment July 1945 (4-bladed propeller)

F6F ▸ Grumman Hellcat fighter

FIDO ▸ fighter director officer

Frances ▸ Yokosuka P1Y twin-engine long range bomber

George ▸ Kawanishi N1K-J Shiden-kai fighter

IJA ▸ Imperial Japanese Army

IJN ▸ Imperial Japanese Navy

Jack ▸ Mitsubishi JM2 fighter

Judy ▸ Aichi D4Y dive-bomber

Kamikaze ▸ Japanese special attack suicide pilot or plane

Kikusui ▸ "floating chrysanthemum," label given to massed kamikaze attacks

LCI ▸ landing craft infantry

LCT ▸ landing craft tank

LSM ▸ landing ship medium

LSO ▸ landing signal officer

LST ▸ landing ship tank

LVT ▸ landing vehicle tracked (nicknamed "Alligator")

MAG ▸ Marine Air Group

MIA ▸ missing in action

Myrt ▸ Nakajima C6N1 single engine reconnaissance aircraft

NAS ▸ Naval Air Station

Nate ▸ Japanese Nakajima Ki-27 fixed-gear fighter

Nick ▸ Kawasaki I1–45 Japanese Army twin-engine fighter

Nugget ▸ fledgling naval aviator

Ohka ▸ Japanese Yokosuka MXY-7 human-guided bomb, code-named "Baka" (meaning "idiot")

Oscar ▸ Nakajima Ki-43 single-engine fighter

PBM ▸ Martin two-engine seaplane

PBY ▸ Consolidated two-engine seaplane

Plank owner ▸ crew member of ship or unit from date of its commission

Rufe ▸ Mitsubishi A6M2-N Zero fighter variant equipped with floats

SB2C ▸ Curtiss Helldiver dive-bomber

SBD ▸ Douglas Dauntless dive-bomber

Section ▸ formation of two airplanes

SNJ ▸ North American advanced trainer

TF ▸ task force

TG ▸ task group

Tojo ▸ Nakajima Ki-44 fighter

Tony ▸ Kawasaki Ki-61 fighter resembling Messerschmitt Bf 109

TU ▸ task unit

Val ▸ Aichi D3A1 fixed-gear dive-bomber

VB ▸ prefix for bombing squadron

VBF ▸ prefix for bomber fighting squadron

VF ▸ prefix for fighting squadron

VMF ▸ prefix for Marine fighting squadron

VP ▸ prefix for patrol squadron

VT ▸ prefix for torpedo squadron
XO ▸ executive officer
YE ▸ homing signal transmitter aboard ship
ZB ▸ homing signal receiver aboard aircraft
Zeke ▸ Mitsubishi A6M "Zero" fighter

U.S. Navy Commissioned Ranks
Fleet Admiral
Admiral (Adm.)
Vice Admiral
Rear Admiral
Commodore (Cmdre.)
Captain (Capt.)
Commander (Cmdr.)
Lieutenant Commander (Lt. Cmdr.)
Lieutenant (Lt.)
Lieutenant junior grade (Lt. [jg])
Ensign (Ens.)

U.S. Navy Enlisted Rates
Chief Petty Officer
Petty Officer 1st Class
Petty Officer 2nd Class
Petty Officer 3rd Class
Seaman 1st Class
Seaman 2nd Class
Apprentice Seaman

CREDITS

All photos shot by U.S. Navy photographers are in the public domain. The painting *Imperial Sacrifice* is reproduced with permission of artist Robert Bailey. The images of Gen. Ushijima and Adm. Ugaki, shot before 1946, are in the public domain according to article 23 of old copyright law of Japn and article 2 of supplemental provision of copyright law of Japn. Source: Chiran Kamikaze Peace Museum.

SOURCE LEGEND
NARA: National Archives and Records Administration
NHHC: Naval Historical and Heritage Command
NMNA: National Museum of Naval Aviation

INDEX

Page numbers in italics refer to illustrations.

Marshall Islands, 48, 125

Martin PBM Mariner seaplanes, 93, 157, 201–3

Mason, Dick, 88–91, 351

Matsuo, Isao, 213

Mauldin, Bill, 289

Mawhinney, Ed, 178, 203

May, Ed, 220–22

Meade, Larry, 22, 351

Meyer, Fred, 236, 280

Michel, John, 264

Midway, Battle of, 8, 18, 41, 92, 106

Mills, Eddie, 89–90

Minami Daito, 46, 88, 208

Minatogawa, 87, 91, 143

Missouri, U.S.S., xiv, *214–15* (216), 223–24, 279–80, 347

Mitajiri anchorage, 108, 133

Mitchell, Spence, 38, 351

Mitscher, Marc, xiii, xiv, 8, 52, 78, 79–81, 110, 135, 150, 156, 161–69, 173–74, 208–11, 217, 223, 317–20, 322, 327–28

Mitsubishi A6M2–N "Rufe" floatplane fighter, 72, 75

Mitsubishi A6M Zero fighters, 24–25, 27–28, 30–32, 88–91, 123, 143, 146–47, 223, 228, 238–40, 242–43, 253, 266–67, 270–73, 275, 279–81, 303, 305–6, 309, 318–20

Mitsubishi G4M "Betty" bombers, 41, 58, 83–91, 226–28, 231, 234–35, 242, 255, 267, 271, 306

Mitsubishi JM2 "Jack" fighters, 223, 240–41

Mitsubishi Ki-21 "Sally" bombers, 325

Mitsubishi Ki-46 "Dinah" bombers, 306–7

Mitsubishi Ki-57 "Topsy" transports, 273

Mog Mog Island, 48, 291–92

Morison, Samuel Eliot, 52, 327

Morris, U.S.S., 149, 151, 225

Morrison, U.S.S., 304–5

Moskala, Ed, 222

Motobu Peninsula, xiv, 217, 247–48

Mullany, U.S.S., 150, 225

Musashi, 25–26, 41, 106, 163

Musashi, Miyamoto, 5

Mussolini, Benito, 302

Nagasaki, xiv, 106, 342

Nakajima, Tadashi, 232

Nakajima B5N "Kate" torpedo bombers, 148, 236

Nakajima B6N "Jill" torpedo bombers, 145, 237, 242

Nakajima C6N1 "Myrt" reconnaissance planes, 276

Nakajima Ki-27 "Nate" fighter, 236, 242, 256–58, 261–62, 266, 277

Nakajima Ki-43 "Oscar" fighters, 148, 238, 264–65, 274, 308

Nakajima Ki-44 "Tojo" fighters, 73–74, 207

Nakajima Ki-84 "Frank" fighters, 337

Nakatami, Kunai, 137–38

Nakatsuru, Tatsuo, 343

Naoto, Kuromaru, 46

Naval Academy, U.S., 18, 36, 259, 270

Navy, Imperial Japanese, xiii, 3, 26, 42, 70, 87, 88, 134, 140, 158, 165, 180, 193; 343rd Kokutai of, 71; in Battle of the Philippine Sea, 8, 81; Combined Fleet of, 41, 102–4, 133, 134, 142, 200; Fifth Air Fleet of, xiii, 42, 85, 343; First Diversionary Striking Force of, 106; losses in Battle of Leyte Gulf of, 29; loss of fleet of, 107, 135; loss of naval air forces of, 83; Okinawa and, 102–9; at Pearl Harbor, 92; Second Fleet of, 133, 134, 199

Navy, U.S., 1, 36, 44, 48, 58, 151, 206, 291, 313, 344; Army issues with, 125, 295–96, 332–33; Corsairs ordered by, 17; Destroyer Squadron 23 of, 163; Fast Carrier Task Force of, *see* Task Force 58; 5th Amphibious Force of, 322; Fifth Fleet of, xiii, 7, 33, 44, 48, 100, 144, 156, 172–73, 225, 249, 294, 308, 322, 327; General Order 99 in,

ABOUT THE AUTHOR

ROBERT GANDT is a former naval officer and aviator, an international airline pilot, a screenwriter, and a military and aviation historian. He is the author of six novels and seven nonfiction books, including *Bogeys and Bandits*, the definitive work on modern naval aviation, which was adapted for the television series *Pensacola: Wings of Gold*. He and his wife, Anne, live in the Spruce Creek Fly-In in Daytona Beach, Florida.

Visit his website at www.Gandt.com.